Traditions of Experiment from the
Enlightenment to the Present

Peter Demetz. (Photo by Michael Marsland. Courtesy of Yale University Office of Public Information.)

Traditions of Experiment from the Enlightenment to the Present

Essays in Honor of
Peter Demetz

Edited by
Nancy Kaiser and David E. Wellbery

Ann Arbor

THE UNIVERSITY OF MICHIGAN PRESS

1995   1994   1993   1992   4   3   2   1

Library of Congress Cataloging-in-Publication Data

Traditions of experiment from the Enlightenment to the present :
  essays in honor of Peter Demetz / edited by Nancy Kaiser and David
  E. Wellbery.
     p.   cm.
  Includes bibliographical references and index.
  ISBN 0-472-10309-1 (alk. paper)
     1. Literature, Modern—History and criticism.   I. Kaiser, Nancy
  A., 1948-   . II. Wellbery, David E.   III. Demetz, Peter, 1922-
  PN710.T65   1992
  809'.03—dc20   92-27453
                                                                 CIP

A CIP catalogue record for this book is available from the British Library.

Acknowledgments

Several people contributed in important ways to this volume, and we wish gratefully to acknowledge their assistance. Michael Jones originally pointed out to us that Peter Demetz was approaching a "round birthday" and that a *Festschrift* would soon be in order. Melissa Vogelsang compiled the selective bibliography of Peter Demetz's writings, and we greatly appreciate her efforts. Marilyn Fries offered opportune advice and assistance.

Without the patient counsel and willing efforts of Jeffrey L. Sammons, our editorial tasks would have been much more onerous. He was genuinely interested and helpful from the very beginning. The cheerful competence of our editor, Joyce Harrison at the University of Michigan Press, sustained us in bringing the manuscript into final form. Our sincere gratitude goes to her. Finally, we wish to thank the contributors for their fine essays in tribute to Peter Demetz.

Contents

Introduction

Nancy Kaiser and David E. Wellbery

The essays collected here under the title *Traditions of Experiment from the Enlightenment to the Present* honor Peter Demetz on the occasion of his seventieth birthday. In both scope and theme, these contributions by colleagues and former students are highly appropriate to the person whose achievements as teacher and scholar/critic they celebrate. The role of experimentation in the history of literature has long been one of Demetz's preoccupations. This abiding interest clearly shapes his most recent book on Italian Futurism and the German avant-garde, and it likewise informs the perspective of such earlier works as the introduction to Karl Gutzkow's critical writings or the investigations of contemporary German-language literatures in *Post-War German Literature* and *After the Fires*. Beyond such thematic connections to his scholarship, however, we feel the productive and provocative tension implied in the title of this volume points to essential features of Peter Demetz's personality. Consistently seeking to establish dialogue between established conventions and marginal practices, Demetz has described himself as "respectful of tradition," yet "not a traditionalist entirely."[1] Not an easy balance to maintain these days, such a position recognizes, respects, and builds upon apparent incompatibilities and incommensurabilities. It prefers the noisy world of intellectual and historical contradiction to the arid consistency of simplifying theories. The troubled history of our century has touched the times and places of Peter Demetz's life in such a way as to strengthen in his writing and teaching what was perhaps an innate distrust of all forms of self-confirming doctrine. He has also always remained open to the provocation of the works of

---

1. Peter Demetz, "Varieties of Phonetic Poetry," in *From Kafka to Brecht and Beyond,* ed. Reinhold Grimm, Peter Spycher, and Richard A. Zipser (Madison: University of Wisconsin Press, 1982), 23.

literature themselves, devoting his seminars "at least occasionally, to the wildest, wooliest, and most radical texts" because of the essential questions they raise about "literary architecture" and about the sensual shaping of language as material.[2]

Peter Demetz's scholarly and academic career presents an impressive trajectory. His first doctorate was granted by Charles University in Prague in 1947, his second by Yale University in 1956—dates and places that alone convey a difficult itinerary of dislocation and reestablishment. The intermediate stages included Zurich, London, Munich, and New York, but Yale University and New Haven, Connecticut, finally became something of a permanent home. In December, 1990, having set a standard of professional excellence rarely attained within the American academy during his thirty-four years of faculty service, Demetz retired from Yale as Sterling Professor of German (Professor of German and Comparative Literature). We refer the reader to the list of selected publications at the end of this volume and to the list of dissertations completed under Demetz's direction, remarkable gauges of his achievements as scholar and teacher. His accomplishments have been recognized through numerous awards and honors: fellowships from the Guggenheim Foundation and the National Endowment for the Humanities; membership in the Berlin Academy of Arts and in the American, Austrian, and German P.E.N. clubs; numerous visiting professorships, including Cornell, Columbia, Princeton, and St. Gallen (Switzerland); a visit as Fellow to the Institute for Advanced Study (Wissenschaftskolleg) in Berlin; the Golden Goethe Medal and the Commander's Cross of the Order of Merit from the Federal Republic of Germany. To say that this was a distinguished career seems, albeit true, hardly adequate: the retirement ceremonies at the cusp of the century's tenth decade marked for many of us who have been associated with German Studies at Yale the end of the Demetz era.

But the motivation of a *Festschrift* does not finally have its source in an array of certifiable honors and accomplishments. Something more elusive and, at the same time, more essential is involved: an intellectual physiognomy, a persistent configuration of action and response, the individual ethos that has impressed itself on the thought and lives of students and colleagues. Of course, as anyone reasonably well acquainted with Demetz can attest, he is not a person one ever ultimately knows. Something—perhaps an instinctive sense of discretion—holds him beyond the horizon

---

2. Peter Demetz, "Reflections of an Emeritus (To-Be)," *Profession*, 1990, 6.

of familiarity. Nevertheless, in our editorial discussions while preparing *Traditions of Experiment,* our joint reflection on the man who had been our most significant teacher began to yield something like a consistent constellation, a texture we found recurring in all our contacts with Peter Demetz. Certainly there is nothing definitive about the image we have come to form, and others, having encountered him in different contexts, would no doubt sketch a different picture. But all such sketches, to the degree they capture something authentic, will involve a dynamic interplay of elements that, on the surface, seem in conflict. "I cannot but accept the internal contradictions of such an approach," he writes in the preface to *After the Fires* with reference to his enterprise of synthesizing sociohistorical and formalist concerns.[3] The productive tension Demetz ascribes to his critical methodology is the salient structural feature of the individual ethos we should like to evoke here. In particular, the force field or configuration that strikes us as specific to Demetz's work and personality is drawn between four poles: an insistent focus on the material construction of the aesthetic artifact; untiring allegiance to the public role and responsibilities of the scholar; a resolutely cosmopolitan perspective; and a rational, analytic mode of criticism that retains a passionate edge.

All of Peter Demetz's work pays careful attention to arrangement and aesthetic detail. His writing betrays what might be termed a constructivist impulse, a desire to regard a work of literature from all sides, to see how it works, how it is made. Like Kurt Schwitters, Demetz takes his materialism literally, attending to the shapes of sound and typography as well as larger compositional patterns. Perhaps such a palpably materialist aesthetic nourishes his discomfort with certain brands of Marxist criticism, in which materialism writ large diminishes the aesthetic object to an exemplum in a historical scheme. Reductionism in any form is alien to his writings; even the most tendentious nineteenth-century novel receives critical attention to particulars of structure and language. As detailed in an article from 1962, for example, the flawed endeavor of Karl Gutzkow's *Ritter vom Geiste* is apparent in the narrative stance as well as in the contradictions of its liberal political message. Gutzkow's political and narrative experiment remains trapped within the confines of Romantic idealism with a penchant for antisocial *Innerlichkeit,* unfortunately not for the last time in the German tradition.

---

3. Peter Demetz, *After the Fires: Recent Writing in the Germanies, Austria, and Switzerland* (New York: Harcourt Brace Jovanovich, 1986), xii.

The attention paid to the material construction of the artefact has placed Peter Demetz at odds not only with numerous representatives of Marxist scholarship, but also with the latter-day proponents of a literary and cultural criticism increasingly removed from the aesthetic object in an adherence to theoretical issues. The Comparative Literature Program at Yale has, of course, been a center of contemporary theory and no one could teach there unscathed, but, in his critical work, Demetz has always insisted upon confronting theory with its ostensible object, the literary text. Long an admirer of Susan Sontag's essay "Against Interpretation," he has kept many of us aware of the sensory deprivation that can result from overexposure to theoretical concerns at the expense of what Sontag calls an "erotics of art." Ever the careful reader, however, he refuses her simple opposition between erotics and hermeneutics. Their very entanglement represents one of the traditions, reaching at least back to Friedrich Schleiermacher, from which Demetz's writing has drawn many innovative impulses. In his 1989 valediction, "Reflections of an Emeritus (To-Be)," he questions the contemporary over-reliance on certain Continental philosophers, notably Nietzsche and Heidegger, and the neglect of "entire batches of other Continental traditions, those attentive to the aesthetic implications of verbal constructs."[4] He insists, in other words, on literature as provocation of its professed theoreticians.

The insistent interest in the material construction of the aesthetic object has often highlighted the practice of artistic experimentation. In all of its variations, artistic experimentation involves a testing of limits, a transgression of culturally sanctioned borders, and Peter Demetz frequently works in such liminal realms. His analyses of modern phonetic poetry, for example, stress the necessity of regarding "language experiments which radically *unbalance* that which we believe to be proper balance, proportion and integrity."[5] The presemantic confrontation with a literary work, as the Russian Formalists well knew and Peter Demetz's work on modern concrete poetry or on Schwitters, Ball, and Dada reminds us, alerts us to an artistic excess beyond, or prior to, meaning. Experimenting with traditional expectations opens insights in both directions, an awareness of the constructed aspect of the tradition and an appreciation for the bold transgression of aesthetic experiment. Not restricted to his work on twentieth-century literature, these insights inform such other areas of Peter Demetz's scholarship as his ambi-

---

4. Demetz, "Reflections," 5.
5. Demetz, "Varieties," 24.

tious essay on Lessing's *Nathan der Weise* (1966). Lessing's deliberate use of blank verse and his equally calculated transgression of the metrical norm are shown to sustain such other innovative aspects of the drama as its transformation of the comic genre and its parti pris on behalf of religious tolerance.

With such studies, which became classic works of postwar scholarship, Peter Demetz combines analysis of structure and aesthetic detail with careful heed to history and social significance. No responsible twentieth-century scholar with firsthand experience of Nazism and Stalinism could retreat into pure aesthetic formalism, and Demetz never has. His 1953 study, *René Rilkes Prager Jahre,* confronted contemporary Rilke scholarship with its obstinate neglect of specific historical, linguistic, and social contexts, as well as with its overwrought readings. The preface to *After the Fires* states clearly the intention "to do justice both to the claims of social life and to the stubborn shapes of writing."[6] In such projects, the heritage of Prague extends beyond the biographical birthplace it was for both Peter Demetz and Rilke. The intellectual legacy of the Prague School of linguistics foregrounds the structured, material character of the work of art while recognizing the interlacing of its semiotic properties with historically variable social contexts. As a teacher, Demetz transmitted an appreciation for the work of such Prague structuralists as Jan Mukařovsky and Felix Vodička. It was an appreciation shared by his teacher, mentor, and close friend, René Wellek, a compatriot and colleague at Yale. In the work of Peter Demetz, the Prague structuralist mediation of social reality and literary text has always been convincingly and vividly accomplished.

Our emphasis on the formalist, even constructivist tendency in Demetz's scholarship and teaching would be reductive were it not balanced by an insistence on the element of social responsibility so central to his career. One of the most important lessons Demetz passed on to his students bears on the intricate linkages between aesthetic and ethical-political concerns so forcefully evident in his writing and professional life. These linkages were never a matter of urgent asseveration. Keenly allergic to doctrinal pronouncements, Demetz thematized his own convictions regarding the political relevance of literature and art only within the scare quotes of wry distanciation. An example of this is his frequent self-stylization as a throwback to the prerevolutionary eighteenth century, which "did not yet believe that an *interesseloses Wohlgefallen* ('disinterested pleasure') was totally incom-

---

6. Demetz, *After the Fires,* xiii.

patible with a citizen's active engagement."[7] Ironically, the historical anach-
ronism Demetz here ascribes to himself issues from historical insight. As
we mentioned previously, the young Prague intellectual suffered through
two waves of ideological violence—Nazism and Stalinism—that sought,
among other perfidious aims, the elimination of that delicate balance
between aesthetic sensibility and civic responsibility the Enlightenment
philosophes had conceptualized and practiced. The political history he lived
through, Demetz occasionally remarked, prevented his becoming a formalist, but it equally precluded his underwriting any body of thought that
subordinates the aesthetic to a sphere of relevance viewed as ultimate or
foundational.

Perhaps the subtlest and most intimate connection between the concerns
of the formalist and those of the citizen is woven in the act of critical
judgment. No doubt this is why Demetz's popular Yale course on literary
theory ("Literature Y") culminated in questions of axiology long before
these became fashionable fodder for discussion. Not only did he recognize
that evaluation is an ineluctable component of literary criticism, he also
acutely sensed how every evaluative act crosses and recrosses the limit
between private sensibility and public norms. This oscillating movement
elicits social answerability from individual preference and, at the same
time, exposes generally accepted codes of value to the invigorating challenge of idiosyncratic tastes. Aesthetic evaluation is an interpenetration of
spheres and, as the aestheticians of the Enlightenment were the first to
recognize, no preexisting order determines how this confrontation of sensibility and sociality will turn out in any given case. Hence the poverty
(and the danger) of a criticism that avoids the risks of evaluation by
shielding itself with an a priori vision of the course of history or with some
other foundationalist dogma. If it is truly to complexify the texture of our
cooperations and deepen the understanding of our isolations, the interplay
of assessment and acknowledgment must remain unforeseeable.

As if to demonstrate the public and political significance of the act of
aesthetic judgment, Demetz has consistently and brilliantly engaged himself in the fray of critical debate for more than thirty years. His reviews
of contemporary literature and his reevaluations of past writers in such
periodicals as *Die Zeit* and the *Frankfurter Allgemeine Zeitung* have established
him as one of the most perspicacious critical voices of postwar Germany.
Since 1986, he has been a jury member for the prestigious Ingeborg

---

7. Demetz, "Reflections," 3.

Bachmann awards, perhaps the single most important literary prize awarded to younger writers in the German-speaking world, and commentators on these often charged and controversial proceedings have noted the flexibility of response and craftsmanlike precision in judgment that Demetz brings to the discussions. In fact, the only such dual career, combining scholarship with journalistic criticism, of equal merit that comes to mind is that of Walter Jens, like Demetz a great admirer of Lessing and an active member of the German P.E.N. Club and the Academy of the Arts. Demetz, the Prague-born resident of the United States, has become, from his outsider position, something of a *praeceptor germaniae*, exemplifying in his essays and reviews the integrity, freshness of perception, and tact that are the requisite virtues of a literate culture.

From the time Peter Demetz entered the world of American university education in 1953 until the present, the educational institutions and sub-institutions associated with the teaching of literature have undergone complex transformations: the universities themselves, especially after Sputnik, have expanded considerably; patterns of funding have altered and the network of interdependencies among universities, foundations, government agencies, and corporations has become intricately knotted; demographic patterns of student selection and faculty and staff hiring have changed; scholarly interest groups have evolved into professional organizations that exercise a variety of social and political functions. There has never been a literature, Ernst Robert Curtius once remarked, that was not supported by some form of educational institution, some framework of regulated instruction in literary techniques and traditions, but, in the postwar world of American (and for that matter European) education, the truth of this aperçu is massive. We mention this here because we believe that the institutional frames of literary education in the United States constitute one of the important dimensions in which Peter Demetz's achievement— the achievement honored in this *Festschrift*—has taken shape. He has held, of course, more than his share of chairmanships at Yale (ten years in the Department of Germanic Languages and Literatures, three years in the Division of the Humanities) and made more than his share of trips to Washington to serve on NEH committees or Fulbright selection boards. He is among the few Germanists to have been elected president of the Modern Language Association (1981), perhaps the most complex such professional organization in the world and certainly the major institutional voice on behalf of literacy, in all senses of the word, in the United States. The MLA presidency recompenses the immense tasks it imposes on its holder with highly visible honors, but Demetz has also worked effectively for many years on the less visible, grass-roots levels of language and literary education, for example in the American Association of Teachers of German. These are important and essential contributions that attest to the concept of social responsibility we would like our sketch to emphasize. Several of Demetz's students and colleagues, however, would probably prefer to stress a less official, but no less significant, aspect of his institutional and educational engagement: his generosity in fostering others' careers, his patience as reader and adviser, his judicious advocacy of the cause of democratization within the academy. Such are his fairness and impartiality, his concrete sense of what needs to be done, that some Yale colleagues referred to him fondly as Peter the Wise.

In speaking about civic responsibility as a defining feature of Peter Demetz's career we called attention to two major domains of activity, the German-speaking world of journalistic criticism and the world of the American academy. Perhaps the most remarkable and singular aspect of Demetz's overall achievement is that it spans the breach between the continents in this way; he is both the respected critic writing for the German-language press and the esteemed American educator. This strikes us as symptomatic of the third major trait we would like our sketch to bring out: Demetz's refusal to define himself within one national sphere of activity, his movement across linguistic and cultural borders, his cosmopolitanism. In some autobiographical remarks presented to the Berlin Academy of Arts, Demetz indicated that one reason he found the United States a congenial place to take up his university career was that the Americans never demanded from him that he become one of their own. Here he could maintain a certain distance from national identity and, at the same time, participate fully in the country's institutions. Perhaps this instinct for multiplicity stems from the polyglot and culturally various ambience of Prague, from which, of course, Rilke and Kafka, two of Demetz's authors, drew the energies of their art. But whatever its source, Demetz's resolute internationalism represents one of the fundamental aspects of his character for all who know him well.

One expression of this is the fact that Demetz has always been a passionate, and even somewhat arcane, traveler. Capable of finding life forms of compelling interest in the flat sunlight of Louisiana evenings (Walker Percy's territory) or in the artificial illumination of a Port au Prince night (where readers, having no electricity in their homes, gather beneath the street lamps), Demetz's fascination for the remote and strange seems intensified when he discovers it embedded within the texture of quotidian occurrences. His richly textured travel essays recount explorations that conform neither to the guidebooks of vacationism nor to the edifying agendas of the *Bildungsbürgertum*. Travel for Demetz, one suspects, is a way of exploding the constraints of entrenched classifications by exposing them to the incomprehensible rustle he hears in the background of foreign scenes, to the shocks of amazement that punctuate his peregrinations. But his wanderings are also a method for testing out different stories of himself, and anyone who has talked with him about Portugal, to cite just one example, knows how he can invent something like the feel of an alternative life from the flux of perceptions a country offers him. With the recent political changes in Czechoslovakia and the lifting of the ban that had prevented his return there for forty years, Demetz's travels can now take him to the place that is perhaps the strangest of all for him. One can be sure that, whatever he will have to say about this at once surprising and familiar Central European world, it will be free of clichés and freshly perceived.

Cosmopolitan, too, is the spectrum of Demetz's literary and artistic interests. At any moment one might encounter among the books assembled for current reading on his coffee table texts by such young writers as the American T. Coraghessan Boyle, modern standards such as the stories of Tommaso Landolfi, curiosities such as the letters of H. L. Mencken, or new editions of such classic authors as Lessing or Varnhagen. He is alert for literary talent wherever it can be found and his reading has never been dictated—as is so often the case in the professorial guild—by the protocols of academic specialization. In fact, one of the most important lessons Demetz taught his students was not to let established canons of taste impair their appreciations. While Thomas Pynchon was to most Germanists a hipster writer (at best) and a pornographer to the overseers of the Pulitzer prize, Demetz proclaimed *Gravity's Rainbow* the most significant novelistic account of World War II on the international literary scene. Long before the lexicon of film criticism came to inform the patois of academic literary study, Demetz was an avid moviegoer whose fascination with the cinema (like that of both Kafka and Wittgenstein, by the way) always had the character of authentic enthrallment. Hence his attraction to such directors as Ken Russell, whose extravagant productions, at the risk of affront, reveal something of the affective force of the film medium. Perhaps it was this same sense of a liberating engagement with the artistic medium that attracted him more recently to the Italian Futurist painters, especially Umberto Boccioni.

Demetz once lamented the tendency in German criticism to ignore "the complicated weave of world literature,"[8] and one could see in this anti-parochial concern for the international texture of literary history the ethos that animates much of his own work as a scholar and critic. Perhaps his book on Fontane (1964) exemplifies this best. By viewing his work against the background of European realism from Walter Scott to Henry James, Demetz virtually rediscovered this most subtle and humane novelist of the German nineteenth century. But the insistence on a cosmopolitan perspective is also forcefully in evidence in his latest book. *Worte in Freiheit* (the title echoes and comments on Marinetti's *parole in liberta*) explores "the futurist affinities that open and link so-called expressionism, which otherwise would remain a concern solely of German literature, to the international discussion of the new possibilities of poetry and language."[9] With magnificent essays on Fernando Pessoa, the Portuguese modernist, and Gabriele D'Annunzio, the poet-prince of Montenevoso, Demetz has recently added to the impressive series of his contributions to the German press calling attention to the world-literary scene. Needless to say, he has also done much, through translations, introductions, and editions, to acquaint the West European world with the achievements of classic and contemporary Czech writers. Clearly, the field of comparative literature, in which he received his Yale Ph.D. and continued throughout his teaching career to participate actively, embodies for Demetz something like a necessity of thought.

The first graduate seminar Peter Demetz taught at Yale was on Lessing and the eighteenth century, as was his final graduate seminar in the fall of 1990. Certainly it is not accidental that the Enlightenment dramatist provided Demetz, as it were, with his entrance and exit lines. The affinities between the two literati are manifold. In a 1971 essay in *Merkur,* the twentieth-century Yale professor probes the challenging legacy of the eighteenth-century man of letters and, in the process, characterizes aspects of his own critical position.[10] In aesthetic matters, Lessing is depicted as ever the *technomorph,* examining the relationship of the artist as artisan to the raw material of his craft. The polemic opening of *Laokoon* takes issue, in Demetz's reading, not simply with Winckelmann, but with idealist aesthet-

---

8. Peter Demetz, "Kitsch, Belletristik, Kunst: Theodor Fontane," *Anmerkungen zur Zeit,* Heft 44 (Berlin: published for the Berlin Academy by Gebr. Mann, 1971), 5.

9. Peter Demetz, *Worte in Freiheit: Der italienische Futurismus und die deutsche literarische Avant-garde, 1912–34* (Munich: Piper, 1990), 154–55.

10. Peter Demetz, "Die Folgenlosigkeit Lessings," *Merkur* 25 (1971): 727–42.

ics and metaphysical exegesis. As the rationalist critic of religion, Lessing is described as subtly refusing the conflation of revelation and rational explanation in any hurried fashion. Remnants of German pietism color his writings, and he is wary of overhasty proclamations of the reign of reason. In fact, Lessing's own sense of historical tempo is best characterized a century later by Melusine in Fontane's *Stechlin,* a novel Demetz interprets as following in the tradition of Lessing: "Alles Alte, soweit es Anspruch darauf hat, sollen wir lieben, aber für das Neue sollen wir recht eigentlich leben."[11] The words aptly characterize the stance of Lessing's *Erziehung des Menschenges-chlechts* as well, and point to a balance of tradition and change also perceptible in Lessing's dramatic writing. Demetz's *Merkur* essay recalls the centrality of Aristotle to Lessing's innovative dramaturgy and the respect for Diderot that parallels his admiration for Shakespeare. The coexistence of innovation and tradition, an Enlightenment aware of its own potentially destructive dialectic, a technomorphic aesthetic, a highly analytic expository style, the gracefully learned and yet direct polemical thrust, the stance of the rationalist *engagé:* we are characterizing both the eighteenth-century writer and the twentieth-century Yale professor and literary critic.

The affinities between Demetz and Lessing are symptomatic of the fourth aspect of the critical ethos we would like our sketch to highlight: Demetz's roots are in the eighteenth century and, however wry or ironic his occasional declarations of allegiance to the attitudes of the Enlightenment *philosophes* might be, they nevertheless reveal something essential about his character. The eighteenth century from which Demetz draws his inspiration has, of course, nothing to do with the aristocratic milieu of snobbishness, superstition, and vicious backbiting so well described by Casanova. His is the world of Smith and Hume, Voltaire and Diderot, Lessing and Mendelssohn: a world, that is, of lucid skepticism combined with elegance and wit; a world in which formalist inclinations predominate in aesthetic discussions and civic responsibility defines the nature of political engagement; a world of urbane cosmopolitanism unclouded by the turgid pronouncements of nationalism. Of course, since the 1960s, *Aufklärung* has become a shibboleth of right-mindedness in Germany, acquiring thereby an oppressively moralistic force that Demetz would be the first to abjure. The Prague-born son of Catholic-Jewish parents could not fail to see through the grandiloquence that makes Enlightenment the historico-

---

11. Theodor Fontane, *Sämtliche Werke,* ed. Edgar Gross (Munich: Nymphenburger Verlag, 1959), 8:251.

philosophical project of modernity. Enlightenment is a style, an attitude, an ethos, and its historical destiny has less to do with the march of modernity than with traditions of artistic and intellectual experimentation that have remained marginal provocations, renewing themselves in the face of the ever-present threat of historical extinction. *Worte in Freiheit, parole in liberta,* words in freedom: perhaps Marinetti's formula for a language of the future is Demetz's definition of an enlightening literature. And perhaps the real theme of his book on the fate of Futurism in Germany (note the dates of the study: 1912–34) is that the liberty that sustains and is sustained by an enlightening literature is a fragile, precarious thing.

A quick look at Demetz's bibliography reveals a rather astonishing fact. Although one of the most significant scholar-critics of the German literary tradition during this century's second half, Demetz has written practically nothing on what is usually held to be the center and apex of that tradition, the classical-romantic era of Goethe, Schiller, Hölderlin, the Schlegel brothers, Novalis, Tieck, Brentano, and Kleist (to mention only some of the major names). Weimar and Jena hold little fascination for him, and, on several occasions, he has exhibited an almost allergic reaction to the philosophical aesthetics of a Schelling, Solger, or Hegel. In our view, this avoidance has nothing to do with the restrictions of scholarly specialization, which Demetz has always happily ignored. Rather, it stems from what might be called Demetz's own strategic view of literary history. However immense its accomplishments, the classical-romantic period nevertheless represents a duplex historical development that runs counter to Demetz's most fundamental literary values: the elimination of the cosmopolitan framework of literary-intellectual discourse that had characterized the Enlightenment and its replacement with the framework of a nationally (and, somewhat later, nationalistically) conceived history; the demise of the constructivist-sensualist aesthetic of the Enlightenment and the ascendence of a hermeneutic-metaphysical conception of art. Moreover, it would be an easy matter to show that the institutionalization of literary education in Germany, with all its stultifying didacticism and its history of dubious allegiances, has, from the mid-nineteenth century until the present day, based itself on the preeminence of classical-romantic works. Viewed in this context, Demetz's scholarship and criticism, moving from the Enlightenment of Lessing to the anticlassicism of Gutzkow and the liberal critics of pre-1848 Germany, rediscovering the international affiliations of Fontane's urbane artistry, attending to the polyglot and, nationally speaking, eccentric backgrounds of the Prague-born writers Rilke and Kafka, tracing the various strands of linguistic experimentation in twentieth-century literature, and, finally, undertaking again and again the risk of aesthetic judgement in his readings and evaluations of contemporary German-language writers, this rich and expansive oeuvre, we want to claim, can be read as the effort to recall and render culturally vital a tradition, or weave of traditions, alternative to the official literary history of Germany. One way of epitomizing this complex critical enterprise would be to see it as a way of keeping alive the Enlightenment values to which Peter Demetz is so profoundly committed.

The aim of *Traditions of Experiment from the Enlightenment to the Present* is to demonstrate our respect and gratitude for that critical enterprise. We wish to call attention to the humane abundance of Peter Demetz's scholarship, to celebrate his achievements as teacher and colleague, and to acknowledge our indebtedness to his generosity of spirit. We wish, even more, to express our eager anticipation of the complexly textured cooperations with Peter Demetz the future holds: the writings and readings, the travels, encounters and conversations, the shocks of amazement. Perhaps the Fontane whom Demetz taught us to savor said it best: "Alles Alte, soweit es Anspruch darauf hat, sollen wir lieben, aber für das Neue sollen wir recht eigentlich leben."

Part 1
Of Enlightenment, Poetic Revolution, and Bourgeois Literature: The Eighteenth and Nineteenth Centuries

Whatever Moves You: "Experimental Philosophy" and the Literature of Experience in Diderot and Kleist

Claudia Brodsky

Some forty years before Kant equated what we know with how we know, the authors of the French Enlightenment looked to the external world and the human mind, discovered no certain connection between them, and attempted to bridge the gap. The rise of natural science, in conflict with Christian dogma, combined with the more flexible perspectives of deism and atheism to form the different materialisms that defined the intellectual tendency of the age. Maupertuis, Buffon, La Mettrie, Helvétius—all appealed individually to the forces of environmental conditions, evolution, and the senses in order to arrive at an empirical description of internal experience, rejecting a priori any metaphysical system smacking of Descartes's God. As traditional theology and philosophy lost their explanatory power to enlightened empiricism, the observation of experience became the new basis for describing what was still called—if now in the context of secular, epistemological investigations—the soul.

An avid surveyor of these developments, Diderot translated the empirical methods of his contemporaries from their application in the natural sciences to speculative philosophy by taking as his focal point the key Enlightenment concept of "experiment."[1] In so doing he not only made philosophical

---

1. The case for the centrality of the concept of "experiment" to Enlightenment philosophy will be made most forcefully by Kant. In the "Vorrede zur zweiten Auflage" of the *Kritik der reinen Vernunlt* (2d ed., 1787), Kant describes his own critical philosophy as an "experiment in imitating" (*zum Versuche nachzuahmen*) the "experiments" (*Versuche*) that, at key historical moments, have revolutionized mathematics and the natural sciences. The "revolution" he is about to effect in metaphysics should be viewed, Kant proposes, as just such an "experiment." See Immanuel Kant, *Werkausgabe*, ed. Wilhelm Weischedel (Frankfurt: Suhrkamp, 1977), B11-21, 3:22-27.

problems into material and aesthetic ones (and vice versa) but gave new form and function to the writing of fiction. This essay will examine literary and literary-theoretical works of Diderot in which the activity he called "experimental philosophy" is formulated and practiced[2]—*La Religieuse, Les Bijoux indiscrets,* and *Le Paradoxe sur le comédien.* Together with Diderot's earliest speculative writings,[3] these works may be seen to constitute the origin of a modern tradition of experiment in literature, that is, a tradition not so much of exploring innovative or changing literary forms—although Diderot also did that[4]—but of making literature the form of a specific kind of exploration, one that attempts, by way of experiments recounted and represented, to fuse empirical with speculative discourse and so to reveal the inner dynamics of experience that routine perception can only obscure.[5] The invisible motions of the soul, mind, or spirit to which Diderot's experiments give verbal form cannot be accounted for either by faith in a prime mover or by the physical uniformity of movement hypothesized by Descartes. They are what moves us in the active, experiential sense, and knowledge of them became an object of literature with and since Diderot. It is this literary tradition of speculating on experience by way of experiment that was soon pushed to its limit in the disassociation of knowledge from action represented in the markedly Diderotian works of Kleist.

Diderot's literary experiments take root in the concept of empirical

---

2. See Denis Diderot, *De l'Interprétation de la nature,* in *Oeuvres complètes,* ed. H. Dieckmann, J. Varloot, and J. Proust (Paris: Hermann, 1975–), 9:28, 32, 35, 43, 45, 71 (unless otherwise indicated, all subsequent quotations from Diderot are from this edition and will be noted in the text as *Oeuvres*; all translations in this essay are my own). Cf. Joachim Ozdoba, *Heuristik der Fiktion: Künstlerische und philosophische Interpretation der Wirklichkeit in Diderots contes (1748–1772)* (Frankfurt: Peter Lang, 1980), in which the notion of Diderot's "experimentation" is limited to the "moral and psychological" elements of his satiric fiction (25).

3. The major premises of some of these early speculative experiments are summarized subsequently. Detailed discussions are included in a book I am completing on the relationship between the Enlightenment and Romanticism.

4. I refer here primarily to his formative conception of *le genre sérieux,* the notion of a mixed, anticlassical drama of "conditions" embraced first in Germany by Lessing and later in France by Constant. See Diderot, *Entretiens sur le Fils naturel, Oeuvres* 10:128–51; G. E. Lessing, "Das Theater des Herrn Diderot" and *Hamburgische Dramaturgie* in *Sämtliche Schriften,* ed. Karl Lachmann and Franz Mucker (Stuttgart, 1886–1919), 8:287–89 and 11.1:179–11.2 respectively; B. Constant, "Réflexions sur la tragédie," in *Oeuvres complètes* (Paris: Gallimard, 1957), 933–67. I owe my own study of Diderot and Lessing in particular, and of Enlightenment literature and theory in general, to Peter Demetz.

5. The model of discursive experimentation described here should be sharply distinguished from the *modèle idéale* of beauty in plastic arts referred to in the *Salons.* Cf. Scott S. Bryon, "Diderot and Kant, or the Construction of 'Truth,'" *Papers in Language and Literature* 21 (1985): 370–82.

"decomposition" explicitly formulated in *De l'Interprétation de la nature* (1753, rev. 1754; *Oeuvres* 9:37, 43–45) and demonstrated in his earlier *Lettre sur les aveugles à l'usage de ceux qui voient* (1749) and *Lettre sur les sourds et muets à l'usage de ceux qui entendent et qui parlent* (1751). The working hypothesis of the speculative experiments described in the *Lettres* is that only a "decomposed" or sensorially deprived subject could provide a proper vehicle for empirical knowledge of the soul precisely because such a subject is compelled by nature to communicate metaphorically. In the absence of one of the natural *portes* to the soul (as Diderot calls the senses [*Lettre sur les aveugles, Oeuvres* 4:34]), the blind or deaf are forced to transport sensory information by way of a substitute medium. The compensatory "symbols" they "invent" throw the relationship between sensory experience and the workings of the soul into relief by exposing the linguistic transformation of experience that fully conventional or naturalized sign systems render imperceptible (4:34). Bereft of the light of nature, the sensorially deprived invent pointedly nonnatural signs that shed "a double light," "the reflected light of metaphor," for while "proper to one sense" these signs are "metaphoric at the same time to another" (4:34). The experience of "decomposition" thus yields enlightening experiments in composition; the compensatory languages described in the *Lettres* are the visible results of experiments that the sensorially deprived are forced to perform on themselves. As such, the inventions of the sensorially deprived are symbols of Diderot's own experimental inventions as well, symbols made to stand for internal activities that the empirical observer cannot otherwise know.

In the *Lettre sur les aveugles,* Diderot's blind Saunderson is just such a symbolic invention,[6] a fictional model of the soul forced by sensory deprivation to speculate on the chaotic force of nature of which it is a product, articulating a vision of endless material permutation that the sighted cannot even imagine (*Oeuvres* 4:48–52). In the *Lettre sur les sourds et muets,* Diderot suggests that the distinct sensory and mental activities of the soul may occur simultaneously, "at exactly the same instant" (4:157). In the course of describing the experimental language of subjects deprived of hearing and speech, Diderot invents two "double" or "metaphoric" models of this internal "paradox" of experiential and reflective simultaneity (157): the sensory model of the soul as ornamental appendage to man viewed as an

---

6. The historical Nicholas Saunderson was professor of mathematics at Cambridge, author of *The Elements of Algebra* (1740–41), and inventor of the tactile calculator described in the *Lettre sur les aveugles.* The deathbed speech attributed to him in *Lettre,* however, is Diderot's own composition or fictional experiment in the experience of "decomposition."

"automaton," or "ambulatory clock" (159); and the linguistic model of the soul as the discourse of "poetry," figured in turn as a "tissue of hiero-glyphs" (169). The sequence of Diderot's early theoretical experiments—which can only be cursorily outlined here—leads from empirical models of the soul revealed through sensory "decomposition" or deprivation, to the model of the soul as hypothetical "paradox," the fiction of a nonsequential, strictly illegible discourse, a simultaneous composition or compilation of hieroglyphs.

But the sequence extending from sensory decomposition to poetry, from discursive experiments in enlightenment to the opaque hieroglyph, is even-tually turned back upon empirical experience. Like the metaphoric sensory and linguistic models of the soul offered in the *Lettre sur les sourds et muets,* that reference takes two related forms. In the *Paradoxe sur le comédien* (pub-lished in 1830) Diderot refers the paradox of the soul to external reality in the form of a theory of a particular kind of experience, the experience of dramatic acting in which that paradox is played out empirically. Here the actor on the stage takes the place of the hieroglyph in the text, and Diderot's notion of sensory and reflective simultaneity[7]—now considered from a different experimental angle—is described, in categorical theoretical terms, as void. Diderot's second form of reference outside the soul—one that must be considered conjointly with the theoretical *Paradoxe*—is the literary form of a novel in which the "paradox of acting" itself is represented discursively. The novel, *La Religieuse,* has traditionally been viewed exclu-sively as a mimetic fiction (of innocence persecuted) rather than a fictional representation of theoretical speculations, or *experimental* fiction (in the Diderotian sense).[8] Yet *La Religieuse* is perhaps the most telling example

---

7. The paradox of the simultaneous mental and sensory composition of experience re-mains central to Diderot's concept of human comprehension; cf. *Eléments de physiologie* (1778), chap. 2, "Understanding": "Objects act upon the senses . . . no sensation is either simple or momentary, for, if I may be allowed to so express myself, [sensation] is a bundle[. . . .]For the simple reason that each sensation is composed, it supposes the judgment or affirmation of several qualities experienced at the same time" (*Oeuvres* 17:462).

8. One could say that the "paradox of acting" has been so skillfully represented in *La Religieuse* that it has been read, praised, and blamed solely in terms of the drama of convent life it stages, a drama in which the heroine and her persecutors are all too sharply defined. For the history of the reception of the novel, see Georges May, *Diderot et La Religieuse* (Paris: Presses Universitaires de France, 1954), 21–34. Modern interpreters of the novel who view it as a human "tragedy"—and these span the gamut from May to Jeffrey Mehlman (see his provocative *Cataract* [Middletown, Conn.: Wesleyan University Press, 1979], 90)—most closely resemble the viewers of a dramatic performance persuaded by the very paradox of which they must remain unaware.

of Diderot's empirical-experimental method because it is a novel that is the product of an actual experiment played out between friends.

Ten years before the publication of *La Religieuse* in the *Correspondance littéraire* (1780–82),[9] Grimm published (in the same journal) the contents of a series of letters that, along with prefatory and closing comments, formed the so-called Préface-Annexe that recounts the empirical circumstances of the novel's creation. Added to the text of *La Religieuse* in every edition of the work since its first book-length publication in 1796, the Préface-Annexe nonetheless has been a thorny subject for Diderot's editors.[10] In the earliest standard edition of Diderot's works (1798), Naigeon characterized it as directly injurious to the "truth" of the novel and argued for the suppression of the document. He compared it to a "scaffolding" that must be "destroyed" if our own "pleasure" in reading is not to be "destroyed" instead, a pleasure always dependent, in part, upon the preservation of "illusion."[11] By a logic of aestheticization opposing art to the empirical that has set the pattern for Diderot criticism, Naigeon considers the truth of the story behind *La Religieuse* destructive of the "truth" within *La Religieuse,* a truth reflected not by reality but by the pleasing impression of reality created by a mimetic fiction.

---

9. The publication history of *La Religieuse* is particularly complex. Diderot reworked the novel as it appeared in installments, and its first publication in book form (the Buisson edition of 1796) does not include all of his alterations. The Dieckmann edition (1975) cited here is based, like the Mauzi (1961) and Parrish (1963) editions, on the recently classified Vandeul collection in the Bibliothèque Nationale, and claims to be the first definitive edition of the text (see Georges May, "Introduction to *La Religieuse,*" in *Oeuvres* 11:12).

10. Herbert Dieckmann has chosen to curtail its title to Préface, arguing that the overtly ambiguous Préface-Annexe, which first appeared in the Assézat-Tourneux edition (1875–77), was probably formulated in response to the remark made at the close of the Préface-Annexe that "most of these letters are posterior to the novel." In addition, Dieckmann cites Diderot's own notation of the words, "preface to the preceding novel," on the extract of the Préface-Annexe that he corrected. Dieckmann explains the second of these equivocal references by the fact that the novel was already being serialized before Diderot corrected the Préface-Annexe; thus "preceding" would refer not to the order in which one is to read the novel vis-à-vis its preface but to the specific moment at which Diderot wrote the word *preceding,* i.e., a moment after the publication of the novel had begun (see Dieckmann, "Introduction to the Préface de *La Religieuse,*" in *Oeuvres* 11:15n). Dieckmann offers no explanation for discounting the first of these equivocal references, and, indeed, it would be difficult to do so, since the statement that the letters are posterior to the novel has been authenticated by Dieckmann himself as authored not by Grimm but by Diderot. Diderot's own indication that the preface should be read at "the end of the work" wraps the novel and preface around each other like a Moebius strip, and is surely the best reason for entitling the preface Préface-Annexe.

11. Naigeon's "Avertissement" is reprinted and contested in the Assézat-Tourneux edition (Paris: Garnier, 1875–77), 5:205–10.

There is, however, precious little reality in the story narrated in the Préface-Annexe to reflect poorly on the pleasurable "illusion" of *La Religieuse*. Or rather, what empirical reality there is has been manipulated by literary friends in service of a prank played on one of their own. According to Grimm, the group of friends gathered around the *Correspondance littéraire* attempted to lure back to Paris the Marquis de Croismare, whose recently developed taste for piety, acquired during a retreat to his country estate, threatened to remove him indefinitely from the company of his Parisian circle (*Oeuvres* 11:26). The actual letters that became the basis of the novel were exchanged in 1760 among the Marquis, a Mme. Madin, and a Suzanne Simonin; this is where—at least textually—Diderot's own experimental fiction begins. For while the Marquis was certainly a real enough historical personage, the same historical reality cannot be ascribed to the events and persons referred to in his letters, as the two female correspondents to whom they are written, are, on the one hand, all but a nominal, and on the other, all but a thematic fiction. Mme. Madin is the real name of a real person, but it is only really to that name, functioning as a kind of post office box, and not to the person that the Marquis addresses and sends his letters. Suzanne Simonin is a fictive name given to the real historical person of a persecuted young nun in whose case the Marquis had really taken an interest. The letters from the fictive Suzanne, a nonexistent nun modeled on a real one,[12] request the Marquis' protection following a fictive escape from captivity. "Mme. Madin" writes to the Marquis in the capacity of the nun's friend in hiding, her confidante and remitter of letters, and the real Mme. Madin, indeed, receives and remits the letters of the Marquis—directly, that is, into the hands of Grimm and Diderot; for it is Diderot who enacts the parts of both these empirically hybrid personae, writing in the roles of the two women to the Marquis. Grimm explains how "this mystification" of the Marquis was routed through the empirical.

We needed an address in order to receive the responses, and we chose a certain Madame Madin, wife of a retired infantry officer, who really lived at Versailles. She knew nothing of our trick, nor of the letters that we subsequently had written for her, and for which we used the handwriting of another young woman. Madame Madin was only advised

---

12. Marguerite Delamarre, whose petition to leave the Longchamp convent was denied by the Parlement of Paris in 1758 (see the account given in May, *Diderot*, 47–76).

that she had to receive and give over to me all letters stamped *Caen.* (*Oeuvres* 11:30, 38; italics in original)

The Marquis, who, Grimm explains, had never met nor known the actual name of the historical nun, is so thoroughly taken by Diderot's impersonations that he eventually invites Suzanne to join him at his estate, thereby forcing his friends, via Diderot's pen, to kill the girl off, terminating a fiction that had amused them over the course of several months. The Marquis eventually returns to Paris, where, Grimm notes, his pious devotion "evaporated, as everything evaporates," and he became "more likeable than ever before" (11:27).

But this return, Grimm states, dates from four years previous to the publication of the letters in the Préface-Annexe, or six years after their original composition, and is attributable, in all true probability [*vraisemblablement*], to real, nondiscursive events: the "successive" deaths of the Marquis' children (*Oeuvres* 11:27). The mixed contents and questionable outcome of this experiment thus raise the following, additional questions. Is the story related in the Préface-Annexe, of the "plot" behind the plot of *La Religieuse,* truly—which is to say empirically rather than artistically— that of an attempt to trick an errantly devout friend back into the social fold?[13] Can the results of an experiment undertaken in the knowledge that it is a fiction—the form of applied duplicity we call a practical joke—be considered in isolation from fiction? Finally, and most significantly, was the plot in fact directed at the truant Marquis to begin with?

Diderot, the actual author if not architect of the experiment, seems to have experienced his own doubts about the nature of the facts involved. In a letter to Mme. d'Epinay, he reports that "the Marquis has responded,"

---

13. A further wrinkle in this "plot" is that it appears to succeed only upon being revealed; Grimm writes of the Marquis, "Since his return to Paris, we admitted this wicked plot to him, he had a good laugh as you can imagine, and the misfortune of our poor nun only worked to tighten the bonds of friendship between those who survived her; however, he never spoke of it to M. Diderot" (*Oeuvres* 11:30). Later in the Préface-Annexe, Grimm admits that the joke was revealed to the Marquis not by plan but by chance. The Marquis happened to encounter the historical Mme. Madin, and the effect produced by this real and uncontrived event was, in Grimm's significant phrase, "a true *coup de théâtre*": "Chance had it that M. de Croismare, after his return to Paris, and about eight years after our sin, found Mme. Madin one morning at the home of one of our female friends who was in on the plot; this was a true *coup de théâtre*: M. de Croismare attempted to get every information about an unfortunate woman who had interested him so much, and of whose very existence Mme. Madin knew nothing. This was the moment of our general confession and absolution" (*Ouevres* 11:38–39).

the experiment is underway, but he continues, "Is all this really true? Is he really mad at heart? Is his head really in the clouds? Isn't there some monkey business about? For I am a bit distrustful of the whole lot of you."[14] Diderot's suspicion is also sounded in the body of the Préface-Annexe itself, which ends by asserting that the letters written by the fictive nun's "generous protector are real and were written in good faith, a fact of which one took all the pains in the world to persuade M. Diderot, who believed himself hoodwinked by the Marquis and by his friends" (*Oeuvres* 11:33). Finally, if the implication of a double deception at work in this discursive experiment did not already wreak havoc with the distinction between speculation and empirical fact, yet another consideration must be written into our understanding of the true story of *La Religieuse,* a discursive *and* empirical fact provided by the handwriting on the wall of literary history, actual manuscripts. In 1952, Herbert Dieckmann published photographic reproductions of two previously unedited manuscripts of the Préface-Annexe. What these manuscripts make visibly evident is that the composition of the Préface-Annexe was reworked and rewritten by none other than Diderot himself.[15] It was Diderot who, writing in the third person, added the observation that "M. Diderot" could not be persuaded *not* to suspect his friends. It was also Diderot who inserted a parenthetical disjuncture that would perplex Diderot scholars for generations to come. Immediately succeeding Grimm's denial that a novel based on the letters had ever been finished, Diderot placed the following anacoluthon: " . . . (and I would add, I who know M. Diderot a little, that he did finish this novel and that it is the memoirs one has just read, in which one must have noticed how important it is to distrust the praises of friendship)" (11:32).

Another reference to the novel written by Diderot similarly inverts the chronology between the letters composing the joke and the novel itself. At the close of the Préface-Annexe, Diderot states, here as always in the voice of Grimm, "If there arise any slight contradictions between the narrative and the memoirs, it is because the majority of the letters are posterior to the novel; and one will agree that if there ever was a useful preface, it is that which one has just read, and that it is perhaps the only one whose reading should be postponed until the end of the work" (*Oeuvres* 11:66–67). The "real" letters, or rather, the original fictions, are described as

---

14. Diderot, *Correspondance,* ed. G. Roth (Paris: Editions de Minuit, 1953–66), 3:18–19.

15. See Herbert Dieckmann, "The Préface-Annexe of *La Religieuse,*" *Diderot Studies* 2 (1952): 21–147.

best read *after* the novel after which they were written; this claim, which Dieckmann identifies as an addition penned in Diderot's own hand, is one he is also at pains to admit.[16] The letters date from early 1760, while Diderot's work on the novel, at least insofar as can be gathered from his correspondence, dates from September of that year. At the same time, there is no conclusive proof that the joke on the Marquis, which might have concealed another joke played on Diderot, did not conceal yet another joke, played on "the whole lot of you," *by* Diderot. Which came first—not simply and symmetrically the facts or the fiction but the facts of a fiction or the fiction derived from those fictitious facts? Why would Diderot, in the course of describing the novel's history, wreak havoc with all possible historical credibility? Why would an author, in preserving the "scaffolding" of his art, destroy the grounds on which a temporal relation between reality and imitation can be reconstructed, invert any sustainable perspective from which the "truth" of his novel's representations can be judged? And why then would he add to this formidable confusion the further suggestion of his own incredulity? Once again, was the joke on the Marquis a joke on Diderot that Diderot himself authored unwittingly? Was Diderot seduced into writing letters meant to seduce a friend or was the circle of friends seduced by Diderot into seducing Diderot . . . and so on.

These are the empirical questions that the Préface-Annexe to *La Religieuse* raises before (or after) one's reading of the novel; as in the question raised by its title about whether it should precede or follow the reading of the work, the fact that Diderot has been discovered to be no less responsible for the Préface-Annexe than for the novel does anything but clear up the opacity— historical as well as theoretical—of the text. To say, with Dieckmann, that Diderot probably considered the Préface-Annexe part of the novel itself, to be rewritten along with the fiction,[17] is obviously, in light of the recently edited manuscripts, true enough, but that conclusion at once precludes the central question of the Préface-Annexe and of the experimental mode of *La Religieuse* as well. For Diderot's experimental fiction centers on the questions of how and if one can derive truth from empirical perception, distinguish good faith from its mere appearance, the internal workings of the soul from the practical appearance of a soul to which they may bear no relation whatsoever.

The place of the soul's practical appearance is a stage, and the answer

16. Dieckmann, "The Préface-Annexe," 29–30.
17. Dieckmann, "The Préface-Annexe," 31.

to the question posed by the Préface-Annexe of *La Religieuse* is found in Diderot's theory of how staged appearances are contrived, the *Paradoxe sur le comédien*. The central premise of the *Paradoxe*, a first version of which was published in the *Correspondence littéraire* in 1770 and which continues to confront contemporary readers with the shock of the new,[18] is that the best actor, contrary to all empirical evidence, is a creature entirely void of "sensibility" [*nulle sensibilité*]; that "the art of imitating everything" requires an absolute absence of the internal experience of anything it enacts.[19] Rather than "actual feeling," what one views on the stage are its "external signs," "accents," and "gestures," which are the "measured" components of a general "system of declamation" (AT *Oeuvres* 8:369). "One says," says the main proponent in this theoretical dialogue (speaking for Diderot), "that actors have no character because in the course of playing characters they lose that which nature gave them, that they become false, as the doctor, the surgeon, and the butcher become hard" (AT *Oeuvres* 8:398). Such a progressive view links internal experience to the experience of acting only negatively, by natural attrition, yet even this attenuated naturalist thesis is categorically rejected by Diderot's speaker: "I think that here one has taken the cause for the effect, and that actors are suited to playing all characters because they themselves have none" (AT *Oeuvres* 8:398–99).

In a successful dramatic performance, the paradox of the hieroglyph, of sensory and reflective ideas that strike the mind simultaneously, is made to appear deceptively clear: one feels that what one sees on stage presents a true picture of a living soul in motion. But the fact of that deception makes acting *more* illegible than "a tissue of hieroglyphs." For the imitations of the soul by which actors sensibly move their spectators are the carefully honed products of their work as "cold and calm spectator" of experience not their own (AT *Oeuvres* 8:365). Acting makes visible what the actor did not and does not experience. The experience of acting thus destroys the mental unity represented by the model of the hieroglyph, and it does so by inverting and mimicking the experience of the sensorially deprived.

---

18. Diderot, "Observations sur une brochure intitulée *Garrick ou les acteurs anglais . . .* Traduit de l'anglais (par Antonio Fabio Sticoti, acteur)," in Diderot, *Oeuvres complètes,* ed. Assézat and Tourneux, 8:339–59.

19. Diderot, *Oeuvres complètes,* ed. Assézat and Tourneux, 8:385 (all quotations from the *Paradoxe* will be from this edition and will be noted in the text as AT *Oeuvres*). Philippe Lacoue-Labarthe sees this exchange of all for nothing as symptomatic of a general logic of mimesis; see "Diderot, le paradoxe et la mimésis," *Poétique* 43 (1980): 273.

Fully endowed with the powers of the senses, actors reverse the dilemma of the sensorially deprived in that they are forced to "borrow" the internal basis of feeling, a "soul" (AT *Oeuvres* 8:404). But, like the sensorially deprived, they must also represent what they lack through compensatory gestures: actors can only portray a borrowed soul on stage by "exaggerating" or "enlarging" its "external symptoms," since, as Diderot reiterates in the *Paradoxe*, all "deeply felt" feelings "are mute" (AT *Oeuvres* 8:386). The sensorially deprived provided Diderot with experimental vehicles for understanding the soul through the "metaphorical" exchanges they performed internally; their emphasis on one sense to take the place of another took the form of "symbols" that could, in turn, be sensorially perceived. But the "theatrical emphasis" (AT *Oeuvres* 8:405) achieved in the experience of acting and perceived by the sighted and hearing public exaggerates signs the actor has not made, signs of a soul as external to him as those signs themselves. What we see when we see the actor acting is the hieroglyph rendered transparent even as its own integrity is consciously dismembered, its simultaneity of sense and reflection torn apart. For the experience of acting imitates the simultaneity of a soul entirely external to it only by proceeding analytically, acquiring and demonstrating—again, entirely externally, through step-by-step rehearsal—signs of experiences it merely observes. Diderot explains why the hieroglyph of the soul, once made visible to the world, takes the soul quite out of the picture; why "the tears of an actor descend from his brain."

> The gestures of [an actor's] despair are memorized and were prepared before a mirror. He knows the precise moment when he will take out his handkerchief and the tears will run; you may expect them at this word, this syllable, neither sooner nor later. This trembling voice, these words broken off, these stifled or trailing sounds, these shivering limbs, these shaking knees, these fainting spells, these furies, [all] pure imitation, a lesson recorded in advance, . . . a sublime aping which the actor maintains in his memory long after having studied it, and of which he is fully conscious at the moment of its execution . . . the illusion [that he is and feels what he plays] is only for you; he knows well that he is not and does not. (AT *Oeuvres* 8:369–70)[20]

The poetic text that the actor performs may appear a more appropriate

---

20. The pronoun "he," used frequently to refer to "the actor" by Diderot, is often employed in the essay for the sake of brevity.

model of the hieroglyph than dramatic acting, but, in the *Paradoxe,* Diderot denies any essential difference between the two, stating that "the great poets, the great actors, and perhaps all great imitators of nature in general . . . are too busy observing, recognizing and imitating to be affected deeply within themselves" (AT *Oeuvres* 8:368). Just as poets are "assiduous spectators of what occurs around them" who exaggerate what they see, creating "imaginary phantoms" and "hippogriffs" instead of "true . . . things as they are in nature" (8:367, 372–73), the actor exaggerates what the poets exaggerate by becoming "the soul," not of any sensory being, but of a "dummy" [*mannequin*] in which he moves enclosed. Diderot's externalization of the paradox of the natural simultaneity of the soul leads from the two models of the paradox proposed in the *Lettre sur les sourds et muets* to the proposition of "three models" of man in the *Paradoxe sur le comédien.*

My friend, there are three models, the man of nature, the man of the poet, and the man of the actor. That of nature is less great than that of the poet, and that of the poet is still less great than that of the great actor. This one mounts upon the shoulders of the last and encloses himself within a great wicker dummy of which he is the soul; he moves this dummy in a terrifying manner, even for the poet who no longer recognizes himself. (AT *Oeuvres* 8:419)

"The man of nature," the first and apparently lowest of these models, is separated by "the man of the poet" from the only soul mentioned in this schema. But that soul is not properly the soul of "the man of the actor"; it is "the soul" the actor becomes when he "moves" about in a nonman, "a great wicker dummy." Here, that which has no feeling at all is granted the simulated movement and interiority of a soul. Diderot's three models of man imply a fourth, that of a soul enclosed within a body deprived of every sense, a "dummy" in the true sense of an inanimate model.[21]

A natural comparison arises in this context between Diderot and Kleist. One textual link between the two authors (to be further developed subsequently) will help clarify the specific connection between Diderot's *Paradoxe* and *La Religieuse.* In *Über das Marionettentheater* (1810), a theoretical and

---

21. This transition from imagined model to material dummy occurs repeatedly in the *Paradoxe.* See Diderot's description of "the model" made by the actress Clairon as the "great dummy which envelops her" on the stage (*Oeuvres* 8:365).

representational prose piece also written in dialogue form that deals with
the performing arts and the artistic performance of inanimate dummies
or marionettes in motion, the story is told of a young man who loses his
natural grace of movement as soon as he catches sight of his own motion
in a mirror.[22] This vision of himself reminds him of a statue he had seen
that imitated a similar motion in static form. Once seen to resemble an
inanimate model, the motion reflected outside him ceases to be part of
him: try as he may to regain "the free play" (*Werke* 2:344) of movement
he had enjoyed, each repeated attempt at recalling that motion, each
conscious act of self-imitation, now mediated by the knowledge of its
representation, only further alienates him from a self he had never known,
or seen reflected, before. Because the boy once had grace, he becomes, in
time, graceless, his body paralyzed, first by the mirrored vision of its
movement and then by the mere memory of that mirrored vision, until
he, whose appearance previously delighted the eyes of others, is hardly
recognizable as the same boy (2:344). Having departed from an unreflective
state of physical grace—a state defined not so much by naive innocence
or a purely internal lack of apperception as by the external accident of
never having seen himself represented, of never having happened to view
himself as modeled on a statue or (in Diderot's terms) on a stage—the
boy can never secondarily acquire its purely external signs. With reference
to the grace of dramatic movement, the *Paradoxe sur le comédien* tells the
same tale in reverse: they that have no character will take one on through
their eyes—first, by observing the gestures, expressions, exclamations, and
movements of others; next, by turning these into external signs for the
characters they are not—for the feelings they do not experience—by remembering, reproducing, and perfecting them, over and over, before a mirror.
Just as Diderot's poet could not compose a poem were he to feel the
emotion his poem is intended to render—"if tears drop, so does the pen

---

22. Kleist, *Sämtliche Werke und Briefe,* ed. Helmut Sembner (Munich: Carl Hanser Verlag,
1984), 2:338–45 (all quotations from Kleist are from this edition, and will be noted in the
text as *Werke*). Hilda M. Brown suggests, in "Diderot and Kleist," *Heinrich von Kleist Studies,*
ed. Alexej Ugrinsky (Berlin: Erich Schmidt Verlag, 1980), 139–45, that the dialogue form
of Kleist's essay may have been modeled on Diderot. Claims for direct influence are hard
to make in this case (cf. Robert Mortier, *Diderot en Allemagne* [Paris: Presses Universitaires
de France, 1954]), and the notion of experiment developed here does not depend on them
in any event. More interestingly, Mark Franko has linked the theoretical premises of the
Paradoxe and *Marionettentheater* by way of the choreographic theory of Oskar Schlemmer, who
admitted his debt to Kleist. See Franko, "Repeatability, Reconstruction and Beyond," *Theatre
Journal* 41 (1989): 56–74.

from the hand" (AT *Oeuvres* 8:386)—the actor who feels nothing will be most successful at inducing feeling in others; unconstrained by the presence of feeling, he is most free to imitate its appearance. The actor who never acts but by calculation, who *is* nothing if not conscious of that fact, appears to embody the motions of the soul precisely by never admitting their absence and self-conscious imitation, by pretending to ignore that there ever was a mirror, that there is an audience, before him. That external signs speak for him is the absolute prerequisite of the actor; for the actor who reveals his knowledge of his art, who says what he does, the play is over, "the wicker dummy" he moves in collapses, the jig is up.

Diderot's "nun" is the actor as narrator. In this experimental fiction played out empirically between friends, Diderot replaces the theory of paradox with its narrative representation, exchanging the conventional and enclosed fiction of the stage (like the metafictional *muet de convention* at first proposed for observation in the *Lettre sur les sourds et muets, Oeuvres* 4:138) for a first-person narrative addressed by a fictive character to a real one. Suzanne Simonin embodies the paradox of acting by doing everything while appearing to know nothing, the paradox of a *comédienne* who narrates her own innocence, who represents the presence of a soul by appealing purely to the senses. Seducing everyone who sees her act while verbally insisting that, in acting, she never knew what she had done, Suzanne is Diderot's "dummy," a fabricated model animated in a particularly "terrifying manner" because, as narrator, this actor says she is constrained by the trappings of her part, the external garments, the dress of a nun.

"Take off my clothes [*Otez-les moi*]!" (*Oeuvres* 11:156). "Oh if only I could rip them off!" (11:154). There is nothing that the nun asks so often and wants so much, and there is nothing that anyone near her wants so much to do. "They stripped me shamelessly" (11:140); "I ripped my garment with my teeth" (11:140); "they stripped my clothes off" (11:141); "they came to strip me" (11:161); "they stripped me to the waist" (11:194); "she undressed me" (11:214); "'Order us to undress her'"(11:139); "'Sister Suzanne, get undressed'" (11:137); "get me out of these clothes, get me out of them" (11:155)—throughout her narration, Suzanne pleads to be and submits to being undressed, the external narrative signs of an internal desire to be freed from the "constraint [*contrainte*]" of holy vows.[23] Com-

---

23. See *Oeuvres* 11:183 for the main thematic statement of Suzanne's teasing desire to be freed from external "constraint." At first, Diderot appears to attribute this speech against the cruelty of forced convent life to Suzanne; at its close, however, he refers it back to its

bined with Suzanne's voluntary descriptions of her generally appealing physical appearance, these external signs make her memoirs into an entirely verbal, but highly visualizable, striptease. Every time Suzanne turns a corner of convent life, with every rise and fall of her fate, those clothes, that habit, are taken off, put back on, stripped from her, ripped from her, unraveled, untied, and unlaced. Whether being undressed to take her vows or to bed down with her Mother Superior, Suzanne flatly reiterates her extraordinary ignorance of—indeed her failure to actually experience—the content of what she does. In emphasizing external signs of the soul while denying any relationship between them and herself, Suzanne's words and actions seduce precisely because they follow Diderot's prescriptions for successful acting to the letter. Of taking her vows she reports, "I was reduced almost to the state of an automaton . . . I know neither what I did nor what I said. Doubtless I was interrogated, and doubtless I responded; I pronounced my vows, but I have no memory of it, and I found myself a nun as innocently as I was made a Christian" (*Oeuvres* 11:123-24). "What an innocent! Ah! What a dear innocent!" exclaims the Superior at Arpajon when, after both experience sexual climax, Suzanne claims utter ignorance of "what was going on inside [her]," and it is in the role of "innocent" that she narrates, as always, candidly, to the Marquis, the gestures of her daily visitations with, and undressings by, the Superior (11:228). The prurient nature of the novel would be comical if it were not consistently misunderstood: the fact that all the scenes Suzanne graphically narrates take place within convent walls has given *La Religieuse* its reputation for a frank portrayal of female homoerotic sex. Those scenes do span a considerable gamut, from sewing parties to acts of sadism complete with chains, whips, ropes, and broken glass, not to speak of the Superior's attempt to explain to her novice the existence of a "language of the senses" that, even when spoken "to oneself alone, is not entirely without pleasure," and of which,

---

context in a legal *mémoire* written by M. Manouri (see *Oeuvres* 11:181, 184). Suzanne, whose powers of reason have been admired by critics of the novel on the basis of this speech, mouths words written by one of her defenders and admirers inside the novel. Robert Ellrich, in *The Structure of Diderot's Major Fiction* (Cambridge, Mass.: Harvard University Library, 1960), notes that this "extremely disconcerting" shift of reference was maintained by Diderot in his revisions of the novel, but dismisses it as "a hopeless confusion" before going on to analyze Suzanne's "forensic rhetoric" (75-99). Jay Caplan characterizes this passage as an "apparent slip in point of view" owing to a moment of emotional confusion on Diderot's part (Caplan, *Framed Narratives: Diderot's Genealogy of the Beholder* [Minneapolis: University of Minnesota Press, 1985], 61). Here, the mere appearance of reasoned argument, even when recognized as such, seems to solidify Suzanne's "character" without denying her hollow status as actress.

Suzanne protests, she does not understand a sentence (11:235).[24] But the scenes themselves, and the sexual activity they portray, are only the mimetic means of Diderot's experiment, the stage on which his "dummy" performs to an audience of readers only too willing to lend it a soul.

It would be easy enough to accuse readers of *La Religieuse* of overlooking the comedy of Suzanne's self-characterization because their eyes, or visual imaginations, are verbally attracted elsewhere, that is, to the always active, anatomically inventoried body of Suzanne. Nor can the failure to see the paradox of Suzanne's self-characterization be limited to male critics or to the heterosexual point of view.[25] A thematic reading that positioned itself in feminist sympathy squarely within the Superior's embrace, believing against belief in Suzanne's explicit and doubly seductive ignorance, would merely switch the gender of a literary stereotype commonly encountered in the next century in Balzac's *Comédie humaine*, that of the unattractive older man who pays for the favors of professional *comédiennes*. For the grotesque fate of the Superior, eventually driven to death for want of her "innocent" (who managed to tell a singularly attentive Father Confessor of the Superior's caresses, the meaning of which, again, she did not comprehend), is also the fate of Balzac's overlusty old men. Whatever the critical and sexual inclinations of its audience and whatever its original effect on the innocent or complicitous Marquis, Suzanne's verbal performance—Diderot's experiment in representing a paradox of acting in which the paradox of sensory and reflective simultaneity is explicitly sundered—has proven an unbroken success.

The question arises, then, why no reader of the novel has publicly noted the pointedly mindless nature of Suzanne's titillating narrative descriptions or has differed substantially from the enamored Superior, who pronounces her "such a pure soul! such an innocent creature!"[26] That Suzanne, who

---

24. The superb irony here is that, in a noneuphemistic sense, "the language of the senses" is the only language this actress of innocence ever speaks.

25. Cf. Vivienne Mylne, *Diderot: La Religieuse* (London: Grant and Cutler, 1981), 41, 43, 54–56, et passim; Rita Goldberg, *Sex and Enlightenment* (Cambridge: Cambridge University Press, 1984), 178, 185, 193. Elisabeth de Fontenay goes furthest in noting that Suzanne's "way of not understanding words and gestures smacks of provocation more than genuine innocence" (de Fontenay, *Diderot: Reason and Resonance* [New York: Braziller, 1982], 141–42).

26. The problem of an innocence that is obviously incongruous with the sexual experience and acts of self-presentation Suzanne describes has been noted most recently by Herbert Josephs ("Diderot's *La Religieuse:* Libertinism and the Dark Cave of the Soul," *MLN* 91 [1976]: 750, 751), Caplan (*Framed Narratives,* 56), and David Marshall (*The Surprising Effects of Sympathy* [Chicago: University of Chicago Press, 1986], 92–98). That innocence itself,

routinely admits to mental blackouts at the most dramatic moments of her narrative (avowing that others "determined to dispose of [her] without [her]" and that she does not "know what was happening in [her] soul" [*Oeuvres* 11:96, 110]), could be Diderot's representation of the actor who seduces for the very reason that he lacks a soul—somehow this seems unthinkable, as if the illusion of the presence of a soul conventionally enjoyed by the audience in a theater cannot be consciously enjoyed by the readers of a narrative confession, especially an overtly erotic one; as if Diderot's experimental fiction worked too well. Sex between women is, of course, a major genre of heterosexual fantasy literature, to which *La Religieuse* adds the erotic charge of religion, of vows of chastity, veils never to be unveiled. But more engaging and inadmissible still is the spectacle of sex between females narrated from the point of view of a woman who knows *only* that she does not know what she is doing. This would be sex as pure surface, gestures reported to be carried out repeatedly without feeling or cognizance, sex as pornography because it is intentionally represented as external, emptied of depth. *La Religieuse* is a novel that narrates sex between women through the voice of a woman who, in her bondage, not only seduces everyone around her but experiences sex without knowing or feeling anything "inside" her, because it is a novel, a fiction written to represent a model of the soul by way of an experiment begun as a practical joke between men.

In the potentially pornographic confession of "the nun," Diderot translated the paradox of acting, the paradox of sensibility imitated and aroused in its unstated absence, into the narrative statement of that absence. And because that statement issues from the actor, the hieroglyph, the embodiment of the paradox itself, it is, paradoxically, a statement the perceiving mind fails to understand. There is no one so "decomposed," so "stripped" of physical senses as to take Suzanne's stated absence of mind literally rather than "see" her stripped and unveiled. Whether Diderot enjoyed the last laugh on his friends can only remain unknown.[27] But the ramifications of the joke enacted in his novel are finally no laughing matter.

---

however, remains unquestioned. Marshall, who, like Ellrich (*Structure*, 81–87), points to Suzanne's consciousness of her own theatrical effect, maintains the realism of her innocence even as "actor," a view he relates to the model of the unsuccessful *comédien sensible* that the *Paradoxe* rejects (99).

27. Given the double dealing described in the Préface-Annexe, Diderot's celebrated comment to a friend (recounted in the Préface-Annexe) that he was "getting upset over" the "story" he was "creating" (*Oeuvres* 11:31) cannot be considered to prove that he regarded his own experience of the novel one way or the other.

La Religieuse is not only the exacting translation of Diderot's theory of the paradox of acting into experimental literary form; it is the narration of Diderot's own empirical observation that the simultaneity of the soul cannot be shown, that its movements threaten to become a spectacle of empty and imitable signs once translated into the external world.

In the final *Post-Scriptum* to her confession, Suzanne, who, now freed of the constraining garments of a nun, works, appropriately enough, in a laundry, states she fears ("this reflection disturbs me") the Marquis "might persuade himself" that she "addresses [herself]" not to his "goodness" but to his "vice," concluding by admitting and immediately resuming the specular role playing at which she hints: "In truth, he would be wrong to impute to me personally an instinct which is proper to my entire sex. I am a woman, maybe a bit *coquette*, what do I know? But this is by nature and without artifice" (*Oeuvres* 11:288). It is also where Diderot calls attention to the "dummy" of a spirit the novel has staged, pulling the plug on his experiment by calling the curtain on his *comédienne*.

The difficulty involved in experimenting without constructing "dummies" or "models of man," in conceiving the soul in any way that does not involve experimental representations, is revealed in Diderot's addition to the *Lettre sur les sourds et muets*, the "Lettre à Mademoiselle..." (1751). Describing the same dilemma Suzanne conceals by revealing her self (and ultimately her "entire sex") as body alone, Diderot makes the following confession.

> You ask me then how we can have many perceptions at the same time. You are at pains to conceive of it. . . . Many times, in the intention of examining what took place in my head, and of *taking my spirit by surprise [prendre mon esprit sur le fait]*, I threw myself into the deepest meditation, withdrawing into myself with all the contemplation of which I am capable; but these efforts produced nothing. It seemed to me that one would have to be inside and outside oneself at once, and to perform at the same time the role of the observer and that of the machine observed. But the case of the spirit is like that of the eye; it doesn't see itself. . . . A monster with two heads fitted on the same neck would perhaps teach us something new. One must then wait for nature, which combines everything, and which brings with the centuries the most extraordinary phenomena, to give us a *two-headed creature [dicéphale]* which

contemplates itself, and one of whose heads can observe the other. (*Oeuvres* 4:197–98; italics in original)[28]

According to this inventive compensation for an admitted structural deficiency, the problem with Suzanne (and all successful actors of souls) would be that they have only one head, with no means of observing or turning in on itself. If that lack defines the conditions of their theatrical success, their singular characterlessness, it also defines the conditions of life off the stage, including Diderot's repeated attempts to know through experiment the simultaneity of experience he hypothesized in the hieroglyph. A look at one last experiment—in terms of literary chronology, Diderot's first— shows Diderot simulating the condition of the *dicéphale* by placing a second observing head someplace else.

Les Bijoux indiscrets (published in 1748) is Diderot's earliest novel and easiest to categorize. Written in neither confessional nor dialogue form, with no appearance of representing reality, it has been classified as a *conte licencieux* or *roman libertin,* and received accordingly.[29] Its "titillating obscenities" and "salacious scenes," considered representative of the genre, have been the object of moral and aesthetic scorn but never the subject of critical debate.[30] To virtually the same degree that *La Religieuse* continues to be admired as a realistic tale of victimization, *Les Bijoux indiscrets* has been dismissed as a fantastic exercise in crude erotic stimulation.[31]

In a technical sense, the basis of these appraisals is the same, for both novels derive from playing out a practical joke. But while the joke involved in the writing of *La Religieuse,* regarded as limited to its origin, receives, at most, a perfunctory nod before the novel "proper" can get underway, the joke of *Les Bijoux indiscrets* intrudes on any attempt to criticize the novel because its enactment comprises the "action" of the fiction itself. This joke,

---

28. Assézat notes, correctly if somewhat unnecessarily (given the extravagance of Diderot's image), that the *dicéphale* proposed here would also fail the test: "The two heads may well be placed on the same body, they will each have a brain and, consequently, a distinct existence" (AT *Oeuvres* 1:402n).

29. For an account of the historical reception of the novel, see Ellrich, *Structure,* 9–12; Ozdoba, *Heuristik,* 20–28; Otis Fellows, "Metaphysics and the *Bijoux Indiscrets:* Diderot's Debt to Prior," *Diderot Studies* 65 (1967): 509–18.

30. Fellows, "Metaphysics," 509, 510.

31. Even Venturi views the novel's only "originality" to reside in its "grossness," deeming it "of very limited importance" to an understanding of the formative ideas of Diderot (see Franco Venturi, *Jeunesse de Diderot (de 1713 à 1753)*, trans. J. Bertrand [Paris: Skira, 1939], 124, 126).

whose practical application makes it appear an unspeakable act of vulgarity, is a fictive attempt to "take the spirit"—here of sensory experience—"by surprise [*sur le fait*]." According to the spare plot of the novel, a sultan named Mangogul who rules the country of Congo from his harem in Banza wants to be distracted from the periodic boredom he experiences in the company of Mirzoza, his *sultane*.[32] Some days, the narrator relates, "Mangogul and Mirzoza had few things to say, almost nothing to do, and, without loving each other less, enjoyed themselves very little" (*Oeuvres* 3:40). What Mangogul says he wants is a way "to get some pleasure at the expense of the women of [his] court"; what that pleasure amounts to is listening to them talk: "to know from them the adventures they have had, and that is all." Told by the resident genie, Cucufa, that his "desire" is an "impossible one," that "to want women to confess their adventures" is to want something that "has never been and will never be," Mangogul nonetheless insists, and the genie produces a magic ring, explaining: "All the women upon whom you turn the stone will tell their intrigues loudly, clearly and intelligibly," but rather than talk "through the mouth" they will talk through "the most honest part within them, and that best instructed in the things you want to know . . . through their *bijoux*" (3:43).

This is just what happens in the novel—in a series of empirical experiments or tests [*essais*], the euphemistic "jewels" are made to speak—and what gives this trivial action theoretical interest is the fact that, while openly grotesque, it is neither obscene nor pornographic. When the *bijoux* speak from beneath billowing skirts, their confounded mistresses are and remain clothed. Instead of describing bodies in motion, when the *bijoux* speak they tell Mangogul stories, picaresque tales composed principally of the names of those they have encountered. Instead of homoerotic tableaux described as empty of experience, the specifically knowledgeable *bijoux* relate histories of experience, stories of whom they have known, remember, and love, which women may tell naturally, if only to other women rather than men. The tales that Mangogul hears are sometimes epic, sometimes lyric, and on one occasion only as long as the simplest transitive sentence. This last case, that of a woman named Eglé who has been cloistered away by a suspicious husband, is surely the most instructive of all. For, to Mangogul's astonishment, the *bijou d'Eglé* says simply "'J'aime Célébi,'"

---

32. This fable is read as an allegory for the court of Louis XV; cf. *Oeuvres* 3:36n; Ellrich, *Structure,* 12.

Eglé's husband, with the effect of making the experimenter think that his magic ring is on the blink (*Oeuvres* 3:137).[33]

The fact that the most faithful woman "tested" in the novel should be exiled by her own husband reflects directly on a misogynist tradition Mangogul's experiments attempt to enforce. The only moral judgment Diderot makes—or invites us to make—in the course of a novel since judged to be immoral is directed against the worn-out stupidity of that tradition, at the moment Mangogul begins to rehearse its prejudices to Mirzoza.

> "I told you that you were all animals."
>
> "Yes, prince, and that is what you still have to prove," added Mirzoza.
>
> "There's nothing simpler," responded the sultan. And then he began to rehash all the impertinent things that have been said and resaid, with the least possible intelligence and wit, against a sex which possesses both these qualities to the highest [*souverain*] degree. Never was Mirzoza's patience put to a greater test; and never in your whole life would you have been more bored than you would be if I related to you all the reasonings of Mangogul. This prince, who didn't lack good sense, was of an absurdity that day which cannot be conceived. As you will judge. (*Oeuvres* 3:127)

The immediate upshot of Mangogul's misogynist fervor is his decision to conduct what Diderot calls "a bizarre experiment" (3:128). Given the strangeness of its larger context, that experiment must be bizarre indeed. It is, but in a specifically significant way: we, the readers, can "judge" the "absurdity" of Mangogul's misogyny by the next action he takes. In order to prove all women "are animals," Mangogul descends to his stables, turns the ring on a mare, and demands from his "secretary, Ziguezague," a complete transcription (3:129). What Diderot's talking *bijoux,* unlike neighing horses, were imagined to provide is a second source of information like that imaged in the (equally grotesque) *dicéphale;* and the premise that divides these indiscrete jewels along with all Diderot's other "models of man" from animals is that, in one way or another, man, in the nongendered, generic sense, speaks. Language is the condition that defines the very possibility of Diderot's experiments, because it alone gives evidence

---

33. The subtitle of this "fourteenth test of the ring" is "The Mute *Bijou.*"

of something in women and men that their "animal" or physical senses cannot circumscribe.

The ostensible plot of *Les Bijoux indiscrets,* in which a passing moment of "boredom" is diverted by a passing fit of misogyny, seems to culminate in Mangogul's wager with Mirzoza that he will not find "a single truly and constantly wise woman" in the land (*Oeuvres* 3:114). The wager, a mere pretext for further experimentation, is, however, soon forgotten,[34] as well it should be, for, as every reader of *Les Bijoux indiscrets* must realize sooner rather than later, such a woman is already right by the sultan's side. For, without the aid of magic, Mirzoza's constancy is made evident by the fact that she continues to put up with, *and* have it out with, the now thoroughly loony Mangogul. But Mirzoza's wisdom is made apparent in a more obvious manner in the novel; in direct contrast to Mangogul's experiments with women reduced to talking sexes, Mirzoza, dressed in what she imagines a philosopher wears (and thereby most resembling, Diderot adds, "a bat"; 3:118), delivers a discourse not on personal sexual experience but on the soul. The long chapter, entitled "The Metaphysics of Mirzoza" and subtitled "Souls," directly precedes Mangogul's attack on women that Diderot deems too boring to recapitulate. Located at the center of the novel and delivered for the most part as an organized monologue, Mirzoza's philosophical disquisition clearly represents the sultan's central blind spot in limiting his desire for knowledge to what he wants to learn from *bijoux.*

Mirzoza's "metaphysics," moreover, imitate Diderot's. She calls her philosophy "an experimental metaphysics" or "metaphysics of experience" [*une metaphysique expérimentale*] because, as she explains, its "foundations" are based not on "obscure" hypotheses but on "experience" or "experiment," both designated by the French *expérience* (*Oeuvres* 3:120, 122).[35] That philosophy describes a "natural," half-capricious, half-directed movement of the soul throughout the body, locating it always in that part of the body on which the activity of the individual is focused.[36] The soul enters all of

---

34. Cf. Ellrich, *Structure,* 24.

35. Mirzoza's explanation of experimental philosophy arises in response to Mangogul's description of "the nature of the soul" propounded by the recognizably Cartesian "philosophers of Monoémugi." According to Mangogul, speaking very much for Diderot, "all their systems" only ended in "uncertain notions, without the internal sense which seems to suggest to me that [the soul] is a substance different from matter" (*Oeuvres* 3:19). On the problem of Cartesian dualism for Enlightenment materialism, see Aram Vartanian, *Descartes and Diderot* (Princeton: Princeton University Press, 1953), 13–15.

36. See *Oeuvres* 3:119–25, including the summation by Mirzoza: "Let us leave aside your

us where we first show movement—"at the feet"—before working its way randomly up to the brain (3:120).[37] But, in some cases, the soul does not make it all the way: thus the soul of a dancer is stuck in the feet, that of a swordsman in an armed hand, and that of one of Mangogul's epic raconteuses in the *bijou*. Whatever the extravagance of this system, it derives the relationship between soul and body from experience. That Diderot thought this was how speculation had now to proceed is demonstrated in the next chapter, in which Mangogul recounts his dream of entering the house of philosophy in the "region of hypotheses" (3:130). That building is filled with oddly shaped creatures, each wearing, as "Plato" explains to Mangogul, a shred of the clothing ripped from the corpse of Socrates. At the end of the dream there enters "a child" who grows through "a hundred diverse forms" to enormous proportions, and who "Plato" identifies as "Experience/Experiment" [*l'Expérience*] (3:131–34). What Diderot makes clear in the middle of this, his first literary experiment, is that the shreds of cloth ripped from the corpse of philosophy will never be put together again. His experimental philosophy embraces that paradox and, in so doing, may produce speculative grotesqueries but never dead forms. This remains as true in the last and liveliest of Diderot's fictions, *Jacques le fataliste et son maître* (published in 1778–80), a monumental experiment in intertextuality that recasts a sentence from *Tristram Shandy* into a means of understanding the world. For the fatalism summarized in the refrain that Jacques ascribes to his captain—that whatever happens on earth has been "written above"—has as its corollary the notion that, paradoxically, anything *can* happen, that experience is its own master and not the slave to anything else we may imagine.

To compare *Jacques*, generally regarded as Diderot's masterpiece, to the embarrassing *Bijoux* may result in cries of critical blasphemy. But if Diderot's first novel is read from the point of view of the experimental philosophy it expounds, rather than the traditional hypotheses of the soul—

---

sages and their great words . . . and with regard to nature, let us only consider it with the eyes of experience, and we will learn from [nature] that it has placed the soul in the body of man as in a vast palace, in which it does not always occupy the most beautiful rooms."

37. One of the sources of Mirzoza's mock-serious thesis has been identified as Matthew Prior's poem "Alma; or, the Progress of the Mind" (1718), a dialogue in which one speaker takes the view Mirzoza proposes: "That Alma enters at the Toes," "Makes the Head her latest Stage" (canto 1, ll. 253, 265), and, "Where Fancy or Desire / Collects the Beams of Vital Fire . . . there" (canto 2, ll. 251–54; see *The Literary Works of Matthew Prior*, ed. H. B. Wright and M. K. Spears [Oxford: Clarendon, 1959], 1:477, 492). On the poem and Diderot's novel, see Fellows, "Metaphysics," 519–40.

Platonic or Cartesian—it tears to shreds, like *Jacques* it can be recognized as one of the most ironic and humorous novels ever written. In the joke that *Les Bijoux indiscrets* carries to fruition, one sense does get to speak directly for itself, indeed it is forced to, and this is Diderot's own dream of the house of philosophy, the fusion of discursivity with empiricism at which his experiments aim. But what Mirzoza's lesson in metaphysics demonstrates is that the joke is a joke, that even its most tireless practice can never be enough. For if by any invention the senses could speak and thereby circumvent the need for speculative reflection, they could only give a parochial or local account of a soul in continual motion, a model of experience that could not even recognize the paradox Diderot's experiments continually re-pose.

If Diderot's efforts initiate a modern tradition in literature of arriving at knowledge from the outside in, of moving from the empirical to discursive models of internal experience and inevitably back again, the writings of Kleist, it should be noted in conclusion, adopt and challenge that tradition almost before it can begin. Mirzoza's speech should resonate loudly for any reader of Kleist's *Marionettentheater.* One of the speakers in that essay also uses the image of individuals with localized souls to defend the thesis that marionettes make better dancers than people do.[38] Living dancers, he argues, have the tendency to get their soul stuck in the wrong place, in the elbow or small of the back, for example, where its weight throws their movements visibly out of balance (*Werke* 2:342). In contrast, marionettes are graceful because their movements follow a "line" described by the manipulation of a central "point of gravity" [*Schwerpunkt*], a nonmimetic source of articulation identified by the external mind of the puppeteer who pulls their strings (2:340). Lacking a soul, marionettes are "without gravity" [*antigrav*], not weightless but unencumbered by mental baggage, the forms of perception and reflection that conflict with the natural gravity of moving bodies (2:342).

Diderot's Mirzoza also saw the soul in bodily terms, not as part of the body itself but as that which "announces" the physical locus of its path of "formation" (*Oeuvres* 3:121). Indeed the empirical opposition set up in Kleist's essay between the soul and physical center of gravity of the body is played out in Diderot's novel by repeated references to people who move

---

38. This argument was taken up again by Edward Gordon Craig in "The Actor and the Über-Marionette," *The Mask* 15 (1908): 3–15. Craig effectively conflates the models of experience developed by Diderot and Kleist by arguing that the first actors imitated marionettes originally modeled on gods.

like "automatons," including a long description of an entire population of "puppets" [*pantins*] on strings (*Oeuvres* 3:127, 276, 237–38). "Isn't it true that we are only marionettes," Mangogul asks as his desire returns to Mirzoza; to which she discreetly responds, "Yes, at times" (3:281). In *De l'Interprétation de la nature,* Diderot also defends the thesis of a controlling "center of gravity." He proposes that the physical properties of any moving body are best understood through the experimental "decomposition of the forces" that "act" upon it (*Oeuvres* 8:59). Once these have been "reduce[d] to a single force," Diderot argues, "one finds that the body proceeds as if the force passed through a center of gravity; and, in addition, that it turns around this center of gravity as if this center was fixed, and that the force acts around this center as around a point of support" (8:59–60). This is the center of gravity around which all bodies without integral souls turn smoothly in Diderot: the spring of his ambulatory clock, the point of support of his actor, of his freshly focused sultan, his "nun." His discursive experiments speculate precisely on whatever it is that moves us in a different direction, throwing the machine out of line, jamming the works. By investigating the "metaphoric" activity forced upon the faulty mechanism of the sensorially decomposed or by imagining functioning organs capable of recounting the forces they have known, Diderot attempts to describe a center of experience off-center to the body, the center or central paradox of a spirit forced to invent its own center of gravity. Moved by internal forces, the path this center describes is the imperfect line of language.

But if Diderot's experiments are carried out to make experience speak, the problem in Kleist is precisely that nobody is talking. The line of discursive experimentation that leads from Diderot's scandalous *bijoux* to modern speculative literature comes up short in the representation of experiences for which no discursive account can be given. Kleist's fictional experiments describe a line that language cannot cross, actions executed in the course of other actions that discourse, emphasizing over and over its own externality to action, can only record. This is as true of Kleist's most eloquent dramatic figures as of narrative characters who hardly speak; as much the fact of experience for Penthesilea and Achilles or Ottokar and Agnes, agents and victims of deadly mistakes, as for Josephe and Jeronimo, condemned by the good fortune of their survival to take the sheer physical occurrence of disaster for signs of a higher spirit at work. Barred from understanding by the very attempt to compensate symbolically for what they do not naturally know, these characters move mechanically. Especially when most passionate, the motion that pervades these experiments with experience is automatic. Its discursive model is that of irony: the representation of the externality of representation to experience, the questioning of the experimental means of language by means of language itself. The irony that defines Kleist's fictions of empirical experience is, in Diderot's terms, the paradox of a narrator who knows that what he is representing is always somewhere else.

Nowhere is this more evident—which is to say empirically inscrutable—than in Kleist's *Marquise von O . . .*, the story that replays the practical joke of *Les Bijoux indiscrets* in reverse. The physical organs endowed with discursive powers of reflection in Diderot's novel are represented in Kleist's story as agents of experience that the reflective mind, including the mind of the reader, does not and cannot know. On the one hand, the celebrated dash—or "—"—of the narrative (*Werke* 1:106) is impossible to understand in representational terms. This *Gedankenstrich* ['thoughtline,' dash] is literally a line acting in the place of discursive thought, a graphic symbol of an entirely mechanical action that no properly linguistic sign can represent, since to say "the Count did" this or that would be just what the Count himself could not say.[39] On the other hand, there is almost no sentence in the story that does not represent that action in some way. As soon as one is informed of the facts of *Die Marquise von O . . .*, the who, where, and when that the Marquise does not know and the Count cannot say, the story appears to narrate nothing so much as its graphic sign. Outside knowledge of the empirical event that Kleist represents purely symbolically—that is, in a dash—colors every action narrated and speech recounted in the story with the displaced meaning of a double entendre.[40] As in Diderot's experimental fictions, these double or metaphoric meanings serve as symbolic compensations for ignorance. But, unlike the symbols produced by Diderot's sensorially decomposed—or even the theatrical signs of his conscious actor or "nun"—these exchanges take place at the external level of narration and serve only to enlighten a reader whose abstract need

---

39. The nearest modern equivalent of Kleist's "—" is probably Broch's *schlafwandeln* ['sleepwalking'], a discursive representation of the paradox of wholly unconscious action that continues in the tradition of Diderot.

40. On the relationship of its double entendres to the ironic structure of the story, see Lilian Furst, "Double-Dealing in *Die Marquise von O . . . ,*" in *Echoes and Influences of German Romanticism,* ed. M. S. Batts, A. W. Riley, and H. Wetzel (New York: Peter Lang, 1987), 85–95. Furst's astute observation of the extraordinary "inventiveness" of Kleist's use of the double entendre (89) recalls Diderot's description of the compensatory symbols developed in the absence of direct sensory experience.

to know bears no resemblance to the immediate, physical quandary of the Marquise. For the Diderotian "double light" reflected throughout this story is created not in the minds of its characters but in those characters' literary and critical third-person narratives, that is, in Kleist's own narrative and the tradition of its reception, the historical transmission of what "—" means. Departing finally from Diderot's premise of knowledge based in experience, we recognize the double entendres of *Die Marquise von O . . .* and understand its displaced meanings because those meanings are not internally produced.

The dash that is the *Schwerpunkt* or center of gravity around which this external act of understanding *Die Marquise von O . . .* revolves also describes the actions of its characters in the manner of manipulated marionettes. The frequent words *verbindlich* ['obliging'], *Verbindlichkeit* ['obligation'], and *Verbindung* ['bond'], ordinarily used figuratively to describe forms of social behavior, instead here convey the mechanical sense of actions literally bound, as if their agents were physically tied to a string (e.g., *Werke* 1:105, 111, 117, 118, 130). Explicit descriptions of actions and speeches as artificial and forced instances of role playing also contribute to the sense that what pass for characters in *Die Marquise von O . . .* are, like the cryptonym of its title, ciphers, mere stick figures or puppets moved by force (e.g., *Werke* 1:106, 100, 111, 112, 139).[41] It is Kleist's tour de force to have represented sensory experience as an oxymoron, a contradiction in terms: to have told a story that begins with the open publication of an unthinkable ignorance, proceeds to narrate the trials of an empirically impossible innocence, and ends with the drawing of contracts for the production of oxymorons to come—the physical conceptions of "a whole series of young Russians" to follow "the first" (1:143). Just as Kleist's dash represents a line of motion that is at once a bar between reflection and the senses, his story makes intimate and physically transforming experience an external matter of speculation. In so doing, Kleist follows Diderot but also puts a new literature of experience to the test. In a tradition of literary experiment that substituted theoretical for chronological development, Kleist would come last. Whatever direction that tradition continues to move in, the series of experiments to follow Diderot and Kleist—like the Marquise's progeny—must follow the first.

---

41. Cf. Furst, "Double-Dealing," 92.

Alexander von Humboldt's Sociopolitical Intentions: Science and Poetics

Gisela Brude-Firnau

"Wie gerne möchte ich nur einmal Humboldten erzählen hören!" notes Ottilie in the *Wahlverwandtschaften*.[1] Her diary entry opens up a threefold perspective. Historically, she refers to the most comprehensive natural scientist of the era, who was equally esteemed in academic, social, and political circles. From the viewpoint of literary history, Humboldt the narrator [*erzählen*] is revered for the linguistic creativity that prompted Goethe's tribute: poetry should claim Humboldt "among its heroes while he still lives on earth."[2] The final perspective comes from the history of ideas; the wish to hear Humboldt talk expresses the conviction of German classicism—especially Goethe's belief—that poetry and science "[sich] zu beiderseitigem Vorteil, auf höherer Stelle, gar wohl wieder begegnen können."[3] Ottilie's wish serves as the departure for this essay's analysis. A sketch of Alexander von Humboldt and Goethe's relationship will be given in order to underscore the literary intentions of Humboldt's last work, the five-volume *Kosmos* (1845–62). Following this outline, the aim of Humboldt's fusion of science and poetry in *Kosmos,* the endeavor to emancipate all classes of society through scientific education, will be examined.

The nearly four-decade relationship, periodically renewed, between Alexander von Humboldt and Goethe was characterized by mutual respect. No other representative of the younger generation was greeted by Hofrat Goethe with such candid openness as the twenty-five-year-old Humboldt.

---

1. Johann Wolfgang von Goethe, *Goethes Werke,* ed. Erich Trunz (Munich: Wegner, 1973), 6:416.

2. Johann Wolfgang von Goethe, *Goethes Briefwechsel mit Wilhelm und Alexander v. Humboldt,* ed. Ludwig Geiger (Berlin: Bondy, 1909), 303.

3. Goethe, *Werke,* 13:107.

Following their first meeting, Goethe wrote, "Da Ihre Beobachtungen vom Element, die meinigen von der Gestalt ausgehen, so können wir nicht genug eilen, uns in der Mitte zu begegnen."[4] Goethe, as it were, placed his bet on the younger man, realizing not only that they held analogous concepts of nature, but also that Humboldt was pioneering an innovative attitude toward nature that Goethe would no longer participate in. Goethe's interpretation of nature remained largely based on intuition, this despite observations and experiments, while Humboldt is among the first to proceed, independently of conjecture, through rational comparison, analysis, and measurement. When, in his last publication, Humboldt returns to the philosophical outlook characteristic of the eighteenth century, his views are nonetheless based on empirically derived results obtained through procedures perfected during the nineteenth century and still followed today.

Like no other scientist, Humboldt was influenced by Goethe, and, like no one else from the Weimar circle, he determined the direction of several developing scientific disciplines. With his *Kosmos,* Humboldt makes the Herculean attempt, long after Goethe's death, to give scientific research in its basic approach a holistic tendency and to create an overall orientation that would encompass all specializations. He attempts to realize Goethe's reflective contemplation [*Denkschauen*], which in the meantime had become his own. This effort acquires renewed relevance in our time as it has become clear that a mode of thinking more oriented toward phenomenal appearances and the concept of unity could serve as a corrective to the devaluation of sensory perception and the mathematization accessible only to specialists that have come to dominate the natural sciences. It is therefore conceivable that the gap between scientists and the general public could have been bridged, perhaps reducing thereby the destructive consequences we face today. Humboldt's *Kosmos* is an early attempt to form a scientific ethos, as well as a reminder of the social preconditions and the social obligations of all scientific research. The work attempted to integrate scientific thought in the human context. What his brother had achieved by reforming classical education at the beginning of the century, Alexander tried to realize for scientific education in the latter half of the nineteenth century. His was not the wish that science should predominate, but the desire to see that the discipline be equal to the humanities: a balanced training and education of society in both fields of knowledge.

The unfinished, five-volume *Kosmos* is, as its subtitle suggests, the

---

4. Goethe, *Briefwechsel,* 292.

"Entwurf einer physischen Weltbeschreibung," that is, a scientific-geographical work from the middle of the nineteenth century but, at the same time, a work in the history of ideas. It not only recounts the phenomena of nature from astronomy to human geography, but, with broad strokes, it sketches the discovery of these subjects. The work thus deals with how nature is mirrored intellectually and artistically in the human mind. The unheard-of success of *Kosmos* in the nineteenth century rests not only on its thematic grandeur, but also on its artful linguistic presentation. The publisher, Cotta, had not experienced a similar success "seit den besten Erscheinungen von Goethe und Schiller," a success "wie er in Deutschland zu den seltensten gehört."[5] In fact, *Kosmos* became the first scientific best-seller of the nineteenth century and was thought to be the most widely read book after the Bible.[6] Although it would hardly reach best-seller status today, the work appeals with new seriousness and relevance in an era in which the threat to nature posed by civilization becomes increasingly apparent. Furthermore, it impresses not only because of its linguistic shaping, but perhaps even more so due to its highly reflected adaptation of literary techniques in the analysis of scientific subjects. Regarding Humboldt's heretofore ignored reflections on this issue, historian Alfred Dove has remarked that there exists almost no other scientific manuscript in which in the preface and "im Verlaufe der Darstellung selbst so häufig und ausführlich von Absicht, Art, Grenzen und Mängeln eben dieser Darstellung gesprochen wird," that here "an Reflexionen über sich selbst . . . übermässig viel geschehen sei."[7] The major elements of this "poetics" and the related intentions should therefore be discussed here.

Humboldt's poetological reflections are primarily to be found in the forty-page introduction, "Einleitenden Betrachtungen über die Verschiedenheit des Naturgenusses und einer wissenschaftlichen Ergründung der Weltgesetze," as well as in the letters to Varnhagen von Ense and to Cotta that accompany the writing. Self-critically yet confidently, the sexagenarian explains in the introduction his position in history and outlines the far-reaching concept that governs his publication. The work will present his

5. Herbert Schiller, ed., *Briefe an Cotta: Vom Vormärz bis Bismarck* (Stuttgart and Berlin: Cotta, 1934), 32–33.

6. Alexander von Humboldt, *Kosmos, für die Gegenwart bearbeitet von Hanno Beck* (Stuttgart: Brockhaus, 1978), v. Beck, however, comments in his Humboldt biography that this was an exaggeration (Hanno Beck, *Alexander von Humboldt* [Wiesbaden: F. Steiner, 1961], 2:230).

7. Alfred Dove, "Alexander von Humboldt auf der Höhe seiner Jahre (Berlin 1827–59)," in *Alexander von Humboldt: Eine wissenschaftliche Biographie*, ed. Karl Bruhns (Leipzig: Brockhaus, 1872), 2:369.

legacy: the entirety of the knowledge and insights acquired in his lifelong pursuit of research gathered in a written document that itself has "cosmic" dimensions. Despite the fact that he foresees employing techniques of description that are partially literary, Humboldt protests against any comparison of his work with contemporary nature- and travel-descriptions: "ich habe gesucht, immer wahr beschreibend, bezeichnend, selbst scientifisch wahr zu sein, ohne in die dürre Region des Wissens zu gelangen."[8] In contrast to the poetic imagination, on the one hand, and to the dry enumeration of facts typical of scientific discourse, on the other, his main concern is "die Komposition, das Beherrschen großer und mit Sorgfalt und genauer Sachkenntniß zusammengetriebener Massen."[9] This composition should not be an encyclopedic rendition of knowledge, but "der Reflex meines Selbst, meines Lebens,"[10] which is to say, his personal, independent worldview.

Although conceived as "die wichtigste literarische Arbeit meines Lebens," to which the author envisioned devoting all his "geistigen Kräfte,"[11] he unsentimentally foresaw the risk of leaving this work unfinished. The thought "daß ein solches Werk nicht vollendet wird von einem aus dem Kometen-Jahr 1769" was to him "sonnenklar,"[12] and it was taken into account in the process of composition. Humboldt wrote individual, self-contained pieces that—as the editor is advised—are to be published soon after they have been written "daß die Käufer doch befriedigt werden, wenn mein Tod die Vollendung unterbräche."[13] This planning did little to influence the printing of the titles, for the first four volumes appeared in 1845, 1847, 1848, and 1850, respectively. Only volume five, with its unfinished sections and meticulous index, was published posthumously, in 1862. The result was rather a series of summaries that ensures an easy overview of the work. The conceptual premises are repeatedly formulated so that each individual volume can be read de facto as a separate treatise. After the first two volumes, Humboldt was able to assume that *Kosmos* was essentially complete, yet even the entire set of volumes gives no impression of fragmentation or garbledness.

8. Alexander von Humboldt, *Briefe Alexander von Humboldts an Varnhagen von Ense aus den Jahren 1827–1858*, ed. Ludmilla Assing (Leipzig: Brockhaus, 1860), 23.

9. Humboldt, *Briefe*, 215.

10. Humboldt, *Briefe*, 91.

11. Schiller, *Briefe*, 2.

12. Humboldt, *Briefe*, 92.

13. Schiller, *Briefe*, 17.

From the point of view of organization and style, the work is decidedly reader oriented. With the first sentence, it is dedicated to "dem deutschen Publikum," later to "meinen Zeitgenossen."[14] The horizon of expectations of these contemporary readers is consequently addressed, challenged, expanded, and modified in order to bring about the necessary receptivity. For Humboldt is less interested in transmitting information than in imparting the capacity for scientific thought and insight; he wants, as it were, to awaken in the reader "Organe . . . , die lange geschlummert haben"(34).

The author envisages two groups of readers and for each he has different didactic purposes. The first is the German public, which he views without differentiation as to class. In this respect rather modern, Humboldt declares: "Was mich am lebhaftesten interessiert, ist der Effekt auf die Massen."[15] Following the appearance of volume one, he admits, "daß an dieser deutschen Stimmung mir, dem Greisen, viel liegt."[16] Clearly, his principle aim is the "Verbreitung der Ideen" in Germany.[17] Therefore, he strives to be intelligible to all, a goal he achieves partially through the "Übertragung der technischen Ausdrücke in glücklich gewählte, beschreibende, mahlerische Ausdrücke."[18] Poetic presentation is the vehicle used to communicate, and, therefore, the task of volume one is to instruct "das deutsche Publikum erst recht über die nicht allein wissenschaftliche Natur" of the work.[19]

But is the reading of *Kosmos* worthwhile to those contemporaries who in their everyday existence are far removed from nature and only infrequently succeed in transcending the "engen Schranken des bürgerlichen Lebens"? Such readers, the author promises, will find "in der Abspiegelung des großen und freien Naturlebens einen der edelsten Genüsse, welche erhöhte Vernunftthätigkeit dem Menschen gewähren kann"(*Kosmos*, 34). It is out of this intellectual pleasure—Humboldt openly argues according to the maxim *prodesse et delectare*—that eventually a different mode of perception and understanding emerges. Humboldt wants to communicate an attitude toward nature that would activate "die Vernunft und das Gemüth

---

14. Alexander von Humboldt, *Kosmos: Entwurf einer physischen Weltbeschreibung* (Stuttgart and Tübingen: Cotta, 1845), v. This dedication can be contrasted with the official inscription to King Friedrich Wilhelm IV. All further references to this edition of *Kosmos* will be indicated parenthetically in the text.

15. Schiller, *Briefe*, 26.

16. Schiller, *Briefe*, 30–31.

17. Schiller, *Briefe*, 27.

18. Humboldt, *Briefe*, 91.

19. Schiller, *Briefe*, 10.

zugleich"[20] and that, without becoming romantic or sentimental, ensures enrichment and education. This would eventually have social consequences, for the reader who has thus acquired such a deepened understanding of nature will more intensively participate in intellectual and industrial progress. The connection between science and economics is already understood here as a given. Clearly, Humboldt intends to counteract the introspection and self-absorption of the educated German bourgeoisie.

The second group of readers to which *Kosmos* is addressed is the experts, the scientists. With a view to them, Humboldt repeatedly stresses the actual scientific relevance of the publication: "es enthält sehr wichtige neue Ansichten."[21] The latest research results are primarily included in volumes three and four, and the author expresses certainty that these titles will stimulate "ein ebenso wissenschaftliches Interesse, als die zwei vorigen ein literarisches erregten."[22] The facts and data expected by the expert are placed, for the most part, in the annotations at the end of each chapter. Humboldt stresses that *Kosmos* does not pretend to be an independent "rationelle Wissenschaft der Natur," but rather "die denkende Betrachtung der durch Empirie gegebenen Erscheinungen, als eines Naturganzen" (*Kosmos*, 31).

Of greater importance than all its more-or-less dated scientific content is the fact that *Kosmos* can be read as an educational program for the mind of the scientist. The work develops those ethical values of science that bind the researcher to society. This, in turn, gives the work renewed relevance today, especially the "Einleitenden Betrachtungen." Employing a diplomatic form of expression dictated by the Restoration era, Humboldt often simply describes his own method, and then shifts to a characterization of the scientist in general in order finally to combine both perspectives in view of certain universally valid principles. His primary concern is that the scientific results be intelligible to all. Referring to Goethe's dictum, "die Deutschen besitzen die Gabe, die Wissenschaft unzugänglich zu machen!" (*Kosmos*, 27–28), Humboldt rejects all too detailed accounts. Much more important is to elucidate the general and all-encompassing relations among the results, for science has progressed to such an extent that its true value is "nicht mehr die Fülle, sondern die Verkettung des Beobachteten" (*Kosmos*, 31). Therefore, the researcher should interpret the

---

20. Schiller, *Briefe*, 27.
21. Schiller, *Briefe*, 18, 7.
22. Schiller, *Briefe*, 45, 25, 31.

results of his work not merely within the context of his own expertise, but also in regard to the general state of knowledge in order to provide "Einsicht in den Geist der Natur" (*Kosmos,* 34). Should this become a generally pursued tendency, Humboldt argues, "kann ein beträchtlicher Theil des Naturwissens Gemeingut der gebildeten Menschen werden, ein gründliches Wissen erzeugen . . . , ganz von dem verschieden, was man bis zum Ende des letzten Jahrhunderts dem populären Wissen genügsam zu bestimmen pflegte" (*Kosmos,* 34). Unmistakably, this statement refers to the condition of the people held in ignorance by the domination of political and clerical hierarchies. With equal insistence, Humboldt rails against traditional and "irrige Ansichten von dem Wesen der Naturkräfte, Ansichten, die durch bedeutsame Sprachformen gleichsam verkörpert und erstarrt, sich, wie ein Gemeingut der Phantasie, durch alle Classen der Nation verbreiten" (*Kosmos,* 17). Such subjective prejudices [*anmaßend wie alles Beschränkte*] must be shattered by the skeptical investigations carried on by a "wissenschaftliche[r] Naturkunde" (*Kosmos,* 17).

The educational and academic jurisdictions of the state are therefore just as much a concern of science as the traditional denial of knowledge to entire segments of society. The scientist's duty to be objective is tied to his obligation of social and political commitment. Here, Humboldt anticipates demands reiterated after the bombing of Hiroshima, to be sure more emphatically, in Brecht's *Galileo.*

Despite the fact that the author's aims vis-à-vis the two groups of readers are distinct, *Kosmos* is ultimately intended for both. Humboldt transcends the difference between the reader-expectations of the two groups by sketching out, as it were, the image of an adequate reader and an ideal mode of reception. He projects, first of all, an emancipated reader by reflecting on his own strategies or, rather, through these reflections he intends to bring about the reader's emancipation. The reader thereby becomes a conscious participant in the unfolding cognitive process, which is therefore adamantly not merely a device of persuasion.[23] Humboldt repeatedly stresses that both the sensory and the intellectual receptivity of the reader are to be challenged. In his view, an author who makes use of the sensuous mediation of poetic techniques should seek to convey the natural phenomena exclu-

---

23. This criticism was leveled against Humboldt by the aging Goethe, who refused to accept Alexander's geological treatises due to their support of the thesis of volcanism. See the letter to Karl Friedrich Zelter, October 5, 1831, cited in Adolf Meyer-Abich, *Alexander von Humboldt in Selbstzeugnissen und Bilddokumenten* (Reinbeck: Rowohlt, 1967), 174.

sively and not his own mood so that he leaves "die Freiheit des Gefühls im anderen unbeschränkt."[24]

The method and goal of his work are combined in an image that can be called the central metaphor, for it determines the work in regard to both its structure and content. The image in question is that of the ascent of a mountain, with the experienced author acting as a guide to readers in their climb upward. In this respect, the author resembles other mountain guides: "Sie rühmen die Aussicht, wenn auch ganze Teile der Gegend in Nebel verhüllt bleiben. Sie wissen, daß auch in dieser Verhüllung ein geheimnisvoller Zauber liegt, daß eine duftige Ferne den Eindruck des Sinnlich-Unendlichen hervorruft, ein Bild, das . . . im Geist und in den Gefühlen sich ernst und ahnungsvoll spiegelt" (*Kosmos,* 38).

The image, which corresponds well to the author-directed and reader-executed process of reading, has its origin in Humboldt's own expeditionary experience: the ascent of a mountain assumed for him on several occasions the significance of a turning point by opening up discoveries in the fields of geography, geology, and climatology that, in part, remain valid today. The most important ascent occurred for Humboldt in the Cajamarca highlands of the Andes. By reaching the peak, he fulfilled his childhood dream of seeing the Pacific Ocean, an experience he describes as "einen unverlöschlichen Eindruck, Gefühle erregend, deren Lebendigkeit keiner vernünftelnden Rechtfertigung bedarf."[25] There in the Andes, the idea of unity, which is the very center of *Kosmos,* was disclosed to him: "auf dem Rücken der hohen Anden erkannte ich, wie von einem Hauche beseelt, von Pol zu Pol nur ein Leben ausgegossen ist in Steinen, Pflanzen, und Thieren und in des Menschen schwellender Brust."[26]

Humboldt's final work was intended to convey this "Einsicht in den Zusammenhang der Erscheinungen" (*Kosmos,* 4) in both a literary and a scientific manner, to make it graspable by both sensibility and intellect. The process of reading becomes, accordingly, the ascent of a mountain, in which the author displays the universe or, more exactly, his epoch's knowledge of the universe. In conformity with classical tradition, Humboldt attributes to such insight an ethical quality: it effects the spirit "läuternd und beruhigend" (*Kosmos,* 23); its significance—entirely in accord with the central

24. Alexander von Humboldt, *Kosmos: Entwurf einer physischen Weltbeschreibung* (Stuttgart: Cotta, 1862), 2:53.

25. Alexander von Humboldt, *Ansichten der Natur,* ed. Hanno Beck (Darmstadt: Wissenschaftliche Buchgesellschaft, 1987), 1:345.

26. Letter to Caroline von Wolzogen, May 14, 1806. Cited in Bruhns, *Humboldt,* 1:417.

metaphor—is "das Streben nach dem höchsten Gipfel, welchen die Vervollkommnung und Ausbildung der Intelligenz erreichen kann."[27] The central metaphor develops such a charge of significance that it becomes a symbol of reflexive knowledge in general. At the same time, however, it refers in its unquestioned valorization of scientific knowledge to Humboldt's historical boundedness: despite his critique of applied, merely "utilitarian" research, it remained unimaginable for him that scientific investigation—including his own expeditions—could have consequences destructive to nature and to humanity. Humboldt's credo, according to which "das industrielle Fortschreiten und die intellektuelle Veredelung der Menschheit" (*Kosmos,* 34), are tightly linked, may already have seemed all too optimistic in 1845. In a time in which industrially exploited research leads through mine fields, it strikes one as sheer illusion.

Other aspects of the central metaphor that refer to mythological and literary parallels enrich its spectrum of meaning. In the poetry of the eighteenth century, the mountainous landscape is transformed from an expressive vehicle of terror to one of majestic sublimity and comes to objectify a feeling for nature that assumes fundamental importance in Goethe's poetry and, in a somewhat altered form, in the poetry of the romantics.[28] The specific quality of Humboldt's concept of nature is revealed through a comparison of his use of the central metaphor with poems by Schiller and Goethe in which the ascent of a mountain and the acquisition of knowledge are likewise at stake. In Schiller's elegy *Der Spaziergang* (1795), from which Humboldt quotes in his "Einleitenden Betrachtungen," the lyrical subject is led, to be sure, to a comprehensive insight into nature and history, but finally recognizes: "es war nur ein Traum, / Der mich schaudernd ergriff mit des Lebens furchtbarem Bilde."[29] In Goethe's *Zueignung* (1794), the mountain peak is the site where "der Dichtung Schleier" is received "aus der Hand der Wahrheit."[30] The scientist Faust expresses his own sense of resignation in the same metaphorical register.

> Geheimnisvoll am lichten Tag
> Läßt sich Natur des Schleiers nicht berauben,

---

27. Humboldt, *Kosmos,* 2:94.

28. Horst S. Daemmrich and Ingeborg Daemmrich, *Themen und Motive in der Literatur* (Tübingen: Francke, 1987), 65–67.

29. Friedrich Schiller, *Schillers Werke: Auswahl aus der historisch-kritischen Ausgabe,* ed. Otto Günter, Georg Witkowski, Albert Köster, Conrad Höfer, Albert Leitzmann, and Franz Muncker (Leipzig: Hesse und Becker, n.d.), 1:46.

30. Goethe, *Werke,* 1:152.

Und was sie deinem Geist nicht offenbaren mag,
Das zwingst du ihr nicht ab mit Hebeln und mit Schrauben.[31]

In stark contrast to this view, Humboldt regards it as the determination of human being "den Geist der Natur zu ergreifen, welcher unter der Decke der Erscheinungen verhüllt liegt" (*Kosmos,* 6). Despite his use of the traditional language of imagery, he does not mean here the illusionary attempt to capture the world in a single formula, but rather the asymptotic approximation of a grand, comprehensive vision. He emphasizes that "jedes Naturgesetz, das sich dem Beobachter offenbart, läßt auf ein höheres, noch unerkanntes schließen" (*Kosmos,* 22). There is no limit to the progress of scientific knowledge, nor does such progress violate or rob nature. The familiar literary imagery conveys the new, purely immanent approach of this concept of nature. Humboldt consciously selected a form of communication intelligible to the bourgeois, literarily educated public.

For this reason, he decisively repudiates the widely held view "daß bei jedem Forschen in das innere Wesen der Kräfte, die Natur von ihrem Zauber, von dem Reize des Geheimnissvollen und Erhabenen verliere" (*Kosmos,* 19); this worry has its source in "sentimentaler Trübheit des Gemüths" or in narrow-mindedness. The sensuous and intellectual experience of nature has rather the character of an enhancement: "das Messen und Auffinden numerischer Verhältnisse, die sorgfältigste Beobachtung des Einzelnen bereitet zu der höheren Kenntniß des Naturganzen und der Weltgesetze vor" (*Kosmos,* 19). The knowledge that gradually forms itself in this manner is the idea of unity, the insight "daß ein gemeinsames, gesetzliches und darum ewiges Band die ganze lebendige Natur umschlinge" (*Kosmos,* 9). Such is the knowledge—in the register of the central metaphor—granted the reader at the peak of the mountain: it stands at the beginning of all investigation just as it is the ultimate scientific goal, perhaps never to be achieved in the course of human history. This idea of unity is, for Humboldt, more a regulatory concept than, as in the case of Goethe, the correspondence between subjective idea and supposedly objective knowledge. Humboldt cites from the pseudo-Goethian fragment *Die Natur* in order to distinguish his own position all the more clearly.

In meinen Betrachtungen über die wissenschaftliche Behandlung einer allgemeinen Weltbeschreibung ist nicht die Rede von Einheit durch

---

31. Johann Wolfgang von Goethe, *Faust,* ed. Erich Trunz (Munich: Wegner, 1987), 28.

Ableitung aus wenigen, von der Vernunft gegebenen Grundprincipien. Was ich Weltbeschreibung nenne . . . ist die denkende Betrachtung der durch Empirie gegebenen Erscheinungen, als eines Naturganzen. (*Kosmos*, 31)

For this alone could "bei der ganz objectiven Richtung meiner Sinnesart, in den Bereich der Bestrebungen treten, die meine lange wissenschaftliche Laufbahn ausschliesslich erfüllt haben" (*Kosmos*, 31).[32]

The central metaphor likewise solves the dilemma that arises from the idea of unity on the one hand and the purely empirical method on the other. Should the author not convey to the reader the entire plenitude of "der durch Empirie gegebenen Erscheinungen" in order then to interpret these phenomena as the sum "eines Naturganzen," thereby making the reader capable of attaining to knowledge of unity? In its function as a solution to this problem, the central metaphor is deployed in a structuring fashion: it supplies "Leerstellen," informational gaps or semantic lacunae. Thus, during the ascent of the mountain "ganze Teile der Gegend" remain "in Nebel verhüllt" from which, nevertheless, "ein geheimnisvoller Zauber" emanates; the indefinite distances veiled in mist awaken "den Eindruck des Sinnlich-Unendlichen," they function as an image that "im Geist und in den Gefühlen sich ernst und ahnungsvoll spiegelt" (*Kosmos*, 38). Obviously, Humboldt is counting here on the activating effect of such "textual enclaves" that "offer themselves up to" emotional and semantic investment on the part of the reader.[33]

Although Humboldt's concept approaches Wolfgang Iser's definition of the "interaction process" of reading, he operates with ellipses in his representation of nature in a manner different than the fictional text. In *Kosmos*, the "Nebelfelder im Naturgemälde" serve the selection of natural phenomena to be represented; they "hide" facts unnecessary to a general understanding or, more precisely, they enable the layman to forget that such facts have not been mentioned. In this way, they render the encyclopedic plenitude superfluous and refer instead to interconnections and coherences. With regard to the reader, the author refers to this carefully selective mode of representation as a sort of semantic nebulousness; with regard to his own position, however, he designates it "das Schweben über

---

32. The correspondence with Varnhagen von Ense explains the polemics against the natural philosophy of the Romantics and Hegel (see Humboldt, *Briefe*, 44–45, 90–91).

33. See Wolfgang Iser, *Der Akt des Lesens* (Munich: Fink, 1976), 266–67.

den Dingen" or as his "aphoristischen Stil."[34] Such gaps have other functions for Humboldt. They commit to obscurity the fact ("wie sollte ich es, bei dem Umfange einer solchen Arbeit, nicht gern eingestehen?" *Kosmos,* 38) that the author himself lacks specialized knowledge in several areas. In other instances, informational gaps can refer the natural scientist to areas that have yet to be investigated. Justifying once again his renunciation of thoroughness, the author summarizes: "Sollte sich nicht in allen einzelnen Theilen das große Naturgemälde mit scharfen Umrissen darstellen lassen, so wird es doch wahr und anziehend genug sein, um den Geist mit Ideen zu bereichern und die Einbildungskraft lebendig und fruchtbar anzuregen" (*Kosmos,* 28–29). The metaphor of the ascent of the mountain, reflected in form and content, thus primarily serves to convey Humboldt's scientific and ethical credo. But it also explains and justifies the representation itself and contributes—along with other images—to the communication between the literarily educated reader and the scientific-didactic intentions of the author.

Humboldt's concept of language owes much, as is to be expected, to the work of his brother, but, in its stylistic application, it is based on original reflections. "Gedanke und Sprache stehen aber in innigem alten Wechselverkehr mit einander," for language has a "belebenden Einfluß auf die Gedankenfülle selbst" (*Kosmos,* 40). Accordingly, Humboldt distinguishes four stylistic levels of *Kosmos* that correspond to the previously explicated intentions: orientation toward the reader, scientific representation, literary metaphorics, and ideal goal.

Immediate orientation toward the reader is served by a "rhetorischen Stil." This style is not merely the product of the writing desk, but, rather, derives from two widely attended lecture series Humboldt held during 1827–28 at the Berlin University and, in a more popularized version, at the Music Academy. Here he tested his own capacity to transmit his ideas to the public, and, during this period, he expressed the idea of maintaining for his work "die Form einer Rede."[35] In the first volume, which appeared seventeen years later, only the "Einleitenden Bemerkungen" recall lectures, "in die sie theilweise eingeflochten waren" (*Kosmos,* x–xi). In fact, these few remaining elements of oral delivery—the use of the first person singular pronoun, references to "diese Versammlung," "Unterhaltungen über die Natur," "meine Vorträge in zwei Hörsälen"—are without significance in

---

34. Humboldt, *Briefe,* 92.
35. Schiller, *Briefe,* 6.

comparison to the rhetorical inspiration engendered by the original public occasion, an inspiration that was directly transferred into the written version. After every lecture, Humboldt used to dictate everything "was durch Lebendigkeit der Sprache mir schien einigen Effekt auf das Publikum hervorgebracht zu haben."[36] The "Einleitenden Betrachtungen" are thus comparable to a literary-conceptual overture that convinces above all by virtue of its stylistic and thematic variety. The landscape sketches that function as vignettes supporting the different lines of thought evince a remarkable literary charm.

While the first stylistic level is determined by the addressee, the second is defined by the object: "das einfach und wissenschaftlich Beschreibende" aims at a precise rendering and should therefore be "bezeichnend, selbst scientifisch wahr."[37] As one might expect, this "deskriptiv wissenschaftliche Stil" characterizes the largest portion of the work, is occasionally developed at great length, and yet, again and again, is allied with the other techniques of representation.

The literary style that the author summarily designates as "das Dichterische" should emerge "aus dem geahnten Zusammenhang des Sinnlichen mit dem Intellektuellen," as Humboldt remarks with regard to natural descriptions generally.[38] As mentioned previously, the literary techniques employed in *Kosmos* are more numerous than the introductory reflections would lead one to anticipate: an elegantly managed multiplicity of perspectives combines objective description with subjective experience, historically changing views of the phenomena with contemporary scientific opinion. This makes it possible for the reader to form both an intellectual understanding and a plastic-intuitive apprehension; thus, to mention one example, in the case of volcanism, the natural appearance is compellingly conveyed. The occasional subjunctive conditional ("wenn die mythische Atlantis aufstiege und Europa mit Nordamerika verbände" [*Kosmos,* 351]) or apparent paradox ("Pflanzen wandern im Ei" [*Kosmos,* 376]) provide additional intellectual stimulation. The self-portrait in Pliny's Roman toga excites the joy of discovery.

The imagination finds aesthetic support, especially in the first two volumes, in a plenitude of quotations extending from the Greek and Roman classics across the Latin Middle Ages to the great European literatures.

---

36. Schiller, *Briefe,* 4.
37. Humboldt, *Briefe,* 92–93.
38. Humboldt, *Kosmos,* 2:53.

For these, Humboldt consulted, as in scientific questions, the experts of his time, most of whom he knew personally. Mythological references, idiosyncratic metaphors, and composite words at certain points make of *Kosmos* a self-sufficient literary work.

And yet Humboldt did not employ these literary techniques in an uncritical fashion: the "Hauptgebrechen" he lamented in his own style was "eine unglückliche Neigung zu allzu dichterischer Prosa."[39] This self-accusation became the point of departure for the detailed stylistic evaluation by Alfred Dove, whose verdict was that Humboldt should not be counted "unter die grossen deutschen Stilisten" and that, in his use of language, he remains a "Dilletant."[40] It is beyond dispute that Humboldt's efforts to achieve a poetic style sometimes have awkward results, above all a certain adjectival excess. Dove's overall condemnation, however, ignores the facts that linguistic expression, for Humboldt, was of considerable, but not primary importance and that the comparison with the great stylists of the German language is therefore unjust. On the contrary, Humboldt himself refers self-consciously to the classics: "man soll nach meinem Tode aus meinen Schriften einmal lesen, mit wem ich gelebt, wer auf mich eingewirkt hat. Darin liegt keine Schande."[41] In his admission of his epigonal relation to Goethe, he is like the majority of contemporary writers whose status has remained unquestioned up to the present day.[42]

Even less appropriate is the criterion of generic purity that leads Dove to the accusation that Humboldt's writing produced "Zwittergestalten halb wissenschaftlicher, halb literarischer Art."[43] Against this view, one must insist that the combination of an objective-descriptive style with literary tropes endows the representation with an intellectual, sensuous, and, at times, spiritual presence and transforms *Kosmos* into a work sui generis, which the best informed Humboldt scholar of our time has designated a "sprachliches Kunstwerk,"[44] "ein Stück Geschichte der deutschen Literatur, das . . . auch von den Vertretern der Literaturhistorie ernstgenommen werden muß."[45]

The fourth stylistic level distinguished by Humboldt is the so-called

---

39. Humboldt, *Briefe,* 23.

40. Dove, "Humboldt," 379, 381.

41. Humboldt, quoted in Dove, "Humboldt," 379.

42. Goethe is praised as "the great master of poetry" whose literary and scientific works inspired his contemporaries to study nature (Humboldt, *Kosmos,* 2:53–54).

43. Dove, "Humboldt," 386.

44. Beck, *Humboldt,* 2:231.

45. Humboldt, *Kosmos, für di Gegenwart,* v.

noble style [*edler Stil*]. This style betrays least the effort of lending the representation "mancherlei Schmuck der Rede und Anspielungen."[46] It derives, as Humboldt himself saw very precisely regarding the unreflected artistic impulse of his own linguistic capacity, from the sensual-aesthetic experience of nature: where the scientist experiences nature primarily as a synthesis of sense impressions and not as a scientific object, nature becomes for him an aesthetic inspiration. "Gefühle veredeln die Sprache," he asseverates. And the intended "Eindruck von der Größe der Natur"[47] still conveys itself to today's reader, although one's reception of such passages, in awareness of the ecological catastrophe that is taking place in South America, is inevitably touched by nostalgia. The degree to which Humboldt consciously made use of the effects of immediate experience while working on *Kosmos* is revealed by a communication to his publisher in which he confides that he likes to inspire himself "durch den unmittelbaren Anblick der Himmelsräume . . . in unserem Riesenrefraktor" on account of the "aesthetischen Einkleidung, die ich dem Ganzen gebe."[48] It would require detailed investigations to demonstrate how the four differentiated stylistic levels succeed—as is summarily claimed here—in forming, interpreting, and conveying the material.

A conspicuous feature of the letters Humboldt wrote parallel to his work on *Kosmos* is that he often emphasizes the significance of the German language for his own work. German is the language in which he feels "das Gute und Schlechte am lebhaftesten."[49] Humorously, he states, "daß es nicht unverdienstlich ist, wenn ein Mensch, der sein Leben mit Zahlen und Steinen zugebracht, sich soviel Arbeit gegeben hat, deutsch schreiben zu lernen"; and he attributes the immense success of the first two volumes of *Kosmos* to "der Bildsamkeit unserer deutschen Sprache."[50] In the case of the polyglot Humboldt, who spent the most creative phases of his life abroad and published the major portion of his works in French, such statements can hardly be attributed to nostalgic sentiments for the fatherland. In opposition to the German nationalism that, from the turn of the century, had become ever more expansive, Humboldt hesitated to affirm "den nationalen Charakter der Sprachen" just as he decisively rejected

---

46. Humboldt, quoted in Dove, "Humboldt," 374.
47. Humboldt, *Briefe*, 47.
48. Schiller, *Briefe*, 48.
49. Schiller, *Briefe*, 20.
50. Humboldt, *Briefe*, 27, 86.

the view "daß die Völker, ein jedes, etwas repräsentieren müssen."[51] It is less a question, then, of the qualifications of the German language than of the German addressees of the work. Humboldt's stylistic efforts in German are motivated by the fact that he wants to convey the political message inscribed in his "demokratischen Kosmos"[52] to as broad a segment of the pre-1848 German public as possible. This political intention was, along with the mastery of his immense theme, the essential aim of his late labors as a writer.

Because of Humboldt's cautious, almost cryptic mode of expression, the political message is difficult to grasp today, but in 1845 it was clearly understood: the royal chamberlain Humboldt was therefore denounced as "unchristlich und demagogisch" before Friedrich Wilhelm IV. Newspapers accused him of "Irreligiosität" and "Pantheismus."[53] And yet Humboldt was by no means a revolutionary. Rather, he endeavored to change the situation in Germany step by step, through enlightenment and incitements to thought and critical reflection.[54] Despite his origins and conduct of life, he saw the future no longer "im Sinne der etablierten höfisch-dynastischen oder aristokratischen Machteliten," but belonged among those voices of the nineteenth century that, in the formulation of Norbert Elias, "den sozialen Glauben, die Ideale, die langfristigen Ziele und Hoffnungen der aufsteigenden industriellen Klassen zum Ausdruck brachten."[55]

The "Einleitenden Betrachtungen" hint at a model of society "im wissenschaftlichen Zeitalter": Humboldt sees science as socially conditioned and as bearing social obligations, its results are to be seen "in ihrer großen Beziehung auf die gesamte Menschheit" (*Kosmos,* 36) and are to be transmitted to all classes. Going beyond the goals of the French Revolution, he states, "Wissen und Erkennen sind die Freude und die Berechtigung der Menschheit" (*Kosmos,* 36). This claim is simultaneously legitimated in terms of the national-economic interests of the state: knowledge and learning are "Theile des National-Reichthums, oft ein Ersatz

---

51. Humboldt, *Briefe,* 43.
52. Schiller, *Briefe,* 29.
53. Humboldt, *Briefe,* 172, 182–83.
54. The letters to Varnhagen and Cotta are particularly informative. See also E.F. Podach, "Alexander von Humboldt als Politiker," *Deutsche Rundschau* 85 (1959): 430–39; Edward Rommel Braun, *The Political Ideas of Alexander von Humboldt: A Brief Preliminary Study* (Madison: published by the author, 1954); Siegfried Kaehler, "Wilhelm und Alexander von Humboldt in den Jahren der Napoleonischen Krise," *Historische Zeitschrift* 116 (1916): 231–70.
55. Norbert Elias, *Über den Prozeß der Zivilisation: Soziogenetische und psychogenetische Untersuchungen* (Bern and Munich: Francke, 1969), 1:xxviii.

für die Güter, welche die Natur in allzu kärglichem Maaße ausgetheilt hat" (*Kosmos,* 36). Wherever education in natural science "nicht alle Classen durchdringt," the country remains economically disadvantaged.

Here, a social model is sketched out that harmonizes the concerns of the individual and the state on the basis of universal scientific education and its industrial application. It is a utopian project that would humanize the emergent industrial age through the ideals of German classicism. The same end is served by the poetic representation that is pleasing to reflection and, therefore, attractive to a broad and stratified readership.

A failed project? Humboldt sought to prevent the limitation of natural scientific knowledge to circles of experts and, therewith, a technocratic form of domination. The contemporary significance of *Kosmos,* therefore, lies in its reference to the possibilities and conditions within which each individual could make natural science his or her personal and, at the same time, a general sociopolitical concern.

Johann Gottfried Seume's Critique of Traditional Society at the End of the Eighteenth Century

Thomas P. Saine

Johann Gottfried Seume may be considered one of the more peculiar personages of the late German Enlightenment, who lived what may perhaps be called an "experimental" life and had an "experimental" career as a writer. At any rate, not many people would want to imitate his life. He first became known to a wider public through the *Spaziergang nach Syrakus*,[1] in which he described his travels from Leipzig through Bohemia and Austria to Italy and back through Switzerland and France. Although he did not walk quite the whole way, he made a point of using his own legs as much as possible. This mode of travel, he later maintained, assured that the traveler would note and become acquainted with the real, everyday life and concerns of those through whose territory he walked, and not occupy himself only with the more conspicuous monuments of the cultural superstructure. When he made a second extended tour, this time through the Baltic regions in the summer of 1805,[2] he once again—although less extensively and systematically than during the Italian journey of 1802— made significant use of his natural means of locomotion. Although he was well educated—he took his "Magister" in law in 1792—and certainly to be accounted a member of the intelligentsia, he cultivated a plebeian image and subsisted on decidedly modest means, and it was from this ground-level point of view that he ultimately offered his sociopolitical critique of traditional German society. While he did not blossom into a social critic

---

1. Johann Gottfried Seume, *Spaziergang nach Syrakus im Jahre 1802* (Braunschweig and Leipzig: Hartknoch, 1803).
2. Johann Gottfried Seume, *Mein Sommer 1805* (Leipzig: Steinacker, 1806).

until relatively late in his life and took what may appear to be some rather questionable interim positions, he deserves recognition for his readiness to advocate the abolition of the old order and the establishment of a new society founded on a truly republican spirit at a time when other reformers only sought to ameliorate social conditions enough to coax Germans into enthusiastic participation in the war of liberation against Napoleonic hegemony.

It is for his willingness to criticize openly the foundations of his own society (and not just of the foreign societies he visited) that Seume deserves to be called a "modern" political writer and a forerunner of better-known nineteenth-century writers and critics such as Heine, Büchner, and Marx. To be sure, Germany had not lacked for "political" writers before Seume, but they can mostly be considered political in a more partisan sense: they criticized one German power on behalf of or in the service of another, they participated on one side or the other in the debates on the condition and the future of the Holy Roman Empire, or they took one side or the other in controversies about the French Revolution and its consequences for Germany. Earlier German political writers, by virtue of their social standing or their partisanship, found a modicum of protection, under-standing, and even patronage for their views. Seume, by contrast, had no patron, no partisan ax to grind, he found no ready-made audience or interest group, and he stood to gain nothing for himself by expressing his views; he affected both to stand alone and to suffer the consequences of his outspokenness. *Mein Sommer 1805* was banned in numerous German territories because of its sharply critical preface. Other writings of Seume's last years, in which he elaborated on his critique of German conditions and on the reasons for the poor showing of German forces against Napoleon and the armies of the French Revolution—his preface to a volume of commentary on difficult passages in Plutarch and his *Apokryphen*—were not published at all during his lifetime.[3] In the preface to *Mein Sommer 1805,* he anticipated criticism while staking out a territory for writers who, like himself, were interested not in partisan issues but rather in the overall good of society.

Wenn man mir vorwirft, daß dieses Buch zu politisch ist, so ist meine

---

3. The "Vorwort zu einem Bändchen Bemerkungen und Konjekturen zu schwereren Stellen des Plutarch," written in Latin, was not published until long after Seume's death. The *Apokryphen* were first published posthumously (in garbled form) as an appendix to the third edition of the *Spaziergang nach Syrakus* (1811).

Antwort, daß ich glaube, jedes gute Buch müsse näher oder entfernter politisch sein. Ein Buch, das dieses nicht ist, ist sehr überflüssig oder gar schlecht. . . . Politisch ist, was zu dem allgemeinen Wohl etwas beiträgt oder wenigstens beitragen soll: *quod bonum publicum promovet.* Was dieses nicht tut, ist eben nicht politisch. Man hat dieses Wort sehr entstellt, verwirrt und herabgewürdigt oder es auch, nicht sehr ehrlich, in einen eigenen Nebel einzuhüllen gesucht, wo es dem ehrlichen, schlichten Manne wie eine gespensterähnliche Schreckgestalt erscheinen soll. Meistenteils gelingt es leider sehr gut.[4]

Seume was not a terribly philosophical writer. He seems to have made little effort to keep abreast of contemporary intellectual developments, and, toward the end of his life, he claimed that he had in fact only been occupied with working out ideas that he had carried around with him for twenty-five years and more. Originally a student of theology, he hardly progressed beyond the views of such early Enlightenment critics of traditional Christianity as Pierre Bayle, Voltaire, and Hermann Samuel Reimarus. His social and political convictions were largely based on the social contract theories of Hobbes and other philosophers of natural law down to Rousseau. He was not very well acquainted with developments in German philosophy, and it would not appear that he was even remarkably well read. Many of the contemporary German writers he mentions from time to time were authors whose books he had helped produce during the years he worked for the Leipzig publisher Georg Joachim Göschen (1797–1801); his knowledge of particular texts would, therefore, seem to be more accidental than systematic in nature.

We normally associate the Enlightenment, from the time of Leibniz on, with some concept of progress (or at least progression) in history. Lessing, Herder, Kant, and Schiller all saw the process of history (in one way or another) as the working out of the destiny of mankind and the perfection of whatever aspect of human nature each saw respectively as the peculiar heritage of the race. Schiller, for example, in his letters on aesthetic education, saw in history the process of attaining human freedom; Kant saw the goal of history (or Nature) in the establishment of a republican constitution; Marx thought that the goal of history was to achieve the classless

---

4. Johann Gottfried Seume, *Prosaschriften,* with an introduction by Werner Kraft (Darmstadt: Joseph Melzer Verlag, 1974), 639. (This edition was first published in Cologne in 1962. It remains the handiest current edition of the prose works, although it contains many misprints and should be used with care.)

society. Seume, in contrast, seems to have had no faith at all in a progressive dynamics of human history, in teleology, or in the inevitability of any particular human development. Enlightenment, for him, was not something that was in the process of being attained, as in the Kantian "Ausgang des Menschen aus seiner selbst verschuldeten Unmündigkeit," but, rather, it was a firm possession and insight that was essentially nonhistorical and timeless: "Aufklärung ist richtige, volle, bestimmte Einsicht in unsere Natur, unsere Fähigkeiten und Verhältnisse, heller Begriff über unsere Rechte und Pflichten und ihren gegenseitigen Zusammenhang."[5] Only a fool or a charlatan could think of standing in the way of such human self-knowledge.[6] Seume's point of view on human society and history was moral, not providential or teleological, and it can be summed up in terms of the recurring demand for "Freiheit, Gleichheit, Gerechtigkeit." These ideals (which, it might be argued, Seume nowhere defines in a truly satisfactory manner) are apparently derived from the teachings of natural law and the contract theory of society, not—for instance—from the example of the French of any other revolution, the revolutionary declaration of the rights of man and the citizen, or contemporary agitation for civil rights or privileges.

Seume seems to have received his most essential inspiration from the study of history, particularly the classical Greek and Roman authors. If we learn little of importance from his works about his reading of contemporary writers, we hear all the more about his reading of the ancients, and, at the end of his life, he claims in his fragmentary autobiography: "Oft pflegte ich und pflege noch jetzt halb im Scherz, halb im Ernste zu sagen: Was ich Gutes an und in mir habe, verdanke ich meiner Mutter und dem Griechischen."[7] The lives, the deeds, and the works of the ancients still had exemplary character and were directly relevant for Seume's own life and times. In the course of his life, however, he came to view the ancients ever more critically because of the contradiction he found there between ideal and reality: the freedom and economic well-being of classical republics had been based on the exploitation of slaves and helots. Seume was especially skeptical of the moral qualities of Roman republicanism,

---

5. Seume, *Apokryphen*, in *Prosaschriften*, 1390.

6. "Wer diese Aufklärung hemmen will, ist ganz sicher ein Gauner oder ein Dummkopf, oft auch beides; nur zuweilen eins mehr als das andere" (*Prosaschriften*, 1390).

7. Seume, *Mein Leben*, in *Prosaschriften*, 103. Seume was working on the autobiography at the time of his death (it ends in midsentence) and had only reached the point of his return from America.

which was so widely admired and imitated in the age of the French Revolution. In his earliest writings on conditions in Russia, he is already unequivocally critical of serfdom, which he compares with conditions in antiquity: "Wo die Sklaverei nur an einem einzigen Menschen gesetzlich bleibt, ist der Staat auf einen Widerspruch gebaut und muß früher oder später sich verbessern oder zu Grunde gehen. Dieses war die Krankheit der alten Staaten, die soviel von Freiheit schwärmten. Die kommenden Jahrhunderte werden lehren, ob die neueren durch den Irrtum der älteren weiser geworden sind."[8] In the *Spaziergang nach Syrakus,* Seume is highly critical of many of the Roman authors he mentions or quotes, especially Horace, whom he regarded as a servile hypocrite. A late essay, "Die Belagerung, Eroberung und Zerstörung von Platäa," condemns the Spartans and Thebans for their barbarity in trying and executing all the defeated Plateans in terms that suggest Seume *may* have seen modern times as more advanced, more humane.

Daß Aufruhr und augenblickliche Volkswut zuweilen so unsinnig handeln, ist zu begreifen und zu verzeihen; aber daß eine Nation, deren Bildung und Menschenliebe man erhebt, einen solchen Prozeß anstellen, ein solches Urteil fällen und dieses Urteil dann kaltblütig ausführen lassen kann, ist nach unsern Begriffen von Kultur kaum denkbar.[9]

All in all, however, Seume seems to have been unable to make up his mind to believe that there was any substantial progress in the history of mankind or in the development of *Humanität* (one of his recurring themes). The French Revolution had *perhaps* inspired a new kind of political thinking:

---

8. Seume, *Zwei Briefe über die neuesten Veränderungen in Rußland seit der Thronbesteigung Pauls des Ersten,* in *Prosaschriften,* 993.

9. Seume, "Die Belagerung, Eroberung und Zerstörung von Platäa: Aus der Geschichte des peloponnesischen Kriegs von Thucydides," in *Prosaschriften,* 1170. Seume concludes the essay with a direct comparison to modern times.

Wenn man auch diese Kriege der Griechen als lauter Bürgerkriege annehmen wollte, welches man doch nach der Verfassung der griechischen Staaten nicht kann, so ist es doch empörend, mit welcher Grausamkeit und Gefühllosigkeit man nach dem Treffen gerichtlich schlachtete. Die blutigsten Szenen unserer Zeit kommen nicht solchen Abscheulichkeiten gleich; denn wenn auch der Parteigeist würgt, so wird doch niemand wagen zu sagen: Das hat die Nation getan. Aber diese Monumente stehen ewig da in der Geschichte der feinsten Nation, zur Schande ihrer gepriesenen Humanität.

One should probably object that Seume overlooks the excesses of French revolutionary "justice" in such cases as Lyons, Nantes, and the Vendée, which would seem directly comparable to the case of Platea.

"Die französische Revolution wird in der Weltgeschichte das Verdienst haben, zuerst Grundsätze der Vernunft in das öffentliche Staatsrecht getragen zu haben. Läßt man diese Grundsätze wieder sterben, so verdient jeder Weltteil seinen sublimierten Bonaparte."[10] The French Revolution had the virtue of having produced the first republicans in the history of the world.[11] But it had produced only individual republicans, not, as yet, a republican society, and at the end of his life—he died in 1810 at the age of forty-seven—Seume seems to have despaired that mankind would ever produce a political organization worthy of itself.[12] Although he came to think of himself as a "republican," it would be wrong to conclude that he identified the idea of republicanism with any specific form of government.[13] He was not an antimonarchist per se, for he considered *every* traditional form of government to be problematic, and he was skeptical that the mass of human beings could be educated or trained to allow themselves simply to be "governed" rather than "ruled."[14] He was rather a pessimist with regard to human nature and, thus, quite uncertain about whether it was the rulers or the ruled who were more to blame for the condition of mankind. "Wenn ich die Menschen betrachte, möchte ich der Despotie verzeihen; und wenn ich die Despotie sehe, muß ich die Menschen beklagen. Es wäre eine schwere Frage, ob die Schlechtheit der Menschen die Despotie notwendig oder die Despotie die Menschen so schlecht macht."[15]

Seume was born at the right time (1763) to experience, feel deeply, and comment incisively (or at least demonstratively) on the events of a crucial period in European history. His life experience, one would think, would have contributed to the development in him of a social-critical consciousness

---

10. Seume, *Apokryphen*, in *Prosaschriften*, 1287.

11. Seume, *Apokryphen*, in *Prosaschriften*, 1321: "Die ganze griechische Geschichte hat wenig Republikaner, die römische keinen einzigen, es müßten denn die Gracchen sein. Die Französische Revolution hat den Vorteil, die ersten Republikaner gestellt zu haben. Ihre Pflanzung wird wachsen, wenn sie auch jetzt vom Unkraut erstickt wird."

12. Seume, *Apokryphen*, in *Prosaschriften*, 1298: "Ich kenne in der Geschichte noch keine Republik im bessern Sinne. Die Franzosen hatten einige Zeit den Anschein, eine zu werden. Es ist ein göttlicher Versuch vielleicht auf Jahrtausende verunglückt."

13. See the very informative discussion of eighteenth-century concepts of the republic in Inge Stephan, *Johann Gottfried Seume: Ein politischer Schriftsteller der deutschen Spätaufklärung* (Stuttgart: Metzler, 1973), 69–76, and her chapter on "Seumes Verteidigung der monarchischen Staatsform" (76–85). Stephan's monograph remains the most important contribution to Seume scholarship—which, unfortunately, is still relatively sparse—during the last twenty years.

14. Seume, *Apokryphen*, in *Prosaschriften*, 1378: "Herrschen ist Unsinn, aber Regieren ist Weisheit. Man herrscht also, weil man nicht regieren kann."

15. Seume, *Apokryphen*, in *Prosaschriften*, 1288.

eager to manifest its purity and righteousness. Recitals of Seume's biography highlight the fate of his father, originally a moderately well-off craftsman, innkeeper, and farmer who was ruined by hard times in the 1770s and ended his life as a tenant farmer hounded by the agents of the aristocratic landowner.[16] Similarly, Seume biographies do not fail to dwell on his "recruitment" into the Hessian army in 1781 and his twenty-two-week voyage to Halifax to join British forces fighting the American colonists.[17] Fortunately, the fighting was already over by the time Seume arrived and he enjoyed a relatively pleasant and peaceful extended stay in and around Halifax before being returned to Europe in 1783. Seeking to desert for fear of being handed over to Prussian recruiters by the Hessians—he and his comrades were now military surplus—Seume was nevertheless captured

16. The recital is always based on what Seume himself wrote in *Mein Leben,* which is our only extensive biographical source. After Seume's death, Göschen published supplements to the autobiography by himself and by Christian August Heinrich Clodius, which were reprinted in Rolf Max Kully's edition of *Mein Leben* (Basel: Gute Schriften, 1972). The massive biography by Oskar Planer and Camillo Reißmann, *Johann Gottfried Seume: Geschichte seines Lebens und seiner Schriften* (Leipzig: Göschen, 1898), is unscholarly and badly flawed, and its treatment of Seume's letters (it contains the largest collection of letters published up to now) is untrustworthy (see Inge Stephan's critique of Planer/Reißmann in her Seume monograph). It is to be expected that the edition of Seume's correspondence currently being prepared by Inge Stephan and Jörg Drews will finally provide reliable texts. Drews organized a Seume exhibition and a working symposium in Bielefeld in November, 1989 (see the catalog, *Johann Gottfried Seume 1763–1810: Ein politischer Schriftsteller der Spätaufklärung* [Bielefeld: Antiquariat Granier, 1989]—the symposium papers are to be published in the near future) and is preparing a new Seume edition to be published in the Deutscher Klassiker Verlag. For short biographical articles on Seume, see Lothar Pikulik, "Johann Gottfried Seume," in *Deutsche Dichter des 18. Jahrhunderts: Ihr Leben und Werk,* ed. Benno von Wiese (Berlin: Erich Schmidt Verlag, 1977), 972–94; Jörg Drews, "Johann Gottfried Seume," in *Deutsche Dichter,* vol. 4, *Sturm und Drang: Klassik* (Stuttgart: Reclam, 1989), 343–53.

17. The circumstances of Seume's recruitment are rather murky, since he nowhere says exactly what happened. He had abandoned the student life in Leipzig and was on his way to see Paris when he was sidetracked. In his autobiography (*Mein Leben,* in *Prosaschriften,* 111) he narrates, somewhat ironically, "Den dritten Abend [after leaving Leipzig] übernachtete ich in Bach, und hier übernahm trotz allem Protest der Landgraf von Kassel, der damalige große Menschenmakler, durch seine Werber die Besorgung meiner ferneren Nachtquartiere nach Ziegenhain, Kassel und weiter nach der neuen Welt." In a third-person *Lebenslauf* presumably prepared by Seume himself for publication in a Leipzig academic register, the *Leipziger gelehrtes Tagebuch: Auf das Jahr 1792,* there is a somewhat different statement. "Als er . . . durch Hessen reiste, wurde er von Werbern genöthiget, unter den Truppen, die damals der Landgraf von Hessen-Kassel nach Amerika schickte, Kriegsdienste zu nehmen" (*Leipziger Tagebuch,* 11—I am indebted to Klaus Weimar and Jörg Drews for bringing this source to my attention). Quite likely, Seume had allowed himself to be "recruited" more or less legally by drinking the health of the ruler and accepting the customary *Handgeld.* He may have regretted his action afterward and tried to get out of the bargain, protesting in vain (as stated in the autobiography) but forcibly reminded of his commitment [*genöthiget*] by the recruiters.

by the Prussians and spent the next four years in *their* army. After two unsuccessful attempts to desert, the second of which almost led to the brutal punishment of being forced to run the gantlet, Seume managed to get permission to take leave (a private citizen in Emden had put up security for him) and never returned. He resumed his studies in Leipzig instead and finished with his degree in law in 1792.

During his early years, Seume certainly experienced some of the most painful discriminations and injustices to be encountered in his society, yet he was not immediately transformed into a *Stürmer und Dränger* full of wrath and self-righteousness. It was only much later, after a decidedly tortuous course of development, that Seume turned into a social critic. During his second incarnation as a student in Leipzig there is hardly any sign that Seume concerned himself overmuch with the French Revolution—at least, during the period from 1789 to 1794 he said and wrote little about it that has come down to us. It is difficult to say with certainty why this is so: he was very busy studying, he had few friends with whom to exchange letters, he had not yet become a writer, and so forth. Instead of immersing himself in the ideals of liberty, fraternity, and equality, he went to Russia at the invitation of the family of a young Russian nobleman he had tutored in Leipzig. He soon became a lieutenant in the Russian army, the adjutant and secretary of Otto Heinrich von Igelström, commander of Russian forces in occupied Poland after the second partition of the country in 1793. The former unwilling conscript was perfectly willing to be an officer.[18]

We possess only two really noteworthy comments by Seume on French affairs before Thermidor. In the summer of 1793, in a treatise (*Über Prüfung und Bestimmung junger Leute zum Militär*) written for General Igelström, he refers in passing to the French leaders as "die jetzigen Schwindlinge an der Seine."[19] The struggle between the Mountain and the Gironde was reaching its climax at the time, and Seume was likely referring to the participants in that conflict, perhaps also to Jacobin agitation for a new constitution to replace the earlier constitution of September, 1791. In a

---

18. So much for any notion that his service in the Hessian and Prussian armies as a common soldier and noncom had soured him on the military life or turned him into a pacifist. Rather, there is a marked military-elitist strain in Seume's thinking. He lost his commission in 1796. On leave in Leipzig to tend to a convalescing Russian nobleman before continuing the trip to Italy, he (along with all other Russian officers who were away from their posts when Catherine II died) was ordered to return to duty but did not receive the order in time to meet the deadline. At various times after 1796, Seume considered the possibility of reentering military service.

19. Seume, *Prosaschriften*, 1403.

letter of November 12, 1793, to his friend Karl Ludwig von Münchhausen, who was stationed with imperial forces in the Rhineland, Seume expressed a strong desire for the end of the war with revolutionary France, indifferent to the claims of both sides in the conflict.

Ich bin völlig Ihrer Meinung! Machen Sie, daß Sie in die friedlichen stillen Hallen Ihrer Väter zurück kehren, und lassen rechts und links und vorwärts und rückwärts die Politik um sich herumtosen. Gott gebe, daß es Friede werde, und daß die beiden Gaskonaden von Seiten bald ihre Endschaft erreichen, daß ein jeder wieder ruhig neben seinem Weinstock und unter seinem Feigenbaum sitzen kann. Himmel, was sind die Menschen für schnurrige Abderitengesichter! Meinetwegen sollen Könige Könige und Prelaten Prelaten bleiben; die Einrichtung ist so ganz gemächlich fürs Ganze, wenn es beide nur nicht zu bunt machen, welches doch warlich wider ihr selbsteigenes Interesse wäre. Und in diesem Falle sagt man ganz glatt weg, das ist eine königliche Narrheit und das ist eine Prelatenschurkerey. Hätte Frankreich nicht seine Könige zu Oehlgötzen gemacht, so würde es nun nicht zur Harpye geworden seyn! Amen. Weg mit dem Zeugs.[20]

In his capacity as adjutant and secretary to General Igelström, Seume was in Warsaw during the spring uprising of 1794. He was captured by the Polish insurgents (actually he managed to surrender safely to Polish officers and avoid the fate of the many Russians who were lynched by Warsaw mobs) and spent more than six months in captivity before Alexander Suworov's forces occupied the city in November. After his liberation, Seume returned to the service of Igelström, who had fallen into disgrace for losing Warsaw and for the policies that had brought on the uprising in the first place, and was rewarded by being assigned to accompany a wounded Russian officer on a trip to Italy. Arriving in Leipzig in 1795 on the way to Italy, Seume ended up staying there the rest of his life. Both before and after the Warsaw uprising he had been privy to confidential diplomatic and military information that served him in his debut as a

---

20. Rolf Kraft, "Unbekannte Briefe Johann Gottfried Seumes an Karl Ludwig Frhr. v. Münchhausen, 1792–1806," *Euphorion* 63 (1969): 171. On the subject of German reactions to the French Revolution and especially to the war with France, see Thomas P. Saine, *Black Bread—White Bread: German Intellectuals and the French Revolution* (Columbia, S.C.: Camden House, 1988).

writer, a piece titled *Einige Nachrichten über die Vorfälle in Polen im Jahr 1794.*[21] Undoubtedly there was some news value in such an eyewitness account, although the impact of the publication was probably vitiated by the fact that Seume—in spite of a certain admiration he expressed for Kosciusko, the leader of the Polish national uprising—was decidedly unsympathetic to the people of Warsaw because of their uncivilized mob behavior and their unchivalrous treatment of the hopelessly outnumbered Russian occupiers. Seume also tried more or less to justify Suworov's ruthless storming of Praga in terms of military necessity, whereas liberal German writers such as Knigge and Rebmann vociferously condemned Russian actions and policy and the third partition that had put an end to Poland's existence as a nation.[22]

While writing his account of the Polish uprising, Seume certainly must have felt some conflict between his liberal conscience and the needs of his Russian employers, but he seems genuinely to have felt that Russia had been justified in intervening in Poland once again. At least he argued that point of view with some consistency in two subsequent pieces on eastern European affairs written in 1797 for his new employer, Göschen, who obviously hoped that publications on this currently interesting subject would sell well.[23] Here, too, Seume showed himself outside the mainstream of German liberal thinking. At a time when German intellectuals had generally turned against the recently deceased Catherine II (who previously had been one of their favorite monarchs) because of her participation in the second and third partitions of Poland and, in particular, because of the brutality with which her forces had put down the Polish uprising of 1794, Seume proceeded to defend her reign and her policies as "enlightened" and to express strong misgivings about the direction in which Russia was moving under her successor, Paul I, who, he feared, would undo Catherine's reforms. In the preface to the piece about Catherine, Seume distanced himself from aristocratic leanings and appealed to the voice of reason as his guide.

---

21. Seume, *Einige Nachrichten über die Vorfälle in Polen im Jahr 1794: von J. G. Seume, Russisch-Kaiserlichem Lieutenant* (Leipzig, 1796).

22. See Gerard Kozielek, "Johann Gottfried Seumes Stellung zum polnischen Aufstand von 1794," *Impulse: Aufsätze, Quellen, Berichte zur deutschen Klassik und Romantik* 2 (1979): 234–58.

23. The first of these, *Ueber das Leben und den Karakter der Kaiserin von Rußland Katharina II: Mit Freymüthigkeit und Unparteylichkeit,* was supposedly published in Altona but actually brought out by Göschen in Leipzig. The second was *Zwey Briefe über die neuesten Veränderungen in Rußland seit der Thronbesteigung Pauls des Ersten, Von J. G. Seume,* supposedly published in Zürich.

Der Verfasser dieses kleinen Aufsatzes ist gewiß nichts weniger als Anhänger der Despotie oder des Aristokratismus; und er hat durchaus keine Aufforderung, weder von innen noch von außen, etwas zu billigen oder zu mißbilligen als den Maßstab seiner vernünftigen Grundsätze, seiner Philanthropie und seines Wahrheitsgefühls. Nach diesen wird er sprechen ohne alle Bedenklichkeit und ruhig sein.[24]

Seume justified Catherine's actions in Poland in terms of the state of nature and the strife between nations, arguing that, whereas within the framework of civil society rulers and ruled are bound by the terms of the social contract, in the absence of binding and enforceable agreements among nations, each nation has the duty to protect its own interests. Poland had been a source of continual danger and instability for Russia since the election of Stanislaus August Poniatowski to the throne, because he had not been able to control the magnates and restore order to the country. Therefore, it had only been prudent of Catherine to exercise her natural right and intervene to remove the danger to vital Russian interests.

Viele Nationen sind unter ihrem Zepter froh und zufrieden gewesen und mit großen Schritten zur höheren Bildung vorwärts gerückt. Der Verfasser glaubt gezeigt zu haben, daß die anscheinenden Beeinträchtigungen ihrer Nachbarn nicht Ungerechtigkeiten, sondern leider notwendige Verflechtungen in dem Interesse der Völker waren. Daß sie sich in der polnischen Königswahl über alle Erwartung nicht geirrt hatte, zog die ganze Kette der großen Begebenheiten nach sich; und daß sie diese Begebenheiten mit Weisheit, Mut und Standhaftigkeit leitete und endigte, gibt ihrem Charakter für ihre Nation den Wert, den sie bei ihr behauptet. Die Geschichte wird gerecht sein, wo die Zeitgenossen es nicht waren.[25]

In a nutshell, Seume regarded the countries of eastern Europe as being still in a less than civilized state. The cities, representing a miniscule part

---

24. Seume, *Prosaschriften,* 1018.

25. Seume, *Prosaschriften,* 1115. Seume goes on to admit that there was some justified criticism of Catherine, but "wo glänzt in der ganzen Menschenkunde ein Charakter ohne Tadel? Selbst Gustav Adolph, der Held und Liebling aller Moralisten, hatte seine Mängel." Curiously enough, perhaps, Seume nowhere discusses the not insignificant role played by Prussia in the second and third partitions of Poland or allows Prussia to share much of the blame for extinguishing the Polish state.

of the total population, were small and undeveloped, containing only a relatively small number of cultured and civilized people together with a large portion of rabble (as we see in his judgments of events during the Warsaw uprising of 1794).[26] The overwhelming majority of the eastern populations were rural, uncultured, ignorant, unfree, and kept in that condition by their exploiters, the aristocratic landowners. (In his writings, Seume displays considerable sympathy for the plight of peasants and villagers in comparison to the urban lower classes.) The aristocrats, however, were also unenlightened, in Seume's opinion, and misguided in resisting change for the sake of preserving their traditional prerogatives and interests: they would benefit both themselves and their clients and serfs if they would allow liberalization of social and economic structures and thus open the way to achievement and productivity in all social classes. In this context, Seume argues, Catherine had been an agent of enlightenment and a civilizing force in Eastern Europe. Seume singles out her tolerance, her administrative reorganization, and her legal reforms for special praise. She had introduced and allowed as much freedom in Russia as was consistent with its state of development: "Nirgends war, selbst bei dem kritischen Zeitlauf, das Gouvernement liberaler als in Rußland."[27] Unfortunately, there was still a long way to go before the people of Russia as a whole reached the level of more fortunate peoples.

> Was die Monarchin für die Rechte und Freiheiten der niederen Volksklasse zu tun willens war, wird aus demjenigen richtig geschlossen, was sie wirklich für sie getan hat. Sowie die Nationen nur stufenweise zur Sklaverei herabgeführt werden, so führt man sie auch nur wieder stufenweise zur Freiheit hinauf. Jeder plötzliche Fall sowohl als jeder plötzliche Versuch zum Schwung bringt hier Konvulsionen hervor, die der Maschine den Untergang drohen.

In forming his judgments about eastern Europe in 1796–97, Seume relied on concepts of natural law and on a distinction between the "civilized" and the "barbarous" to ground his critique of sociopolitical conditions. (His attitude toward the mass of the population is particularly evident in his frequent discussions of the Russian military and the rela-

---

26. Seume's judgments of the Warsaw uprising correspond quite closely to what other German publicists had had to say about mob scenes in Paris at the height of the French Revolution.

27. Seume, *Prosaschriften*, 1117.

tionship between the relatively civilized generals, such as Suworov, and the brutish common soldiers.) Whoever sought, like Catherine II, to bring civilization and enlightenment to the unenlightened and uncivilized was worthy of praise. His firsthand observation of conditions in Eastern Europe seemed to confirm the correctness of his point of view. During his tour of Italy in 1802, however, he was confronted with the paradox of civilized territories that had relapsed, or threatened to relapse, into a state of feudal barbarism as a consequence of what might be called an "overenlightened" intervention in their affairs that had not been carried through to the end. Napoleon Bonaparte had scored his first smashing successes in Italy, wresting many of its fragmented territories from their feudal rulers—among them the pope—and founding French-oriented republics. This, in the eyes of Seume and other liberal-minded observers, had been on the whole a boon for the Italian peoples who thereby recovered much of their freedom (although the French had also made use of their conquest to loot the country and send innumerable treasures home to their museums). By 1802, however, at the time of Seume's trip, Napoleon had made his peace with the Roman church, restoring the papal possessions in Italy and allowing the return to power of ruling families earlier dispossessed by the establishment of the Italian republics.

Everywhere he went in Italy, once he had passed beyond Austrian-controlled Venice, Seume noted the triumphant return of the old order. He was especially critical of the situation in Rome and southern Italy: Rome was now again firmly under the thumb of the pope, robbers infested the countryside of Naples and Sicily, and monks and landowners lived well while the people suffered. Sicily, in particular, appeared depressed and ruined,[28] exploited ruthlessly by the government. Seume quotes a Sicilian tax official who had naively described his duties as though collecting taxes were the most straightforward profession in the world: "Wir müssen, sagte er, in der Insel herumreisen, die rückständigen Steuern einzutreiben, und im Namen des Königes den Leuten Kleider, Betten und das übrige Hausgeräte wegnehmen, wenn sie nicht zahlen können."[29] On his return to

---

28. See especially the poem "Trauer der Ceres," which Seume inserted at the end of the account of his stay in Sicily, but also his comments in various other passages of the *Spaziergang nach Syrakus*. Seume's depiction of Sicily is in stark contrast to the picture later painted by Goethe in the *Italienische Reise* (based on his travels there in 1787).

29. Seume, *Spaziergang nach Syrakus im Jahre 1802*, ed. Albert Meier (München: Deutscher Taschenbuch Verlag, 1985), 192. Meier's edition, from which I continue to quote in the following, includes a very helpful commentary.

Naples from Sicily, Seume notes the lack of affection Neapolitans evidence for their king, who has Russian soldiers to protect him "weil man ganz laut sagt, daß er sich auf seine eigenen Soldaten nicht verlassen kann."[30] If that is truly the case, according to Seume, then the king has only himself to blame, since the Neapolitans are "eine der bravsten und besten Nationen. . . . Was ich hier und da schlimmes sagen muß, betrifft nur die Regierung, ihre schlechte Verfassung oder Verwaltung und das Religionsunwesen." Back in Rome after his visit to Naples and Sicily, Seume immediately launches into a tirade against Bonaparte's concordat. "Dank sei es der Frömmelei und dem Mamelukengeist des großen französischen Bannerherrn, die Römer haben nun wieder Überfluß an Kirchen, Mönchen, Banditen. Er hat uns zum wenigsten wieder einige hundert Jahre zurückgeworfen."[31]

Seume claimed to have followed Bonaparte's career closely, practically from the very beginning.[32] (There is no conclusive body of evidence either to support or to disprove the contention.) At any rate, Bonaparte did not become a prominent figure in Seume's writing until his trip to Italy and the *Spaziergang nach Syrakus,* but, from then on, his effort to come to terms with the late stages of the French Revolution (represented by Bonaparte) and its consequences for Europe played a crucial role in Seume's thinking. It is not too much to claim, in fact, that Seume was fixated on Bonaparte and worked him into most of his attempts at historical explanation. He identified the course of history very much with the prominent actors in that history, as we have already seen in his views on Catherine II. Bonaparte became, for him, the world-historical figure par excellence; his career traced the course of the hopes and disappointments of contemporary humanity.

During his tour of Italy, Seume could observe both the benefits Bonaparte and the Revolution had promised and the devastating blow to those expectations produced by the concordat and the subsequent French withdrawal from most of Italy. In the Italian part of the *Spaziergang nach Syrakus,* Seume refers repeatedly to Bonaparte and his policies but without launching into any detailed discussion of his career and development. In the section

---

30. Seume, *Spaziergang,* 213.

31. Seume, *Spaziergang,* 214.

32. "Ich bin dem Mann von seiner ersten Erscheinung an mit Aufmerksamkeit gefolgt, und habe seinen Mut, seinen Scharfblick, seine militärische und politische Größe nie verkannt. Problematisch ist er mir in seinem Charakter immer gewesen" (Seume, *Spaziergang,* 273).

of the work describing his (much less lengthy) travels in France, however, Seume begins to sketch his picture of Napoleonic times. He finds little to criticize in Bonaparte's dissolution of the Directory and the institution of the Consulate; in the beginning, it was perhaps necessary for Bonaparte to gather the reins of power in his own hands in order to gain control over the warring factions. But in Seume's eyes, the battle of Marengo (June, 1800), where Bonaparte had defeated the Austrians decisively and forced a temporary end to the continental war, had marked a critical point in Bonaparte's career. Rather than turning to the task of reviving and strengthening the Republic, Napoleon had used the opportunity to enhance his own status at the expense of the Republic.

Aber nun fängt der Punkt an, wo sein eigenster Charakter hervorzu-treten scheint. Seitdem hat er durchaus nichts mehr für die Republik getan, sondern alles für sich selbst; eben da er aufhören sollte irgend etwas mehr für sich selbst zu tun, sondern alles für die Republik. Jeder Schritt, den er tat, war mit herrlich berechneter Klugheit vorwärts für ihn, und für die Republik rückwärts.[33]

Bonaparte had had the potential to be the greatest man in the history of the world, but he had failed the test. "Er hatte aber dazu nicht Erhabenheit genug und setzte sich herab mit den übrigen Großen auf gleichen Fuß. Er ist größer als die Dionyse und Kromwelle; aber er ist es doch in ihrer Art, und erwirbt sich ihren Ruhm."[34] That is, Napoleon was not an imposing monarch who could be respected for the manner in which he represented the interests of the state, but a tyrant and despot, a usurper of power rather than a legitimate wielder of it. The Bonaparte who had saved the Revolution and the Republic from anarchy had given Seume great cause for hope. "Ich habe vorher ganz ruhig dem Getümmel zuge-sehen und immer geglaubt und gehofft, daß aus dem wildgärenden Chaos endlich noch etwas vernünftiges hervortauchen würde."[35] Bonaparte's sub-sequent betrayal of freedom and the Republic had awakened in Seume the (perhaps largely elegiac) feeling of belonging to the republican party him-self. "Seitdem Bonaparte die Freiheit entschieden wieder zu Grabe zu tragen droht, ist mirs, als ob ich erst Republikaner geworden wäre."[36]

---

33. Seume, *Spaziergang,* 273–74.
34. Seume, *Spaziergang,* 274.
35. Seume, *Spaziergang,* 275.
36. To all intents and purposes, Seume's perception of Bonaparte did not change sig-

Though Seume had apparently viewed developments in France from 1789 on with a great deal of skepticism (the "Schwindlinge an der Seine"), he was still convinced of the justness of the French Revolution and he was convinced that the Revolution had brought momentous change for individual French citizens (it had brought forth the first true republicans) and for French society: aside from the periods of instability and civil strife (above all the Terror and the Jacobin dictatorship), he judged that its impact on France had been largely beneficial. Immediately after crossing from Basel into France, he noted that "[alles war] merklich wohlfeiler und man war durchaus höflicher und billiger. . . . Mir tut die Humanität und das allgemeine Wohlbefinden besser, als der wohlfeile Preis."[37] The Revolution had created a sense of community and belonging in France, transforming the people into a true "nation" that would not easily be dissolved again, even if enthusiasm for the Revolution and revolutionary ideals should wane or even disappear. Seume's conviction that the Revolution had made of the French a united people and an indomitable European force became even stronger when he contrasted France with the condition of Germany in the aftermath of Bonaparte's victories.

In the years after 1802, Seume inevitably changed his mind somewhat on the question of whether the French had truly become or were still a true nation as he had originally represented them in the *Spaziergang nach Syrakus*. He came to see them—at least the soldiers in Bonaparte's armies— as a collection of subjects mesmerized by a magnetic and domineering personality who threatened to rob them completely of their own republican will and commitment. At the time of his stay in Paris in July, 1802, Seume already noted the symptoms of impending restoration. Clergy who had been exiled under the Republic were returning from abroad, Bonaparte was making concessions to the aristocracy in order to win their support for his self-aggrandizing aims, and Seume thought he could see that the common people—the true republicans—were in danger of losing all that they had previously gained by their sacrifices. He commented with special bitterness on the creation of the Legion of Honor, which he interpreted as

nificantly after 1803. In the *Apokryphen,* he only developed the same thoughts further. For example: "Moses, Christus und Mohamed waren wirklich große Heilande der Völker, jeder in seinem Kreise. Bonaparte hätte ein größerer werden können, aber er hat nicht gewollt. Er hatte zu viel Eitelkeit und Ehrgeiz und nicht Stolz genug" (*Prosaschriften,* 1290). "Wenn Bonaparte die Stimme der Vernunft und Freiheit und Gerechtigkeit gehört hätte, er wäre die Sonne der Humanität. Er hat in sich selbst das schönste, reinste, höchste Ideal verdorben, das das Schicksal zum Heil der Menschheit aufstellen zu wollen schien" (1337).

37. Seume, *Spaziergang,* 263.

being aimed at mollifying the aristocrats for the sake of consolidating Bonaparte's position in France.

> Die Errichtung der Ehrenlegion mit Anweisung auf Nationalgüter ist der erste beträchtliche Schritt zur Wiedereinführung des Lehnssystems; das ward allgemein gefühlt: aber niemand hat die Macht, dem Allmächtigen zu widerstehen, der den Bajonetten befiehlt. . . . Wo die Regierung militärisch wird, ist es um Freiheit und Gerechtigkeit getan. Rom fiel, sobald sie es ward. Die Geistlichkeit spricht wieder hoch und laut.[38]

Still, in spite of the signs of impending restoration, French enthusiasm for the republican cause remained an all-conquering force. When he saw French troops on parade on Bastille Day in 1802, he found them physically and militarily unimpressive, concluding that they had won victories not because of their strengths but rather by virtue of their republican spirit. "[Ich kann] mir in den französischen Soldaten, ich mag sie besehen wie ich will, immer noch nicht die Sieger von Europa vorstellen. Wir sind mehr durch den Geist ihrer Sache und ihren hohen Enthusiasmus, als durch ihre Kriegskunst geschlagen worden."[39]

Seume's tour through Poland, Russia, and the Baltic in the summer of 1805 took him to regions untouched as yet by the conflict between revolutionary France and the European powers, and the account of his travels—*Mein Sommer 1805*—deals hardly at all with the big picture of the situation in Europe. He was content, for the most part, to describe conditions in their local and regional context. (He did come to the important conclusion—contrary to what he might have expected earlier on the basis of his belief that government by Russia would bring enlightenment to Polish society—that the Poles had not benefited in the least, socially or economically, from Russian domination.) By the time the book was published, however, in early 1806, Bonaparte's armies had defeated the Austrians and their Russian allies at Austerlitz yet again, on December 21, 1805. Bonaparte had extended his military dominance across the Rhine and was soon to force the dissolution of the Holy Roman Empire, spelling the end of Germany as it had existed since the early Middle Ages. In the

---

38. Seume, *Spaziergang,* 276–77.

39. Seume, *Spaziergang,* 273. In referring to "wir," Germans in general, Seume seems to mean the whole history of French superiority over German and imperial forces since 1792–93, not just the latest French successes over the Austrians, which had led to the current (short-lived) peace.

preface to *Mein Sommer 1805,* dated January 3, 1806, Seume, for the first time, turned his critical gaze on Germany to describe its humiliation and the path it would have to take if it was to rise up again and save itself from French domination. "Eine so traurige Rolle, als wir seit den letzten zehn Jahren gespielt haben, liegt kaum in den Annalen; und noch schlimmer ist es, es ist durchaus keine Aussicht, daß es je im einzelnen und im ganzen besser werde. Wir sind wirklich nun ein Spott einer Nation, die uns seit Jahrhunderten mit ihren Torheiten gegängelt hat."[40]

How had this come to pass? Seume's explanation of the situation begins with the fact that "die Franzosen . . . seit fünfzehn Jahren erst zur Nation im höheren Sinne des Wortes geworden [sind]; freilich durch eine furchtbare Wiedergeburt, um die sie niemand beneiden wird, aber sie sind es geworden."[41] The Germans, in contrast, continue to be oppressed and weighed down by their feudal past.

> Bei uns zerstörten die Freiheiten die Freiheit, die Gerechtigkeiten die Gerechtigkeit. Jedes Privilegium, jede Realimmunität ist ganz gewiß der erste Schritt zur Sklaverei, so wie es die erste öffentliche Ungerechtigkeit ist. Das ist unser Urteil. Das sehen alle Vernünftigen; aber niemand hat den Mut, den Anfang zur Gerechtigkeit zu machen. So mögen wir denn die Schmach unsrer Schwäche tragen! (*Prosaschriften,* 642)

Seume had earlier considered Poland and Russia to be socially and politically backward, the victims of their irrational feudal systems, and he explained their ills in terms of that backwardness; Germany now sinks into the same status as its eastern neighbors in comparison with the French achievement of the previous fifteen years.

> Der Franzose ohne Unterschied schlägt für ein Vaterland, das ihm nun lieb geworden ist, das ihm und seiner Familie eine gleiche Aussicht auf

---

40. Sueme, *Prosaschriften,* 640–41. Seume's strong patriotism becomes evident in his writings after 1806. Space does not permit a discussion of the nature of this patriotism. Although he was later to be claimed by German nationalists as one of their own, he distanced himself from the patriotic liberation movement, refusing a request, for example, to compose songs for the cause. It would seem that his critique of traditional German society was so thoroughgoing that he hardly thought mere "patriotism" or the uniting of the mass of Germans against Bonaparte without radical reforms in German society would be sufficient to rejuvenate Germany.

41. Seume, *Prosaschriften,* 642.

alle Vorteile vorhält und diese Vorteile wirklich gewährt. Nur der Mann wird gewürdigt nach dem, was er gilt, bei uns wird die Schätzung genommen nach dem, was das Kirchenbuch spricht, der Geldsack des Vaters wiegt oder das Hofmarschallamt vorschreibt. Für wen soll der deutsche Grenadier sich auf die Batterie und in die Bajonette stürzen? Er bleibt sicher, was er ist und trägt seinen Tornister so fort und erntet kaum ein freundliches Wort von seinem mürrischen Gewalthaber. Er soll dem Tode unverwandt ins Auge sehen, und zu Hause pflügt sein alter, schwacher Vater fronend die Felder des gnädigen Junkers, der nichts tut und nichts zahlt und mit Mißhandlungen vergilt. Der Alte fährt schwitzend die Ernte des Hofes ein und muß oft die seinige draußen verfaulen lassen; und dafür hat er die jämmerliche Ehre, der einzige Lastträger des Staats zu sein, eine Ehre, die klüglich nicht anerkannt wird! Soll der Soldat deshalb mutig fechten, um eben dieses Glück einst selbst zu genießen?[42]

Seume's description, in the preface of *Mein Sommer 1805*, of the lot of the ordinary German differs very little from his description, in the text itself, of the lot of the common Baltic, Russian, or Polish serf. Germany, for all its "culture," remains a primitive land as long as it has not become a nation in the sense in which the French have become a unified nation since the beginning of the Revolution.

In the preface to *Mein Sommer 1805*, Seume is no longer at all equivocal on the subject of Bonaparte: he is a tyrant and the destroyer of the Republic, but he has understood how to awaken and harness the energies of a great nation in his service.

Er verstand es, die aufgeregten Riesenkräfte einer großen, schönen, wackeren, liebenswürdigen Nation zusammenzufassen und sie nach seiner Neigung zu richten. . . . Ohne sein Verdienst und seine Größe zu schmälern, muß man der Nation die ihrige lassen. Seine Sache war, bloß das Gute der Revolution zu sammeln und es zu seinen Zwecken zu leiten. Was die Nation dabei gewinnt oder verliert, kann erst ein künftiges Jahrhundert entscheiden. (*Prosaschriften*, 648)

Seume sees no hope for Germany if it does not imitate the best of the French Revolution while seeking to avoid its excesses. There is no sense

---

42. Seume, *Prosaschriften*, 646.

waiting for the French flame to burn itself out, as some might perhaps hope ("Anstatt daß wir, philosophischer und humaner als sie, zu ihnen hinaufsteigen sollten, hoffen wir verkehrt genug, sie werden wieder zu uns herabsinken" [*Prosaschriften*, 649]); it is time for radical reform to raise Germany to the full potential of its humanity, which has been retarded by the injustice and inequality preserved in its economic and social system. As long as the few have privileges, rights, and property and the many have none, the Germans will be unable to withstand the French. Exactly two years later, after Bonaparte had completed his conquest of Germany by destroying the Prussian army at Jena and Auerstedt, Seume continued his critique in his "Vorwort zu einem Bändchen Bemerkungen und Konjekturen zu schwereren Stellen des Plutarch."[43] He blames the situation of Germany—more desperate than it has ever been before—squarely on the outmoded feudal system that had prevented the development of a united nation of citizens such as the Revolution had produced in France.

Ja, diese Fäulnis, Seuche, Pestilenz und Vernichtung ist eine Folge der Prärogative, der Ausnahmezustände und der Privilegien. Jeder für sich, keiner für das Vaterland. Je mehr Vermögen jemand besitzt, um so mehr strebt er nach Privilegien, damit er die übrigen quälen, unterdrücken, wie Klötze und Dummköpfe behandeln kann. Es gibt nur *eine* Gerechtigkeit, *eine* Freiheit, nämlich gleiches Recht für alle; bei uns nennt man in mehr als barbarischer Weise Gerechtigkeiten und Freiheiten alles, was Vernichtung und Untergang der Freiheit, der Gerechtigkeit und des Gemeinwesens ist.—Das ist unser Elend, daher unsre Tränen. Überall gibt es bei uns despotische Ansprüche, Königreiche, Herrschaften, Dynastien, Grafen, Barone—Namen, barbarisch wie ihre Bedeutung; einen gesetzlichen bürgerlichen und militärischen Oberbefehl gibt es nirgends, nirgends eine Bürgerschaft. Der Name Bürgerschaft ist ein Verbrechen, der Name Bürger eine Schande. . . . Aus der Barbarei haben wir uns nicht emporheben können; daher war es notwendig, daß wir in Knechtschaft versinken mußten. *Eins sei das Volk, eins die Oberherrschaft, eins die Staatsgewalt, eins die Autorität und die Majestät des Vaterlandes!*[44]

It is difficult to reconcile the moral principles Seume claimed to uphold

---

43. Dated January 1, 1808, and written in Latin, the Plutarch preface was suppressed by the censors.

44. Seume, *Prosaschriften*, 1175–76.

with all the positions he argued at the beginning of his career as a writer. Though espousing Enlightenment and human rights in the abstract, he defended Catherine's subjugation of helpless Poland and condemned the Warsaw uprising of 1794. No less a person than Goethe saw Bonaparte, after Jena and Auerstedt, both as the guarantor of European order and stability and as the embodiment of "das Dämonische," a force of nature that it is useless to seek to judge according to the usual moral norms. At the end of his life, however, after following the career of Bonaparte, a much more threatening foe of individual and national freedom than Catherine had ever been in a position to be, Seume—abstracting from his perception of what the French people had gained, in spite of all the costs, from their republic and their revolution—concluded that the only freedom and equality was freedom and equality for all. The absence or decay of civil liberties and justice sapped a nation's strength and might invite foreign intervention, like Catherine's in Poland or Bonaparte's in Italy and Germany (and Russia, which Seume did not live to see), but did not justify it. The only remedy was to operate on the nation and make it whole again by removing the cause of the weakness. Johann Gottfried Seume, the intrepid pedestrian, deserves to be remembered, if only for learning this lesson of the French Revolution.

"Poesie und Philosophie sollen vereinigt sein": Friedrich Schlegel's *Lucinde* as Experimental Novel

Michael T. Jones

Friedrich Schlegel's only novel has recently inspired such appellatives as "subjectivistic," "nonepic," and "ironic"; the labels "allegorical novel" and "romantic book" have been added to the older judgments of monstrosity and obscenity.[1] If *Lucinde* really does deserve the characterization of "the most widely read German romantic novel today,"[2] one wonders about the reputation of the German romantic novel, for its formal structure is surely unique. In adding "experimental" to the list of *Lucinde* descriptions, I offer a reading based on the goal the author set for himself: a literary enactment of philosophical tensions. As is well known, Schlegel participated in the general philosophical and literary enthusiasm that greeted Fichte's *Wissenschaftslehre* of 1794. Agreeing (i.e., with Novalis and Hölderlin) that Fichte had taken a decisive step beyond the limitations of Kant with his insistence on the centrality of the productive imagination, Schlegel, by 1797, contended that the most advanced literary efforts must

---

1. For allegorical, see Ernst Behler, "Friedrich Schlegel: Lucinde (1799)," in *Romane und Erzählungen der deutschen Romantik*, ed. Paul Michael Lützeler (Stuttgart: Reclam, 1981), 112; for subjectivistic, see Margret Eifler, *Die subjektivistische Romanform seit ihren Anfängen in der Frühromantik: Ihre Existentialität und Anti-Narrativik am Beispiel von Rilke, Benn und Handke* (Tübingen: Niemeyer, 1985), 26ff.; for non-epic, see Esther Hudgins, *Nicht-Epische Strukturen des romantischen Romans* (The Hague: Mouton, 1975), 44ff.; for ironic, see Cornelia Hotz-Steinmeyer, *Friedrich Schlegels Lucinde als "Neue Mythologie": Geschichtsphilosophischer Versuch einer Rückgewinnung gesellschaftlicher Totalität durch das Individuum* (Frankfurt: Lang, 1985), 48ff.; for romantic book, see Eric A. Blackall, *The Novels of the German Romantics* (Ithaca: Cornell University Press, 1983), 21ff.

2. Simonetta Sanna, "Schlegels Lucinde oder der ästhetische Roman," *Deutsche Vierteljahresschrift für Literaturwissenschaft und Geistesgeschichte* 61 (1987): 457.

take account of German Idealism. This position never left him during the early Romantic period, but it is most explicit in *Lyceum* 115.

> Die ganze Geschichte der modernen Poesie ist ein fortlaufender Kommentar zu dem kurzen Text der Philosophie: Alle Kunst soll Wissenschaft, und alle Wissenschaft soll Kunst werden; Poesie und Philosophie sollen vereinigt sein. (*KA* 2:161)[3]

But how to do it? How to turn Fichte's spare, abstract, abstruse account of the vicissitudes of ego and non-ego into something resembling *Poesie?* The magnitude of this challenge inspires respect for the endeavor, if not necessarily admiration for its result. Along with Hölderlin and Novalis (and Hegel at an early stage), Schlegel settled on love as a concept that could reproduce duality and *Wechsel* as well as unity, for love was to be efficacious for depicting both empirical experience and transcendental speculation. It was to be an empirical manifestation of the principle of unity in multiplicity.

But the decision to place love at the center of the novel does not, in itself, dissolve the disparity of medium between literature and philosophy. Using the background provided by Schlegel's Jena lectures on transcendental philosophy of 1800–1801, I will examine the function, in two significant segments of *Lucinde,* of the two most characteristic concepts of poetry (in the broader sense) and philosophy. These are, respectively, the concepts of representation and reflection. Schlegel himself underscored their importance in the two *Athenäum* fragments that are omnipresent in critical discussions of early Romanticism—116 and 238: the one circles around reflection, the other around representation.

The irony of these two fragments in the present context, however, is their chiasmatic effect. Fragment 116, which centers on reflection, is the most famous characterization of romantic poetry.

> Nur sie [romantische Poesie] kann gleich dem Epos ein Spiegel der ganzen umgebenden Welt, eine Bild des Zeitalters werden. Und doch kann auch sie am meisten zwischen dem Dargestellten und dem Dar-

---

3. *Kritische Friedrich Schlegel-Ausgabe,* ed. Ernst Behler, Jean-Jacques Anstett, and Hans Eichner (Paderborn: Schöningh, 1958–). References to this edition are included in the text as *KA* and provide volume and page number. Schlegel's voluminous italics have not been reproduced.

stellenden, frei von allem realen und idealen Interesse auf den Flügeln der poetischen Reflexion in der Mitte schweben, diese Reflexion immer wieder potenzieren und wie in einer endlosen Reihe von Spiegeln vervielfachen. (*KA* 2:182–83)

Here is prefigured what will become of reflection in *Lucinde,* which will include the literal, mirror-connected meaning of the word as well as the higher, philosophically potentiated one. The philosophical concept makes possible such potentiated poetic representation. Fragment 238, on the other hand, adduces poetry as transcendental poetry "nach der Analogie der philosophischen Kunstsprache" (note the chiasma). Just as transcendental philosophy represents [*darstellt*] "das Produzierende mit dem Produkt" and thereby "eine Charakteristik des transzendentalen Denkens," so must poetry, by employing poetic theory and artistic reflection, "in jeder ihrer Darstellungen sich selbst mit darstellen, und überall Poesie und Poesie der Poesie sein" (*KA* 2:204).

These famous statements become no clearer by being endlessly repeated. They are anything but a finished recipe for what "Transzendentalpoesie"[4] as "Poesie der Poesie" would actually look like in reality. Schlegel uses them as retrospective justification for his bold, audacious experiment in plot, genre, and philosophy. In the sphere of content, he forsakes the traditional plot structure by having the novel begin with the ideal love relationship rather than end with it, and thereby risks boring his readers. His experiment with form—the arabesques of varying genres surrounding somewhat traditional narration—was and remains innovative, despite its reiteration in voluminous critical literature. What remains little appreciated and little understood is the function of reflection on representation and the representation of reflection in the novel.

At the conclusion of his Jena lectures on transcendental philosophy in 1800–1801, Friedrich Schlegel sketches a model of "philosophy's return into itself" based on an ontology of apparently radical skepticism: "die Wahrheit ist relativ"; since "alle Philosophie ist unendlich" and "alles Wissen ist symbolisch," it follows "daß die Form der Philosophie unendlich ist" (*KA* 12:92–93). The latter claim is made less obscure if we recall Schlegel's description of Lessing's "symbolic form" in the 1801 conclusion to his Lessing essay: "Gibt es wohl ein schöneres Symbol für die Paradoxie

---

4. Roland Heine, *Transzendentalpoesie,* 2d ed. (Bonn: Bouvier, 1985).

des philosophischen Lebens, als jene krummen Linien, die mit sichtbarer Stetigkeit und Gesetzmäßigkeit forteilend immer nur im Bruchstück erscheinen können, weil ihr eines Zentrum in der Unendlichkeit liegt?" (*KA* 2:415).[5] Infinity is surely a familiar romantic concept, to be approached only in the mode of "infinite approximation," but literary critics, untrained and uninterested in the morass of idealist philosophy, often limit the notion's applicability to knowledge about art.

Thus, Schlegel's claims here, which are not aesthetic-critical but epistemological, are quite radical. From his three axioms, he proceeds to deduce (1) "daß die Philosophie durchaus historisch seyn soll," and (2) "daß die Philosophie nothwendig polemisch zu Werke geht" (*KA* 12:93). The term *Polemik* is to be understood literally, as a tension between negations.

> Die Wahrheit entsteht, wenn entgegengesetzte Irrthümer sich neutralisiren. Absolute Wahrheit kann nicht zugegeben werden; und dies ist die Urkunde für die Freyheit der Gedanken und des Geistes.
>
> Wenn die absolute Wahrheit gefunden wäre, so wäre damit das Geschäft des Geistes vollendet, und er müßte aufhören zu seyn, da er nur in der Thätigkeit existirt. (*KA* 12:93)

This freedom, the infinite exertion that constitutes philosophy, confronts "die Aufgabe, den Organismus aller Wissenschaften und Künste zu konstruiren" (*KA* 12:94). This process is a destruction as well as a construction. Again, there is a parallel claim in Schlegel's writings about Lessing, this time from "Vom kombinatorischen Geist" in his Lessing anthology. Here, while praising Lessing, Schlegel denounces "eine durchaus falsche Anordnung und Konstruktion der Künste und Wissenschaften" and appeals to the "Idee einer eignen Wissenschaft, welche die Einheit und Verschiedenheit aller höhern Wissenschaften und Künste und alle gegenseitigen Ver-

---

5. The mathematical sign for this in the notebooks is the parabola, "an ellipse whose closure is only a theoretical or mystical concept because its second focus is infinitely removed from the first" (Marcus Paul Bullock, *Romanticism and Marxism; The Philosophical Development of Literary Theory and Literary History in Walter Benjamin and Friedrich Schlegel* [New York: Lang, 1987], 37). It is well known that Schlegel did not distinguish carefully between symbol and allegory, as was done later in the wake of Goethe. For an account that epitomizes the valorization of symbol over allegory despite its appearance of neutrality, see Doris Starr, *Über den Begriff des Symbols in der deutschen Klassik und Romantik* (Reutlingen: Hutzler, 1964). The emphasis on allegory in *Lucinde* parallels the characterization of symbol from the 1801 conclusion of the Lessing essay. On the entire topic of the romantic use of mathematics, see Marshall Brown, *The Shape of German Romanticism* (Ithaca: Cornell University Press, 1979).

hältnisse derselben von Grund aus zu bestimmen versucht" (*KA* 3:82). Necessary for this "encyclopedia" are not only commentary but also criticism, he declares, a criticism that could function as "das Organon einer noch zu vollendenden, zu bildenden, ja anzufangenden Literatur," a *Kritik* "die selbst produzierend wäre, wenigstens indirekt durch Lenkung, Anordnung, Erregung" (*KA* 3:82). It is the kind of criticism where "ein kühn kombinierender Geist sichtbar ist. Dieses Kombinatorische ist es, was ich vorhin im Sinne hatte, und als wissenschaftlichen Witz bezeichnete" (84).

In his combinatory, "witty," polemical construction of that "encyclopedia" that does not yet exist, Schlegel, in his lectures, refuses to be intimidated by what he calls the "dogmatism of logic."

Der Satz, daß alle Wahrheit relativ sey, könnte leicht auf eine allgemeine Skepsis hinleiten. Z. B. Wenn alle Wahrheit relativ ist, so ist auch der Satz relativ, daß alle Wahrheit relativ sey. Wenn alles richtig verstanden wird, so kann man dies auch zugeben. Es ist damit nichts gewonnen; man kann nicht nur diesen Satz zugeben, sondern auch das, daß das ganze System der Philosophie relativ sey. (*KA* 12:95)

Schlegel's critique of logic (in the form of the principles of identity, sufficient reason, and contradiction) is one of the constants of his thought that I cannot follow further here except to note that it finds its way into the *Athenäum* fragments and that the principle of contradiction particularly draws his ire.

Der Satz des Widerspruchs ist auch nicht einmal das Prinzip der Analyse, nemlich der absoluten, die allein den Namen verdient, der chemischen Dekomposition eines Individuums in seine schlechthin einfachen Elemente. (*KA* 2:178)

The paradox, the witty combination of the incomparable, are the despair of the logician but the joy of the romantic Schlegel, who—as is well known—developed his theory of irony from such oppositions and did so because the structure of the world demanded it: "Alle Realität ist das Produkt entgegengesetzter Elemente" (*KA* 12:8).[6] The combinatory, Socratic method of

6. ". . . die Dialektik im künstlerischen Schaffensprozeß, der transcendentale Akt in seiner ästhetischen Bedeutung und die poetische Reflexion als synthetisierendes Vermögen,—diese Gedanken stehen offenkundig in Beziehung zu Schlegels Definition der Ironie als 'logische

philosophy strives, through the destruction of error (again the bane of the austere logician: how can one speak of error without [absolute] truth?), to achieve the potentiated and infinite "philosophy of philosophy" (*KA* 12:100), a parallel to the "Poesie der Poesie" of *Athenäum* 238. He actively separates logic from philosophy in order to free it for combinatory constellations ripe with reflection on their representation. This method and procedure of the combinatory *Geist* is explicitly experimental. "Wie das Denken als Experimentiren zu behandeln sey, hieße den combinatorischen Geist bestimmen; wir haben das nicht erst nöthig, unsere ganze Art zu philosophiren war schon so" (*KA* 12:102).

In this descriptive context of the experimental construction of the philosophy of philosophy, another conceptual dyad emerges that is also central for *Lucinde:* that of *Mitteilen* and *Darstellen*. One of Schlegel's earliest critiques of Fichte was his claim that Fichte's system was necessarily indifferent to being communicated (which hardly meant that the man himself was indifferent to public response): "Der ächte Mystiker will seine Meinung gar nicht mittheilen. . . . Fichte ist so sehr Philosoph als es der Mystiker nur sein kann" (*KA* 18:4).[7] Combinatory experimentation, in opposition to the thoughts of the "genuine mystic," must be communicated, both to achieve concrete form in language and to dispel illusions of results or absolute truth.

Ein absolutes Verstehen ist nach unserer Ansicht gar nicht möglich. . . . Gäbe es eine absolute Wahrheit, so gäbe es auch eine abso-

Schönheit'" (Ingrid Strohschneider Kohrs, *Die romantische Ironie in Theorie und Gestaltung*, 2d ed. [Tübingen: Niemeyer, 1977]: 51). That the phrase "logische Schönheit" from *Lyceum* 42 (*KA* 2:152) breaks the bounds of Aristotelian logic by aestheticizing it is evident. Rüdiger Bubner ("Zur dialektischen Bedeutung romantischer Ironie," in *Die Aktualität der Frühromantik*, ed. Ernst Behler and Jochen Hörisch [Paderborn: Schöningh, 1987], 85–95) makes the important point that Schlegel's denial of absolute truth, and his concomitant contention that truth emerges from the mutual relativization of error, is precisely what *differentiates* him from Fichte. "Fichtes Wissenschaftslehre beginnt mit einem absoluten Prinzip, das der Ironiker für notwendig noch ausstehend hält" (92).

7. The opening notations of the "Philosophische Lehrjahre" contain this characterization of Fichte the mystic as opposed to other philosophical types, the skeptic and the eclectic. For an account of Schlegel's understanding of these types, see Kurt Röttgers, "Fichtes Wirkung auf die Frühromantiker, am Beispiel Friedrich Schlegels: Ein Beitrag zur 'Theoriepragmatik,'" *Deutsche Vierteljahrsschrift für Literaturwissenschaft und Geistesgeschichte* 51 (1977): 55–77. Röttgers does not regard the distinction between Fichte and Schlegel as so radical as does Bubner; rather, he claims that Schlegel's primary reservation about Fichte was "die Frage nach der Kommunikabilität, die er in die Form einer Frage nach dem Sinn der Unterscheidung von Geist und Buchstaben einer Philosophie kleidet" (72).

lute Verständlichkeit. In der Verständlichkeit ist zweyerley enthalten, (1) der falsche Begriff der absoluten Verständlichkeit, (2) die Forderung an den der mittheilt, daß er es auf eine gewisse Weise thun soll, wie es in dem Begriff der Verständlichkeit liegt. Nun giebt es kein anderes Medium als die Darstellung. Durch Darstellung soll das in dem andern vorgehen, was in uns vorgieng, so hat sie den Zweck der Mittheilung erreicht. In der Mittheilung soll enthalten seyn, nicht immer eine Darstellung der Resultate, sondern der Art und Weise, wie es entstanden ist, die Darstellung soll also genetisch seyn. Die wahre Methode der Darstellung ist demnach genetisch, oder historisch. (*KA* 12:102)

Schlegel typically plays with superficial notions (truth, comprehensibility) in order to "represent" the task of infinite approximation. Absolute truth and absolute comprehensibility (one thinks of "Über die Unverständlichkeit") are impossible to achieve, but that does not diminish the necessity that *Mitteilung* become *Darstellung*. *Mitteilung* would provide the mere "results" of thought, whereas *Darstellung* demonstrates the "Art und Weise, wie es entstanden ist." By imitating or mimicking development, genetic evolution, or "history," *Darstellung* is better able to achieve (but never absolutely, of course) the "Zweck der Mitteilung" than a mere enumeration of the "results" could reach. All these considerations will have widereaching consequences for the experimental novel *Lucinde*.[8]

As handed down in the questionable form of an auditor's notes, the Jena lectures make an extraordinarily modern impression today. They show a philosophical *bricoleur*,[9] rummaging about in the conceptual repertoire of contemporary thought, rearranging elements in new and surprising ways. The unifying theme is Schlegel's explicit effort to combine Fichte and Spinoza, but, as the manuscript's finder and first editor admits, its value is based not so much on the originality of the thoughts but, rather, lies "am bunten, das dispositionelle Gerüst bis zur Unsichtbarkeit umwuchernden Rankenwerk, das nach Inhalt und Form wie eine Fortsetzung der

---

8. The most detailed account of the unification of poetry and philosophy in *Lucinde* is Karl Konrad Polheim, "Friedrich Schlegels *Lucinde*," *Zeitschrift für deutsche Philologie* 88 (1969 Sonderheft): 61–90. Polheim concentrates on the novel's relation to the "Brief über den Roman," thus building on his authoritative investigations of key Schlegelian poetic concepts in *Die Arabeske: Ansichten und Ideen aus Friedrich Schlegels Poetik* (Munich, Paderborn, and Vienna: Schöningh, 1966).

9. Jacques Derrida, "Structure, Sign, and Play," in *Writing and Difference*, trans. Alan Bass (Chicago: University of Chicago Press, 1978), 285ff.

Athenäumsfragmente anmutet."[10] One example of the experimental use of idealist categories is the early section on "epochs of truth," which reverses the Kantian valorization of *Verstand* and *Vernunft*, insisting that epoch 1 (*Einsicht* = Enlightenment?) is characterized by *Bestimmtheit* but yet still runs the danger of dogmatism; epoch 2 (*Vernunft* = German Idealism?) is the epoch of ideas, idealism, and knowledge, and seems to close the "history of consciousness"; yet epoch 3 (*Verstand*) is the "return of all epochs," the point that corresponds to the (obviously transcendental) "philosophy of philosophy" with which the lectures close (*KA* 12:13).

To this cycle of epochs correspond the concepts of finitude and infinitude and—paralleling a similar text in *Lucinde*—determinacy and indeterminacy. The infinite is the originary but utterly indeterminate "Chaos"; then: "aus dem Unendlichen entsteht das Bewußtsein, wenn das Unendliche unendlich endlich wird. Und wenn im Bewußtsein des Ich und Nichtich, und die Vereinigung der beyden erreicht ist, entsteht das Unendliche" (*KA* 12:25). In these epochs are a multitude of concepts that, as any student of Schlegel knows, tend to proliferate endlessly. What interests me in the context of the lectures is the attribution of speculation to Spinoza and of reflection to Fichte. I summarize: analysis (dividing a phenomenon into its elements) confronts two phenomena, consciousness and the infinite. The infinite is then divided; its "known" element is the indeterminate [*das Unbestimmte*], from which emerges ("ergiebt sich durch den Gegensatz") *das Bestimmte*. Schlegel calls the definition of the infinite positive and genetic. Consciousness is the opposed phenomenon and is divided into two elements: *Ich* and *Nichtich*. This phenomenon he calls negative. "Die Dedukzion: das Bestimmte bestimmt sich immer mehr, bis es sich zum Unbestimmten und ins Unbestimmte bestimmt": this last *Unbestimmtes,* he elaborates, represents the "höchste[n] Gipfel der menschlichen Besonnenheit, des Verstandes" (*KA* 12:26). A fragment elaborates the Fichtean side of the contrast: "Das Gute in Fichte's Form ist das SETZEN, und dann das Aus sich herausgehn und In sich zurückkehren—d.h. die Form der Reflexion" (*KA* 18:476).[11]

---

10. They were found and first published by Josef Körner in his edition of *Neue Philosophische Schriften* (Frankfurt am Main: Schulte-Bulmke, 1935), who describes them in his introduction (57–58).

11. It was the achievement of Walter Benjamin's dissertation, "Der Begriff der Kunstkritik in der deutschen Romantik," to place reflection at the center of the Romantic conception of art, and this based on a paucity of appropriate texts. Its authoritative status was often invoked but not questioned until recently, by Bullock (*Romanticism and Marxism*) and Winfried

That the little text "Eine Reflexion" in *Lucinde* is a playful sexual experiment with Fichte's philosophy is a commonplace.[12] Only the moral evaluation has changed; Kluckhorn said, "Eine künstlerische Geschmacklosigkeit, über die sich kein Wort zu verlieren lohnt, die uns aber mahnt, die eigentlichen Gedanken Schlegels von dem zweideutigen allegorischen oder libertinistischen Gewande zu trennen, in welchem es ihm gefällt sie auszudrücken."[13] Anstett and Eichner are less judgmental: ". . . un exposé un peu piquant de l'idéalisme fichtéen"; ". . . eine metaphysische Phantasie, 'Reflexion,' in der Schlegel in parodistisch angewandter Fichtescher Terminologie über das Thema der Zeugung und die Allgegenwart des Geschlechtsunterschiedes in der Natur reflektiert."[14] The text is a parodistic and witty experiment with an off-color version of Fichtean philosophy, then, that has something to do with the novel's theme of love, although exactly how it is connected remains somewhat puzzling. Anstett's "close reading," to which critics usually refer, makes apt points but chiefly in the mode of paraphrase.

The narrator-observer invokes, in the first paragraph, the passive stance of his *Gemüt* ("meinem Gemüt nicht selten sonderbar aufgefallen"); in the second, his active *Geist* ("dann fragte mein Geist"). The former term appears often in Idealism as a synthetic unity of mind and body, intellect and feeling. What "occurs" to it is the enigmatic energy of "verständige und würdige Menschen," who endlessly repeat the eternal yet useless

Menninghaus (*Unendliche Verdopplung: Die frühromantische Grundlegung der Kunsttheorie im Begriff absoluter Selbstreflexion* [Frankfurt: Suhrkamp, 1987]). In particular, Menninghaus offers a carefully nuanced critique of Benjamin while accusing most of the rest of Schlegel scholarship of quoting him but never really wrestling with him. Any future consideration of the problem of reflection will have to consider these matters, but I must restrict myself in the present context to the novel and omit the problem of Romantic criticism. An important point of future study will be the affinity of notions of "groundless reflection" with Derridian modes of thought, an exploration begun by Menninghaus (115ff.). See also the excellent account of philosophical reflection in German Idealism and thereafter in section one of Rodolphe Gasche, *The Tain of the Mirror: Derrida and the Philosophy of Reflection* (Cambridge, Mass.: Harvard University Press, 1986). Gasche also mentions that "this kind of criticism [Derrida] originated in early German Romanticism. The reciprocal dissolution of opposing concepts or contradictory strata within a text, which this criticism promotes, must be traced back to the Romantics' attempt at a transcendental poetry that was to represent an amalgam not only of all different genres but also of all the hitherto separate disciplines" (139).

12. A single study is devoted solely to this little text (see J.-J. Anstett, *"Lucinde: Eine Reflexion,* Essai D'Interpretation," *Etudes Germaniques* 3 [1948]: 241–50). Because of the brevity of "Eine Reflexion," I dispense with specific page references to it.

13. Paul Kluckhohn, *Die Auffassung der Liebe in der Literatur des 18. Jahrhunderts und in der deutschen Romantik,* 3d ed. (Tübingen: Niemeyer, 1966), 368.

14. Anstett, "Essai," 245; Hans Eichner, Vorwort to *KA* 5:xliv.

"play" while coming no nearer to the goal. Fichte immediately comes to mind, which in view of what follows is eminently justified (and Novalis did something similar with his "ernster Mann" in *Die Lehrlinge zu Sais*). Fichte's endless circling around the subject-object relation in the *Wissenschaftslehre* claims to give an account of cognition through the emphasis on reflective self-determination in mutual limitation of ego and non-ego.[15] The original and unitary *Gemüt*, then, regards this as frenetic *Tathandlung* that leads nowhere, whereupon *Geist* regards what that activity *should* be accounting for—the non-ego or nature—as making fun of it. In fact, nature, "die überall so viel denkt, die List im Großen treibt und statt witzig zu reden, gleich witzig handelt,"[16] evinces all the activities attributed to the self-positing ego: *denken* and *handeln*, and does so "wittily" in both senses of experimental combination and of poking fun at the naïveté of "educated speakers" in matters—sexual. For nature knew all along that the ego and non-ego dyad (along with such Fichtean categories as *Trieb* and *Gefühl*) were sexual as well as epistemological. That is certainly true for the concept of *Wechselbestimmung*, despite the fact that Fichte's "naive intimations" leave the beast unnamed.

The third paragraph complements the standard mind-nature dualism with a second one of ancients and moderns: the more repressed the moderns, the greater the tendency to crack jokes about sex, whereas the dignity of the ancient gods included "shamelessness" in the constitution of mythology in ancient art. But a simple appeal to the old mythology is insufficient, and, thus, Schlegel's call for a "new mythology" that is shortly to follow (in *Gespräch über die Poesie*) is also a call to include ancient shamelessness in the "desired ideal."

Thus far, the somewhat informed reader will have had little trouble following Schlegel's paradoxes and oppositions. The fifth paragraph opens the theme of reflection proper and, characteristically, immediately "potentiates" it: "Das Denken hat die Eigenheit, daß es nächst sich selbst am liebsten über das denkt, worüber es ohne Ende denken kann." The process or activity of thinking itself—subjectivity—is in its own turn subjected to

---

15. The important term for mutual limitation is *Wechsel* and its more dynamic counterpart *Wechselbestimmung*. See the discussion in Fichte's "Grundlage," in *Johann Gottlieb Fichte's sämmtliche Werke*, ed. J. H. Fichte (Berlin: Veit und Comp, 1845): 1:196ff. In J. G. Fichte, *The Science of Knowledge*, ed. and trans. Peter Heath and John Lachs (Cambridge: Cambridge University Press, 1982), the translators render this important term as "interplay" (178f.).

16. Anstett's conviction ("Essai," 246ff.) that the role of nature in this text leads inexorably to Schelling seems to me an exaggeration.

thinking and thereby becomes object: this is the meaning of "reflection" that Fichte introduced into idealist philosophy. The dualism of *Geist* and nature or mind and body is reproduced on a higher level. Thinking reflects upon itself *and also* upon the infinite.

Darum ist das Leben des gebildeten und sinnigen Menschen ein stetes Bilden und Sinnen über das schöne Rätsel seiner Bestimmung. Er bestimmt sie immer neu, denn eben das ist seine ganze Bestimmung, bestimmt zu werden und zu bestimmen. Nur in seinem Suchen selbst findet der Geist des Menschen das Geheimnis welches er sucht.[17]

The swirling wordplays leave the reader breathless at first but are eminently comprehensible and reveal surprising latent possibilities in German. Note the chiasma in the first sentence: "gebildet" and "sinnig" recalls mind and body, but then "Bilden" and "Sinnen" as nouns propose a similar (not identical) juxtaposition yet reverse the connotations, so that the forms of *Sinn,* previously associated with the senses [*sinnlich*], are now connected with mind, while *Bilden* has been severed from its metaphorical association with "cultured" and recovers its original concrete meaning by virtue of its place in the new opposition. Playing with the combinatory possibilities of his language, Schlegel reenacts through chiasma the theme of *Wechsel-bestimmung* that he is approaching in the mode of infinite approximation or *Suchen.* Moreover, the parallel between *bilden* and *sinnen* on the one hand and the larger contexts of representation and reflection on the other is evident.

"Bestimmt zu werden oder zu bestimmen" repeats the fundamental mechanism of ego and non-ego that lies at the basis of the *Wissenschaftslehre,* a mechanism that is, for the early Schlegel, one of infinite striving. But Fichte is himself constantly tempted to recuperate the tension-filled state of reciprocal determination, or, in other Fichtean terms, the unstable equilibrium of centrifugal and centripetal forces, in a "higher" synthetic unity of ego that would be the Absolute. As he writes near the conclusion of the *Grundlage:* "Man kann diesen Trieb nennen *den Trieb nach Wechselbestimmung* des Ich durch sich selbst, oder den Trieb nach absoluter *Einheit*

---

17. The interplay of *bestimmen* and *bestimmt zu werden* is also described in Fichte as centripetal and centrifugal forces. See Jeffrey Barnouw, "'Der Trieb, bestimmt zu werden': Hölderlin, Schiller und Schelling als Antwort auf Fichte," *Deutsche Vierteljahresschrift für Literaturwissenschaft und Geistesgeschichte* 46 (1972): 248–93, esp. 267ff.

und Vollendung des Ich in sich selbst."[18] Schlegel recognized this perfectly clearly: "Eine Antinomie zwischen mehren Theilen der menschlichen Bildung ist kein wahrer Dualismus, sondern nur eine Wechselbestimmung" (*KA* 18:301). Furthermore, "in meinem System ist der letzte Grund wirklich ein Wechselerweis. In Fichte's ein Postulat und ein unbedingter Grundsatz" (521). But Schlegel has endured decades of critical abuse for his scatalogical use of the primordial opposition provided by nature—that of male and female—to depict reciprocal determination in a philosophical allegory that is also a concrete description of the sex act. The interplay of *das Bestimmte* and *das Unbestimmte* is quite determinate in their manifestation of male and female qualities: *geheimnisreich, reizende Verwirrung,* and *vergängliche Schönheit* are female attributes, *Zauberkraft, erhabene Bildung,* and *vorübergehende Energie* are male ones. Retrogressive and unbalanced as such language sounds to modern ears, the theoretical aim is an eternal symmetry that can function as "Mittlerin" and "allegorische Miniatur," pointing toward infinity and the universe even while never achieving it ("sich dem Unendlichen zu nähern und ihm zu entfliehen").[19]

---

18. Fichte, *Werke* 1:326.

19. The novel's implications for male-female relationships are not my topic, but a few remarks are in order. A measure of the necessity for feminist criticism is Polheim's statement ("Schlegels *Lucinde,*" 70) that, with regard to the theme of love, "haben Kluckhohn und Eichner so grundlegend gehandelt, daß wir für Weiteres darauf verweisen dürfen." When women began to find a critical voice, there turned out to be a great deal "Weiteres." The early days of feminist criticism produced a denial that there was anything liberating at all for women in the novel, that critics have simply taken over traditional notions of women as eternal (see Baerbel Becker-Cantarino, "Schlegels *Lucinde*: Zum Frauenbild der Frühromantik," *Colloquia Germanica* 10 [1977]: 128–39). At the same time, some critics were eager to "actualize" the novel, particularly its "scandalous" praise of indolence, as foreshadowing present subversive modes of living (see Gisela Dischner, *Friedrich Schlegels* Lucinde *und Materialien zu einer Theorie des Müßiggangs* [Hildesheim: Gerstenberg, 1980]). For a trenchant, clear-eyed account of both utopian, forward-looking moments in the novel and its ongoing retrogressive aspects, see Henriette Beese, "Nachwort" to Friedrich Schlegel, *Lucinde,* and Friedrich Schleiermacher, *Vertraute Briefe über Schlegels* Lucinde (Frankfurt: Ullstein, 1980). A common claim about the love relation in the novel is that its unparalleled innovation for its own time is the emphasis on dialogue: "Nur in der Antwort seines Du kann jedes Ich seine unendliche Einheit ganz fühlen" (*KA* 5:61). Jochen Hörisch (*Die fröhliche Wissenschaft der Poesie: Der Universalitätsanspruch von Dichtung in der frühromantischen Poetologie* [Frankfurt: Suhrkamp, 1976], 110f.) sees in the novel the "Möglichkeit versöhnter Intersubjektivität" epitomized. Yet there is precious little dialogue in it and none that contradicts Julius, who nevertheless can attribute to Lucinde such sentiments as "Ich weiß, auch du würdest mich nicht überleben wollen, du würdest dem voreiligen Gemahle auch im Sarge folgen . . . " (*KA* 5:11). That does not prevent Julius, when he believes Lucinde dead, first contemplating "following her" and then stopping for reflection: "Schon eilte ich, dir zu folgen, aber plötzlich hielt mich ein neuer Gedanke an, und ich sagte zu meinem Geist: 'Unwürdiger, du kannst nicht einmal

This symmetry is the originary and even humorous symmetry of nature itself. "Auch in dieser Symmetrie offenbart sich der unglaubliche Humor, mit dem die konsequente Natur ihre allgemeinste und einfachste Antithese durchführt." The notion of symmetry of contradictions is also crucial to what may be the single most trenchant definition of "romantische Poesie" from the *Gespräch über die Poesie.*

Ja diese künstlich geordnete Verwirrung, diese reizende Symmetrie von Widersprüchen, dieser wunderbare ewige Wechsel von Enthusiasmus und Ironie, der selbst in den kleinsten Gliedern des Ganzen lebt, scheinen mir schon selbst eine indirekte Mythologie zu sein. (*KA* 2:318–19).

What is important for our present purposes is less the biological than the philosophical ramifications of this simple and "funny" antithesis: it is a matter of limitations and borders, the setting of limits (of male and female) and their abolition.

The free act of *Bestimmen,* of epistemological determination, is also necessarily a setting of borders. But Schlegel foreshadows his great antagonist Hegel; to set borders is already to transcend them. In translating Fichte's tortured, circling epistemology into a witty reflection on sex, Schlegel also presupposes a post-Hegelian mode of the thinking of difference without synthesis.[20] In the passage at hand, the setting of borders is male and their abolition female.

Mit leisen aber sichern Fortschritten erweitert das Unbestimmte seinen angebornen Wunsch aus der schönen Mitte der Endlichkeit ins Grenzenlose. Das vollendete Bestimmte hingegen wirft sich durch einen kühnen Sprung aus dem seligen Traum des unendlichen Wollens in die Schranken der endlichen Tat und nimmt sich selbst verfeinernd immer zu an großmütiger Selbstbeschränkung und schöner Genügsamkeit. (*KA* 5:73).[21]

---

die kleinen Dissonanzen dieses mittelmäßigen Lebens ertragen und du hältst dich schon für ein höheres reif und würdig? Geh hin zu leiden und zu tun was dein Beruf ist . . . '" (*KA* 5:69). Lucinde's "Beruf" as "Priesterin der Freude" (5:66) would apparently end with her husband's death.

20. The affinity of such thought not only to Derrida's attempts to think *différance* but also to Adorno's negative dialectics is evident. For an account of Schlegel's relation to Fichte and Hegel that culminates in Adorno, see Klaus Peter, *Idealismus als Kritik: Friedrich Schlegels Philosophie der unvollendeten Welt* (Stuttgart: Kohlhammer, 1973), esp. 128ff.

21. The "Schranken der endlichen Tat" are not so evident in other pathos-filled outbursts

The last sentence, of course, is a pithy summary of the "Lehrjahre der Männlichkeit," describing the course of apparently necessary male *Bildung* from infinite desire to an acceptance of limitations and finitude. The term *Selbstbeschränkung* resonates with one of Schlegel's most renowned definitions of the creative process, that of *Lyceum* fragment 37. The fragment describes the tendency of young geniuses to blurt out everything at once; they must learn "den Wert und die Würde der Selbstbeschränkung," a result of "Selbstschöpfung und Selbstvernichtung" (*KA* 2:151) or, in the terms of the *Gespräch,* of "Enthusiasmus und Ironie."

With the description of *das Unbestimmte,* however, we are on far less familiar territory: an opening and expansion from finitude toward the limitless, in a process ("leise aber sicher") not immediately perceptible. *Das Unbestimmte* turns out to be "bestimmt" from the outset by its limited position (in the "beautiful middle," a term with sexual overtones, but limited nevertheless), from which it must expand toward the infinite. For *das Bestimmte,* which begins as indeterminate desire, that opening toward the infinite becomes in turn the limits [*Schranken*] it requires. Thus, the transcendental act of determination—from indeterminacy through determination to a higher indeterminacy that results from reflection on the first determination or the "thinking of thinking"—is recapitulated on an individual empirical level by sex and reproduction, and by the reflection upon it that is this text. "Durch diese Individualität und jene Allegorie blüht das bunte Ideal witziger Sinnlichkeit aus dem Streben nach dem Unbedingten." Schlegel never made the common mistake of confusing the empirical and the transcendental; here, concrete individuality (of *this* relation) along with its abstract counterpart allegory both contribute to the paradox of "witty" (intellectual) sensuality. But the individual takes over reflection and momentarily forgets itself, presumably in the sex act.

---

regarding Julius's determination to perform heroic deeds: "Ich fühlte nie mehr [than now, with our love] Zuversicht und Mut, als Mann unter Männern zu wirken, ein heldenmäßiges Leben zu beginnen und auszuführen und mit Freunden verbrüdert für die Ewigkeit zu handeln" (*KA* 5:65–66). The "friend" turns out to be Eduard rather than Antonio: "Ich entsage dem zarten Genuß und stürze mich in den wilden Kampf des Lebens. Ich eile zu Eduard. Alles ist verabredet. Wir wollen nicht bloß zusammen leben, sondern im brüderlichen Bunde vereint wirken und handeln" (5:76). How this resolution is to be reconciled with the withdrawal into domesticity and the idyllic countryside remains a mystery. Bernd Bräutigam (*Leben wie im Roman: Untersuchungen zum ästhetischen Imperativ im Frühwerk Friedrich Schlegels [1794–1800]* [Paderborn: Schöningh, 1986]) offers a trenchant analysis of these and other matters (i.e., the Prometheus-Hercules opposition) and notes that the pathos-filled declarations tend "in unfreiwillige Komik auszugleiten" (89). The most "heroic" *Tathandlung* of this novel may well be the experimental transposition of Fichte into love and *Poesie.*

The higher function of delimitation is thus attributed to the female principle, but, as the epilogue shows, Lucinde and Juliane do not understand it. The epilogue turns into a defiant, almost insolent defense of male clumsiness, of the unnamed (the penis), of Julius's intention to turn the content of sexual clumsiness into an art work, of what they will learn from it, and—generously—that they can say whatever they like about it, with the implication that it will make no difference. The female principle may be higher, but individual females, in this reflection, are not encouraged to talk back.

"Eine Reflexion" appears late in the novel and represents thinking to a "higher power," the Fichtean "thinking of thinking" that represents a potentiation of the determinate cognitive act. But not only is the metaphorical meaning of reflection present in the novel; this little text "potentiates" an earlier one, *Metamorphosen,* where it retains its literal, mirror-related meaning; "In süßer Ruhe schlummert der kindliche Geist und der Kuß der liebenden Göttin erregt ihm nur leichte Träume" (*KA* 5:59). The repose of dream is a common theme in the novel, which opens with a dream that must be interrupted. Here, the dream is narcissistic: "So schaut das Auge in dem Spiegel des Flusses nur den Widerschein des blauen Himmels . . . und die eigne Gestalt des in sich selbst versunkenen Betrachters" (*KA* 5:60). But the text asserts that Narcissus is attracted by his own grace, whereas "Liebe ist höher als Anmut" (60). It concludes with a recapitulation of the interplay of determinacy and indeterminacy.

Nicht der Haß, wie die Weisen sagen, sondern die Liebe trennt die Wesen und bildet die Welt, und nur in ihrem Licht kann man diese finden und schauen. Nur in der Antwort seines Du kann jedes Ich seine unendliche Einheit ganz fühlen. (61)

Here, the mechanism of primordial unity, determinate division and individuality, and renewed unity ("ein harmonisches Meer der Vergessenheit," [60]) is impelled by love. But here, love is identified with light and determinacy, not with night and death as in "Sehnsucht und Ruhe" ("eine große Liebesnacht wird sich ewig ruhig fühlen," [*KA* 5:80]). It is also identified with dialogue and interchange; the phrase "Antwort seines Du" has misled even sharp-eyed critics into ruminations about dialogue and intersubjectivity. While Schlegel understood that the novel as he had published it ("Erster Teil") was written totally from a male perspective and, therefore, planned to continue it from Lucinde's, nevertheless the conclusion of "Eine Reflexion" remains typical for Julius's propensity for anticipating possible disagreement and disarming it in advance. Genuine disagreement seems to belong to male friendship ("Julius an Antonio") but not to love as depicted here.

Reflection in the form of the narcissus theme appears earlier in the novel, in the "Idylle über den Müßiggang." As Helga Slessarev has shown, romantic irony functions, here, as a means for treating the theme of idleness, in accordance with the mechanism of *Selbstschöpfung und Selbstvernichtung* or enthusiasm and irony. The opening enthusiastic outburst is a product of purely narcissistic self-reflection.

> Ich saß, da ich so in mir sprach, wie ein nachdenkliches Mädchen in einer gedankenlosen Romanze am Bach, sah den fliehenden Wellen nach. Aber die Wellen flohen und flossen so gelassen, ruhig und sentimental, als sollte sich ein Narcissus in der klaren Fläche bespiegeln und sich in schönen Egoismus berauschen. (*KA* 5:25)

But the narrator does not remain like the "thoughtful girl" for long, because the novel's central theme—"die Möglichkeit einer dauernden Umarmung" (*KA* 5:25)—presents itself as a more noble goal that interrupts the navel gaze. Slessarev thinks of the "Buffo" of *Lyceum* 42 and comments that "so sehr jedoch dieser Buffo seine Vernunft anspannt, er kann das Problem nicht lösen, und so fällt er denn wieder in den Zustand des nachdenklichen Mädchens zurück, dessen gaukelnde Gedanken sich allerdings weiter mit dem Liebesspiel befassen."[22]

After the thoughtful girl, interrupted temporarily by the exertion of reason, the next figure is the Oriental "mystic": "Gleich einem Weisen des Orients war ich ganz versunken in ein heiliges Hinbrüten und ruhiges Anschauen der ewigen Substanzen, vorzüglich der deinigen und der meinigen" (*KA* 5:26). Once again, repose, dream, "heiliges Hinbrüten" at the outset threaten, as here, to become "halbbesonnene Selbstvergessenheit" (26) or indeterminacy and must be interrupted by the "light" of determination and "thought." But here the thought is one that got Schlegel into much trouble: the praise of indolence, and the polemic against the simpletons who have not understood that. *Denken* and *dichten,* he insists,

---

22. Helga Slessarev, "Die Ironie in Friedrich Schlegels 'Idylle über den Müßiggang,'" *German Quarterly* 38 (1965): 292.

are possible only through passivity, but "freilich ist es eine absichtliche, willkürliche, einseitige, aber doch Passivität" (*KA* 5:27).

One more textual example will make possible a transition from the topic of reflection to a second central topic of the novel, representation. The novel's opening letter, "dieser in seiner Art einzige Brief" (*KA* 5:9), also enacts the mechanism of (enthusiastic) dream and (ironic) interruption, but it includes a meditation on the act of writing itself. Daydream, admission that it was a daydream, then a contingent interruption [*Zufall*] and concomitant resolution not to narrate traditionally and in a boring fashion ("in klaren und wahren Perioden vor dir aufzurollen") all constitute an attempt to use and (paradoxically) control or mold *Zufall*. The interplay of determinacy and indeterminacy is already prefigured here, in the exchange between contingency and purpose ("mein unbezweifeltes Verwirrungsrecht"—Lucinde is not asked about her doubts) or, as in "Idylle," between passivity and intent. *Athenäum* 51 expresses the ironic interchange of conscious intent and passive instinct.

Naiv ist, was bis zur Ironie, oder bis zum steten Wechsel von Selbstschöpfung und Selbstvernichtung natürlich, individuell oder klassisch ist, oder scheint. Ist es bloß Instinkt, so ists kindlich, kindisch, oder albern; ists bloße Absicht, so entsteht Affektation. Das schöne, poetische, idealische Naive muß zugleich Absicht, und Instinkt sein. (*KA* 2:172–73)[23]

The "Studium des Müßiggangs" ironically recommended by Julius (*KA* 5:27) in the form of an "Idylle" is therefore yet another example of poetic reflection at the higher, Fichtean level.

The central passage on representation in the novel occurs in the "Allegorie von der Frechheit." The narrator's guide, "der wahre Witz," has just renewed for him the old *Schauspiel* of the four novels and accompanied it with his own interspersed commentary. The narrator's first reaction is the Wertherian return into the self—"Ich kehrte in mich selbst zurück und in den neuen Sinn, dessen Wunder ich schaute"—yet this narcissism is now enriched by a greater sense of the world—"Ich erkannte bald die

---

23. The difficulties inherent in the interplay between instinct and purpose should not be underestimated. "Naive" here becomes the vanishing point or point of indifference (the "second center" of the parabola): the point of irony. The paradox is similar to that of *Gemüt* and *Geist* in "Eine Reflexion" and the claim in the opening letter to "mold" contingency ("den rohen Zufall zu bilden"). At stake is the self-understanding of the early Romantics as well as the question of what they were actually able to achieve.

Szene der äußern Welt wieder, aber reiner und verklärt..." (*KA* 5:19).
From somewhere, from the voice of fantasy, he perceives these words: "Die
Zeit ist da, das innre Wesen der Gottheit kann offenbart und dargestellt
werden, alle Mysterien dürfen sich enthüllen und die Furcht soll aufhören"
(5:20). Shortly thereafter, it is the familiar voice of wit once again that
explains and interprets fantasy.

> "Du mußt das unsterbliche Feuer nicht rein und roh mitteilen wollen,"
> sprach die bekannte Stimme meines freundlichen Begleiters. "Bilde,
> erfinde, verwandle und erhalte die Welt und ihre ewigen Gestalten im
> steten Wechsel neuer Trennungen und Vermählungen. Verhülle und
> binde den Geist im Buchstaben. Der echte Buchstabe ist allmächtig und
> der eigentliche Zauberstab." (*KA* 5:20)

A great deal could be said about this passage, but space allows only
schematic comments. First, the central antithesis is that of *Mitteilen* ("rein
und roh") and *Darstellen*. The reference to letter one is unmistakable, in
which the narrator forsakes the well-worn ruts of straightforward narration
("in klaren und wahren Perioden..., die von Stufe zu Stufe allmählig
nach natürlichen Gesetzen fortschreitende Aufklärung..." [*KA* 5:92]) for
the "Recht einer reizenden Verwirrung" that he claims for himself. The
concept of *Darstellen* is elsewhere central for Schlegel. I noted previously
that his chief criticism of Fichte the mystic (in his notebooks) was the
problem of communicability; but he was always fulsome in his public praise
of Fichte, for example in the opening text of his Lessing anthology, "An
Fichte."

> Der Unterschied der Prosa und der Poesie besteht darin, daß die Poesie
> darstellen, die Prosa nur mitteilen will.... Dargestellt wird das Unbes-
> timmte, weshalb auch jede Darstellung ein Unendliches ist; mitteilen
> aber läßt sich nur das Bestimmte. Und nicht das Unbestimmte, sondern
> das Bestimmte ist es, was alle Wissenschaften suchen. In der höchsten
> aller Wissenschaften aber, die nicht irgend etwas einzelnes Bestimmtes
> lehren soll, sondern das Bestimmen selbst überhaupt zu bestimmen hat,
> ist es eben deswegen nicht hinreichend, das Gedachte schon fertig zu
> geben. Es will diese Wissenschaft nicht dieses oder jenes Gedachte,
> sondern das Denken selbst lehren; darum sind ihre Mitteilungen
> notwendigerweise auch Darstellungen, denn man kann das Denken
> nicht lehren außer durch die Tat und das Beispiel, indem man vor

jemandem denkt, nicht etwas Gedachtes mitteilt, sondern das Denken in seinem Werden und Entstehen ihm darstellt. Eben darum aber kann der Geist dieser Wissenschaft nur in einem Werke der Kunst vollständig deutlich gemacht werden. (*KA* 3:48)

The lengthy quote (from 1804), dedicated to Fichte and purportedly describing Lessing, provides a striking commentary to the *Lucinde* passage. While prose is here identified with *Mitteilen* and with *Wissenschaft* (and therefore philosophy), *Poesie* is *Darstellung* of the finite and determinate; it evokes the infinite, which it can never depict as "present" [*bestimmen*]. *Darstellen* is connected to the infinite and the indeterminate; philosophy remains in the realm of the determinate and of *Mitteilen;* "darum sind ihre Mitteilungen notwendigerweise auch Darstellungen" for the "höchste aller Wissenschaften." The unification of poetry and philosophy is conceived in terms such that poetry is the potentiation of philosophy, the ironic transcendence of determinacy toward indeterminacy. Later in the Lessing anthology, however, this progression will be questioned by the "essence of criticism," for it is criticism that must attend or precede the work of art, equally dependent on *Darstellung* yet conceptual and also inspirational for the production of art.

Second, what is the role of time—"Die Zeit ist da?" Somewhat mysteriously, these magical words suddenly precipitate an uproar in the "bones" of the narrator. I recall no critic who has expressed wonder about this sentence. Yet it seems clear from my previous remarks that temporality, at least its concept, violently yanks the narrator away from his eternal temptation of purely narcissistic self-reflection toward the necessity for combinatory creation, "die Gesänge des Geistes nachzubilden" (*KA* 5:20).[24] These "songs" must necessarily be connected with temporality, and they cannot be reproduced by the activity of "rein und roh mitteilen," because such communication only aims at results, at *das Bestimmte*. In order to mimic or reenact [*Nachbilden*] the flights of spirit toward the final goal

---

24. The connection of allegory and temporality is one of de Man's most well-known theses (Paul de Man, "The Rhetoric of Temporality," in *Interpretation: Theory and Practice*, ed. Charles S. Singleton [Baltimore: Johns Hopkins University Press], 173–209). The attempt by David E. Wellbery ("Rhetorik und Literatur: Anmerkungen zur poetologischen Begriffsbildung bei Friedrich Schlegel," in Behler and Hörisch, *Die Aktualität*, 161–73) to reread aspects of Schlegel's poetics in light of de Man could be expanded by considering the role of allegory in the novel. With regard to de Man's sharp distinction between allegory and symbol, however, there is nothing in Schlegel that would correspond to de Man's concept of symbol.

that always eludes it (*das Unbestimmte*), the narrator must learn (in letter one he claimed he had already learned it) to combine, in ongoing paradoxes, to connect and distinguish. Only by means of such linguistic strategies can spirit and can time itself (and therefore transcience, mutability, and history) be *dargestellt.*

Third, what of the romantic dyad of *Geist* and *Buchstabe?* Both publicly and privately, Schlegel always defended the dignity of the letter: "Apologie des Buchstabens, der als einziges ächtes Vehikel der Mittheilung sehr ehrwürdig ist" (*KA* 18:5). In *Athenäum* 93, he states, "Die Lehre vom Geist und Buchstaben ist unter andern auch darum so interessant, weil sie die Philosophie mit der Philologie in Berührung setzen kann" (*KA* 2:179). In the interplay of *Geist* and *Buchstabe* in Schlegel's writings, one is never confused with the other. In its combinatory possibilities, language can never completely reproduce its object but only mimic and reenact it, because the object is *das Unbestimmte*. It eludes language by definition. Still, combinatory language nevertheless possesses the quality of the magic wand [*Zauberstab*] to evoke indeterminacy, yet not in philosophical *Mitteilung* but only in the linguistic work of art.

From these remarks, it is clear how poorly equipped is a prevalent conceptual dyad of our day—that of presence and absence—to grasp the complexity of early German Romanticism. The early romantics, Schlegel in particular, had no illusions about "presence" in the form of conclusions or results that one can carry home: these were, for him, "klare und wahre Perioden" susceptible to an activity of "rein und roh mitteilen," and they were an important but not the highest form of language. There remains the dignity of the letter, which, properly employed, can transcend determinacy and reenact the indeterminate: its highest calling. Yet the dignity of the letter never permits the confusion of it for the thing it signifies: "Verhülle und binde den Geist im Buchstaben." There is no mystification of language here: it ties spirit down rather than setting it free; it conceals rather than reveals. But in its highest manifestation as *Darstellung,* it is what we have. That is the more realistic, ironic conclusion of the foregoing enthusiasm: "Die Zeit ist da, das innre Wesen der Gottheit kann offenbart und dargestellt werden..." (*KA* 5:20). Only in the mode of the bound spirit can this occur. There is both a sense of the limitations of the letter and also trust in its power to strain toward its own transcendence.

Der echte Buchstabe ist allmächtig und der eigentliche Zauberstab. Er ist es, mit dem die unwiderstehliche Willkür der hohen Zauberin Fantasie das erhabene Chaos der vollen Natur berührt, und das unendliche Wort ans Licht ruft, welches ein Ebenbild und Spiegel des göttlichen Geistes ist, und welches die Sterblichen Universum nennen. (*KA* 5:20)

Fantasy, as the combinatory faculty, touches nature, calls upon infinity in the word (the word is *love*), but never brings it to presence, because it cannot. Such a fantasy would amount to trust in *Mitteilung*, which would be a bringing to presence. Schlegel's clear rejection of determinate *Mitteilung* in favor of indeterminate *Darstellung*, even accompanied by his defense of the letter, places him beyond oversimplified oppositions, ready to be reread.

The foregoing remarks help clarify the necessity for one of the most spectacularly experimental novel forms of German prose.[25] They help explain the paucity of traditional narrative in the novel.

Andeuten will ich dir wenigstens in göttlichen Sinnbildern, was ich nicht zu erzählen vermag.... [E]s bleibt immer etwas zurück, was sich nicht darstellen läßt, weil es ganz innerlich ist.... Auch in dem was reine Darstellung und Tatsache scheint, hat sich Allegorie eingeschlichen, und unter die schöne Wahrheit bedeutende Lügen gemischt. Aber nur als geistiger Hauch schwebt sie beseelend über die ganze Masse, wie der Witz, der unsichtbar mit seinem Werke spielt und nur leise lächelt. (*KA* 5:58–59)

Traditional narrative would be determinate in the deficient sense. The

---

25. I cannot deal here with the question of the novel as "fragment" or "totality" as work of art. The concept of "work" in its usual connection with (organic) totality is ideological. One of the earliest investigations of the antithetical structure of the novel's apparent chaos was Wolfgang Paulsen, "Friedrich Schlegels *Lucinde* als Roman," *Germanic Review* 21 (1946): 173–90. But Paulsen's innovative (and correct) insistence on the novel's unity as a "work of art" includes such statements as "Der von Anfang an gewählte Ton wird durchaus beibehalten, selbst dort, wo der Verfasser sich von seiner 'romantischen Ironie' verleiten läßt, anstatt über das Thema des Buches über die Darstellung des Themas im Buche ('Allegorie von der Frechheit') zu meditieren" (180–81). The implication is clear: romantic irony is inimical to the organic work of art; the verb *verleiten* is indicative of the critic's own characteristic prejudices, which lead him to condemn a central section of the novel whose unity he sets out to demonstrate. With regard to the question of conclusion or closure, there is widespread critical acclaim for Eichner's formulation (*KA* 5:xliv) that "der Roman in einer immer dünner und transparenter werdenden Prosa verschwebt und sich gleichsam in Nichts auflöst." Most readers would also agree with Behler ("Schlegel: *Lucinde*," 116), in view of the designation "Erster Teil," "daß sich diesem Roman nichts mehr hinzufügen läßt und die dichterische wie thematische Potentialität der *Lucinde* in dem vorliegenden Teil absolut erschöpft ist."

famous Romantic mixing of genres, the encapsulation of a rather traditional narrative section by ornamental arabesques, and the potentiated reflection on representation that is also representation of reflection—all these qualities of *Lucinde,* many of which have infuriated readers from 1799 to the present day, contribute to an evocation of what cannot be represented in language. Allegory as "significant lies" invented by the fantasy of wit appears as the *Oberbegriff.* It hovers indeterminately over its object, the signified, as a linguistic representation (specifically of time and mutability) without illusions of presence but satisfied with its ironic self-consciousness.[26] The satisfaction may not be terribly modern, but the ironic self-consciousness surely is.

That the novel *Lucinde* itself falls far short of its author's grandiose intentions is a critical commonplace not to be gainsaid. Nevertheless, the Romantic concept of art as exemplified here remains our own: the work of language art employs the significative medium of "determinacy" (and the Saussurian insistence on differential signification varies Hegel's insight that all determination is negation) to evoke the indeterminate. It thus inspires infinite reading and interpretation that take the manifest form of criticism. While some formulations hint at a teleology (from indeterminacy through determinacy to a goal of indeterminacy), the emphasis on criticism, itself an aesthetic yet conceptual form, entails infinite interplay between *Poesie* and *Philosophie,* with the "highest of all sciences" hovering in the tension between them.

The two sections on reflection and representation, along with the programmatic opening letter, constitute the most explicit examples in the novel of the attempt to represent the productive faculty and process along with the product. Their position in the novel is not entirely arbitrary, in accordance with the narrator's "Verwirrungsrecht" to place this or that "ganz an die unrechte Stelle" (*KA* 5:9). "Eine Reflexion" follows the passages on narcissistic self-reflection and further valorizes the concept of reflection. The passage on representation concludes the "Allegorie," arguably the central genre for representation in Schlegel's sense. An understanding of the function of these concepts is crucial to an appreciation of this excessively conceptual, disappointingly abstract, yet curiously inviting experiment in nonnarrative.

---

26. Schlegel's characteristic emphasis on hovering [*schweben*], familiar from *Athenäum* 116, is epitomized conceptually in the titular concepts of the penultimate text, "Sehnsucht und Ruhe." One pole of the dyad is never recuperated into the other and, thus, into unity.

The Society of the Dead: Allegory and Freedom in Lenau's Poetry

James Rolleston

In the fifth and sixth of his letters *Über die ästhetische Erziehung,* Schiller offers this evocation of contemporary society.

> Die losgebundene Gesellschaft, anstatt aufwärts in das organische Leben zu eilen, fällt in das Elementarreich zurück. . . . Ewig nur an ein einzelnes kleines Bruchstück des Ganzen gefesselt, bildet sich der Mensch selbst nur als Bruchstück aus, ewig nur das eintönige Geräusch des Rades, das er umtreibt, im Ohre, entwickelt er nie die Harmonie seines Wesens, und anstatt die Menschheit in seiner Natur auszuprägen, wird er bloss zu einem Abdruck seines Geschäfts, seiner Wissenschaft. . . . Und so wird denn allmählich das einzelne konkrete Leben vertilgt, damit das Abstrakt des Ganzen sein dürftiges Dasein friste, und ewig bleibt der Staat seinen Bürgern fremd, weil ihn das Gefühl nirgends findet.[1]

The entire structure of aesthetic education comes into being as the dialectical negation of this dystopia, and, perhaps for that very reason, Schiller's agenda retains a powerful resonance for all subsequent attempts to conceptualize art's social function. For the conditions Schiller sketched— dehumanization of labor, specialization of human faculties—clearly intensified as capitalism became better organized; at the same time, while Sengle stresses that Biedermeier thinking viewed idealist systems as passé, he is equally emphatic that the need for coherence between private and public,

---

1. Friedrich Schiller, *Über die ästhetische Erziehung des Menschen,* in *Sämtliche Werke* (Munich: Hanser, 1960), 5:580, 584, 585.

past and present, remained essential to the language of the period.[2] So the very eclecticism of Biedermeier made it receptive to Schiller's diagnosis of dysfunctional modern life, a diagnosis implicitly subjecting his remedies to an advance survival test and insuring their independence from mere "subjectivity."[3] Indeed these remedies are already active, as declared allegiances, in the articulation of the dystopian present; they are best described as positive versions of human time, joining forces conceptually to confront what Schiller perceives as the ruin of time.

There is first the "classical" insistence on the sensuous moment, present time lived as full harmony with nature ("Harmonie seines Wesens"); no matter how skeptical Schiller becomes of the possibility of such living, this idea retains its regulative force: "der Weg zu der Gottheit, wenn man einen Weg nennen kann, was niemals zum Ziele führt, ist [dem Menschen] aufgetan in den *Sinnen.*"[4] Second, the concept of history is becoming structurally central ("aufwärts in das organische Leben"): Schiller's quest is for a history in overt opposition to the French Revolution, yet, of course, the very urgency of the quest is rooted in the fact of the Revolution, in the new vision of "created" history. So the notion of organic history is fissured from the outset—the organism is artificial—which in no way prevented the idea from becoming a commonplace in the nineteenth century (through Wilhelm von Humboldt, among others). Third, in productive tension with this historical temporality, Schiller invokes the familiar, "timeless" idea of humanity ("Menschheit"): this concept becomes, for the nineteenth century, a point of intellectual stabilization, an image to contain the havoc wrought on every other value by historical change.

---

2. Sengle's evocation of Biedermeier liberal politics gives an especially vivid idea of the domestication of "organic" images of history: "Potenzierter Harmonismus war die Erwartung der Liberalen, die sich einbildeten, die Beseitigung der alten Ordnung werde ganz von selbst zu einer neuen, besseren führen.... Das heilsgeschichtliche Denken wird hier zur Idee einer naturgesetzlichen Entwicklung.... Das Wissen um die menschliche Unvollkommenheit und Tragik drohte ganz verlorenzugehen" (Friedrich Sengle, *Biedermeierzeit* [Stuttgart: Metzler, 1971], 1:78).

3. The persistent impact of Schiller's ideas on the next literary generations was acknowledged by Goethe in his antitheoretical fragment of 1812, "Epoche der forcirten Talente." Katherina Mommsen summarizes: "Mit seinen *Briefen* brachte Schiller, besonders durch das gemeinsame Auftreten mit dem allgewaltigen Kant, Goethe eine der grössten Niederlagen seines Lebens bei" (Mommsen, "Goethe über die schädigende Wirkung der Schillerschen Dichtungstheorie," in *Friedrich Schiller: Ein Symposium,* ed. Wolfgang Wittkowski [Tübingen: Niemeyer, 1982], 395). Sengle also stresses Biedermeier self-distancing from Goethean individualism.

4. Schiller, *Werke,* 603.

Celebrating the sensuous moment, promoting an organic understanding of history, and confronting empirical experience with a "higher" model of human life—these three versions of time take us, both separately and together, to the center of the Biedermeier imagination. The systematic relationship among them, which Schiller sought to work out, is, to be sure, forgotten; the links of Biedermeier poets either to the "Greek" heritage of sensuous immediacy or to currently evolving philosophies of history are masked and oblique. Moreover, the struggle for an imagery of social coherence, crucial for Biedermeier consciousness, must occur within the discourse of a history announced in advance as disintegrative and potentially dystopian. Schiller's three zones of fulfilled time, smoothly unified in his language, are now felt as centrifugal, threatening to undermine each other. Thus, poems acquire a new mission: to embody the very process of temporal integration, the self-conscious movement from the intense moment to its completion as idea. Mörike's poetry has long been understood in terms of such a process.[5] But if my argument about the persistence of Schiller's aesthetic project is to be convincing, it must be tested in the context of poetry very unlike Mörike's. Nikolaus Lenau's work occupies a wholly different expressive register; indeed, at first glance, it seems perverse to connect Lenau in any way with Schiller's vision.[6]

Lenau's poems stand at a point of extreme polar opposition to those of Mörike. It is worth quoting a few characteristic lines of Mörike (from the beginning of "An einem Wintermorgen") in order to recall the kind of imagery that is inconceivable in a Lenau text.

Einem Kristall gleicht meine Seele nun,

5. See Christiaan L. Hart Nibbrig, *Verlorene Unmittelbarkeit: Zeiterfahrung und Zeitgestaltung bei Eduard Mörike* (Bonn: Bouvier, 1973); also see James Rolleston, *Narratives of Ecstasy* (Detroit: Wayne State University Press, 1987), 45–56.

6. Lenau's literary ancestry has proved problematic for Lenau scholarship, doubtless because the tired antithesis derivative versus spontaneous has tended to frame the argument. Thus, Hugo Schmidt finds Lenau's links to eighteenth-century poetry to be tenuous, except in the case of the Göttinger Hain (Hugo Schmidt, *Nikolaus Lenau* [New York: Twayne, 1971]). Richard Dove, on the other hand, sees these links as overwhelming, casting Lenau as an attitudinizing fraud, "far more a survivor of the eighteenth century than a proto-Surrealist. . . . Lenau exploited nature, as he exploited so much else, in order to extract "das Erhabene," an ultimately *literary* value which, as Longinus said, showers the beholder with reflected glory" (Richard Dove, "The Rhetoric of Lament: A Reassessment of Nikolaus Lenau," *Orbis Litterarum* 39 [1984]: 233, 241). So many questions are begged by such statements that it is a relief to turn to Hansgeorg Schmidt-Bergmann, *Ästhetismus und Negativität: Studien zum Werk Nikolaus Lenaus* (Heidelberg: Carl Winter, 1984). I am much indebted to this study, which pioneers several new perspectives.

> Den noch kein falscher Strahl des Lichts getroffen:
> Zu fluten scheint mein Geist, er scheint zu ruhn,
> Dem Eindruck naher Wunderkräfte offen . . .

Although, as the product of ceaseless oscillations, Mörike's self is hardly stable, it is indisputably at the center of his world, both giving and receiving images; moreover, it is a self imbued with futurity, with the potential to "crystallize" into something new, and this intimate temporality is grounded in a working relationship between the permanent possibility of aesthetic harmony and a longing of the writing consciousness for oneness with natural processes (oneness is never achieved, but a kind of aesthetic benevolence in nature persists, fueling the "nahe Wunderkräfte" and guaranteeing the writer's "Annäherung"). To summarize Mörike's articulation of time and ideality is to recognize the viability of Schiller's aesthetic program in the new century: a concept of self heightened through momentary intensities, an exploration of the past culminating in a will toward the future, and a casting of the creative act as an approximation of the inherited, in principle timeless, idea of the human (in principle because, in practice, the idea is accessible only through aesthetically energized time).

This entire, fundamentally harmonious aesthetic is meaningless to Lenau. To put it as forcefully as possible, neither self nor future carry any weight in his poetics. Lenau has been called an early aesthete because of his acknowledged transfer of all his emotional energy into art, leaving him with very little "life" to live. But it needs to be stressed that this transfer was not effectively compensatory in the modernist sense with which we have become familiar; Lenau has no fantasy self, à la Baudelaire, able to transmute the world's base metal into aesthetic gold. On the contrary, the speakers of his poems pursue the baroque tradition of dissolving all glittering illusions back into the basest metal of all, into death; they contribute nothing of their own, certainly not baroque religious faith and no very clear subjective story either, just the given tableau of a natural scene or a station on a journey. Like the character Faust in his first epic poem, Lenau's speakers are "discovered" examining corpses, and Mephistopheles later confirms, in the context of a murder Faust has committed, that Faust's initial contemplative posture already contains all the "truth" the world has to offer: "Die Wahrheit steht an dieser Leich' und schaut / Ins Antlitz dir . . . "[7] Whence, then, Lenau's undoubted productive energy? Why pursue "knowl-

---

7. Nikolaus Lenau, *Sämtliche Werke und Briefe,* ed. Eduard Castle (Leipzig: Insel Verlag, 1911), 2:71. All Lenau citations are to this edition.

edge" that is already fixed and deathly without hope of an aesthetic escape from that knowledge? A sentence of Adorno's points to the resources on which Lenau seems to draw: "Art possesses expression not when it conveys subjectivity, but when it reverberates with the primal history of subjectivity and ensoulment."[8] The "history of subjectivity" is Lenau's theme, drawing him ever more intensely into the long historical epic-dramatic-lyric hybrids that culminate in his greatest work, *Die Albigenser;* the one viable escape from the despair and risk of silence inherent in the rigid limits of his personal subjectivity was—duplication, multiplication, re-production of the endlessly repeated despair of the past. This perspective is summarized toward the end of *Die Albigenser.*

> Doch weile auf der Vorwelt unser Blick,
> Die Vorwelt soll uns tief im Herzen wühlen,
> Dass wir uns recht mit ihr zusammenfühlen
> In *ein* Geschlecht, *ein* Leben, *ein* Geschick.
>
> (*Werke* 2:398)

The intensity of this vision may suggest why Lenau's work stands in a relation of polarity rather than simple contradiction to that of Mörike. The choric rigidity and reproducibility of Lenau's selves are utterly remote from Mörike's microdramas of depths and surfaces; for Lenau there is essentially a taboo on that "future" that is everywhere to be felt in Mörike. But the third temporal mode, the enduring "idea," is explicitly affirmed by Lenau. This idea lacks verifiable ethical or social content, but it is not simply synonymous with the aesthetic. Lenau's "aestheticism" drew him *toward* history, not away from it. In a highly idiosyncratic sense, his use of the term *Geist* in his later works is derived from Hegel, as he suggests in his remarkable 1842 comment on Hegel.

Ich war bis vor einem Jahr einer der heftigsten Gegner Hegels, damals studierte ich aber ein paar Werke von ihm und erkannte, dass doch nur auf der von ihm gebrochenen Bahn die Menschheit kann befreit werden. Überhaupt ist es doch etwas Schönes um die Zeit, wo alles, woran Jahrtausende geglaubt und fortgebaut haben, in Frage gestellt wird.[9]

---

8. Theodor W. Adorno, *Aesthetic Theory* (London: Routledge and Kegan Paul, 1984), 165.
9. Conversation with Max von Löwenthal, quoted in Schmidt-Bergmann, *Ästhetismus,* 150.

That Lenau's Hegel reading was an experience not of conversion but of confirmation, an act of appropriation for a not-yet-theorized poetics, is suggested by Hansgeorg Schmidt-Bergmann's interpretation of this passage in his excellent study of Lenau.

> Die radikale Umwertung des Tradierten, der Umsturz der gültigen Wahrheiten und Dogmen, diese von Hegel "gebrochene Bahn" ist es, die Lenau von der Hegelschen Philosophie für sich übernahm.... Hegel korrigierend verweigert sich Lenau den affirmativen Konsequenzen der Hegelschen Dialektik, was in der Restaurationszeit innerhalb der Hegel-Rezeption ohne Beispiel dastehen dürfte. Lenau beharrt auf Nichtidentität, auf der Legitimation des Besonderen und sperrt sich gegen eine falsche Versöhnung.[10]

The agency that presses for a "reconciled" history, in Hegel as in modernity generally, is, of course, the self in both its needful singularity and its recapitulatory power. In breaking open the self, permitting the voices of the past to push it aside, Lenau is under no illusions: he is cloning his own confinement and despair. But the powerful term *freedom* [*befreit*], inherited from Kant and Schiller, is also in play; the "Legitimation des Besonderen," in Schmidt-Bergmann's apt phrase, implies some kind of aesthetic Last Judgment, a raising of the dead that will link that moment of self-understanding they achieve in dying to all other comparable moments.[11] Thus the fundamental repetitiveness of death insights is no drawback, since it is the equally fundamental repetitions of literary language that make possible this raising of the dead.

Lenau's resurrection of the specifics of history, then, is remote from the romanticizing embrace of, say, Walter Scott. Much "research" went into the writing of *Die Albigenser;* yet is could not conceivably be read for "local color"—all detailing is magnetized by the varied yet ultimately predictable horrors of the deaths that the poem documents. There is, thus, a tremendous

---

10. Schmidt-Bergmann, *Ästhetismus,* 150.

11. Freedom, for Lenau, is the inescapable "value" of his own time, a value that it would be historically meaningless to reject, but that he refuses to see as the final word of the dialectic. In a remarkable fragment on the Bible, Lenau subverts New Testament values much as, in his view, Hegel subverts all inherited beliefs.

Das alte Testament ist die unorganische Welt, das Reich des Gesetzes; das neue Testament ist die organische Welt, das Reich der Freiheit. Der Zug zu der unorganischen Welt; der Klang der Glocken, der Reiz des Alpengebirges—was ist es? Dies ist das Reich der Wahrheit, Lüge ist nur im organischen Reich; jenes ist das Reich der Treue. (*Werke* 4:63)

productive tension between the "Legitimation des Besonderen" and Lenau's explicit goal of generating *"ein* Geschlecht, *ein* Leben, *ein* Geschick." One might say that Lenau is striving for a counterhistory, Benjamin's "tradition of the oppressed" (who are, for Lenau, heretics); except that the peculiar rigor of his poetics preempts any kind of extended empathy with his subjects—or indeed systematic antipathy. Simon de Montfort, the ruthless oppressor of the Albigensians, receives both frequent excoriation and momentary tributes to his effective generalship. He also receives a vivid but banal death moment, felled by an anonymous stone from the city he is besieging. Specificity in Lenau is thus always haunted, a moment that comes to life *because* it is wholly controlled by death. Lenau's poetic production, for all its experimental fascination, remains necessarily repetitious and self-absorbed because his evident need for multiple historical figures derives from the empty immediacy of their dying rather than from any quest for historical meaning. For that "meaning" is already given in its utter absence.

"Geist," for Lenau, thus appears to be a regulatory concept, a Hegelian telos without Hegelian movement designed to prevent the implosion of all experience into the terrifying oneness of death. When he tries to give the term imaginative content, as in the fourth of the 1843 *Waldlieder,* the rather ingenuous text obeys the exact laws of longing intensifying toward a death moment that govern Lenau's vision generally.

> Sehnsüchtig zieht entgegen
> Natur auf allen Wegen.
> Als schöne Braut im Schleier,
> Dem Geiste, ihrem Freier.
>
> . . . .
>
> All ihre Pulse beben,
> In ihm, in ihm zu leben,
> Von ihm dahinzusinken,
> Den Todeskuss zu trinken.
>
> (*Werke* 1:449–50)

Geist . . . Freier, spirit as liberator: one is tempted to see Lenau's use of these words as linguistic in the narrowest sense, without any of their customary connotations. Yet they are the opposite of decorative. These verbal embodiments of the human idea hold his poetics in place, linking it once again to the idealist temporality of aesthetic education that Lenau cannot evade, even as he rejects every one of Schiller's premises. For, of course, a taboo on the future means a taboo on "education." And yet, in Lenau's terminology,

nature is "liberated" into literary language. The only word for such liberation is *aesthetic,* and the only transformation literature necessarily
imposes on experience is repetition. For a poet such as Mörike, the tendency of language to schematize, make generic the intimacy of the moment,
is to be resisted, manipulated, disguised. The nuances of each unique
instant can be adequately captured only in a language of multiple shifts
in rhetoric and perspective. But, for Lenau, linguistic repetition is to be
accentuated as the sole guarantor of continuous consciousness. To him,
the isolated intense moment—the very definition of experience as he understands it—is also the ultimate illusion, because its given structure of longing
is destined to explode into nothingness. As we have seen, Lenau does,
indeed, move "outside" the invariance of the self into the collective past.
But what emerges from this visionary quest still lacks the linear quality
inherent in the words *memory* and *history.* To generate a text as *Organischlebendiges* (his own term),[12] Lenau must move to the third temporal zone,
the "timelessness" of "Geist," where a concept of history as a gigantic,
hopeless simultaneity can be authorized as the only true version of human
living: ceaseless intensities rendered intelligible by their common substratum, death.

The distinction between Mörike's and Lenau's poetics clearly corresponds to the opposition between symbol and allegory articulated by Paul
de Man in "The Rhetoric of Temporality."[13] Symbolism is the consciously
modern style (Goethe, Coleridge), its energy deriving from the new priority
of historical thinking: "The philosophy of history never justifies the world
as the created world but only as a world still to be produced."[14] A modern
allegorical intention, however, while rejecting the potent dreams of future
meaning derived from symbols, is not free of the historical requirement
to "produce the world." Lenau's rhetoric of liberation into the zone of

---

12. The word occurs in Lenau's only literary review, of *Lyra und Harfe* by Georg Keil
(1834): "Die wahre Naturpoesie muss unseres Bedünkens die Natur und das Menschenleben
in einen innigen Konflikt bringen, und aus diesem Konflikt ein drittes *Organischlebendiges*
resultieren lassen, welches ein Symbol darstelle jener höhern geistigen Einheit, worunter
Natur und Menschenleben begriffen sind" (*Werke* 6:33). As with *freedom,* Lenau seeks to drive
the word *organic* beyond its conventional, complacent resonances, to heighten our awareness
of the ceaseless deadly conflicts with and between all organisms.

13. "Whereas the symbol postulates the possibility of an identity or identification, allegory
designates primarily a distance in relation to its own origin, and, renouncing the nostalgia
and the desire to coincide, it establishes its language in the void of this temporal difference"
(Paul de Man, "The Rhetoric of Temporality," in *Blindness and Insight,* 2d ed. [Minneapolis:
University of Minnesota Press, 1983], 207).

14. Hans Blumenberg, *The Legitimacy of the Modern Age,* trans. Robert M. Wallace (Cambridge, Mass.: MIT Press, 1985), 58.

Geist is both inseparable as such from Schiller's rhetoric of aesthetic *Veredlung* and destined in practice to reenact ceaselessly its assault on the illusions of symbolism. Where Mörike conceals, "naturalizes" a stylized image through apparent informality, Lenau reiterates it, forces its threadbare quality into the open—whereupon his intensity becomes inescapable. Mörike initiates the drama of symbolic harmony with his very first word; Lenau's texts, by contrast, rarely begin strikingly, relying as they do on remorseless repetition in order to become metapoems, undermining their own images.

"Die Rose der Erinnerung" opens in the following manner.

> Als treulos ich das teure Land verliess,
> Wo mir, wie nirgend sonst, die Freude blühte,
> Mich selbst verstossend aus dem Paradies
> Voll Freundesliebe, holder Frauengüte.
>
> (Werke 1:107)

The reader's attention is held only by the "psychological" question of motive-for-leaving that is never answered, the Lenau poetic self being a setter of scenes, a traveler, an organizer of momentary intensities, but *not* a continuous psyche. This text is typical rather than especially successful in that the power of repetition is not felt for several stanzas. In stanza 4, a rosebush addresses the speaker.

> "Nicht in den Staub, o Freund, hier weine hin,
> Hier auf die weichen Blätter dieser Rose!"

The conceit is hardly inspiring in itself, but it offers Lenau what he needs to initiate the process of motivic deconstruction. Stanza 6 brings his characteristic fusion of allegorical detachment with an extended death moment, here the death of the rose.

> Der Rose inniglicher Duft entschwand,
> Es ging die frische Farbenglut verbleichen;
> Sie ruht so blass und starr in meiner Hand,
> Des Unverwelklichen ein welkes Zeichen.

But it is only at this point, in the poem's last two stanzas, that Lenau is able to imbue his conventional imagery with a hallucinatory power. Stanza 7 opens: "Des Unverwelklichen?—sie rauscht so bang, / Will meine Hand die Rose wieder wecken." The apparatus of the "journey" is forgotten, instead the rose's death is desperately extended as the speaker's senses are skewed from the (conventional) sight and scent into the unexpected zone of sound. The sound emanating from the rose confounds the easy "baroque" move toward "das Unverwelkliche," drowning out every other response in the speaker (all the various German words for sound crowd into these lines), until the poem consumes itself, the ceaseless tramping of its own linguistic movement revealed as its sole, exclusive truth.

> Ein leises Schreiten der Vergänglichkeit,
> Hörbar geworden plötzlich meinem Lauschen!

On occasion, as in another rose poem, Lenau can achieve the power of repetition without a lengthy exposition of conventional imagery.

> *Welke Rose*
>
> In einem Buche blätternd, fand
> Ich eine Rose welk, zerdrückt,
> Und weiss auch nicht mehr, wessen Hand
> Sie einst für mich gepflückt.
>
> Ach, mehr und mehr im Abendhauch
> Verweht Erinn'rung; bald zerstiebt
> Mein Erdenlos, dann weiss ich auch
> Nicht mehr, wer mich geliebt.
>
> (*Werke* 1:419)

The second stanza is clearly an intensification of the first, with close parallelisms in the thought sequences. Yet Lenau permits two readings of the emotional tone: either the "ich" makes a typically baroque move toward intensity, as it focuses on its own transience—or detachment is maintained throughout, with the parallelism in what is "known"/not known registered, as it were, clinically. Although Lenau's view of the self as fundamentally unstable and passive means that both readings are in play, the special quality of the poem derives from the second one, from the thought that intensification is no more than repetition. To intensify is not merely to rupture the moment and ensure its death—it points to a collapse of meaning at the heart of language itself. For if the speaker's earthly life dissolves, what *is* the "ich" that "no longer knows" its emotional past? "Wer mich geliebt" would seem to be an intensification of the hand that plucked the rose, but it is actually an empty phrase depending on a verb (*weiss*) deprived of any imaginable content. The reader is left with a purely *gestural* language, an attempt by the speaker to witness his own death as a process [*zerstiebt*] exactly analogous to the disintegration of the rose. Lenau turns a metaphorical verb (*verweht*) back toward its literal meaning: memories are being blown away like rose petals. Thus, even as he appears to reenact the baroque move from the empirical to the spiritual, he effectively reverses it, forcing the reader to confront the sheer materiality of consciousness.

Tradition is indispensable to Lenau, he knows no other way of writing. But he treats it as, in his expressed opinion, Hegel treated past belief systems, uprooting it, setting it adrift. Repetition, quotation, the dominance of gesture, all are essential techniques for this productive process. In "An der Bahre der Geliebten," the speaker remembers an idyllic past moment when he had declared "Ich liebe dich ewig!" and the beloved's response had been unsatisfactorily muted.

> Schmerzlich berührt von deinem Schweigen, frug ich,
> Ob vernommen das Wort du meiner Seele,
> Und du nicktest hold; doch es dünkte mir dein
>   Nicken zu wenig.
>
>   (*Werke* 1:90)

The speaker permits the reader to see his own faint ridiculousness, but without abandoning the emotional tone; the power of the poem derives entirely from the repetition of this nonevent in the present.

> Meine gebrochne Stimme ruft dir bange
> Nach: "Ich liebe dich ewig!" O wie selig
> Wär, ich nun, antwortete meinem Schmerz dein
>   Leisestes Nicken!

We are in the world of romantic hyperbole, of *Komödianten* and *Kulissen,* so deftly punctured by Heine. But Lenau's "irony" does not free him from his own scene setting, and this unfreedom is the source of his power. The reader mentally enacts the "story" from the dead woman's perspective, outlining love's triviality with a clarity made possible by the speaker's theater. All culminates in the grotesquerie of *Nicken.* But the repetition of this gesture causes the rest of the scenery to disappear: the girl's earlier melancholy fuses irrevocably with the mechanical nodding of a death's head. The repeated nodding is true, the repeated "Ich liebe dich ewig!" is false: all the speakers's "Glühende Tränen" and "Schmerzen" dissolve in the unyielding clarity of this symmetry. As in "Welke Rose" the reader feels uneasily deprived of the nominal basis of lyric expression, a speaker whose continuity would be guaranteed by the responsibility he takes for his words. Instead, the self drowns in its own obsessive images.

The way beyond this reductive poetics took Lenau to various forms of *Rollengedicht* (poems on Ahasver, the wandering Jew, on the Indians glimpsed during his journey to America, on such ethnic figures from his native Hungary as the famous "Die drei Zigeuner") and ultimately to the verse epics. As we have seen, this enabled him to develop a technique of duplication, producing a shock of identity between nominally dissimilar or exotic narratives. Lenau's power derives from the fact that such apparent moves "outside" the self are liberating only in the strictly aesthetic sense of enabling textual production; psychically, there is no outside, the exploration of others' stories merely opens up hitherto unnoticed cells in the poet's own mental prison. As Lenau put it in 1838, "Die Geschichte der Menschheit wiederholt sich konzentrativ in der Geschichte des Menschen. Ich spüre was ich versäumt, verschwendet, verfehlt habe, und das ist mein Übel."[15] "Die Heidelberger Ruine," written during his 1833 American journey, embodies an interesting attempt to hold the historical past as a simultaneity within the momentary intensities of the self's contemplation. A self thus pluralized need not be endowed with specific "experience," with some twinge of hope that would require dismantling; this dispersal of the subject enables Lenau to begin his text much more strikingly, with a *Zeilenkomposition* that seems to anticipate Trakl.[16]

> Freundlich grünen diese Hügel,
> Heimlich rauscht es durch den Hain,
> Spielen Laub und Mondenschein,
> Weht des Todes leiser Flügel.
>
> (*Werke* 1:98)

The second stanza, to be sure, veers sharply from Trakl-like enigma, but compresses vividly (*konzentrativ* is Lenau's word) the baroque version of human life into a series of metaphoric "signs," images of action that are merely hinted at before being swept aside.

> Wo nun Gras und Staude beben,
> Hat in froher Kraft geblüht,
> Ist zu Asche bald verglüht

---

15. Lenau, *Werke* 4:151.

16. For a discussion of the Lenau-Trakl relationship, see Walter Weiss, "Nikolaus Lenau und Georg Trakl: Ein Vergleich ihrer Metaphorik," in *Lenau-Forum* 1985: 81–89.

Manches reiche Menschenleben.

The poem is a long one and does not maintain this concision. Lenau's goal is to transcend the baroque antithesis of recurrent nature versus death-bound humanity. Instead, he makes nature complicitous in the whole death process, evoking its springtime thrust through military and other strictly human metaphors.

> Über ihrer [der Blüten] Schwestern Leichen,
> Die der rauhe Nord erschlug,
> Nehmen sie den Freudenzug,
> Gibt der Lenz sein Siegeszeichen.

Living humanity is then brought on stage, its delusions qualitatively indistinguishable from nature's own; the speaker discerns its activity far below, from his viewpoint beside the ruined castle.

> Auf der Taten kühnen Fechter—
> Winkt hinab voll Bitterkeit
> Die Ruine dort, der Zeit
> Steinern stilles Hohngelächter.

This is the tenth stanza. By delaying the substantive appearance of the ruin, Lenau has achieved for it a subtle ambiguity: does the castle, in the useless persistence of its stone, simply embody the vanity of all human projects? Or is it emblematically shaking its fist against destiny, summoning us to an awareness of time transcending springtime banality? Lenau immediately brings on another stock figure, the nightingale, to explore this ambiguity. Initially, the nightingale simply laments, "warning" all who listen against the delusions of springtime hope. Then it falls silent. In stanzas 14 to 20, the speaker beautifully postulates a content to that silence: the dead are *almost* resurrected, summoned by "des Frühlings mächtig Wort" to revisit the scene of former joys. They do not quite materialize, but pour all their longings for expression into the nightingale, which gradually begins to sing their desires. At this moment of aesthetic "liberation," the dead are reconciled to their return to the death realm—and the speaker no longer views the energy of springtime as sheer futility.

> Blüten seh' ich niederschauen;
> Die mein Klagen roh und kalt
> Gegen die Gestorbnen schalt,

Jetzo muss ich sie bedauern;

Denn mich dünkt, ihr frohes Drängen
Ist der Sehnsucht Weiterziehn,
Mit den Blüten, die dahin,
Um so bälder sich zu mengen.

This shift is of the utmost importance for Lenau's poetics: if he can overcome the dualism between nature and humanity, as well as that between self and other, then, without in any way changing his baroque tropes of *vanitas,* he can achieve a new texture, a "liberation" of deluded perception into a rigorous language of death. One simply has to decode everything that happens, especially in a season of spring, as a moment in the dying process. Then the essential gesture, whether cosmic or intimate (here the blossoms gusting to the ground), is isolated, probed, aesthetically centered. And we will learn how to look directly at death instead of flinching away from it or falsely conceptualizing it as otherness.

Although Lenau's vision remains allegorical, devoid of any conciliatory impulse, the three temporalities of Schillerian aesthetics are indispensable to his program, which is to rewrite dynamic history as static truth. First, the moment of sensuous immediacy isolates and "purifies" an event from the flow of dailiness, recreating it as coded gesture. Second, history is actualized, not as a meaningful organism but as the legions of the dead clamoring to be heard, whether through a retelling of their story or through recognition of their presence in nature. And finally, the timeless idea of humanity (Lenau's reimagining of Hegelian *Geist*) emerges into truth, not as an alternative or harmonious domain, but as a structure of simultaneity releasing the imprisoned dead (and the psychically imprisoned living) from linear emptiness.

It is through the nightingale's silence that the speaker of "Die Heidelberger Ruine" hears the return of the dead. And silence becomes central to Lenau's death imagery; silence both isolates the moment from the prevailing noise and links it to the larger historical fate to which a death moment belongs, namely, indifference and forgetting. Only through this dialectic can what Lenau calls the "Kunde" be heard, the truth of history that, so far, resides in the *word freedom,* in the possibility of imagining such a value and the pursuit of its traces in the lives of the long dead. The first poem of the 1843 *Waldlieder* cycle concludes with stanzas showing vividly why "nature" remains vital to Lenau's quest.

Natur! will dir ans Herz mich legen!

Verzeih, dass ich dich konnte meiden,
Dass Heilung ich gesucht für Leiden,
Die du mir gabst zum herben Segen.

In deinen Waldesfinsternissen
Hab ich von mancher tiefen Ritze,
Durch die mir leuchten deine Blitze,
Den trüglichen Verband gerissen.

(*Werke* 1:446)

As with the structuring of time, Lenau's relationship to nature stands in a curious symmetry with the classical tradition: nature remains the zone of pure truths, the origin to which the needs of the ego in society block access. But these truths are concerned exclusively with death: the worst temptation is to seek "Heilung" from the wounding visions that nature inflicts. Nature's overtly cyclical rhythms conspire with the human everyday to obscure the death truths, which are revealed only in moments, as "Blitze." The moments occur, of course, more frequently in the fall; in the springtime fullness of "Die Heidelberger Ruine," the path of truth is devious. But in the fall the distorting self-pity of melancholy has to be resisted. The final poem of *Waldlieder* should be quoted in full, as perhaps Lenau's finest single text.

Rings ein Verstummen, ein Entfärben;
Wie sanft den Wald die Lüfte streicheln,
Sein welkes Laub ihn abzuschmeicheln!
Ich liebe dieses milde Sterben.

Von hinnen geht die stille Reise,
Die Zeit der Liebe ist verklungen,
Die Vögel haben ausgesungen,
Und dürre Blätter sinken leise.

Die Vögel zogen nach dem Süden,
Aus dem Verfall des Laubes tauchen
Die Nester, die nicht Schutz mehr brauchen,
Die Blätter fallen stets, die müden.

In dieses Waldes leisem Rauschen
Ist mir, als hör' ich Kunde wehen,
Dass alles Sterben und Vergehen
Nur heimlichstill vergnügtes Tauschen.

(*Werke* 1:455–56)

The customary passivity of Lenau's speaker here finds fulfillment. He has become identical with the sense perceptions of seeing and hearing, is exclusively the witness of nature's "Entfärben" and "Verstummen." Even natural events are, in principle, singular: one can only hear single sounds and see single objects. But Lenau manages to reverse all sensory "impact" through his technique of repetition. Sounds lose definition, objects (the bird's nest) withdraw from existence even as they come into view, like a film in reverse. And so the silence occurs in which nature can tell its "Kunde": that its processes are a kind of play, requiring a subjective word, an abstract summation of mood [*vergnügt*], to express their truth. Lenau's reduction of self to its sensory core is justified by the "need" of nature for his consciousness. A symmetrical inversion of Schiller's *Spiel* is evoked, that state in which the familiar dualism between human and nature ceases to limit the possibilities.

For Lenau, of course, such moments of fusion are inseparable from the dying process. Throughout his *Die Albigenser* he focuses on his figures' deaths rather than their lives; and it is remarkable how frequently the death scenes are shrouded in silence, as if the sound track were turned off and the possibility being explored that the abstract movements might yield that "Kunde" toward which, for Lenau, all consciousness is directed. In the section "Der Besuch" we hear of a mother and child freezing to death in the sudden extremity of the physical and spiritual winter.

> Sie irren in der Schneenacht hin und wieder
> Und sinken endlich müde, schläfrig nieder!
> Sie schlafen ein, und stille wird ihr Schmerz,
> Erbarmend legt die Nacht sich an ihr Herz
> Und saugt ihm leis unspürbar aus der Wunde
> Das Leben aus, wie Gift, mit kaltem Munde.
>
> (*Werke* 2:359)

The neutrality of perspective is striking, indeed, with life equated with poison;[17] but it is not so much objective (the language is full of "human" commitment) as *attentive*. As with the falling leaves of the *Waldlieder*, the narrating consciousness must strip itself down in the face of historical deaths: if death has a truth to reveal, it will certainly not coincide with the response human fear of death has always imposed.

Lenau is also attentive to the "Sage," to the bare narration that constitutes his tradition. The lives of the heretics cannot be "rescued" if they

---

17. Richard Dove would call this "the uncanny amorality of his worldview" (Dove, "Rhetoric," 246).

are subjected to reinterpretation, that is, exploited for modern needs. In this passage on the battle of Carcassonne, the poet integrates his techniques of gesture and silence to produce an image as in a medieval tapestry; the violence is so intense that it can no longer be heard, it has become a sheer patterning of spiritual fury.

> Die Sage spricht: dort ballte das Verderben
> Im Kampfe sich, dort war so dichtes Sterben,
> Dass irr die Seelen die von dannen wallten,
> Im wilden Kampfgewühl zusammenprallten
> Und dann, noch krank von ihres Hasses Toben,
> Mit Grauen weithin auseinander stoben.
>
> (*Werke* 2:365)

Can an immortal soul be "sick?" We have seen earlier that a self-undermining language is deployed by Lenau at crucial moments. Here it is part of his attentiveness to the source: in this supremely wasteful catastrophe of the Christian era, did something happen to faith itself? Were these deaths so horrible that some wholly discordant "truth" escaped the medieval cosmos, reverberating still for the ear ready to listen? A sick, hating immortal soul is no immortal soul at all.

In "Beziers," Lenau stages his own desire for silence, turning off the sound track and isolating a "natural" image that, to him, is ultimately not in conflict with the military tumult.

> Wenn still und lautlos ginge dies Zerstören,
> Man müsste aus den Wunden hier das Blut
> Gleich einem Bach im Walde rauschen hören,
> Doch wie ein Meer im Sturme schreit die Wut.
>
> (*Werke* 2:366)

The silence is, so to speak, underneath the noise, defining it, as each successive death eliminates the entire world that was that warrior's consciousness. As Lenau listens to the "Sage," the silence of the dead seems to swell, resisting the apparent meaninglessness assigned to it by "history." In the town of Lavaur, the entire populace is massacred (except for a young girl who then loses her mind) and left unburied.

> Das Gras im Burghof zu Lavaur
> Wuchs einsam, ungestört empor,
> Schon überhüllt es und umschattet
> Gebein, zerstreut und unbestattet; . . .

> Der dunkle Himmel scheint zu trauern.
>
> *(Werke* 2:382)

Toward the end of *Die Albigenser,* the speaker listens to participants who themselves view the events as past. They certainly cannot speak the story's truth, but their reactions belong to it. A monk, disgusted by the violence of the Papacy, renounces his calling, declaring that the meaning of Jesus' life and death has not yet been formulated. The knight with whom he is conversing links the battle just past to their own future deaths, perhaps in quietness and solitude, as controlled by a single *Geist.*

> Die Schar der kühnen Streiter schwand zusammen,
> Schon wird es still; der Geist, der sie gelenkt,
> Er liebt, zu sinnen bald, in sich versenkt,
> Und bald in Kämpfen herrlich aufzuflammen.
>
> *(Werke* 2:393)

Again the attentiveness/neutrality predominates: the battle deaths have no intrinsic meaning. Yet they remain, in some ultimate and frankly visual sense, "herrlich." Drawing back from the events a little further still, "ein Greis" does, after all, find intrinsic meaning in them.

> Noch die Freiheit war es nicht;
> Dunklen Gruss, verworrne Kunde
> Brachte nur von ihrem Licht
> Die vorausgeeilte Stunde; . . .
>
> *(Werke* 2:395)

Lenau's "Schlussgesang" makes clear that, in some sense, this is also his viewpoint. "Freedom," the great idea of modernity, cannot be devoid of meaning. And, indeed, Lenau hears its *Kunde* in both nature and history, the possibility of change at the center of the most unchanging of all events, death. But the inextricable linkage of freedom and death in Lenau's mind means that the term must always be understood dialectically. It is the value that can only be stated negatively, as that which has never been realized. But it is also imposed on us as a responsibility inherent in our very existence as remembering and anticipating beings. As Walter Benjamin puts it, "For every image of the past that is not recognized by the present as one of its own concerns threatens to disappear irretrieveably."[18] The "present," how-

---

18. Walter Benjamin, "Theses on the Philosophy of History," in *Illuminations,* ed. Hannah Arendt (New York: Schocken, 1969), 255.

ever, for Lenau as for Benjamin, is itself nothing but isolated moments, its "concerns" permeated with death. Lenau's last significant fictional voice, Don Juan, sums this up in lines designed to fob off a former girlfriend: "Ein Augenblick hat ewigen Gehalt, / Und sein Gedächtnis mögen wir bewahren" (*Werke* 2:426). The double meaning of "Gedächtnis," as living memory and as frozen memorial, seems essential: the road to freedom, for Lenau's "Augenblick," lies through death. And this road points away from introspection toward the public truth that is repressed in both daily life and history. Don Juan also remarks: "Die Selbstvertiefung wollte nie behagen" (*Werke* 2:439), which surely characterizes his author. The restless traveler and melancholic found his vocation through intensive listening: exploring both nature and history, Lenau strove to make himself into a conscientious, attentive instrument, cleaning away the noise that obscures all deaths and recreating the silence as free text, without promise but also without despair.

Charles Sealsfield: Innovation or Intertextuality?

Jeffrey L. Sammons

Charles Sealsfield's location in literary history has always been a problem. Still unsettled is the question of whether he is to be regarded as an American or German (i.e., Austrian, Swiss, European) writer. He obtains a place as easily in the *Oxford Companion to American Literature* as in the *Oxford Companion to German Literature*.[1] It is, in fact, symptomatic of the symbiosis of American and German culture in the nineteenth century that the great surge of curiosity about Sealsfield in the United States around 1844 was instigated by a few admiring lines in Theodor Mundt's continuation of Freidrich Schlegel's history of literature.[2] One of the most important recent studies of him appeared in a series on "Anglo-Saxon Language and Literature" and strongly insists on regarding him as an American and, especially, a Southern writer.[3] Austrian Americanist Walter Grünzweig has

All quotations from Sealsfield's novels are cited from Charles Sealsfield, *Sämtliche Werke*, ed. Karl J. R. Arndt et al. (Hildesheim and New York: Olms Presse, 1972-), in parentheses as *Werke* with the edition volume number, original volume number in brackets (where necessary), and page number. All quotations from letters and documents are cited from Eduard Castle, *Der große Unbekannte: Das Leben von Charles Sealsfield (Karl Postl), Briefe und Aktenstücke* (Vienna: Karl Werner, 1955), in parentheses as *Briefe* with page number.

1. Henry Garland and Mary Garland, *The Oxford Companion to German Literature* (Oxford: Clarendon Press, 1976), 791–92; James D. Hart, *The Oxford Companion to American Literature*, 4th ed. (New York: Oxford University Press, 1965), 755. The latter also contains an entry for Friedrich Gerstäcker (311), but no one to my knowledge has claimed that he was an American writer.

2. Theodor Mundt, *Geschichte der Literatur der Gegenwart* (Berlin: Simion, 1842), 425–26. See Nanette M. Ashby, *Charles Sealsfield: "The Greatest American Author," A Study of Literary Piracy and Promotion in the 19th Century* (Stuttgart: Charles Sealsfield Gesellschaft, 1980).

3. Jerry Schuchalter, *Frontier and Utopia in the Fiction of Charles Sealsfield: A Study of the Lebensbilder aus der westlichen Hemisphäre* (Frankfurt am Main, Bern, and New York: Peter Lang, 1986), 86, 304.

objected to seeing him exclusively as a German-language and Austrian writer,[4] while Friedrich Sengle has implied that he was a Swiss writer[5] and a recent, ambitious study that goes farther than any other in presenting him as having come to be passionately anti-American, portrays him as primarily Austrian and European.[6] The problem, of course, was initially generated by Sealsfield himself, who actually spent only a few years of his literary career in the United States, published only one of his novels, and that an apprentice work, in English, lived most of his life in Europe, primarily in Switzerland, published all the rest of his novels in German there, and yet insisted to his dying day and even beyond it upon his American identity.

Those allergic to the pigeonholing of literary phenomena may ask what of it. But the problem is not so easily waved off, for it is a component of the continuing insecurity in the apprehension of Sealsfield, despite a considerable amount of erudite scholarship in recent years. His literary-historical placement bears upon the question of what kind of writer he was, generically, creatively, and qualitatively. For whatever theorists may say, the contextualization of texts affects judgment.[7] The curious effect of the modern surge of attention has been to cause his image to undergo substantial alterations depending upon the location assigned to him.

Sengle and his disciple, Franz Schüppen,[8] have been able to locate Sealsfield in the category of the Biedermeier because that category is so capaciously defined. In Sengle's scheme, one of its characteristics is a

---

4. Walter Grünzweig, "'Where Millions of Happy People Might Live Peacefully': Jacksons Westen in Charles Sealsfields *Tokeah; or, the White Rose,*" *Amerikastudien/American Studies* 28 (1983): 236; see also Alexander Ritter, "Charles Sealsfield: Politischer Emigrant, freier Schriftsteller und die Doppelkrise von Amerika—Utopie und Gesellschaft im 19. Jahrhundert," *Freiburger Universitätsblätter* 75 (1982): 55.

5. Friedrich Sengle, *Biedermeierzeit: Deutsche Literatur im Spannungsfeld zwischen Restauration und Revolution 1815–1848,* vol. 3, *Die Dichter* (Stuttgart: Metzler, 1980), 762.

6. Günter Schnitzler, *Erfahrung und Bild: Die dichterische Wirklichkeit des Charles Sealsfield (Karl Postl)* (Freiburg: Rombach, 1988), 12, 128. See also Peter Michelsen, "Americanism and Anti-Americanism in German Novels of the XIXth Century," *Arcadia* 11 (1976): 277.

7. In my essay ("In Search of Bonaventura: The *Nachtwachen* Riddle 1965–1985," *Germanic Review* 61 [1986]: 50–56), I tried to show that the evaluation of the *Nachtwachen* has often been dependent upon the status of the assumed author. Now that Ruth Haag ("Noch einmal: Der Verfasser der *Nachtwachen von Bonaventura,*" *Euphorion* 81 [1987]: 268–97) has supplied documentary evidence that Ernst August Klingemann was the author, it will be interesting to see whether Klingemann will now be revalued or whether his reputation as a *Trivialschriftsteller* will cause a devaluation of the *Nachtwachen.*

8. Franz Schöppen, *Charles Sealsfield, Karl Postl: Ein österreichischer Erzähler der Biedermeierzeit im Spannungsfeld von Alter und Neuer Welt* (Frankfurt am Main and Bern: Peter Lang, 1981).

mixture of styles and tones, an absence of authoritative generic and stylistic models. Thus, anything loose and baggy, as Sealsfield's novels certainly appear to be, can be accommodated. Sengle also points to Sealsfield's theological origins, his patriarchal social pattern, his ultimate withdrawal and resignation, and his detail realism as Biedermeier qualities.[9] There may indeed be "Biedermeier" authors with whom Sealsfield might plausibly be compared, the most likely, I should think, being Gotthelf.[10] One might also think of Willibald Alexis.[11] But surely Sealsfield's most prominent characteristics—the energy and violence of his writing, the political detail of his narrations, their engagement with questions of liberty, property, monetary policy, banking and credit, mob rule, the rise of working-class agitation, and so forth—do not cause the term *Biedermeier,* in its more usual understanding, to spring readily to mind, as Sengle indeed acknowledges.[12] Nor does expanding the "Biedermeier" category to encompass Young Germany help us very much, notwithstanding Sealsfield's own acknowledgment of the Young Germans as contemporaries (*Werke,* 21[1]:52–54), for hardly any Young German novel, with the exception of Heinrich Laube's *Die Krieger* and possibly Mundt's *Madonna,* can compare with his in their differentiated engagement with current, public events of the time. Thus, the occasionally encountered resistance to Sengle's colonization of Sealsfield is not without reason.[13]

As modern inquiry evolved, an awareness grew of a need to try to see him in an American literary environment. But, until relatively recently, this was not easy to do. The American authors of that age best known to Germans are Irving and Cooper, whose names have been adduced from time to time, though not with notable precision. It would not be easy to detect in Sealsfield any affinity with Irving, especially not in the work that takes place largely in Irving's Dutch New York landscape, *Die Deutsch-amerikanischen Wahlverwandtschaften;* Sealsfield, moreover, was quite hostile to Irving (see *Werke,* 10[1]:86). While there are doubtless Cooperesque

---

9. Sengle, *Biedermeierzeit,* 3:758–60, 764–65.

10. See Hubert Fritz, *Die Erzählweise in den Romanen Charles Sealsfields und Jeremias Gotthelfs: Zur Rhetoriktradition im Biedermeier* (Bern: Herbert Lang; Frankfurt am Main and Munich: Peter Lang, 1976). Sealsfield's own feelings about Gotthelf were mixed; he found *Die Käserei in der Vehfreude* too "pfarrerisch" (*Briefe,* 322).

11. See Sengle, *Biedermeierzeit,* 3:809.

12. Sengle, *Biedermeierzeit,* 3:757.

13. E.g., Alexander Ritter, *Darstellung und Funktion der Landschaft in den Amerika-Romanen von Charles Sealsfield (Karl Postl)* (Stuttgart: Charles Sealsfield Gesellschaft, 1969), 48, 311; Schuchalter, *Frontier,* 110.

elements in Sealsfield's first novel, especially in its primitive English version, his pioneer ideology of manifest destiny comes to move quite far away from Cooper's elegiac resignation, and Sealsfield became quite critical of Cooper also (*Werke,* 10[1]:15). The trouble is that the writers likely to be most relevant in Sealsfield's environment—among them Timothy Flint, James Kirke Paulding, Anthony Ganilh, John Pendleton Kennedy, Catharine Maria Sedgwick, Lydia Maria Child, George Tucker, and William Gilmore Simms—are largely unknown today except to specialists in American studies; with the possible exception of Simms, they have been decanonized and overshadowed by the protomodern masters Poe, Hawthorne, Melville, and Whitman. For many years there were limited, source-hunting excursions into this material; now, after initial probes by Schüppen,[14] we have an extensive, wide-ranging study by Grünzweig.[15] However, in his effort to situate Sealsfield as firmly as possible in the context of antebellum American literature, Grünzweig displays such a vast amount of what I believe today is called intertextuality and used to be called plagiarism that one begins to wonder whether any degree of originality can actually be ascribed to Sealsfield.

The charge of plagiarism is an old one; in fact, it was once, apparently unjustly, raised by Simms himself.[16] It has long been known that Sealsfield borrowed from Flint one tale of a village idiot and his fearsomely competent wife for the story *Christophorus Bärenhäuter* and another of a kidnapped child for the third chapter of *Pflanzerleben* 1, a segment of Balzac's *Gobseck* for a scene in *Morton,* an anonymous Texan memoir for the perilous ride of Colonel Morse in *Das Kajütenbuch,* and an Irish anecdote of Samuel Lover for "Der Fluch Kishogues" in the same work, as well as a number of other items.[17] Closer attention to these passages has tended to relieve Sealsfield of the odium of plagiarism. For example, it has been shown that he did not take over the stylistic elements of the Texan memoir and that he expanded and elaborated the Balzac text.[18] A major Sealsfield scholar

14. Schüppen, *Sealsfield,* on Flint: 19–20, 120–21; on Irving, Paulding, and Cooper: 222–32; on Simms: 235–36.

15. Walter Grünzweig, *Das demokratische Kanaan: Charles Sealsfields Amerika im Kontext amerikanischer Literatur und Ideologie* (Munich: Fink, 1987).

16. See Karl J. Arndt, "Plagiarism: Sealsfield or Simms?" *Modern Language Notes* 69 (1954): 577–81; see also Grünzweig, *Das demokratische Kanaan,* 105–6.

17. See Otto Heller, "Some Sources of Sealsfield," *Modern Philology* 7 (1909–10): 587–92; Eduard Castle, *Der große Unbekannte: Das Leben von Charles Sealsfield (Karl Postl)* (Vienna and Munich: Manutius Presse, 1952), 451–53; Grünzweig, *Das demokratische Kanaan,* passim.

18. Fritz, *Die Erzählweise,* 20–22, 24–25. The, in my opinion, not very healthy influence

of the older generation concluded that Sealsfield was "a borrower, but not a plagiarist."[19] Grünzweig himself observes that Sealsfield shifted the import of Flint's story of the kidnapped child and altered the tale of Christophorous Bärenhäuter in favor of the Irish shrew and against the German oaf.[20] He also makes the point that inexperienced antebellum writers regularly borrowed themes, motifs, and images from one another.[21] But, although Grünzweig's account is by no means undifferentiated, the overall implication is one of such extensive intertextuality that Sealsfield seems to be a reduplicator of his American literary context.

In such matters, the Germanist is naturally inclined to yield to the Americanist. But, in trying to follow the Americanists' lead, especially Grünzweig's, I have obtained a somewhat different impression of Sealsfield's location. He appears to me quite unlike his American contemporaries in three crucial matters: structure, tone, and ideology. In short, his novels are not *formed* like the American novels; they do not *sound* like the American novels; and they do not make the same claims for the American experience.

This literature is a product of a kind of American enlightenment and is, in a sense, pre-Romantic, despite the occasional wildness of its setting. It precedes the journeys into myth and romance—into the twilight zone, so to speak—of Melville, Hawthorne, or Poe. It is not to be thought of, however, as primitive or undercompetent. With the exception of Tucker's amateurish, anemic, and priggish *Shenandoah* (1824), it is, for the most part, a well-written and well-formed literature. Some of it strikes me as excellent. Catharine Maria Sedgwick's *Hope Leslie* (1827) is more than competent; it is a finely written novel of real distinction, and the novels of Paulding are marked by a controlled, ironic humor, even if the irony is somewhat reactionary. On the whole, narration is linear and free of notable complexities. It is true that Kennedy's *Swallow Barn* (originally 1832), said to be the first plantation novel, presents itself as a kind of antinovel, narrated in a leisurely, apparently arbitrary manner that may owe something to the example of Fielding. But nowhere does one find the characteristic Chinese-box construction of encapsulated first-person nar-

---

of Balzac on the *Morton* fragment as a whole is a topic that has not been pursued as much as it might be.

19. John T. Krumpelmann, "Sealsfield and Sources," *Monatshefte* 43 (1951): 324. See also Schuchalter, *Frontier,* 87.

20. Grünzweig, *Das demokratische Kanaan*, 97–105; see also Walter Grünzweig, "'The Italian Sky in the Republic of Letters': Charles Sealsfield and Timothy Flint as Early Writers of the American West," *Yearbook of German-American Studies* 17 (1982): 15.

21. Grünzweig, *Das demokratische Kanaan,* 31.

rations, nor the sheer sprawl, the sense that the texts are all middle without beginning or end, characteristic of Sealsfield. For example, Flint's *Francis Berrian* (1826) is an encapsulated first-person narration, but well within the established conventions of frame stories. The inner narrator is a well-educated Harvard man on the Texan frontier, which brings us to the next point.

The Americans write a middle style with a decorum tending to refinement, a drawing-room style; even when the matter is far away from domesticity, the point of view, on the whole, is not on the frontier, but at a point of observation distant from it. Sealsfield's rawness, his enthusiasm for violence, the loudness of his volume, are not modeled in the American texts, even in the places where one might expect to find it: not in Flint's extremely popular biography of Daniel Boone,[22] almost certainly known to Sealsfield, written in a dignified but not ornamented middle style with graceful, rhythmic periods, nor even in Flint's edition of the hair-raising adventures of the hapless Westerner James O. Pattie,[23] nor yet in Paulding's *Westward Ho!,* a tale of the most primeval Kentucky frontier.[24] Something more like Sealsfield's often rough, masculine tone, his delighted dilation on the vulgar and boorish, might be found in Simms. But Simms presents chronological difficulties. He was thirteen years younger than Sealsfield, and the beginnings of his literary career are so closely contemporaneous with Sealsfield's writing decade that a direct influence seems unlikely, especially as he would have had to acquire at least some of Simms's works in Switzerland. Simms's own suspicion of plagiarism, noted above, has been refuted partly on the grounds of chronology. Just as plausible would be influences from subliterary sources, such as the tall tales and humorous yarns surrounding Davy Crockett or Mike Fink.

The difference in tone extends to the ideological aspect. Sealsfield's ideological message is more insistent, more obtrusive, more single-minded than anything in the putative American models known to me. This difference is clearest in the matter of slavery. In much of the Sealsfield scholarship of the past, the topic of slavery has been more or less systematically obfuscated. The first critic to give a truly satisfactory account of Sealsfield's representation of slavery is Schuchalter, who not only is quite

---

22. Timothy Flint, *Biographical Memoir of Daniel Boone,* ed. James K. Folsom (New Haven: College and University Press, 1967). Originally published in 1833.

23. James O. Pattie, *The Personal Narrative of James O. Pattie,* [ed. Timothy Flint, 1831] (Philadelphia and New York: Lippincott, 1962).

24. James Kirke Paulding, *Westward Ho! A Tale* (New York: J. and J. Harper, 1832).

clear that Sealsfield was racist, but makes the less commonly perceived point that he was more racist than the antebellum American writers.[25]

In fact, this point may seem somewhat surprising. From today's viewpoint, those American writers who, like Paulding, Kennedy, Tucker, and Simms, opposed abolition and defended the slaveholding society, must appear racist insofar as they must postulate black inferiority, whatever their views might be on the reasons for or the permanence or impermanence of this inferiority. They may, indeed, portray blacks in a comical or grotesque light in many places. But in no case known to me do they portray blacks as *subhuman,* as Sealsfield was wont to do. This is the point that has been consistently evaded. Much has been written about Sealsfield's replication of the proslavery arguments: that Southern agriculture could not be maintained without slaves; that slaves could not be emancipated without the total destruction of civilization and, in any case, could not look after themselves; that they were happier and better treated than European or Northern wage laborers; that slavery was an evil imposed upon Americans by the British, leaving the Americans with a grave but unavoidable responsibility; and, a point about which Sealsfield was particularly obsessive, that slavery was a form of private property and, therefore, could not be justly interfered with by law or in any other manner (see, especially, *Werke,* 14:118–60). These are arguments familiar from that brand of Southern or Southwestern Jacksonianism to which Sealsfield became obdurately attached from his first experience of America; traces of them are found in many of the American novels.

But Sealsfield goes beyond these ideological positions. He consistently presents blacks as ridiculous, disgusting, and animalistic. They all speak the same barely intelligible, ungrammatical, and inarticulate jargon, "ob man sie in den Sklavenstaaten antrifft oder in der mexikanischen Provinz

---

25. Schuchalter, *Frontier,* 188–213, esp. 189, 192. A fair recapitulation of Sealsfield's representations of slavery will be found in Paul Duncan Hartley, "Society and Politics in Europe and America in the Works of Charles Sealsfield" (Ph.D. diss., University of Leeds, 1986), 154–82. Others see "contradictions" or "ambiguities" in Sealsfield's position; e.g., Bernd Fischer, "Form und Geschichtsphilosophie in Charles Sealsfields *Lebensbilder aus der westlichen Hemisphäre,*" *German Studies Review* 9 (1986): 249; Grünzweig, *Das demokratische Kanaan,* 138–43; Schnitzler, *Erfahrung,* 167. I see no ambiguities in Sealsfield's position, except as they faithfully reflect the irrationality of the slaveholding ideology. Gunter G. Sehm, perhaps owing to his South African vantage point, is more sensitive to the real state of affairs: Sealsfield was "kein Demokrat...und dazu ein Anhänger der feudalen Sklavenhaltergesellschaft" (Sehm, *Charles Sealsfields Kajütenbuch im Kontext der literarischen Tradition und der revolutionär-restaurativen Epoche des 19. Jahrhunderts* [Stuttgart: Charles Sealsfield Gesellschaft, 1981], 3).

Texas, in Pennsylvania oder in New York";[26] in fact their lips are too thick to allow them the use of human language (*Werke,* 13:18). The oddest of the anatomical claims is that their calves are in front of their legs rather than in back (*Werke,* 13:14). Constantly they are compared to animals; they are like monkeys and odious orangutans because they imitate white dress (*Werke,* 13:8, 13–14); they are demons, cobolds, a subterranean force; their children resemble piglets (13:67, 71–72). They are so much like animals that it is difficult even to raise them to the level of slavery (*Werke,* 15:386–87). They are liars and thieves, so stupid that a male exhorted to love Jesus believes Christ is a woman and is astounded to hear otherwise, while an inattentive mother causes her baby to die; they are violent: one bites off another's nose and a drunken, orgiastic group plots a genuine rebellion, a scene that may well have been influenced by the rebellion of Nat Turner in 1831 (*Werke,* 13:61–62, 79–81, 86–87, 95, 135–46).[27] Throughout there is an undercurrent of fear of black sexuality and a horror of miscegenation. The scene in "La Chartreuse" in chapter 2 of *Die Farbigen,* with its disturbingly sensual girls, is the most salacious in Sealsfield's generally prudish fiction (*Werke,* 14:223–80). *Farbig* in his usage means mixed blood, and he leaves no doubt, here or elsewhere, that racial mixture leads to degeneration.[28] Schuchalter points out the absences also: Sealsfield's narrator Howard "never mentions the beauty of the spiritual, the power of the slave service, the remarkable creativity of the slave dance. He never sees the expressiveness of the slave's verbal art, its wealth of stories, proverbs, and verbal games."[29] It might be added that the author does nothing to compensate for the limited vision of his narrators. Rather, it appears, in *Nathan,* that reconciliation to slavery is a sign of true Americanism and republicanism (*Werke,* 15:376–77).

None of this is in the American novels supportive of slavery. Not only is it not to be found there; it seems anxiously to be avoided. Instead we see the most imaginably cordial, affectionate, and loyal relations between masters and slaves; it appears that the uprising of Nat Turner, rather than depositing in fiction an awareness of a revolutionary undercurrent among the slaves, led instead to elaborate denial. In Kennedy's *Swallow Barn,* all is mildness and domesticity (*this* is Biedermeier in an American setting);

---

26. Max L. Schmidt, *Amerikanismen bei Charles Sealsfield* (Ph.D. diss., Bonn, 1937), 24.

27. On the possible influence of Turner's *Confessions,* see Grünzweig, *Das demokratische Kanaan,* 140.

28. See Schuchalter, *Frontier,* 232–52.

29. Schuchalter, *Frontier,* 198.

the blacks are usually called not slaves, but negroes or servants.[30] The whole of chapter 46, titled "The Quarter," is a depiction of the slave quarters suffused with good humor and loyalty; the blacks are well taken care of, for they are helpless in their present condition, which makes emancipation impossible. Slavery is wrong, but it is the Southerner's responsibility and cannot be changed.[31] In the following chapter there is the story of Abe, a bad slave, corrupt and criminal, who is sent away to sea instead of to prison, whereupon his character improves. He becomes a good seaman and displays courage on a rescue mission in a storm, eventually losing his life. It is, a character comments, "a gallant sight to see such heroism shining out in an humble slave of the Old Dominion."[32] In Paulding's *The Dutchman's Fireside*, a faithful slave of the past is praised, though it is said that there are no more such since the "meddlers" have come;[33] in *Westward Ho!*, in the preface to which the author asserts that he "yields to none in respect for the motives of those who are sincerely anxious to rid this country of the embarrassments of slavery; and none more heartily wishes the thing were possible, at a less risk to the happiness of both master and slave,"[34] the slaves are grotesque and happy; one of them refuses freedom, and, when exhorted by an abolitionist in Philadelphia, he sees that the freed blacks are beggars, depraved women, and criminals, and realizes that he is better off in his enslaved condition.[35]

In *Woodcraft* (1854), Simms repeats the motif of a slave refusing emancipation, in this case on the grounds that he and his master are bound to one another: "*You* b'longs to *me* Tom, jes' as much as me Tom b'long to *you*; and you nebber guine git *you* free paper from me long as you lib."[36] Of all the writers, Simms came to be the most vigorous defender of slavery and the Confederate cause; *Woodcraft* is a rejoinder to *Uncle Tom's Cabin*.[37] Interestingly, no other writer in this group portrays blacks so humanly.

30. John Pendleton Kennedy, *Swallow Barn; or, A Sojourn in the Old Dominion*, rev. ed. (New York: Putnam, 1853), reprinted with an introduction by Lucinda H. Mockethan (Baton Rouge and London: Louisiana State University Press, 1986), xxv.

31. Kennedy, *Swallow Barn*, 453, 455, 458.

32. Kennedy, *Swallow Barn*, 483. Schuchalter (*Frontier*, 192) also calls attention to the figure of Abe.

33. James Kirke Paulding, *The Dutchman's Fireside: A Tale* (New York: Harper, 1831), 44.

34. Paulding, *Westward Ho!*, 4.

35. Paulding, *Westward Ho!*, 58, 64–65.

36. W. Gilmore Simms, *Woodcraft; or, Hawks about the Dovecoat* (New York: Redfield, 1854), 509.

37. J. V. Ridgely, *William Gilmore Simms* (New York: Twayne, 1962), 97.

In *The Yemassee* (1835), the blacks volunteer to fight with their masters (the protagonist has no hesitation in arming them), and they refuse emancipation.[38] In *Woodcraft*, they are faithful, competent, brave, and loyal—for example, "The negro guides did their duty with the exactness and promptitude of persons who knew exactly what was required of them, and what was the object of the arrangement"; on one occasion, they form an impromptu jury, and the master promises to be buried together with his beloved cook, Tom.[39] This is a writer who was explicitly racist in the modern sense; one character, very likely speaking for the author, argues that whites and Indians can never be reconciled, for "the very difference between the two, that of colour . . . must always constitute them an inferior caste in our minds. Apart from this, an obvious superiority in arts and education must soon force upon them the consciousness of their inferiority."[40] Thus it appears that a similar ideology of racism can lead to very different fictional portrayals.

No one today, of course, will exculpate the antebellum American writers on these grounds. It is clear that their portrayals are just as biased and distorted as Sealsfield's; the gentle, humanized, even admiring depictions of blacks served the preservation of slavery as an institution and contributed to the body of antiabolitionist discourse. One might argue, to be sure, that Sealsfield is merely more realistic, that he is reflecting the true tone of Southern white attitudes. This appears to be the view of Grünzweig, who argues that Sealsfield reflects the ambiguities of the Southern intellectual climate and that he was freer, with his European audience, to depict them.[41] There is, furthermore, the question of voice, of what we are to make of his habit of splintering his narration among so many differentiated first-person narrators. Grünzweig, for example, interprets George Howard, one of Sealsfield's most persistently racist figures, as an unreliable narrator.[42] But we should be careful not to be too ready to apply our modernist

---

38. [William Gilmore Simms], *The Yemassee: A Romance of Carolina* (New York: Harper, 1835), 204, 217, 225, 229, 231. Sealsfield's hero, Andrew Jackson, incidentally, though he supported slavery on economic and political grounds, had no compunctions about arming *free* blacks and insisting on equal pay for them in the defense of New Orleans; thus, even Jackson may have been less racist than his disciple. See Robert V. Remini, *The Life of Andrew Jackson* (New York: Harper and Row, 1988), 92.

39. Simms, *Woodcraft*, 121, 154, 183.

40. Simms, *Yemassee*, 106–7.

41. Grünzweig, *Das demokratische Kanaan*, 150, 143–44; see also Schnitzler, *Erfahrung*, 167–68.

42. Grünzweig, *Das demokratische Kanaan*, 152.

sensibilities to a writer of the past. There can be no doubt that Sealsfield complicates his perspective with his multiplicity of narrators, but it is not certain that he does so to undermine the narrators' authority. Another scholar argues that Sealsfield's texts do not sharply distinguish between author and narrator and that the narrator can speak in the author's voice;[43] he refers to Sengle, who sees the unclear juncture between author and narrator as a Biedermeier characteristic.[44] The difficulty would be to find the countervoice. The abolitionist in *Pflanzerleben*, Vergennes, is portrayed as a shallow hothead and a potential terrorist in his association with the French Revolution. Schuchalter points out that "all of Sealsfield's narrators are profoundly unsympathetic to the plight of the slave."[45] Nor do matters change when he switches to a third-person mode; the old black Priam in *Die Deutsch-amerikanischen Wahlverwandtschaften* is barely human in form, with the face of an orangutan and parts that do not fit, his nose resembles a pickle, his nostrils open outward, his mouth is that of a frog, his lips are like snails, his feet like fly swatters; he is stupid, pompous, and evidently deranged besides (*Werke*, 23[4]:19–21). Indian children also look like monkeys (*Werke*, 6[1]:85), and the Indians in Mexico like orangutans (*Werke*, 8[1]:78). Mexicans are the product of miscegenation between Indians and whites and, therefore, have the worst qualities of both races (8[1]:298–99); Mexican soldiers are skinny, dwarfish, and weak (*Werke*, 16:28).

Sealsfield was an intensely intolerant man. Estimates of his personality that indicate he was overbearing and opinionated are not implausible.[46] His racially pure communities are democratic only internally; toward all other peoples, from the slaves within to the Spanish, Mexicans, Indians, Irish, or Germans without, they are hostile and contemptuous; only the French Creoles, for some reason, are potentially educable to American superiority. Occasionally there are traces of anti-Semitism (e.g., *Werke*, 8[2]:44; 9[2]:291–92, 306–7). The doctrine of the conquering superiority of the Norman race, elaborated by the Alkalde in *Das Kajütenbuch* and adumbrated elsewhere (e.g., *Werke*, 6[1]:236), is merely another one of the items that Sealsfield snatched from a Southern ideology of a patriarchal and feudalized society.[47] But he tended to absolutize them and make them

43. Fritz, *Die Erzählweise*, 30.
44. Friedrich Sengle, *Biedermeierzeit: Deutsche Literatur im Spannungsfeld zwischen Restauration und Revolution 1815–1848*, vol. 2, *Die Formenwelt* (Stuttgart: Metzler, 1972), 982–84.
45. Schuchalter, *Frontier*, 207.
46. E.g., the police spy report composed after his flight (*Briefe*, 73).
47. Rollin G. Osterweis, *Romanticism and Nationalism in the Old South* (Gloucester, Mass.: Peter Smith, 1964), 6, 48.

loom larger in the ideological fabric of his fiction than they did in his environment.

A good example of this is his treatment of Catholicism. His intense hostility to Catholicism is a prominent feature of his texts and may at first look like the zealotry of the lapsed monk.[48] But here, as elsewhere, he is drawing upon an element from his American social and political environment, for there was a vast amount of anti-Catholic agitation in his time. This movement was part of American nativism, a posture that Sealsfield, with his hostility to immigrants, especially the Irish, also assumed. He twice refers with gratification to one of the most spectacular events of this epoch, the burning by a mob of the Ursuline convent in Charlestown, Massachusetts, on August 11, 1834: once in *Die Deutsch-amerikanischen Wahlverwandtschaften* (*Werke*, 22[2]:315), and once in *Das Kajütenbuch,* where the narrator, Colonel Morse, remarks that "das amerikanische Volk" burned such places down "mit dem sichern Takte, der es stets leitet" (*Werke*, 16:36). However, despite the noisiness and vigor of the anti-Catholic agitation, it never became a successful political force; when it became organized in the Know-Nothing party, it foundered in ridicule after a few electoral successes.[49] Furthermore, so many of those in the forefront of the movement were such evident crackpots that it is troubling to see Sealsfield in their company.

The anti-Catholic theme is naturally most prominent in those texts dealing with Mexico and Texas: *Der Virey,* "Die Prärie am Jacinto" in *Das Kajütenbuch,* and *Süden und Norden.* Here, too, one might look at American literary models, such as Timothy Flint's *Francis Berrian* (1826) or Anthony Ganilh's *Mexico versus Texas* (1838). These texts also depict a superiority of American culture over the Mexican that justifies Texan independence as, in part, a confrontation with the obscurantist, repressive, superstitious hold that the Catholic church maintained over the Mexican people. But if we look more closely, we shall find once again that the American writers have a more nuanced perspective. Flint, who was himself a Protestant

---

48. Although there is no direct evidence, I think it not improbable that he may have converted to a Protestant denomination and may even have been ordained; he did, after all, identify himself as a "clergyman" on his passport (*Briefe,* 109). Grünzweig (*Das demokratische Kanaan,* 192) doubts that Sealsfield's anti-Catholic affect is to be interpreted biographically. Schnitzler (*Erfahrung,* 27), on the other hand, argues that Sealsfield's identity as a Catholic priest determined his perceptions at all times.

49. Ray Allen Billington, *The Protestant Crusade 1800–1860: A Study of the Origins of American Nativism* (Gloucester, Mass.: Peter Smith, 1963), 380–429. On the burning of the convent, see 68–95.

clergyman, takes a sufficiently condescending view of the Spanish culture in Mexico, and one of his main characters is an evilly intriguing priest. Yet he is able to see the situation also through Spanish eyes: "They had been accustomed to consider us as a nation of pedlars and sharpers, immoderately addicted to gain, and sordid in the last degree; that we were a kind of atheistic *canaille,* on an entire level, without models of noble and chivalrous feeling; in short, a kind of fierce and polished savages, whose laws and institutions were graduated soly with a view to gain."[50] To this it is replied, not altogether fairly, that only lower-class Americans have such prejudice against the Spanish.[51] But at least there is a comparative view of intolerance. Flint's novel ends with a Protestant-Catholic marriage in a Catholic ceremony; the boys are to be raised as Protestants, the girls as Catholics, and the narrator remarks, quite in contrast to Sealsfield's views of miscegenation, that "crossing the breed," as in agriculture, "is considered a great improvement."[52] Ganilh's novel, no less insistent on Mexican backwardness in the grip of Catholic bigotry, begins and ends with mixed marriages; the consequence of the first liaison is a protagonist who is raised as a Mexican aristocrat, thus providing a contrasting point of view to that of the Texans, internal to the Mexican cause, for much of the novel. In one place, the author introduces a refugee from anti-Catholic persecution in the United States who makes a direct reference to the notorious convent burning and predicts that all Catholics will emigrate to Texas when Mexico has completed its conquest;[53] thus we see how bigotry cuts both ways.

What I am endeavoring to argue here is that the question of whether Sealsfield is to be located in a European or an American literary tradition is wrongly put; rather, I suggest, he is not to any significant extent in any literary tradition at all. He is a writer who wittingly and zealously placed himself in an ideological context and drew indiscriminately on all resources to nourish it: personal experience (about which we know almost nothing); atmospherics (Jacksonianism, anti-Catholicism, defenses of slavery); elaborated doctrine (an example would be Jefferson's *Notes on the State of Virginia,* a passage from which he applied, or rather, misapplied as a motto to *Der*

---

50. Timothy Flint, *Francis Berrian or the American Patriot* (Boston: Cumming, Hilliard, and Company, 1826), 103.

51. Flint, *Francis Berrian,* 104.

52. Flint, *Francis Berrian,* 266.

53. Anthony Ganilh, *Mexico versus Texas, A Descriptive Novel, Most of the Characters of Which Consist of Living Persons, By a Texian* (Philadelphia: N. Siegfried, 1838), 157–58. Ganilh, incidentally, was clearly, if ironically and obliquely, opposed to slavery; one of his characters is a learned and philosophical escaped slave of considerable wit and dignity.

Legitime und die Republikaner [*Werke,* 6(1):iv] and which may have been a major source of his racism);[54] and fiction, which for Sealsfield's purposes has a status no different from that of any other stimulus. A modern study on the development of racialist ideas as an ideology of white, "Anglo-Saxon" imperialism as manifest destiny shows with total clarity how faithfully Sealsfield reproduced the terms of public discourse in his environment. Whether it is a matter of the destiny of the superior white race "to bring good government, commercial prosperity, and Christianity to the American continent and to the world"; the acceptance of violent energy, addiction to conquest, and intolerance of the race; the association of blacks with animals (especially orangutans); the argument that Indians could not be domesticated, would have to be removed, and were doomed to extinction; the inclusion of the "Normans" into the racially exclusive heritage; the view that other peoples are unfit for self-government and that the Mexicans in particular were doomed to lose the struggle with the Anglo-Saxons "because they were a mixed, inferior race with considerable Indian and some black blood"; the depiction of Mexican men as shiftless and feeble but of Mexican women as sensual and desirable—it is all there, verbatim in the environment.[55] Horsman points out that the picture of the Indians given by the writers of the time, even Simms, was more positive than the image predominating in popular discourse.[56] I believe that the point could be expanded to all the elements in Sealsfield's ideological substance. Thus, his intertextuality is with the totality of public and popular discourse (including what passed for scientific discourse of the time in matters of race and ethnology), not primarily with literature.

His attitude to literature, and therefore to his own vocation as a writer, is not altogether easy to recover. His commentary on literature is scattered, for the most part occasional, and not infrequently banal; Ritter regards Sealsfield's mentions of authors as name dropping.[57] Indeed, in his letters,

---

54. Jefferson, as is well known, mulled the "hypothesis" of black inferiority; see Thomas Jefferson, *Notes on the State of Virginia* (1787 edition), ed. William Peden (Chapel Hill: University of North Carolina Press, 1955), 137–43. Schuchalter (*Frontier,* 166) remarks: "Implicit in the Jeffersonian vision was the idea of a slaveocracy."

55. Reginald Horsman, *Race and Manifest Destiny: The Origins of American Racial Anglo-Saxonism* (Cambridge, Mass.: Harvard University Press, 1981), 2, 72, 100, 142, 108–10, 164–66, 182, 210, 233–34.

56. Horsman, *Race,* 191.

57. Ritter, "Sealsfield," 51. Ritter also comments on Sealsfield's dubious literary judgments in "Charles Sealsfields 'Madonnas of(f) the Trails' im Roman *Das Kajütenbuch;* Oder: Zur epischen Zähmung der Frauen als Stereotype in der amerikanischen Südstaatenepik zwischen 1820 und 1850," *Yearbook of German-American Studies* 18 (1983): 92.

Sealsfield is often such a philistine that it is hard to detect the novelist at all, and one may be inclined to credit the early rumor that he had murdered the actual author and appropriated his works. Once in a while, for example, in his haggling with Cotta, he sounds as though he were writing primarily for money; late in life, in 1861, when he was worried about his finances, he grumbled, perhaps ironically, "Wird es recht schlimm, so greifen wir wieder zur Feder" (*Briefe*, 148, 154–55, 323). Schuchalter has speculated that if Sealsfield had not gone bankrupt as a planter, he might never have become a writer.[58] Some of his comments seem to make no sense at all. For example, when describing *Tokeah* to Cotta, he said, "das ganze ist in einen *Roman* auf die Art wie *Corinna* eingekleidet" (*Briefe*, 144). Neither *Tokeah* nor any other Sealsfield novel bears any detectable resemblance to Madame de Staël's *Corinne,* except insofar as the fiction in the latter is a pretext for the communication of travel impressions and doctrine. To be sure, certain literary antecedents were of some value to him. One was Bulwer-Lytton's *Pelham,* which Sealsfield praised several times and which had a detectable influence on *Die Deutsch-amerikanischen Wahlverwandtschaften.*[59] Sealsfield himself, however, put the most stress on Scott as his model. In his draft of an article for the Brockhaus encyclopedia in 1854, he credits himself with being the creator, "im nationalen oder höheren Volks-Romane," of a form in which the whole people is the hero (*Briefe*, 291), a concept that seems to derive from Scott, especially as, in his other extended passage of literary criticism, the preface to *Morton,* he claims that only Scott has raised the prestige of the novel, that he is now quoted by American and English statesmen like Horace or Tacitus, and that he is much superior to Goethe "in sittlich-patriotischer Hinsicht" (10[1]:6, 9). Scholars have tended to follow Sealsfield's lead and to acknowledge his discipleship to Scott.

But the question is whether Sealsfield's novels resemble Scott's in any significant way. Surely they do not in narrative tone. Scott is close to us readers and distanced from his subject; Sealsfield is inside his subject, across from us, like a teacher across from his pupils. One might ask whether Scott is not one more item that he snatched out of his American environ-

---

58. Schuchalter, *Frontier,* 36. We do not, it seems to me, certainly know that Sealsfield went bankrupt or even that he actually was a planter.

59. On the influence of *Pelham,* see my essay, "Charles Sealsfields *Deutsch-amerikanische Wahlverwandtschaften:* Ein Versuch," in *Exotische Welt in populären Lektüren,* ed. Anselm Maler (Tübingen: Niemeyer, 1990), 55–57. Sealsfield especially praised *Pelham* in the introduction to *Morton* (*Werke,* 10[1]:16).

ment. For Scott was very popular in the antebellum South as a neofeudal model; he was the genuine predecessor of Simms.[60] In contrast, the more populist and egalitarian Dickens was rejected in the South.[61] Sealsfield, too, came to have little regard for Dickens. In his Brockhaus article, he rejected as frivolous any claim that he was a disciple of Dickens, and, in a letter of 1860, he denounces Dickens's writing as "ein miserables Geschreibsel, absolut ekelhaft, ohne Geist" and asserts that he should have quit with *Nicholas Nickleby,* that is, with his third published novel near the beginning of his career (*Briefe,* 292, 316).

There is good reason to think that Sealsfield regarded literature as just another resource of the phenomenal world, "clothing" reality and ideas, as he remarked correctly of *Corinne,* in fictional guise. In 1847, he employed some contemporary American novels to retain impressions and estimate conditions, "wenn sich auch aus denselben wenig oder gar nichts benützen läßt" (*Briefe,* 218). In the *Morton* preface, he asserted that his tendency was higher than novelistic; it was historical, and his type of novel was designed to affect "die Bildung des Zeitalters" (*Werke,* 10[1]:18–19). For the Brockhaus article, he defined his purpose as depicting "die Republik der V. St. dem deutschen Publikum im Romangewande." The conventional materials of fiction—"Liebesszenen und Abentheuer"—were but a foil to the representation of the public and private life, past and future, of the American nation in order to provide a supplementary resource to history (*Briefe,* 291–92). However, these utterances seem to be somewhat reticent in regard to his actual purpose. For his novels are not only reportorial and (allegedly) mimetic; they are intensely didactic in their propagation of the Jacksonian, agrarian-patriarchal, internally democratic but externally hostile and aggressive, internally disciplined but externally anarchic society of the South and Southwest, with its values of life, liberty, and the pursuit of property as a new dispensation in human history, a utopia held up to forlorn contemplation by the backward, ossified, shackled societies of Europe. Consequently, just about all modern authorities, though they may differ considerably in details and perspectives, are in agreement that, when historical developments made this vision of America untenable, he abandoned his literary career, thus explicitly or implicitly giving support to the view that, for him, artistic creativity was wholly subordinate to the figu-

---

60. Osterweis, *Romanticism,* 17, 26, 47. Bulwer-Lytton was also popular in the South (29–30, 114). See also Horsman, *Race,* 39–41.

61. Osterweis, *Romanticism,* 38.

ration and transmission of ideology.[62] It would be fair to say, however, not that it was the Jacksonian movement that failed him, but that he was unable to live up to the Jacksonian movement's potential of democracy— that strand traced out in Arthur Schlesinger's classic study[63] that led to the widening of political participation, to the Locofocos, and to the administration of Martin Van Buren. It is true that any admirer of America might have been dismayed by the increasing crudity of political discourse and the shenanigans of the election campaign of 1840, memorably portrayed in *Die Deutsch-amerikanischen Wahlverwandtschaften,* but it is also true that Sealsfield was unable to show the working-class mobs—the Locofocos *were* the Jacksonians of the 1840s—as much tolerance as he had shown to the boorishness of Kentuckian Ralph Doughby, and he became wholly hostile to Van Buren, who, despite his fastidious tastes, so irritating to the public, was one of the most radically democratic presidents in U.S. history. Thus, novelist Sealsfield became a victim of his inflexibility, which strangled his creativity.

In itself this may not seem so remarkable. There are doubtless many cases in the history of letters where creativity subordinated to ideology fails when ideology, for one reason or another, is unable to sustain it. But the case becomes more curious if we find unusual literary quality in the writer. In the past, this was not much of an issue. Older critics did not think very highly of Sealsfield as an artist, finding him of interest for other reasons. He was regarded as slovenly in composition and macaronic if not rebarbative in style. But with the collapse in modern times of normative expectations brought to the novel, stronger claims have been made for his literary excellence. A transitional view was held by Norbert Fuerst: " . . . the strange thing is that, in spite of such primitive qualitative means,

---

62. Cf. Ritter, *Darstellung,* 235, n. 1, 314; Walter Grünzweig, *Charles Sealsfield* (Boise: Boise State University, 1985), 42; Schuchalter, *Frontier,* 56; Schnitzler, *Erfahrung,* 359. It should be remembered that Sealsfield did not conclude his writing career as abruptly as it may appear. According to Karl J. R. Arndt ("Newly Discovered Sealsfield Relationship Documented," *Modern Language Notes* 87 [1972]: 450–64), he may have been writing for New York newspapers as late as 1856 or 1857. In 1862, he thought about dictating his memoirs (*Briefe,* 330–31). More important, in the mid-1840s, he repeatedly refers to two works he has written but cannot yet publish (*Briefe,* 210–11, 215–16, 225, 228, 246). It is not clear why these works did not appear or why Sealsfield did not pursue publication more vigorously. Sengle (Biedermeierzeit, 3:793n), in keeping with his thesis of 1848 as a caesura in literary history, argues that Sealsfield was incongruent with the programmatic realism. But the documents suggest that the hindrance to publication was political, and that publication was held up by Sealsfield's publisher, Metzler (*Briefe,* 235, 246).

63. Arthur M. Schlesinger, Jr., *The Age of Jackson* (Boston: Little, Brown, 1946).

he achieves—in every volume—areas of sheer intensity, where his theme and his technique, his obsessions and his very shortcomings coalesce into a crude and boisterous fulfillment."[64] Ritter's study of Sealsfield's landscape depiction elevates him well above this level and makes strong claims for formal excellence.[65] Even stronger claims are made by Günter Schnitzler, who brings Sealsfield primarily into connection with the visual arts, with the landscape painting of Salvator Rosa, Claude Lorrain, and the Hudson River school.[66] Schuchalter speaks of "the loftiness of Sealsfield's intention" as "the progenitor of a new kind of novel" and defends his attention to form.[67] I, too, hold with these views. I submit that Sealsfield's excellence lies where his originality is found—in the ingenuity of form and the incomparable vitality of tone.

This does not mean, however, that he is locatable in literary history. His case may resemble that of Wilhelm Hauff, as it has recently been described. "Es kommt dann zu dem auf den ersten Blick paradoxen Befund, daß Hauffs Erzählen zwar zahlreiche literarische Einflüsse aufnimmt, Abhängigkeiten von anderen Autoren, ja Plagiate unschwer nachzuweisen sind, die Gesamtanlage wie die Struktur und Zielsetzung seines Werkes jedoch fast traditionslos dastehen."[68] Bernd Fischer, while acknowledging in a review of Grünzweig's study that there may be many parallels with American literature, recognizes "ein m. E. ungewöhnliches Maß an Risikobereitschaft . . ., die dann doch etwas an den jungdeutschen Roman erinnert."[69] Schuchalter argues that Sealsfield's "political vision . . . places his work firmly within the genre of utopian fiction."[70] But, if so, this is an assignment that we make retrospectively; there is no evidence that the

---

64. Norbert Fuerst, *The Victorian Age of German Literature: Eight Essays* (University Park and London: Pennsylvania State University Press, 1966), 44–45.

65. Ritter, *Darstellung.* Bernd Fischer ("Baumwolle und Indianer: Zu Charles Sealsfields *Der Legitime und die Republikaner,*" *Journal of German-American Studies* 19 [1984]: 86) opposes Ritter's aesthetic evaluation, at least for *Der Legitime.*

66. Schnitzler, *Erfahrung,* passim. Schnitzler was preceded by Beate Jahnel (*Charles Sealsfield und die Bildende Kunst* [Stuttgart: Charles Sealsfield Gesellschaft, 1985]), who compared Sealsfield's landscape descriptions to the paintings of the Hudson River school.

67. Schuchalter, *Frontier,* 215, 308–9.

68. Michael Limlei, *Geschichte als Ort der Bewährung: Menschenbild und Gesellschaftsverständnis im den deutschen historischen Romanen (1820–1890)* (Frankfurt am Main, Bern, New York, and Paris: Peter Lang, 1988), 78.

69. Bernd Fischer, review of *Das demokratische Kanaan* by Walter Grünzweig, *German Quarterly* 62 (1989): 126. As I indicated previously, I believe that Sealsfield puts every Young German novel into the shadow.

70. Schuchalter, *Frontier,* 310.

genre of utopian fiction was one of the sources of Sealsfield's imagination. His work might also be seen as an example of "authoritarian fiction," defined as "written in the realistic mode (that is, based on an aesthetic of verisimilitude and representation), which signals itself to the reader as primarily didactic in intent, seeking to demonstrate the validity of a political, philosophical, or religious doctrine."[71] The abrupt end to Sealsfield's literary career is all the more striking in view of the clear signs that his last works were growing stronger and more experimental. *Die Deutsch-amerikanischen Wahlverwandtschaften* is certainly the wittiest of his novels, and it contains an account of a storm at sea that might fairly be set beside Joseph Conrad's *Typhoon*;[72] ominously, it breaks off as a fragment at a scene hyperbolizing the donnybrook of a New York election campaign. *Das Kajütenbuch*, though certainly weak in its last sections, contains the most widely admired and best known of his writings, "Die Prärie am Jacinto." The last novel, *Süden und Norden,* is an extraordinary account of the disarray that can befall consiousness in an alien environment. Sealsfield himself rightly called it "ohne Zweifel das poetischste meiner Werke" (*Briefe,* 252). It is a novel that is, to a large extent, still to be discovered.[73] Yet this increase in artistic possibilities seems to have given no satisfaction; it could not compensate for the increasing untenability of the superintending ideological construct.

All literature lies in an order of literature, and all literature is determined and informed by its social, political, and historical context. But literary history must recognize that cases differ in their proportions. Sealsfield is strongly shifted away from the order of literature. Yet it is for this very

71. Susan Rubin Suleiman, *Authoritarian Fiction: The Ideological Novel as a Literary Genre* (New York: Columbia University Press, 1983), 7. Suleiman's reiterated insistence that the authoritarian novel be unambiguous in meaning and interpretation (54, 59, 67, 71) would not apply to Sealsfield.

72. To be sure, storms or calms at sea were staples in the German emigration novels. See Juliane Mikoletzky, *Die deutsche Amerika-Auswanderung des 19. Jahrhunderts in der zeitgenössischen fiktionalen Literatur* (Tübingen: Niemeyer, 1988), 205–12. But it should be remembered that Sealsfield comes very early in the sequence of this genre.

73. For a thoughtful interpretation, see Andreas Peter, *Charles Sealsfields Mexiko-Romane: Zur raum-zeitlichen Strukturierung und Bedeutung der Reisemotivik* (Stuttgart: Charles Sealsfield Gesellschaft, 1983). Peter believes that the novel images the collapse of a private utopia and, therefore, signals the renunciation of Sealsfield's career (117). A similar position, without going into the novel in any detail, is taken by Harald Eggebrecht, *Sinnlichkeit und Abenteuer: Die Entstehung des Abenteuerromans im 19. Jahrhundert* (Berlin and Marburg: Guttandin und Hoppe, 1985), p. 160. Eggebrecht argues that Sealsfield's enduring value lies not in his political realism but in his probes into the "Zwischenraum" of the imagination (see esp. 149).

reason that it is in his literary artistry that his originality lies. His inter-textuality relates not to literature as such, but primarily to the ideological public discourse of the antebellum South, of which literature is only a part, and by no means the most privileged part. It is here that his intentionality was overtly centered, but also here where he is least original. Thus, this innately gifted, mentally energetic, eccentrically innovative writer ulti-mately missed his vocation in two ways. He came to occupy a subordinate and eventually rather obscure place in the history of literature because he was unable or unwilling to invest in the artistry potentially at his command, and he lost the thread of his purpose as an enlightener and liberator because he allowed himself to become so ideologically frozen into a historical moment as to be unable to cope with its dynamic and dialectic. Schuchalter observes: "In not believing in America, Sealsfield could not fully believe in himself. He thus became a fractured, fragmented personality."[74] Seen in this light, he is perhaps a cautionary case.

---

74. Schuchalter, *Frontier,* 56.

Experiment in Denial:
A Reading of the *Gartenlaube* in
the Year 1890

Peter Gay

From its first appearance in 1853, the *Gartenlaube* presented itself as a family magazine and promptly elected itself a member of the family it proposed to serve. Ernst Keil, its founder, sounded the note of good-humored intimacy in the opening number in an address to his readers: "*Grüss Euch Gott,* dear folks in the German land!" He was offering them a present, to be added to those the Christ Child had brought the week before: a "new little sheet—*ein kleines Blättchen!* Peruse it in a quiet hour!" It was to be read "in the circle of your loved ones during long winter evenings, by the snug stove," or "in the spring, with a few friends in the shady arbor, when the white and red blossoms drop from the apple tree." His magazine, he wrote, was intended for "home and family"; it was "a book for big and small, for everyone who has a warm heart beating beneath his ribs, who still takes pleasure in the good and noble. Far from all disputatious politics [*räsonnierende Politik*] and from all conflicts of religious or other opinions," the *Gartenlaube* aimed to introduce its readers to "the history of the human heart and of the nations," to provide them with "a knowledgeable guide to the workshop of human knowledge," to tell them about "the beautiful secrets of nature, the artful construction of man and his organs," and whatever might be of interest in human activity. "So we want to entertain you, and in entertaining, instruct you. And over all shall hover the breath of poetry, like fragrance on the blooming flower, and you shall feel homey in our arbor—*es soll Euch anheimeln in unserer Gartenlaube,* in which you will find good German *Gemütlichkeit.*" This is the garrulous intrusiveness of the hearty, widely traveled uncle recounting his discoveries in exotic climes, of the well-meaning aunt worried about the children's health, of the dashing cousin bursting to enumerate his conquests in love and war.

Keil's manifesto was prophetic of much that was to come. If its coziness seems a little strained now, the *Gartenlaube* was, after all, not written for twentieth-century cultural historians. In its day, and for its public, the manner pleased and the formula worked. Keil assembled, and after his death in 1878 his successors retained at least for some years, a stable of contributors—novelists, biographers, travel writers, didactic physicians— who worked in the same vein and to the same purpose: to entertain and, in entertaining, instruct. All had the unmistakable tone of the *Gartenlaube*. And at the end of each issue, the editors sustained the general harmony with unsigned commentaries: glosses on the more important illustrations, biographical information on a noted author, solicitations for a monument to a forgotten German hero or a pension to ease the lonely old age of a neglected German writer, and, on occasion, sober but satisfied reflections on the rise of the magazine to unrivaled eminence.

Concluding the last number for 1890, when the *Gartenlaube* was an old and trusted member of the family, the editors permitted themselves one of these self-referential retrospects. They had every right to feel complacent: with a print run of about 300,000 copies, they could safely count on a readership of well over a million faithful. This meant that the *Gartenlaube* far outstripped rival periodicals, like *Daheim,* and, for that matter, most daily newspapers. Its circulation reflected not some sudden upsurge of popularity, but a persistent capacity to please. As the editorial fondly noted, families who had begun their subscriptions in the 1850s had kept them up through the decades and evidently taught their children to imitate them in this, as in so much else. The editors did not affect astonishment at this gratifying state of business. They saw their journal as the kind of fare a decent family would want to consume: now, as ever, the *Gartenlaube* kept away from "everything immature and unclean." Moreover, it had secured long-lived loyalties by judiciously mixing reverence for tradition with interest in innovation. "To enable such connections to persist, from one family generation to the next, requires a faithful clinging to goals established as good and just, and resolute progress on well-tried paths."

The editorial was, as usual, chatty, confiding, insinuating, talking man to man, or man to woman. Its prose is as bland as the recipe it outlines, and the editors, almost as if sensing the risks of torpor implicit in such writing and such aspirations, found it useful to underscore their alert commitment to modernity. "It is not as though the *Gartenlaube* narrow-mindedly rejects the new: that would be to misunderstand the qualities that made it great, and to misunderstand the tasks placed before it." They were, after all, imposing tasks: in addition to being mature, clean, conservative, and liberal, the *Gartenlaube* also undertook to be comprehensive in its cultural concerns. It "ever was and should be" a "mirror of its age and a guide to its age." However we choose to read this rather awkward pair of metaphors, they stake out ambitious aims. The *Gartenlaube* bravely refused to be judged as mere escape literature; it presumed to look at its world with open eyes, responsibly and candidly, seeing it all. And in the Germany of 1890, there was much to see.

As everyone knows, 1890 was a critical year for the Empire. In mid-March, Wilhelm II, who had succeeded to the Imperial and the Prussian thrones less than two years before, compelled Bismarck to hand in his resignation. It was, almost literally, a stunning event. Bismarck had become, partly by his own doing and partly with the aid of assiduous admirers, a legend in his lifetime. He had practically invented the German Reich and had dominated Prussian—and, with that, German—politics for more than twenty-seven years. Most Germans, and many foreigners, found a Germany without Bismarck inconceivable. It had seemed that only God could remove him. Now Emperor Wilhelm II, already notorious for his prodigious energies, ubiquitous interest, and tactless speeches, had anticipated the divine decree. Within a few months, Bismarck's abrupt disappearance into the wings of history generated far-reaching changes in foreign and domestic policy: an end to Bismarck's stabilizing diplomacy, the cautious maneuverings of a satiated empire, and an end to the Anti-Socialist law, on the books for twelve years. With that, the Social Democratic Party reemerged as a legal and increasingly authoritative spokesman for Germany's working class. This, in turn, implied new initiatives in (or at least new talk about) what was called "the social question," which, of all questions, troubled thoughtful Germans most. The departure of Bismarck did not have to wait for historians to seem a historic moment for the German Reich. Tenniel's often reprinted cartoon in *Punch,* depicting the venerable pilot departing from his post, permits us to recapture the depth and immediacy of the shock it records.

In literature and in the arts, too, there was more life, more controversy, in 1890 than there had been for decades. The brute realities of urbanization, the social dislocations inherent in innovative technology, the persistent conflicts between capital and labor were beginning to make their way into the theater and the novel. It was in January, 1890, that Otto Brahm launched his *Freie Bühne für modernes Leben,* a weekly at once civilized and aggressive, that, as its name suggests, stood for experimentation, for frank naturalism, for the uncompromising acceptance of the modern. "Art," Brahm promised in the first number, "shall stand in the center of our aspirations; the new art which looks at reality and the life of the present." The word inscribed on its banner, he wrote, was *truth;* the mortal enemy was, logically enough, "the lie." If the rhetoric was scarcely an innovation, the intent behind it was; as Brahm sought to monopolize the truth for his party, playwrights sympathetic to his cause were making ready to offend the establishment and painters to affront the academy. The dismissal of Bismarck, pregnant with great consequences, was a reflection, a highly visible symptom, of a Germany in turmoil, of a society beset with uncertainty and anxiety.

Yet in the pages of the *Gartenlaube,* mirror and guide, all was placid. In its twenty-eight issues for 1890, there is no divorce, no slum life, no religious bigotry, no political confrontation. There are no Social Democrats; the only reference to the "Red Specter" appears in a backward glance, in an unsympathetic, even horrified account of the Paris Commune, now safely nineteen years in the past. There is still a trade in slaves in remotest central Africa; but while the *Gartenlaube* permits itself a show of indignation, this residue of barbarism, it cheerily notes, is on the wane. And there is still the scourge of disease—indeed, much of the tension and charm would have gone out of the *Gartenlaube* if some miraculous cure-all had banished illness from the world. But disease, too, is now retreating; thanks to such medical pioneers as Robert Koch, to whom the *Gartenlaube* devotes a worshipful article, one of the most vicious of maladies, tuberculosis, seems now curable. The march of modern science, *German* science, offers the *Gartenlaube* grounds for realistic rejoicing and patriotic pride. Koch had discovered the antituberculosis vaccine not by a "lucky accident," but through "the most organized, most strenuous labor." And it seemed to the *Gartenlaube* that it was precisely this quality of deliberation and effort that imprinted his achievement with "the stamp of *German* science." But the writer immediately—I am tempted to say hastily—adds, "Where the welfare of humanity is concerned, there are no national barriers. Honor to the good, wherever its origins! Yet we Germans can still be proud to call this man, who has accomplished so great a thing, a son of our fatherland." The *Gartenlaube* of 1890 is nothing if not patriotic, but even patriotism is most acceptable when it is least aggressive; national pride must not obstruct international concord. This kind of modest boasting is an essential element in the implicit message and deliberate policy of this "illustrated family paper": all is well, and getting better, and all will continue to get still better to the extent that one can please oneself without displeasing others.

Culture, for the *Gartenlaube,* is predictably as harmonious as politics or society and far less eventful. The *Gartenlaube* knows no debates, let alone quarrels, among schools of poets, painters, or composers. Contentions between rebellious Naturalists and respectable literary conservatives are so distant that their noise does not penetrate to its domain. In all of the 898 folio pages that make up the volume for 1890, the *Gartenlaube* devoted, in addition to the usual commentaries on its pictures, a bare dozen articles relating more or less directly to the arts. They turn out to be celebrations and commemorations prompted by anniversaries, birthdays, or the unveiling of a monument. Some are obituaries, like the expansive piece on one Karl Eulenstein, late virtuoso on the mouth harmonica. And some of them are barely disguised self-advertisements: an essay on Theodor Fontane's seventieth birthday happily coincides with the serialization of his novel, *Quitt;* an appreciation of the popular poet Herman Lling calls attention to a regular contributor. Clearly, the *Gartenlaube* of 1890 liked to remember anniversaries, praise its authors, perhaps best of all, to bring wreaths to funerals. Hegel's epigram about philosophy, that belated discipline, applies to the *Gartenlaube* in the year of Bismarck's capitulation: in its pages, the owl of Minerva spread its wings only with the coming of the dusk.

Not even Bismarck's fall could ruffle its composure. Its first allusion to that momentous event came in the shape of a portrait, on the front page, of the new chancellor, von Caprivi—a superb piece of diplomatic deviousness. In its customary commentary on the engraving, the *Gartenlaube* devotes a few sentences to Caprivi's illustrious predecessor, cast in the breathless style German writers normally adopted when they had occasion to speak of Bismarck: he was "a man unprecedented in the history of our nation, almost unprecedented in the history of humanity." Quite explicitly, the *Gartenlaube* refuses to dig beneath the surface of contemporary politics. "This is not the place to discuss the reasons and the frame of mind that induced Prince Bismarck to return his posts to the hands of his Emperor. Suffice it to say: he departed." Thus, the *Gartenlaube* chose to present the polite and palpable fiction of Bismarck's voluntary resignation as the literal truth. This was not just the embarrassed subterfuge of an editorial staff too shocked to respond properly. In its next issue, the *Gartenlaube* printed an engraving depicting "Bismarck's Farewell to Berlin," noted in pathetic tones the "great chancellor's" decision to "conclude his days in rural retirement in Friedrichsruh," and reported deep emotion among the people of Berlin, "penetrated by the conviction . . . that the chancellor *wanted* to leave" and certain that "the Emperor felt his decision as strongly as the most enthusiastic supporter of the departing man." This was an adroit displacement of emphasis from the writers in the *Gartenlaube,* and from the protagonists in the high drama, to the Berlin populace. Yet, for all these disclaimers and soft deceptions, it is as incredible that the *Gartenlaube* was trying to mislead its readers about the true circumstances of Bismarck's retirement as that these readers should be dim enough to mistake a dismissal for a resignation.

I call it a ritual to emphasize the share of convention in this transaction. It was not a lie in the ordinary sense, for a lie is designed to deceive. It was, rather, a thoroughly understood though tacit manner of facing the world by not facing it or, at least, by facing it through the mists of an obsessive optimism. If there was deception here, it was a self-deception in which both partners shared. Certainly, the ritual contained an admixture of magical thinking, as do all rituals not wholly reduced to a mechanical exercise: the anxious hope that gentle talk will somehow smoothe the edges of rough reality, and that the reiterated proclamation of concord will somehow lower the temperature of conflict. Such willed gentility, whatever its consequences, is not a sign of unrealistic unawareness. Quite the contrary, gentility is a search for safety, and one seeks safety only when one senses danger. Reticence is not a synonym for ignorance; it suggests, rather, a *longing* for ignorance that suggests an uneasy awareness of unwelcome, or at least problematic, realities.

The *Gartenlaube* of 1890 did not wholly banish such realities; it is possible to extract a consistent set of political and social views, or at least attitudes, from its pages. The magazine was ostentatiously devoted to the Imperial house: the two-page engraving of the Empress Auguste Victoria that presided over the first issue was emblematic of a loyalty firmly held—at least, persistently displayed. Yet at the same time, as I have noted, the *Gartenlaube* was conciliatory in its nationalism, earnestly hopeful for social peace at home and pacific diplomacy abroad. Its celebration of the newly acquired isle of Helgoland, transferred by treaty from England to Germany in the summer of 1890, is characteristic. "It is rare in our day," the journal notes, "that a piece of European territory changes hands from one state to another, not after a bloody clash of arms but a free, diplomatic agreement." A triumphant *Gartenlaube,* it would seem, rejoiced in the manner of this acquisition at least as much as in the acquisition itself. Its enthusiasm for the promise of science, medicine, and technology is entirely congruent with such a lack of militancy: it is the arts of peace, far more than the arts of war, that will bring the progress for which the *Gartenlaube* professes to stand. Thus it can grow quite as lyrical over so prosaic a theme as the electric works of Berlin as it does over England's surrender of Helgoland: the power plant embodies the miraculous energies of nature harnessed and the possibility of great things to come—a veritable "fairy land world" of clean, safe light. Most of the magazine's causes are safe enough. Neither the lists of missing persons for which the *Gartenlaube* was famous nor its appeal for a monument to Hoffmann von Fallersleben, the author of Germany's best-known nationalist anthem, was exactly controversial. But there are occasions when a writer takes an advanced position. In a well-reasoned, businesslike essay on the place of women in medicine, Professor Dr. Hermann v. Meyer refutes the standard charges against women as physicians—their presumed physical weakness, intellectual incompetence, and moral susceptibility—and advocates their unrestricted admission to medical schools and medical practice. At such moments, the mirror becomes the guide.

In 1890, the *Gartenlaube* remained faithful to the digestible didactic program it had outlined over thirty-five years before: to entertain and, by entertaining, instruct and thus to enlarge the circle of culture. Its rare, cautious ventures into political and social controversy do not pretend to be penetrating analyses or searching criticisms; they are invitations to *Bildung*. In his long, perceptive review of *Rembrandt als Erzieher*, Julius Langbehn's anonymous, notorious diatribe against "modern leveling," Johannes Proelss, a regular and versatile contributor, poet, essayist, and novelist, complains of Langbehn's feeble scholarship, narrow-minded parochialism, ill-tempered tone, and, principally, his false populism. While Langbehn celebrates the *Volk*, Proelss notes, his only possible readers are the highly educated; Langbehn thus grossly "underestimates" how far "the popularization of knowledge and of art" has already gone. It is a shrewd hit and an instructive self-appraisal. For saleable as Langbehn's manifesto proved to be, it neither drew from nor appealed to the plain people it hailed as the root of all German virtue. And what Proelss diagnoses as Langbehn's failure—to be truly popular—was, he implies, precisely the *Gartenlaube*'s success.

Yet, at least in 1890, success of this kind did exact the price of denial. What little politics there is in the *Gartenlaube* is hazy and inconsequential. There are a few observations, a few moments of recognition, but nothing more. A substantial and sympathetic review of Edward Bellamy's *Looking*

Backward asks rhetorically, "Who today, whether in America or Europe, fails to take an interest in that great question, the possible settlement of social conflicts which, year by year, kindle into ever more dangerous flame the struggle between interest groups in modern society? In the princely castle and the peasant's hut, among the whirring wheels of our industrial cities and the soft noise of a pen in the quiet study of the scholar—everywhere this greatest of questions about human progress finds its echo." But in the *Gartenlaube*, the echo is faint. It raises the social question but immediately retreats from possibly inconvenient answers by insisting that Bellamy's utopia is a fable rather than a serious proposal for social policy or political reform. Feeble as the *Gartenlaube*'s recognition of social conflicts may have been, its will to action fell short even of that.

The *Gartenlaube*, to be sure, never intended to be a political journal. But its political pieces are consistent, in intention and presentation, with the rest of its offerings—its travel pieces, its biographical articles, its reportage on natural history and natural science, its fiction, and its art. In each of its departments, the *Gartenlaube* performed the rituals of denial with equal deftness. Discretion is king. Evidently, the publisher judged the curiosity of his readers to be unquenchable, for he sought to gratify their appetite with exotic fare: meticulously illustrated series on deep-sea fauna, boyish reminiscences of African adventures, and wide-eyed explorations of medical science, that inexhaustible source of astonishment and hope. With its peculiar mixture of commercial calculation and pedagogic earnestness, the *Gartenlaube* liked to open windows to the unknown—and the unthreatening. It was pieces on "Stanley in Darkest Africa" or birds in battle over German lands that its youthful readers would recall decades later as memorable introductions to tantalizing mysteries. Dependable and informal, these articles interested many and offended no one. And wherever appropriate, their authors would add reassurance to instruction: an article on the wounds that modern military technology can inflict opens with an invocation to peace and the prayer that a future war be "postponed to some unforeseeable distance." Even so obviously political and potentially controversial a subject as German colonialism is translated, in the *Gartenlaube*, into an anodyne essay in biography and soothing prognosis. An article on imperialist prophet and activist Karl Peters suggests that the "Sturm und Drang period of our colonial activity is now over," and the "era of a calmer, constructive labor has begun." There is, for the readers of the *Gartenlaube*, much to learn and nothing to worry about.

At first glance, the melodramatic stories and novels of the *Gartenlaube* seem in striking contrast to the deliberate restraint of the rest. But only at first glance. The fictions of the *Gartenlaube* are palpably that, fictions; it is not necessary, indeed hardly possible, to suspend disbelief for them. In these tales, imaginary characters yield to all the emotions and act out all the aggressions that the *Gartenlaube* consistently edited out of its treatment of the real world. The novels are safe; as with the articles on German Imperialism or technical innovation, nothing follows from them. The oaths, the blood, the poetic justice are displacements, pure—or, rather, impure—theater.

There is certainly a great deal of activity in this fiction. Fathers curse sons, sons kneel at the feet of their mothers, lovers shower passionate kisses on their beloved's upturned face, handsome men suffer hideous mutilation, fierce pride produces obstacles to careers or marriages, noble soldiers falsely accused of treachery redeem themselves with superhuman feats of heroism. Authors set the stage swiftly, usually in the opening paragraph, after providing a bit of *Stimmung* with an anthropomorphic allusion to nature: sunshine dazzles, storms threaten, birds wing their way into the unknown. This symbolic freight is heavy but not bulky; authors are intent on plunging rapidly into a confrontation and etching, with brusque economy, the characters that will keep the faithful reader company for some weeks. Everything tells, everything serves to divide the cast into heroes and villains, instantly. Work of features, quality of voice, style of speech settle, without delay and without appeal, the fictive actor's place in the tale. The characters rarely disclose themselves expressively; their creators present their puppets to the readers, permitting them little play for imagination and virtually no room for interpretation. Novels in the *Gartenlaube* are not strangers to development: a headstrong protagonist learns to value the virtues of his stern and distant father; a cool heiress melts, at long last, under the warmth of love. But such journeys from ignorance to insight, superficial flaws to underlying goodness, are built into the beginning of the story and present no surprise to the alert consumer. They *are,* by and large, the story, arousing the pleasing anxiety of bearable suspense, bearable because readers can confidently predict that their hero will learn his lesson, his heroine discover her heart.

The sound effects accompanying these characters are as unmeasured as the actions into which they plunge. The pages of *Gartenlaube* novels are awash with terrible, wild laughter, ear-splitting screams of horror, and uncontained floods of despairing tears. And they provide the Freudian with a feast. When the tall and vital adolescent protagonist of E. Werner's

Flammenzeichen first meets and recognizes his mother, after a long banishment to which his unbending father had consigned her years before, the boy throws himself into her outstretched arms and lets her "overwhelm" him with "hot caresses" and "sweet, tender endearments." For some time, "everything else vanished from sight in the floods of this stormy rapture." Still more telling is the opening scene of Hermann Heiberg's *Ein Mann:* a willful, spoiled young lady, much given to such boyish pursuits as hunting, accidentally discharges her gun and shoots out an eye of her father's valued associate. Castration proves prelude to infatuation. Incredibly noble, the victim never reproaches the girl for his disfigurement, falls in love with her, and is loved in return. But the couple's road is far from smooth; they are kept apart by false shame and misplaced pride. It is only when blindness threatens the man's remaining eye and a risky operation becomes imperative that the girl rushes to the rescue. "Richard Tromhold did not tremble under the physician's instrument. With quiet composure, Susanna's hand held his in her own; a steadying power streamed from her into his nerves, while the decisive work was accomplished." The operation is a success, and Tromhold's sight is preserved. Two weeks later, when Susanna meets him at the hospital, "they sank onto one another's breast in the stormy overflow of their feelings, intoxicated with happiness. And from the saved eye of the man there streamed hot tears of love and unutterable gratitude to destiny." It is, with the best of intentions, one of the most repellent endings in modern German literature.

The novelists of the *Gartenlaube* were no more stereotyped than its readers, but, like those readers, made up a distinct, recognizable family. That occasional visitor, Theodor Fontane, was, of course, a far more distinguished writer than regular feeders of fiction like E. Werner or Hermann Heiberg, and none of these remotely reached the almost charismatic appeal of Keil's fortunate discovery, E. Marlitt, who, from the late 1860s on, regularly supplied the *Gartenlaube* (and markedly increased its circulation) with novel after novel. Yet all of these novelists had much, or were tailored to have much, in common. They all aimed at rapidity of development, vehemence of action, simplicity of characterization. Fontane's *Quitt* was, like *Unterm Birnbaum,* his earlier contribution to the *Gartenlaube,* a tale of crime and punishment, and, in any event, the editors relentlessly pruned its bulk and excised its refinements to fit their perception of their readers' tastes. They even forced on it their favorite signature—the last sentence of the novel recapitulating its title—by cutting Fontane's original ending and concluding, predictably, with the word *Quitt.* When the tried recipe of the *Gartenlaube* clashed with the individual production of its novelists, it was not the recipe that was compelled to yield.

It would have been surprising if, in a family magazine as carefully nurtured and closely supervised as the *Gartenlaube,* its art should have escaped the reigning formula. In his opening statement of 1853, Ernst Keil had announced that his *Blättchen* would bring its readers "decorative and explanatory illustrations by recognized artists," and he always paid attention to its visual presentations. By 1890, the *Gartenlaube* offered its readers, in addition to a generous sprinkling of vignettes, meticulous maps, full-page and sometimes two-page engravings, two-color reproductions of "original paintings." The first of these, presented "to its readers" as an "Easter greeting," is a sentimental rustic scene, *Young Life:* a little girl offering a bunch of spring flowers to a young peasant woman. The second, its pendant, presented at Christmas, moves from country to city and childhood to young womanhood. *Zum Weihnachtsball* has a certain pathos of its own: the debutante stands in her most formal gown, stiff, touchingly nervous in her long gloves, fur piece, and holding a fan, being observed by an elderly couple, probably her parents, with a mixture of pride and concern.

These special gifts were representative of pictorial art in the *Gartenlaube.* Many of the engravings, to be sure, made no pretense of decorating and tried only to explain. And they explained very well. A biographical article on Samuel Smiles and a piece on the seventy-fifth anniversary of the *Burschenschaften* gain much by the accompanying portraits; the articles on nature history or modern industry are, as I have noted, intelligently and accurately illustrated. Vignettes showing interesting inventions or unusual trees are as lively as they are informative. An article commemorating the 450th anniversary of printing has no fewer than seven illustrations, including four large and readable specimens of early typefaces. But most of the art in the *Gartenlaube* was for art's sake. And that art constitutes a denial, not only of life, but of art itself. It would not be possible to infer from these reproductions even a breath of controversy, let alone widespread turmoil, among painters. The editors' rage to educate their readers obviously did not extend to this domain. Avoidance of tension happily went hand in hand with real preferences. There is good reason to believe that both editors and readers really liked the narrative, decorous, wholly academic art that covered page upon page of the *Gartenlaube.* But it remains striking to note how consistently the magazine, both in its articles and its reproductions, ignored the newer schools active both abroad and in Germany. On the rare occasions that a rebellious Impressionist such as Max Liebermann or a romantic classicist such as Arnold Böcklin got access to the *Gartenlaube,* its choice invariably fell on one of their least venturesome productions, made still less venturesome by the engraver's tools. Only three of the many painters exhibiting in the *Gartenlaube* of 1890 have secured as much as a footnote in the history of art: Franz Defregger appears twice with characteristic peasant scenes; Franz Stuck once, with a symbolic, coarse vignette; and Eduard Grützner, who specialized in gourmandizing priests, with a typical example of his cheerful and monotonous anecdotal art.

Neither these, nor any other reproductions, jar the artfully composed harmony of these pages. The readers of the *Gartenlaube* obviously enjoyed the kind of humor that would bring a knowing smile, or the pathos that would bring a sympathetic lump in the throat: a visit to the marriage broker elicited the first of these responses, the unhappy widow sacrificing her last cherished remembrance the second. These readers also enjoyed seeing children and animals and, even more, children with animals. They enjoyed a touch of terror: the fabulous Lorelei luring her bewitched lover to his horrific end; the boy shepherd lost on the perilous mountainside and staring into the abyss. But best of all, they enjoyed pictures of love, in all its varied presentable—which is to say, respectable—forms: the classically garbed young woman shaking cupid from the tree; the sumptuously dressed lady holding a *billet doux;* the innocent young thing dreaming, perhaps, of forbidden matters; the lover departing—or advancing.

Far rarer, but for the historian possibly more instructive, are engravings that have art itself as its subject. *The Judgment of Paris,* depicting a priest holding an apple and pondering three rustic Italian beauties grouped picturesquely around a well, splendidly exemplifies a favorite genre: the humorous, trivializing treatment of a classic theme. Such a picture at once flatters its public with the broad hint that, of course, it understands the literary allusion while, at the same time, it provides a mild erotic thrill: the priest's comic dilemma is set off by the virile soldiers standing by him, appraising the nubile girls. Whatever we might call such, and similar, illustrations, the *Gartenlaube* would have scorned the label of philistine for itself. One of its large reproductions shows a picture gallery, crammed with paintings, copyists, and visitors young and old displaying a variety of attitudes toward the art around them. The gloss on this picture demonstrates that neither its painter nor its commentator has the slightest patience with art that refuses to be anecdotal, sentimental, or heroic. Yet the commentator singles out one person in the painting, the one bravely, dutifully following his catalog, as a "good philistine." Like many other Germans locating themselves in their culture, the *Gartenlaube* unhesitatingly distanced itself from the uncultured and defined the philistine as Someone Else. At least in its own eyes, then, the *Gartenlaube* held no reasonable doubt that it possessed, and had a mission to diffuse, *Bildung*. Nor could anyone else doubt that, at least in 1890, the periodical had realized the aim first announced in 1853: it stayed away from all disputatious politics. In the year of Bismarck's dismissal, the *Gartenlaube* indirectly, but emphatically, solicited its family of readers to practice the politics of denial.

Just reading the *Gartenlaube* is too easy; placing it in imperial culture is far more difficult. Its calculated evasions, its strenuous triviality, appear to be symptoms, and perhaps causes, of that familiar figure of fun and lamentations, the apolitical German, ill-prepared to confront, in fact thoroughly trained to overlook, unpleasing social realities. But, as usual, appearances are deceptive. The *Gartenlaube* of 1890 cannot presume to represent the *Gartenlaube* of earlier years. We know that Ernst Keil had launched his magazine promising to keep it clear of political involvement. But this explicit abstention from politics was, in itself, a political act. Keil had conceived the idea for the *Gartenlaube* in the fortress of Hubertusburg, to which he had been sentenced for printing offensive cartoons in one of his earlier journalistic ventures. An inventive publicist, a proud and nostalgic liberal driven by memories of the temporary triumphs and ultimate disasters of 1848, Keil was also a responsible family man and, in his way, a minor—a very minor—nineteenth-century Voltaire. He would rather trim and publish in freedom than offend and languish in prison. When he emerged from Hubertusburg, he undertook to give the censor no trouble with his proposed family periodical and waited for better times. They came in the 1850s, when censorship in Saxony was somewhat relaxed. Keil promptly burst forth from his self-constructed nonpolitical cage. In 1859, the nationwide festivals celebrating Schiller's hundredth birthday served as the occasion for an outpouring of liberal and nationalistic sentiments, and Keil participated in the orgy of political rhetoric. Commissioning a special article from his trusted collaborator, Max Ring, he specified that the piece must describe, "in glowing, enthusiastic language," the poet who, "more beautifully, more enthusiastically" than any other, had "battled for the highest possession of the people, for freedom and nationality." In the article, Keil specified, description must not drown out politics, especially in regard to "the question of German unity and freedom."

Experienced in the ways of sailing close to the wind of the forbidden, Keil implicitly instructed his contributor by expressing confidence that Ring, himself no novice, would know how to mix rousing advocacy with prudent reserve and thus keep the article on Schiller "printable" [*druckfähig*]. From these heady days onward, the share of politics markedly increased in the pages of Keil's journal, and the circulation increased with it, quite as markedly. By 1860, Keil could proudly tell his readers that the *Gartenlaube* was printing over 100,000 copies, and he attributed this unrivaled circulation to "its popularization of the sciences," but even more to its "aspiration to be, through and through, a *German* paper." Evidently it paid, at least in those years, to have progressive, if respectfully formulated, views on politics. The muffled tones and anodyne attitudes of 1890 were something relatively new.

Whatever else they may demonstrate, the political years of the *Gartenlaube* do not support the proposition that a nonpolitical stance was part of the German bourgeois character. This has not been lost on the literary historians who have studied the journal, and they have resorted to a plausible explanation. While the readers of the *Gartenlaube* were not born nonpolitical, they had the nonpolitical posture thrust upon them. "Under the impress of the German victory of 1871," the liberal impulses that had informed the early *Gartenlaube* gave way with almost indecent speed. The novels of E. Marlitt, with their tendentious juxtaposition of corrupt aristocrats and honorable bourgeois, maintained a measure of social rebelliousness and political liberalism for some time, at least in the sphere of amorous confrontation. But Marlitt's fellow artists and writers, like their successors in fiction, staged a massive flight from reality and from even the faintest social criticism, dropping instead into bland descriptions of contemporary life and swooning adulation of the Imperial house. Thus, the *Gartenlaube* became a willing instrument for what has been called the "self-deception of the bourgeoisie." Whether the editors of the magazine were manipulators or inhabitants of their sunny realm of dreams, whether they were exploiters or victims, their cheerful periodical potpourri, filled to bursting with deference and optimism, was a splendid—which is to say, depressing—exemplar of how *Kultur* can be abused as a mask for *Politik*. However well meaning its initial progressivism, with the advent of Empire, and increasingly in the 1880s, the *Gartenlaube* family became a complacent, probably an actively conniving, accomplice in the perfection and the propagation of German chauvinism.

This caustic analysis is not wholly wrong. Certainly, the quantity of political commentary decreased and its quality declined with the late 1860s and never recovered. We can document, from about 1867, a marked veering toward Bismarck, an increasing commitment to his policies, to say nothing of his person. And certainly by 1890, as I have shown in detail, the denial of politics was in the saddle. But while this caustic analysis is not wholly wrong, it is not wholly right either. Two sets of realities, one sociological and the other psychological, require us to refine and revise it.

Sociology first. The critical students of the *Gartenlaube* from whom I have drawn in the last few moments, envision its "family" as a coherent slice of German society. They see it as bourgeois and, more restrictedly, as petty bourgeois; to them, it was the *Mittelstand* that mainly subscribed to the periodical and enforced its apolitical and servile tone. In this view, the archetypal reader of the *Gartenlaube* appears as a neighborhood retailer, a small wholesale merchant, a self-employed craftsman, a white-collar worker or minor bureaucrat complete, of course, with adoring wife and numerous children. This archetype is hard working, worried about money, and super-ficially educated though with some pretensions to high culture; a thoroughly domesticated animal, he is given to ceremonious family outings, occasional concerts, large quantities of beer, and larger quantities of cake. As a good burgher, he defers to constituted authority right down to the policeman who directs his movements with a wave of his hand, he respects his betters even though they may be fairly low on the social ladder themselves, in turn, he condescends to his domestic help, he half fears and wholly despises the working class, especially the militant Social Democrats. He is a born sub-ordinate and, hence, imperious with those who are subordinate to him.

Apart from its tendentiousness (for the petty bourgeoisie has become a pariah, a veritable scapegoat, in much recent historical literature), this description seems plausible enough. Indeed, the contents of the *Gartenlaube* suggest that it recruited its most faithful public from the *Mittelstand*. The nonacademic tenor of its articles coupled with the unquestioning academ-icism of its art, the undemanding level of its fiction, and the bluff heartiness of its communications imply readers neither avant-garde in their taste in art nor sophisticated in their way of life. Its persistent didacticism points in the same direction; it implies subscribers intent on discovering the world without too much strain after a day's hard work. Its examination of sensible budgets would appeal, not so much to comfortably situated bourgeois, who scarcely needed such lessons, as to those who could not aspire to con-spicuous consumption. The kind of book the *Gartenlaube* was likely to recommend was, like Johannes Scherr's *Bildersaal der Weltliteratur,* designed for circles of the people "delighting in culture" [*bildungsfreudig*], and explicitly aimed not at "specialists" [*Leute vom Fach*] but the widest possible public. And the kind of social club the *Gartenlaube* thinks its readers will want to know about and emulate is one called "Prunklosia," a small circle that caters, as its name implies, to the unostentatious; it is composed of "scholars, artists, officers, officials, and private persons" who courageously reject the reigning fashion of giving ambitious parties and, instead, hold informal and inexpensive dinners every other week. If, in its novels, the *Gartenlaube* gave its readers license to indulge in expansive fantasies, in the rest of its pages it exhibited, and extolled, a sobriety that could only gratify those modestly placed in the world, folk who were doubtless heartened by the spectacle of scholars, artists, and their like sitting down to a simple roast and vegetables. Perhaps they were not missing so much in life after all!

But, in fact, the publishers of the *Gartenlaube* aimed their product at a far wider readership, both socially and geographically, than all these inferences would suggest. In 1895, they demonstrated this self-perception in one of those rare glimpses behind the curtain. An illustrated article on the dispatch office of the *Gartenlaube,* caught at the moment a new issue was ready to be distributed, shows a cluster of persons waiting for their copy and others, already in possession of their precious journal, eagerly reading it. At the window of the dispatch office we see "a lady" with hat, "a woman of the people" wearing a kerchief, and "a gentleman" sporting a white mustache and bowler; others on the scene include well-dressed young people, evidently students and apprentices and ladies from the comfortable classes. The *Gartenlaube* was not content to address the *Mittelstand* alone. And they cast their net far beyond Germany: in 1888, advertising its annual calendar for 1889, the *Gartenlaube* thought it "equally useful to Protestants and Catholics in Germany and Austria-Hungary, to Russians and Jews alike." Letters came to the editor from all parts of Germany, from London and Moscow, Riga and Vienna, Australia and Latin America, and the United States. When they emigrated, Germans gave up much but not, it seems, the *Gartenlaube;* certainly, the many articles that the magazine devoted to Germans abroad attest that emigrants made up a significant portion of its readership.

The social diversity of that readership emerges from a series of slight but telling clues. It included Austrian chemists working for their navy in Italy, Protestant ministers in small towns, and rural teachers in the German provinces and the Brasilian jungles. One reader, reminiscing in 1928, recalled that his grandfather, a highly cultivated *Pfarrer* and a friend of Keil's, had contributed poems to the *Gartenlaube,* and that his parents, evidently solid middle-class citizens, had continued to subscribe to the magazine and to have its volumes bound. "In the house of my parents, the *Gartenlaube* had its firm place, as with all educated bourgeois families" [*wie bei allen gebildeten bürgerlichen Familien*]. At the other end of the economic spectrum, among working-class families, the *Gartenlaube* had its faithful readers as well: August Bebel read the journal, at least in the late 1860s, when he was already prominent in the burgeoning labor movement. And in 1879, the *Gartenlaube* noted the twenty-fifth anniversary of a *Gartenlaube-Verein,* formed in 1854 by a group of weavers in Chemnitz, who had jointly subscribed to a copy that they would circulate, and had continued this practice for a quarter-century. Social Democrats might be a menace, but working-class readers were welcome, as welcome as members of the cultivated bourgeoisie—the *Bildungsbürgertum.*

It is essential to remember, moreover, that the *Gartenlaube* did not merely address itself to many kinds of families, but to everyone *within* the family as well. The rationing of politics and the absence of smut have something to do with that. It was a *family magazine* in the literal sense of the term. After World War I, the *Gartenlaube* became, most emphatically, a magazine for women, delivering heavy doses of domestic advice, fashions, and recipes. But in the Empire, its reach was wider than this. Here and there, in asides and in reminiscences, we catch confirmation of the predictable: the men seeking out articles on inventions, the boys swallowing accounts of African explorers and military campaigns, the women and adolescent girls weeping over the serialized novels. But far more common was the *Gartenlaube* that everyone read, all the way through. For young men eager to impress dancing partners, the novels provided useful insights and material for conversation; for young women, especially those aspiring, however timidly, to a measure of independence, articles on women physicians provided possible models for conduct. Moreover, this was still an age of reading aloud, especially in small towns, remote villages, or distant colonial outposts, and in these family sessions there was no discrimination by sex or age: one read out the *Gartenlaube* from beginning to end.

This sociological account should help to enrich and complicate the categorical condemnation of the *Gartenlaube* as an adjunct to imperialism. And some psychological considerations will complicate matters still further. As I have documented, it was not just the absence of politics that is striking, but the *form* of that absence: a denial of troubles, a strenuous evasion of the problematical, that characterized this periodical during the Empire. The mechanism of denial springs into action only where there is uneasiness too exigent to be managed by rational conduct. Here I am, I know, on slippery ground, on the thin ice of meager evidence. I am offering suggestions for research rather than dogmatic conclusions. It seems to me highly likely that the Germany of Bismarck, and even more the Germany of Wilhelm II, was in the grip of profound and pervasive anxieties. The very men in charge of policy—of diplomatic, military, and social policy— came to behave like anxious children grasping at fantastic solutions. This sense of unreality—the hallucination of encirclement, the fantasy of being choked, the need to be first lest one be last, above all the sense that the world is, quite simply, out of control—emerges over and over again. Policies such as the Schlieffen plan have the meticulous precision characteristic of paranoid constructions; earlier, the political rhetoric of Bismarck and his followers displayed a kind of unmeasured, inappropriate violence that betrays not mastery but drift. The fear of Red Revolution, no doubt fostered by the uncompromising pronouncements of the Social Democratic leadership, was real enough, but it was hardly rational. Socialists were good burghers displaying, more and more as time went on, what Lenin would later denounce as sheer "trade union consciousness." Liebknecht, Bebel, and the others talked revolution, but, as any sensible observer could have seen—would have seen if he had not been overwhelmed by anxiety— had no intention of making, no way of making, a revolution. Indeed the friend-enemy psychology that dominated so many Germans at the time suggests a regressive flight into literally childish ways of seeing the world.

The readers of the *Gartenlaube,* I submit, shared the anxieties of the age as much as its triumphs. Apparently settled and contentedly domestic, they were in many ways lost in a new world of vast cities, aggressive-sounding trade unions, and blood-curdling talk of the great world conflagration to come. Hence, what I have called the calculated evasions of the *Gartenlaube* betray not merely a self-satisfied surrender to the powers that be, but also, and significantly, a way of coping with a deeply felt, often deeply concealed need: the need to be reassured that all was, after all, well.

Part 2
The Twentieth Century: Language, Technology, Intertextuality

German Cinema and the Sister Arts:
Wegener's *The Student of Prague*

Brigitte Peucker

The body in films is also moments, intensities, outside a single constant
unity of the body as a whole, the property of a some *one;* films are full of
fragments, bits of bodies, gestures, desirable traces, fetish points.
—Stephen Heath

Early speculations concerning the nature of film hovered uneasily around
the subject of movement, around issues of life and lifelessness, body and
soul, the fantastic and the uncanny effect. "The essence of cinema," Georg
Lukács wrote in 1913, "is movement itself,"[1] and he was already reflecting
a widespread belief. Earlier, a Grand Café program advertising films by
the Lumière brothers describes in detail what these films record, namely,
"all the movements which have succeeded one another over a given period
of time in front of the camera and the subsequent reproduction of these
movements by the projection of their images, life size, on a screen"—all
before the titles of the films are mentioned.[2] Wildly affirmative of cinema,
in which he saw the basis of all new directions in the arts, Expressionist
poet Yvan Goll proclaimed, in 1920, that cinematic movement would have
the catalytic effect of ozone or radium upon all media and genres, which
for the moment were "dead and mute."[3] With Viking Eggeling and perhaps

Epigraph from Stephen Heath, "Body, Voice," in *Questions of Cinema* (Bloomington: Indiana University Press, 1981), 183.

1. "Das Wesen des Kinos ist die Bewegung" (author's translation). Georg Lukács, "Gedanken zu einer Asthetik des Kinos," in *Kino-Debatte: Texte zum Verhältnis von Literatur und Film 1909–1929,* ed. Anton Kaes (Tübingen: Niemeyer, 1978), 113. References to other essays in this volume will cite *Kino-Debatte.*

2. Early film catalog quoted in Stephen Heath, "The Cinematic Apparatus: Technology as Historical and Cultural Form," in *The Cinematic Apparatus,* ed. Teresa de Lauretis and Stephen Heath (London: Macmillan, 1980), 1.

3. Yvan Goll, "Das Kinodram," in *Kino-Debatte,* 137.

Hans Arp in mind, Goll speculated that the future would soon bring *Kinomalerei* ['movie painting'] into existence. A year earlier, another writer, Carl Hauptmann, theorizing about Rodin against the historical backdrop of the *Laokoon* controversy, made the claim that sculpture's desire to suggest movement—indeed, the desire of all of the visual arts to transcend the moment—could now be realized in cinema.[4]

But the introduction of movement into the realm of visual representation was thought to have consequences that were not always viewed in a positive light. Cinematic bodies—the human figures subjected to motion in films— were generally perceived as attenuated, as "merely" the sum of their actions and movements, and were often contrasted negatively with so-called theatrical bodies. Eleonora Duse's is a frequently cited example of the stage actor's body, the theatrical body capable of projecting "full presence" or "soul," or—as even Lukács put it—a body in which "being" and "acting" were indissolubly one.[5] As observed in theatrical performances, the actor's body was thought to be redolent of "fate," "mystery," and "tragedy," whereas, according to Lukács, bodies in films should not even be considered "human," but rather as constituting "life" of a wholly new and fantastic kind.[6] Thus, cinematic representations of the human body were adjudged to be "unmetaphysical" and "soulless," to constitute one-dimensional creatures whose life is a life of pure surface—to be somehow monstrous or unnatural—precisely because visual representations, the stillness of which the limits of technology had made to seem natural, were now capable of being subjected to movement. Nevertheless, Lukács's reading differs from some insofar as he felt that the cinematic representation of human beings ought not to be perceived as inadequate, as founded upon a lack, but rather simply as a consequence of the *principium stilisationis* of cinema. According to Lukács, neither fate nor causality determines cinematic "life," since, as he believes, movement alone constitutes or defines the cinema, he is able to argue that, while the human figures represented on the screen may have lost their souls, they have precisely for this reason regained their bodies.

---

4. Carl Hauptmann, "Film und Theater," in *Kino-Debatte,* 124.

5. See Lukács, "Gedanken," 113. In *Kino-Debatte,* see also Paul Ernst, "Möglichkeiten einer Kinokunst," 118–23; Hauptmann, "Film und Theater," 123–30.

6. In an argument grounded in idealism, Lukács asserts that "das Phantastische ist aber kein Gegensatz des lebendigen Lebens, es ist nur ein neuer Aspekt von ihm: ein Leben ohne Gegenwärtigkeit, ohne Schicksal, ohne Gründe, ohne Motive; ein Leben, mit dem das Innerste unserer Seele nie identisch werden will, noch kann; und wenn es sich auch—oft— nach diesem Leben sehnt, so ist die Sehnsucht nur die nach einem fremden Abgrund, nach etwas fernem, innerlich Distanziertem" ("Gedanken," 113).

During this period of silent cinema, it comes as no surprise that the "body language" of pantomime and gesture occupied a central position in the discussion of the place of film with regard to the established arts. For some, the presence of the body on stage, contrasted with its actual absence from the cinematic frame, ensures the primacy of even theatrical pantomime over film, not to mention the primacy of drama, with its access to the spoken word.[7] Others, such as Carl Hauptmann, claim that it is in body language that the soul is best expressed; Hauptmann sees in the foregrounding of gesture [*Gebärde*] a kind of privileged primal domain of signification [*Urbereich, Urmitteilung durch Gebärde*] available to cinema.[8] Usually, however, it is suggested that the silent cinema's muteness contributes to the uncanniness and "soullessness" of its figures. Sometimes the facial expression of cinematic figures, whether exaggerated or blank and—in either case—masklike, is seen as contributing to the uncanniness of these figures. It is this effect, as Walter Benjamin reminds us, that Charlie Chaplin uses to such advantage; his "mask of uninvolvement" makes Chaplin into a "marionette in a fair sideshow."[9] Contributing also to this marionettelike effect are Chaplin's body movements, his "exercises in fragmentation," as Miriam Hansen puts it; utterly self-conscious about the effects of the cinematic apparatus on the representation of his body, Chaplin is the film actor par excellence who, by "chopping up expressive body movement into a sequence of minute mechanical impulses, . . . renders the law of the apparatus visible as the law of human movement."[10] But Chaplin's recuperative strategy of exposing the fragmentation of the body to the view was a personal solution to a perceived threat, not a strategy that could find universal application.

Unnatural Conjunctions: The Heterogeneous Text

In 1916, Paul Wegener's lecture, "The Artistic Possibilities of the Cinema,"[11] with its emphasis on the "kinetic lyricism" of the cinema and on

---

7. Ernst, "Möglichkeiten," 119.

8. Hauptmann, "Film und Theater," 125–26. See also Egon Friedell's "Prolog vor dem Film," which also insists that verbal language not be given hegemony—that glances, gestures, and the way the body is held signify more than verbal utterance in the modern age (Egon Friedell, "Prolog vor dem Film," in *Kino-Debatte*, 43).

9. Walter Benjamin, "Rückblick auf Chaplin" (1929), in *Kino-Debatte*, 173: "die Maske des Unbeteiligtseins macht ihn zur Marionette in einer Jahrmarktsbude."

10. Miriam Hansen, "Benjamin, Cinema, and Experience: 'The Blue Flower in the Land of Technology,'" *New German Critique* 40 (Winter, 1987): 203.

11. Wegener's lecture is quoted in Lotte Eisner, *The Haunted Screen: Expressionism in the German Cinema and the Influence of Max Reinhardt*, rev. ed. (Berkeley: University of California Press, 1977), 33.

the play of pure motion for its own sake, established Wegener as a forerunner among the artists and filmmakers—including Hans Richter—who would develop the abstract film in Germany. Wegener's interest is in what he calls the "fantastic domain" of "optical lyricism," a term perhaps not as far from Gilles Deleuze's concept of the "movement-image" as the nearly seventy years that separate their two texts might suggest; for Deleuze, too, the lure of filmmaking lies in the possibility of reproducing pure movement "extracted from bodies or moving things,"[12] movement as a function of a series of equidistant instants reproduced in a sequence of shots. Not surprisingly, however, it was the tantalizing implication of movement suggested by series photography—comic photographs of a man fencing with himself and playing cards alone—that originally drew Wegener to the cinematic medium in 1913, and, at the same time, suggested to him the suitability of the cinema for transmitting the fantastic tales of E. T. A. Hoffmann.[13]

Series photography is considered to be one of the several "primitive" stages in the evolution of the cinema. In the United States, Eadweard Muybridge published photo sequences to illustrate his studies of animal locomotion, and was already using an invention of his own, the zoopraxiscope, to project short sequences during his lectures on animal locomotion in 1880. Thus, living bodies, especially human figures, came to be linked with movement—indeed, were vehicles for portraying movement—in series photography from its very inception.[14] It is probable that the images of the fencer that Wegener saw were very much like those produced by Muybridge, and that their subject was given a sword as a prop in order to enable him to demonstrate not only the graceful postures assumed by the human body while fencing, but also to demonstrate both a certain set of movements and the manner in which the camera could record them sequentially. What Wegener saw additionally, however, is the absence of

---

12. Gilles Deleuze, *Cinema 1: The Movement-Image,* trans. Hugh Tomlinson and Barbara Habberjam (Minneapolis: University of Minnesota Press, 1986), 23ff. It should be noted that Deleuze takes the writings of Henri Bergson as his point of departure, thus making the similarity of concern between Deleuze and Wegener less surprising.

13. Eisner, *Haunted Screen,* 40.

14. In a fascinating article on Muybridge and Méliès, Linda Williams traces the beginnings of the cinematic mise-en-scène in the props and situations that Muybridge gives to his human figures in order to better illustrate certain movements made by the body, and argues that the presence of women in the frame engenders "a fetish response on the part of the male image-producer to restore the unity which this body appears to lack" (Williams, "Film Body: An Implantation of Perversions," in *Narrative, Apparatus, Ideology: A Film Theory Reader,* ed. Philip Rosen [New York: Columbia University Press, 1986], 522).

an opponent in these photographs, and he immediately made the connection between this uncanny absence in the photographic frame and the potential of film to express uncanny effects. I shall return to the nature of these effects later.

While I shall finally be concerned here with the connection between Wegener's interest in cinematic motion and his representation of the body by means of what Deleuze calls the "fixed primitive image,"[15] it is nevertheless clear that Wegener's interest in itself is of a more abstract order. There is one particular aspect of the fascination with the abstract play of shapes dissolving into one another, with motion subjected to temporal rhythms such as we find in the films of Richter, that fixes his attention. That is the possibility of conjoining the "natural" with the "artificial": "I can imagine," writes Wegener, "a kind of cinema which would use nothing but moving surfaces, against which there would impinge events that would still participate in the natural world but transcend the lines and volumes of the natural."[16] The images produced by the conjunction of the organic and the inorganic—of the natural or "living" and the artificial or "dead"—could, by means of the camera and of montage, become moving images emphasized as such. For Wegener, it is "pure" motion, divorced from the actual status of the object as inherently animate or inanimate that is of interest, and this, naturally, is the kind of motion that cinema is capable of rendering—even in its early period.[17] Further examples that Wegener puts forward—as when he suggests that "microscopic particles of fermenting chemical substances could be filmed together with small plants of various sizes"[18]—strongly confirm the impression that it is the ontological status of such composite images, liberated from the binary link of being and nonbeing to life and death, that is at least in part the object of his fascination. It is, furthermore, precisely the potential for such a juxtaposition of natural and artificial in Hanns Heinz Ewers's filmscript for *The Student of Prague* that Wegener claims to have found so compelling: "*The Student of Prague*, with its strange mixture of the natural and artificial . . . interested me enormously."[19]

---

15. Deleuze, *Cinema 1*, 25.

16. Eisner, *Haunted Screen*, 33.

17. "The spatial and fixed shot tended to produce a pure movement image" (Deleuze, *Cinema 1*, 25).

18. Eisner, *Haunted Screen*, 33.

19. See Eisner, *Haunted Screen*, 40. The director of this film was technically Stellan Rye, a Dane, who worked with Ewers, with the cameraman Guido Seeber, and with Wegener, a

The natural and artificial: this pairing and its permutations take on great resonance for this film on several levels, including, of course, the thematic one suggested by the various "supernatural" elements of the plot, to which I shall return. It finds expression very intriguingly, for instance, in the manner in which the film is an assemblage of varying spaces, spaces that do not generally coexist as jarringly in later narrative cinema as they do here. Kracauer's distinction, in *Theory of Film,* between the "two tendencies" of cinema—the "Lumière tendency," with its documentary interest in the natural, recording the details of the physical world, and the "Méliès tendency," with its formative interest in the artificial, in theatrical vision[20]—is aptly illustrated by several different sequences of *The Student of Prague,* pointing to the way in which early cinema, in its desire for a uniquely cinematic space, appropriates the spaces and modes of as many of the arts as it can press into service, with the consequence of presenting itself repeatedly as a mixed mode, a heterogeneous text.

Not surprisingly, given such emphases, *The Student of Prague* is utterly self-conscious about its position vis-à-vis the more established arts; to see this, one need only examine the opening images of the film, which seem almost to constitute a setpiece made up of nineteenth-century mourning pictures, including a weeping willow with a tombstone. On this tombstone is inscribed the text of Alfred de Musset's "La nuit de Décembre," a poem that establishes the centrality of the themes of mimetic artifice, the double and of death. To say nothing of its recognizable allusion to the visual arts, the literary space that this short sequence announces—the poem as epitaph, the space of writing at the moment at which it most obviously marks an absence, a text "signed" by the poet, as one might find it in an anthology— appears again at the end of the film, as though to enclose the cinematic narrative in literary brackets, to frame the moving images of its narrative with the static spaces at once of writing and of death. (In some prints, this opening sequence survives only as the text of the poem itself, which

---

Max Reinhardt actor; it has become a convention, however—though not one practiced by all film historians—to consider this film to be "Wegener's"; it is just such a blurring of the question of authorship that reminds us most vividly of the collaborative nature of filmmaking. For further background information, see Heide Schlüpmann, "The First German Art Film: Rye's *The Student of Prague,*" in *German Film and Literature: Adaptations and Transformations,* ed. Eric Rentschler (New York: Metheun, 1986), 9–24.

20. Siegfried Kracauer, *Theory of Film: The Redemption of Physical Reality* (1960; reprint, London: Oxford University Press, 19–78), 28–40. See also Gerald Mast, "Kracauer's Two Tendencies and the Early History of Film Narrative," in *The Language of Images,* ed. W. J. T. Mitchell (Chicago: University of Chicago Press, 1980), 129–50.

is then less clearly distinguishable from the film's title cards, but nevertheless still serves to stress the status of the literary as writing.) The student Baldwin, the central character of the film played by Wegener, is able to enter this preliminary scene. However, its function in the narrative is to foreshadow his tragic end, and the melancholy movements of his body and that of the willow itself, staged and stagy, suggest that the scene as a whole is more than a mere illustration of the poem: it is meant pointedly to predict that the film will animate writing, will "bring it to life."

Immediately following this is another sequence whose space is also uncinematic and easily identifiable: it is a credit sequence that introduces each actor in turn, in costume and on a theatrical stage with a curtain. The lack of backdrop scenery here and the attempt to present the theater as theater, not as a space where technological illusions are created, seem designed to emphasize the fact that all movement in the theater—unlike film—must be generated either by the bodies of the actors or by overtly mechanical means—such mechanisms, for example, as the swing used for the deus ex machina, mechanisms that had become sophisticated in the nineteenth century but would suddenly seem archaic from the standpoint of cinema. In this connection, a further speculation of Wegener's concerning the conjunction of natural and artifical seems pertinent. He hoped that film would make it possible to use "marionettes or small three-dimensional models which could be animated image by image, in slow or rapid motion depending on the speed of the montage," thus giving rise "to fantastic images which would provoke absolutely novel associations of ideas in the spectator."[21] Once again, the reader is made aware of Wegener's fascination with film's capacity to animate the inanimate and with the frisson that this capacity evokes in both filmmaker and spectator. Though this effect may have been felt more intensely during the early period of cinema, it is arguably still produced today; as one critic has noted, "the experience of film involves a mysterious equivocation between terror and the sense of a utopia in which divisions between life and death are effaced."[22]

One might well see in the marionettes mentioned by Wegener equivalents of the automata that recur in Hoffmann's stories, figures that generate uncanny effects and tend to be connected in one way or another with crises of perception and of desire. Wegener's formulations seem to imply not

21. Eisner, *Haunted Screen,* 35–36.
22. Paul Coates, *The Story of the Lost Reflection: The Alienation of the Image in Western and Polish Cinema* (London: Verso, 1985), 12.

only that film offers technical possibilities for the animation of puppets, but also that the apparatus of cinema naturalizes the movements of the marionettes because, once they become images in a film, their movements—"animated image by image"—are no more mechanically produced than the movements of human actors. (Especially when viewed from this perspective, Wegener's remark obviously evokes Kleist's "Über das Marionettentheater" ["On the Marionette Theater"] as well, to which I will return later.)

For today's spectator, the rapid juxtaposition of the film's two opening sequences—the literary-painterly space with the theatrical space—occasions a feeling of Brechtian alienation, a feeling that, however, he or she had probably already experienced while reading the two cards that follow the film's title, the first announcing "A Romantic Drama in Six Acts," the second proudly informing us that the film was shot on location—"in Castle Belvedere in Prague, Palace Fürstenberg, Lobkovitz, and other historic places." As we see once again, the claim of romance, with its Méliès-like insistence on artifice and the film's self-proclaimed generic identity as drama are relativized by the counterclaim of photographed reality reminiscent of Lumière, a reality that, moreover, is placed within a historical context and thereby given a temporal dimension. The narrative itself, which opens with a short series of genre scenes of student life, is thus placed within a series of brackets that raise conflicting expectations and make conflicting claims about the status of the text and its generic identity.[23]

As Thomas Elsaesser acknowledges, Wegener, Wiene, Murnau, Lang, and many others involved in the early phase of German filmmaking very self-consciously addressed themselves to the task of elevating the cinema to the status of an art form, and he astutely observes that it is within the confines of the so-called German art cinema that the forms of the fantastic flourish.[24] In a later essay, Elsaesser stresses the predominance of aesthetic

---

23. Thomas Elsaesser, in his provocative essay "Social Mobility and the Fantastic: German Silent Cinema" (*Wide Angle* 5, no. 2 [1982]: 14–15), to which I will refer frequently, has made the claim that *The Student of Prague* sets up generic expectations that link it with two of the most popular commercial genres of the German cinema of this period, the comedy and the musical, both of which the film then works to disavow (17). Although these genres are certainly alluded to, the conflicting generic "bracket" in which the narrative is enclosed, with the reference to Musset, at least, pointing to "high culture," makes one question to what extent the spectator could ever have thought he or she was watching an "entertainment" film.

24. Elsaesser, "Social Mobility," 20.

self-consciousness or filmic effects in German cinema of the silent period, noting that, in this cinema,

> the authority, origin and control of the act of narration was constantly foregrounded, and in a manner that had no equivalent in contemporary silent cinema of other countries. The profusion of nested narratives, framed tales, flashbacks, *en abîme* constructions and interlacing of narrative voices emerges as an index of the very difference that singled out German silent cinema as historically specific.[25]

I would like to suggest that an obvious explanation for this phenomenon lies precisely in the self-conscious attempt to develop a new art form to which Elsaesser referred in his earlier text and that an important consequence of this attempt can be located in the barely formulated theoretical issues buried in essays and films such as Wegener's, issues expressed, for example, in formulations suggesting the sort of boundary crossings between natural and artificial that I have been discussing. These textual passages suggest that film, at the moment of glorying in its capacity to introduce movement into—or narrativize—the visual arts and to give visual expression to narrative, is at pains to contain an uneasiness about its hybrid nature, an uneasiness that is nevertheless repeatedly embodied in image and metaphor.

For the contemporary spectator—and, I suspect, also for the spectator of 1913—there is one scene in *The Student of Prague* that stands out most vividly for the juxtaposition of its spaces—and for the intricacy with which it poses the problem of the interrelation of the arts. It is the second sequence of the film, which the title identifies as the "Preparation for the Hunt." Typical of early cinema, it is extremely short and begins with an interior scene of what appears to be the breakfast room at the Count's castle. The frame is determined by a frontal point of view and, as in a stage set, we see a back wall only, a wall covered from floor to ceiling by tapestrylike paintings, with a door at the center. For a few instants only, the eye is allowed to linger upon the two figures in the foreground (the count and his daughter) in riding attire, whereupon almost immediately a third figure, the master of the hunt, enters through the door. It is at that moment that

---

25. Thomas Elsaesser, "Film History and Visual Pleasure: Weimar Cinema," in *Cinema Histories/Cinema Practices,* ed. Patricia Mellencamp and Philip Rosen, The American Film Institute Monograph Series, vol. 4 (Frederick, Md.: University Publishers of America, 1984), 66.

the space of the scene is radically disrupted. What had been a tableau scene typical of early cinema, appropriate to its theatrical space, is relegated to being "merely that," for when the door opens, it reveals another space— an actual birch wood, not a set. Oddly, the door opens immediately into nature without the mediation of a hallway, stair, or any other kind of architectural space. For the spectator, the impression is one of a theater flat (the wall with the door) having been imposed upon a natural scene, as though a stage had simply been set up in the middle of a birch grove. The effect is startling and it is heightened even further when all three characters leave by this door and enter the deep space of the wood. Despite the presence of a servant who has entered the room, and who moves about in the foreground, the door is allowed to remain wide open and our eyes follow the receding figures as they wend their way among the trees. The scene is held another few seconds; as we watch, the servant is busily occupied with clearing the table at one side of the room, thus enabling us to gaze simultaneously upon the beauty of the revealed natural scene and upon the tapestrylike mural that covers the whole wall of the room. Tellingly, this mural has for its subject matter the hunt.

There follows a cut and our next view is of figures moving out of deep space and toward the spectator—from background to foreground—in a movement that seems magically continuous with the movement of these same figures from the foreground to the background in the previous frame. Here, in fact, there occurs one of those moments in which movement seems almost to exist independently of the figures that produce it. As they approach, we see that they are the huntsmen on horseback, surrounded by a pack of hounds, leaving the castle grounds through a fence with a wrought iron gate in the foreground; they emerge as though leaving the constraints of a frame, ever more animated, the bodies of horses and hounds in constant motion. A montage of shots follows that not only reveals an extraordinarily beautiful landscape, full of the play of light and shadow with trees reflected in bodies of water in the manner that Danish directors had already learned to project on screen, but serves also to impart the intoxication that the filmmaker so obviously feels with what we might call, following Deleuze, the "emancipation of the image."[26] Considering the fact that this sequence serves no diegetic purpose, this montage of shots is relatively long; the camera is placed in various positions (it is not yet mobile) and horsemen and dogs pass in front of it at various distances, their bodies passing in and out of the cinematic frame with increasing

---

26. Deleuze, *Cinema 1*, 23.

speed. Repeatedly, these figures evoke offscreen space, the space outside the cinematic frame on which André Bazin bases his distinction between cinema and painting.[27]

Obviously, what is at issue here is the manner in which the figure is of the body released from the tableau space of theater with its relatively fixed perspective and, more particularly, from the space of the tapestrylike wall mural that entraps and contains it. The film brings the mural of the hunt to life, as it were, surpassing even a *tableau vivant* in its capacity to introduce the presence and movement of the body into the work of art— and going beyond that to generate the movement from frame to frame that is produced by changes in camera position. The dramatic organization of the sequence of shots, with its ever-faster motion, suggests building to a triumphant crescendo and leaves no doubt that this moment is particularly designed to proclaim the cinema as an advance over earlier, more culturally established art forms.[28] Wegener's radical departure from the circumscribed theatrical space of the castle interior celebrates film's ability, in the words of Kracauer, to "record the visible world" and even to transcend it in the play of "pure movement" Wegener admired. And yet it is apparent, as I suggested before, that the possibility of rendering visual representation movable was not seen only as a cause for celebration by the early filmmaker; rather, the conjunction of the visual and the narrative modes in the moving image constitutes a cause for anxiety as well.

"Its Strange Mixture of the Natural and Artificial": The Presence of Kleist

It is at this point that I would like to return to Kleist's "Marionette Theater," which seems almost uncannily to form a subtext, not only for Wegener's

---

27. André Bazin, "Painting and Cinema," in *What Is Cinema?* ed. and trans. Hugh Gray (Berkeley: University of California Press, 1967), 1:164–69.

28. Taking up Elsaesser's point that this film, like the other films of the fantastic in German silent cinema, both represents social conflicts and disguises them, I would like to point out that the presence of the servant in the scene I described obviously serves to underscore the problem of a rigid social hierarchy that Elsaesser discusses. In fact, his presence reminds us that the tapestrylike mural of the hunt represents essentially feudal social relations directly, and also points to tapestry making itself as a collective art form that is also dependent upon such relations (the drawings for tapestries were usually done by established artists or masters, while they were executed by groups of skilled workers). Recalling Erwin Panofsky's comparison between cathedral building and filmmaking ("Style and Medium in the Motion Pictures," 1934), a comparison also made by Walter Benjamin ("The Work of Art in the Age of Mechanical Reproduction," 1935–36), we may well wonder whether any parallel is intended here between tapestry making and film.

lecture on "kinetic lyricism," of his search for a "pure" motion that transcends the limitations imposed upon the human body by virtue of its physical limitations and the problem of consciousness, but also simply for various images within the film itself.[29] As readers of Kleist will recall, this dialogue relates several narratives, the first of which, told by the dancer, makes the somewhat outrageous claim that marionettes [Gliederpuppen] have more grace—more *Anmut*—and greater fluidity of motion than human dancers. The second narrative, the only one told by the "I" of this exchange, tells the story of a young man who, happening to glance into the mirror one day while bending over to dry himself, tells his companion that he sees a resemblance between himself and the famous Spinario sculpture of a young man extracting a splinter from his foot. Although his companion has also just made the same observation, he does not admit this and, on the contrary, tells the young man rather brusquely that he is seeing things—literally, ghosts ["er sähe wohl Geister"].[30] From this moment on, the young man is wholly changed; he begins to spend all of his time contemplating his reflection in the mirror, and, in the process, is alienated from himself and loses his natural grace. In the third of the three narratives, the idea of reading body movements is also of central importance; here, it resides in the capacity of a bear to discern thrusts from feints while fencing.

Each of these narratives appears to leave its traces either in *The Student of Prague* or in Wegener's essay. The language of mechanics that Kleist's speaker uses to describe the movements of the marionettes, language concerning the curves that their motions are said to describe, the rhythms of these motions, and the "machinist" who is said to control them, renders them both abstract and technological, much like the cinematic motions described by Wegener in his essay. The film combines images from the other two narratives, placing the student Baldwin, Prague's most skillful fencer, before a mirror and allowing him to thrust and parry with his mirror image, an image that will become, in effect, one of the "ghosts" in the remark with which Kleist's narrator had dismissed his friend's observation. (Ironically, the phrase "er sähe wohl Geister" dismisses uncanniness at the very moment of suggesting it.) Additionally, there is, in the Kleist text, a

---

29. Peter Gay points out that Kleist's popularity in Germany increased during this period, and that later, during the Weimar years, Kleist actually became a cult figure (Gay, *Weimar Culture: The Outsider as Insider* [New York: Harper and Row, 1970], 61).

30. Heinrich von Kleist, "Über das Marionettentheater," in *Sämtliche Werke und Briefe*, ed. Helmut Sembdner (Munich: Hanser, 1961), 2:343.

passage that Cynthia Chase has called "an appendage" to these narratives,[31] a remark by the dancer to the effect that the newly available artificial limbs enable human dancers to execute their steps more gracefully than they could with their natural limbs. Not only does the dancer suggest the substitution of marionette for human dancer, as noted above, but he also sanctions that monstrous conjunction of artificial (dead) and natural (living) parts that forms one of the central concerns in this film, a site at which Wegener locates an important aspect of cinematic experimentation.

As will have become clear, not only in the "appendage" but in all three of the narratives in the "Marionette Theater," the discourse of the body occupies a more central position than most have recognized.[32] Paul de Man has commented upon the (humorously ironic) connection between the Spinario figure removing a thorn from his foot to which the young man in the second narrative fancies he bears a resemblance, and the *Laokoon* group that has been the object of so much attention from those who seek, like Lessing, to delineate the boundaries between the arts: both sculptures portray their subjects in pain,[33] pain that has been repeatedly idealized in the case of *Laokoon* commentators, and that has also evoked sublimated feelings of sexuality (in Winckelmann, for example). The connection between the visual work of art and sexuality is not absent in the Kleist text, either: the narrator of the story has, after all, been observing the young man in a public bath and has prefaced his anecdote with the words: "Ein junger Mann von meiner Bekanntschaft hätte, durch eine blosse Bemerkung, gleichsam vor meinen Augen, seine Unschuld verloren."[34] It is not only a fall into self-consciousness that is at issue here, as this suggestive wordplay on losing one's virginity makes clear; the loss of innocence is very pointedly occasioned by the narrator of the story: it is effected by language, by "a mere remark." But the latent eroticism of the Kleist essay is not my topic here. I am concerned, rather, with the manner in which the young man of the second narrative, an erstwhile beholder of the sculpture and now

---

31. Cynthia Chase, "Mechanical Doll, Exploding Machine: Kleist's Models of Narrative," in *Decomposing Figures: Rhetorical Readings in the Romantic Tradition* (Baltimore, Md.: Johns Hopkins University Press, 1986), 146.

32. A noteworthy, if somewhat surprising, exception is Paul de Man's "Aesthetic Formalization: Kleist's *Über das Marionettentheater,*" in *The Rhetoric of Romanticism* (New York: Columbia University Press, 1984), 263–90.

33. As de Man puts it: "The splinter-extracting ephebe thus becomes a miniature *Laokoon,* a version of the neoclassical triumph of imitation over suffering, blood, and ugliness" ("Aesthetic Formalization," 280).

34. Kleist, "Marionettentheater," 343.

beholder of his own image in the mirror, is no longer in control of that image just when he most desperately seeks to "embody" the work of art, with the result that he is not only alienated from his image, but from his own body as well.

The nature of the young man's narcissism requires some elaboration here.[35] Though he is not wholly subsumed by a mirrored self at whom he gazes and who confirms his gaze, gazing back in a mutually sustaining erotic relation, he is alienated from a beloved image. What Kleist's young man sees as he loses one grace after another ("immer ein Reiz nach dem anderen verliess ihn")[36] is the degree to which he is other than his desired mirror image, Spinario's figure. Yet perhaps the situation more closely resembles a grotesquely skewed version of the Lacanian mirror stage, in which the haunting presence of the sculpture in the memory is substituted for the confirming gaze of the mother, and this "presence" causes the self to appear ever less idealized. Here, I would suggest, is an analogue for the fragmented imaginary of early cinema that, searching for an identity while gazing into the mirror, sees the presence of the arts that have engendered it, but cannot, as yet, visualize an idealized version of itself in the mirror's surface.

"Bits of Bodies:" The Fragmented Image

Like the young man of the anecdote, Baldwin, the central character of Wegener's film, has lost control of his mirror image (he has, in fact, sold it), and, in Baldwin's case, it returns to pursue and haunt him as his double. There have been various readings of the return of and to the double during the fin de siècle, usually having to do with the effects of industrialization and mass production,[37] but quite clearly the function that it takes on in *The Student of Prague* has at least as much to do with the anxiety created by the production of the moving image itself as with the technology of this production, and must be seen within the experimental— and potentially problematic—context of movement both attached to and divorced from the body. In *The Student of Prague*, the image producer (Baldwin, Wegener) loses control of his image, which then chases and pursues him—flaunting its mobility all the while—until the end of the

---

35. See de Man, "Aesthetic Formalization," 277; Chase, "Mechanical Doll," 143.
36. Kleist, "Marionettentheater," 344.
37. Coates, *Lost Reflection*, 12.

film, when its destruction (staged as a duel between Baldwin and his mirror image) also occasions the end of the narrative and of the film. Obviously, such a reading positions the double within a group of fantastic figures familiar to us from other early German films. As Elsaesser has pointed out: "One of the most typical figures of the fantastic in the German cinema is that of the sorcerer's apprentice, i.e., the creation and use of magic forces which outstrip their creator and over whom he loses control";[38] Elsaesser connects these figures very convincingly with the double (here the mirror image) read as a part of the self that emancipates itself and turns against its creator (i.e., the "whole" self). But it strikes me that the motivation for the production of these monsters, creatures, or split selves can be accounted for by means other than those of Elsaesser, who reads them as figures for the alienation of the producer from his product in capitalism.[39] As if to remind the spectator that this is cinema in its primitive phase, the anxiety expressed in the narrative of Wegener's film would seem to have much in common with that of primitive peoples who fear that the camera will "steal" their image and, hence, possess them.[40]

It calls to mind other primitive fears as well, such as the feeling of uncanniness described by Jentsch and somewhat disparagingly quoted by Freud in his essay "The 'Uncanny,'" concerning "doubts whether an apparently animate being is really alive; or conversely, whether a lifeless object might not be in fact animate."[41] As we recall, it is precisely this

---

38. Elsaesser, "Social Mobility," 19.

39. Elsaesser makes the point that

one way of recovering the historical dimension of the uncanny motif, therefore, is to point not so much to the emergence of the machine but to the changing relations of production during the Romantic period, especially as they affect the artists and intellectuals increasingly thrown upon the market with their products and finding there that they no longer control the modes of reproduction and distribution of their works. For many of Hoffmann's tales, notably the *Sandman* or *Mlle. de Scuderi* and the goldsmith Cardillac, apply what Marx wrote as early as 1830 about consumerist fetishism, namely, that in the capitalist production process, the product confronts the producer as something alien, and his own person comes to seem to him uncanny. ("Social Mobility," 20)

One might also remark that, in *The Student of Prague,* the moving cinematic image—the mirror image—is sold, as though in an allegory of the consumer-dependent nature of this new art form.

40. It is a well-known fact that Otto Rank was inspired to pursue his study of the double by *The Student of Prague,* and that he formulates his ideas using the work of such romantic writers as Hoffmann, Lenau, Heine, and Dostoyevsky. See Otto Rank, *The Double: A Psychoanalytic Study,* trans. and ed. Harry Tucker, Jr. (Chapel Hill: University of North Carolina Press, 1971).

41. Sigmund Freud, "The 'Uncanny,'" in *On Creativity and the Unconscious: Papers on the*

boundary between animate and inanimate that is the focus of Wegener's interest: "uncanniness" would seem to describe the effect produced upon him by cinematic motion. Although Freud goes on to cite Jentsch's claim that "the impressions made by wax-work figures, artificial dolls and automatons" in particular elicit this kind of response,[42] he is eager to substitute the castration complex as the origin of the Uncanny for the tamer speculations concerning an "intellectual uncertainty" evoked by such figures put forward by Jentsch. And yet, even as Freud asserts the primacy of his theories over those of Jentsch, the theme of motion remains present in Freud's thinking as, for instance, in the contention that "dismembered limbs, a severed head, a hand cut off at the wrist, feet which dance by themselves—all these have something peculiarly uncanny about them, especially when, as in the last instance, they prove able to move of themselves in addition."[43] Mutilation, fragmentation, and movement—all will be shown to have a role to play with regard to the manner in which the spectator perceives the cinematic image. The body is too much the terrain threatened by the "cutting" of film to be left conveniently out of the picture.

Clearly, the theme of the double, as it is figured in *The Student of Prague,* expresses cinema's fascination with the ontology of the image and poses questions concerning the nature of cinematic representation, especially with regard to the manner in which narrative and visual coherence in films are anchored in the human body. It is true that Wegener was fascinated, as we recall, with the detachment of movement from the body, with the possibility of leaving the domain of narrative cinema, bound as it is to the human figure, for that of *kinetische Lyrik* ['kinetic lyricism'].[44] And in Wegener's essay, as in the Kleist text, it is implied that increased formalization will produce increased aesthetic pleasure,[45] and that the cinema machine, the product of modern technology, can successfully realize the dancer's interpretation of the marionette theater as a place where movement is unencumbered by Kleist's "Trägheit der Materie."[46] But it should be noted notwithstanding—lest it is not already apparent—that *The Student of*

Psychology of Art, Literature, Love, Religion, ed. Benjamin Nelson (New York: Harper and Row, 1958), 132.

42. Freud, "The 'Uncanny,'" 132.
43. Freud, "The 'Uncanny,'" 151.
44. Eisner, *Haunted Screen,* 33.
45. See de Man, "Aesthetic Formalization," 272.
46. Kleist, "Marionettentheater," 342.

Prague is by no means the abstract film that Wegener envisions, but rather one in which the (doubled) body is prominent.

As I explained previously, early instances of animating visual representation—an enterprise shared by Wegener—tended to involve photographic studies of the human body in motion; the human model, after all, was the most easily controllable object for such experimentation. In series photography, each photograph tends to represent the whole body, which is centered within the frame, and early narrative cinema displayed the whole human figure within its frames as well. The close-up of a body part had to be "invented," of course, and the story about the occasion on which Griffith chose for the first time *not* to include the whole body of an actor within the frame records the shock that was felt at this act of "mutilation": "You'll cut off his feet" was the enraged cry of Billy Bitzer, the cameraman.[47] The Hollywood moguls put it another way: "We pay for the whole actor, Mr. Griffith. We want to see him."[48] Unlike theater, which (generally) puts the actor's whole body on display on the stage, cinematic space is created as bodies move into, across, and out of the frame and are "fragmented" in the process. Close-ups, pans, and tracking shots: it is in the interest of the camera to dismember the human body as it creates the film, perversely playing on the spectator's desire for "the whole actor" during the process. We might also call to mind a French film described in a 1913 essay, a film in which a wooden horse assembles itself out of many pieces and then proceeds to gallop away in what is surely a commentary on the nature of the image.[49] Seen in this context, Wegener's gesture of splitting— or fragmenting—the actor and thereby effectively doubling him should be read simultaneously as a figuring of cinema's tendency to fragment the body and as an effort to shore it up by duplicating its wholeness.

Film is at its most uncanny, one early theorist claimed, where "connecting limbs" [*Zwischenglieder*]—frames or sequences necessary to the continuity of motion and of action—were omitted.[50] In statements such as these, film itself is figured as a body whose organic wholeness is tampered with, an object that has lost a limb [*Glied*]. If cinematic narrative is, in fact, a "mechanism entailing mutilation,"[51] as I think it is in some sense,

47. Billy Bitzer, quoted in Heath, "Body, Voice," 184. Heath's source is Lillian Gish, *The Movies, Mr. Griffith, and Me* (London: W. H. Allen, 1969), 59–60.

48. Heath, "Body, Voice," 184.

49. Ernst, "Möglichkeiten," 122.

50. Ernst, "Möglichkeiten," 120.

51. See Chase on Kleist: "The puppet theater is a model of the text as a system for the

it is only fair to point out that mutilation, cutting, or decoupage function only as one set of terms in a dialectic, function over and against suturing and montage to create cinematic narrative and cinematic space. In this context, I find it useful to cite Roland Barthes on Diderot's notion of the tableau.

> Diderot is for us the theorist of this dialectic of desire; in the article on "Composition," he writes: "A well-composed picture [tableau] is a whole contained under a single point of view, in which the parts work together to one end and form by their mutual correspondence a unity as real as that of the members of the body of an animal; so that a piece of painting made up of a large number of figures thrown at random on to the canvas, with neither proportion, intelligence, or unity, no more deserves to be called a *true composition* than scattered studies of legs, nose and eyes on the same cartoon deserve to be called a *portrait* or a *human figure.*" Thus is the body expressly introduced into the idea of the tableau, but it is the whole body that is so introduced—the organs, grouped together and as though held in cohesion by the magnetic power of the segmentation, function in the name of a transcendence, that of the *figure,* which receives the full fetishistic load and becomes the sublime substance of meaning.[52]

The student of Prague's body is "split" (the mirror image or reflection is severed from the body that produces it) and "doubled" (the mirror image acquires a life of its own); the film contains, therefore, a figure of its own hybrid status as text, its discomfiting suspicion that it is its own body that is not all of a piece. Early cinema suspects that the arts of which it is comprised set it at odds with itself; it suspects that it is composed of scattered limbs that do not quite come together as a figure. In the earliest of Fritz Lang's Dr. Mabuse films, a minor character (the Countess's brother) is tagged as "decadent" and "weird" because he is "a Cubist"—because, in effect, he admires paintings in which "legs, nose, and eyes" do not, in fact, come together in the customary way. In this same film,

---

production of figures. That system would need to be understood, were we to follow the implication of the dancer's appended explanation, as a mechanism entailing mutilation; the puppet-theater text would be a mutilating machine" (Chase, "Mechanical Doll," 146).

52. Roland Barthes, "Diderot, Brecht, Eisenstein," in *Image, Music, Text,* trans. Stephen Heath (New York: Hill and Wang, 1977), 71–72.

Hugo Balling—an obvious allusion to Hugo Ball, the Dadaist—is one of the evil personae of Dr. Mabuse himself. Clearly, these references both are and are not admiring, for film is envious of avant-garde painting and poetry and quotes them in order to place itself on the cutting edge.

György Kurtág's *Kafka Fragmente:*
Kafka in Pieces

Ruth V. Gross

Nichts dergleichen.
Nein, nein, nichts dergleichen!

In 1948, a young Czech Germanist named Peter Demetz contributed an article to the Austrian periodical *Plan* entitled "Zur Interpretation Franz Kafkas," in which he summarized the significant Kafka scholarship of the day and provided his own reading of Kafka's "Das Urteil." In that article, Demetz explained the problem of placing Kafka in the scheme of national literatures and was one of the first to ask whether it was at all possible to attribute Kafka to one nation, one language, and one national literature. Kafka, who, for obvious reasons, has alternately been classified as an Austrian, German, Czech, and Jewish writer, clearly belongs to that category known as the world author; but he is also a European writer belonging to the world of "Mitteleuropa," a world that perished when East and West as separate designations (and ideologies) for Europe became a reality after World War II (and that, as of this writing, is quite rapidly reemerging).

With Kafka there is another dimension. Until May, 1963, fifteen years after Demetz's article, Kafka was officially unsanctioned in the postwar Marxist or Eastern European world. Dismissed as a "modernist," Kafka was seen as presenting a nihilistic fatalism in his works that was detrimental to the progress of socialist development in Eastern Europe.[1] In 1963, after years of "official" neglect in the Eastern bloc, a Congress on Kafka was convened in Libliça Castle near Prague to reassess the significance and influence of Kafka for the Marxist world. The host of the conference was

---

1. Georg Lukács, "Franz Kafka or Thomas Mann?" in *Realism in Our Time,* trans. J. Mander and N. Mander (New York: Harper and Row, 1964).

Eduard Goldstücker, at the time Czechoslovakia's leading expert on Kafka; the discussions included writers and critics from most Eastern European countries, as well as two Western Communists—Ernst Fischer from Austria and Roger Garaudy from France. What resulted was a general reappraisal of Kafka by all who participated in the conference except the East Germans (who, even if they acknowledged Kafka's stylistic genius, continued in their belief that Kafka had nothing to say to contemporary socialism).[2]

In the almost thirty years since that conference, many critics from the Eastern bloc have dealt with Kafka. Recognizing his importance as a literary figure for both East and West, some Marxists have revised their ideas on alienation and realism to incorporate Kafka's texts into their canon.[3] It is not surprising, then, that an Eastern European, to be precise, an Hungarian, would be among those composers who have recently set Kafka to music. The phrase "Kafka set to music" sounds strange, almost comical, perhaps because it has been done with such mixed success and with little public acknowledgment.[4] Because Kafka is not a lyric poet or a storyteller in any traditional sense, his words are not naturally suited as texts for lieder or opera librettos. His prose jolts, startles, subverts its meaning. How can it be appropriate for a song cycle? Any answer to this question must lie in the composer and his or her choice of text.

György Kurtág, born in 1926 (two years after Kafka died), in a part of post–World War I Rumania that was strongly rooted in Hungarian language and tradition, has become Hungary's most important living composer. His opus 24, *Kafka Fragmente: Meine Gefängniszelle, meine Festung,* an enormous, seventy-five-minute-long piece for soprano and violin, is Kurtág's third song cycle.[5] This immense work is dedicated to one of

---

2. Cf. Kenneth Hughes, "The Marxist Debate, 1963," in *The Kafka Debate,* ed. Angel Flores (New York: Gordian Press, 1977), 51–59.

3. Hughes especially notes Ernst Fischer and Roger Garaudy ("Marxist Debate," 53, 56–57).

4. My thanks to Eva Gruhn of the Staatliche Hochschule für Musik in Hannover, for researching no fewer than forty-five compositions, mostly by German composers, that take Kafka stories, fragments, and letters as their basis. The earliest settings are by Max Brod and Ernst Krenek and, more recently, such composers as Lukas Foss, Gottfried von Einem, Alberto Ginastera, Hans-Werner Henze, Bruno Moderna, and Gunther Schuller have tried their hand at "Kafka-Vertonung." Few of the works have achieved the prominence that Kurtág's opus 24 has.

5. My analysis of the piece is based on a facsimile completed in 1986. *Kafka Fragmente: Meine Gefängniszelle, meine Festung* will be published by Boosey and Hawkes in 1992. On August 5, 1988, the American premiere of György Kurtág's *Kafka Fragmente: Meine Gefängniszelle, meine Festung* was performed at the Monadnock Music Festival in Francestown, New Hamp-

Kurtág's mentors and friends, Marianne Stein, with whom he studied during a year spent in Paris in 1957-58. During that year he also studied with Olivier Messaien and Darius Milhaud and became particularly intrigued by the music of Anton Webern. Much of opus 24 recalls the short, compressed, fragmentary elements of Webern's music (cf. Webern's First Cantata op. 29). It was Stein, a psychologist specializing in work with all kinds of artists—painters, architects, musicians, and theater people—who changed the course of Kurtág's musical path. His encounter with her caused him to reject all his previous work and begin again. She got Kurtág to concentrate, above all, on tiny units in his musical thinking, units not deductively determined by overlapping and wide-reaching formal connections, but rather little, surveyable complexes that express something both in themselves and as part of a larger context. Through Stein's influence, Kurtág became a master of the "little form," and, thus, it is so appropriate that he dedicated this particular work to her. According to one musicologist, Stein discovered something about the essence of Kurtág's composition that he had not yet known himself—that in each microcosm of musical expression Kurtág could create a macrocosm of profound emotion.[6]

Kurtág and Kafka intersect most obviously in this idea of "the little form." Kurtág selected his texts for this cycle from Kafka's diaries, letters, and aphorisms. Indeed, because these Kafka texts are so diverse, plentiful, rich, and noncohesive one to another in Kafka's oeuvre, we may say that Kurtág is the real author of his text here, while Kafka's writings provide the language for Kurtág's conception. We know that both composer Kurtág and writer Kafka reveal similar characteristics in their style of work as well as their background. Kurtág, like Kafka, has a very strong self-critical streak. For that reason, the quantity of published works is fairly small for both men. Both men grew up in cultures that were profoundly multilingual and multicultural—in the unique and passing world of Mitteleuropa, where diverse nationalities have provided us with great art, great music, great literature, and, of course, great wars and great hatred in this century. (In this regard, Kurtág's score for *Kafka Fragmente* is characteristic—German,

---

shire. A few days later, the same work was performed at the Tanglewood Festival in Lenox, Massachusetts, and a large American audience had the opportunity to hear these musical settings of Kafka's prose.

6. Hartmut Luck, "'Dezembers Gluten, Sommers Hagelschläge . . .': Zur künstlerischen Physiognomie von György Kurtág," in *György Kurtág,* ed. Friedrich Spangemacher (Bonn: Boosey and Hawkes Musikverlag, 1986), 31.

Hungarian, Italian, and French markings, remarks, and subtitles are intermingled, apparently because Kurtág felt that whatever he meant could best be expressed in the particular language he chose.)

Kafka's Prague no longer exists, but it was a city where Germans and Czechs confronted each other for centuries. For Kafka, Prague was the microcosm that represented the Austro-Hungarian Empire. Within that society, the Germans were aggressive and nationally conscious, which, ironically, made the Jews of the city (whose language was German) nationally conscious Germans. Modernism's debt to the "nationality problem" that fueled World War I should not be underestimated. It is within this complex of many languages and cultures that Kafka's literary production arises. György Kurtág also grew up in a multilingual, multicultural environment of interwar nationalistic tensions and wartime catastrophe. Thus, for both Kurtág and Kafka, there is a simultaneous awareness and suspicion of words and the fixed aspect of language that must be overcome. They experience the same crisis of language confronted by Austrian authors of the fin de siècle. The aphorism or fragment had served as a kind of linguistic mask for many writers in fin de siècle Austria that they used as a weapon against the meaninglessness and shallowness of common expression. Aphorisms and fragments expressed, for them, a sense that physical and psychic reality are in no way stable or eternally definable. A continually changing perspective recognizes the unsystematic over the systematic; the bureaucratic immobilism of the Castle and its Law must be subverted. Given this constant verbal fluctuation, a *Sprachkrise* as the concrete medium for these perceptions emerged.[7] The fragmentary or aphoristic expression responded to the tensions of modernity by simultaneously taking them into account and trying to overcome them. What resulted was the kind of skepticism about the value of reason and thought apparent in Kafka's life and art, shaped by the same crises and questions. Although skeptical of language, he is driven to communicate the inexpressible. The internal world can only be lived, not described, yet Kafka wants to communicate precisely this internal world, and so he does through the kinds of self-observing, self-critical writings in his notebooks and diaries. For Kafka, truth lies in the details and not in the whole. In a letter to Max Brod, Kafka wrote: "I shall only describe the externals since I cannot speak of more than I could see. But all one actually sees is the most minute details;

---

7. Richard T. Gray, *Constructive Destruction: Kafka's Aphorisms, Literary Tradition and Literary Transformation* (Tübingen: Max Niemeyer Verlag, 1987), esp. 135–59.

and this is indeed significant in my opinion. It testifies to sincerity, even to the worst idiot. Where truth is, all one can see with the naked eye is such minute details."[8] In other words, for Kafka, truth is the empirically perceptible; totality, a series of fragments.[9] For Kurtág, too, the whole is very much a series of fragments. Nowhere is that clearer than in his creation of *Kafka Fragmente,* a major musical achievement.

Kafka Fragmente consists of forty individual pieces divided into four parts of different lengths. The first part contains nineteen fragments, all extremely brief. Part 2 is one longer fragment that Kurtág subtitled "Homage-Message à Pierre Boulez," the French composer and conductor who is one of Kurtág's recent champions. Part 3 contains twelve fragments, eleven of which are brief, but the twelfth, like part 2, is once again a well-developed piece. And part 4 is made up of eight fragments, also ending with a longer one. (In the overall structure, part 2 could be seen as the finale of part 1, thus presenting three symmetrical sections, each ending with an extended fragment.) As in previous works (such as the *Attila Jozsef-Fragmente,* opus 20), Kurtág shows a great talent for the miniature, giving us a collection of what British music critic Stephen Walsh has called "emotional snap-shots."[10] The title of the work echoes one of the fragments—"Meine Gefäng-niszelle, meine Festung"—and shows the fluctuating perception of both the composer and writer regarding creative solitude. Because some of Kurtág's recent song cycles have been about various kinds of failure, Walsh, in his review of the work, described *Kafka Fragmente* as "a series of generalised vignettes about the futility of existence, the misery of joy, and perhaps even the joy of misery."[11] He finds the work fundamentally pessimistic, expressing a basic existential nihilism, in which "the work's greatest image of failure is the inability of the voice to match the violin in graphic or expressive bravura."[12] I tend to disagree with his assessment of the general meaning of the work and the vocal line. His tendency to allegorize the voice and the violin is too simple; I think that he underestimates the strength of the positive side of the work.

---

8. Franz Kafka, *Letters to Friends, Family, and Editors,* trans. Richard Winston and Clara Winston (New York: Schocken Books, 1977), 119–20.

9. Gray, *Constructive Destruction,* 153.

10. Stephen Walsh, "Kurtág's 'Kafka Fragments,'" *Hungarian Musical Quarterly* 1 (1989): 15.

11. Walsh, "'Kafka Fragments,'" 15.

12. Walsh, "'Kafka Fragments,'" 16.

Each of the Kafka fragments chosen for this work, like Kurtág's music, exists both in a microcosm and as a macrocosm. The words express one meaning on their own, but, as a collection, they undertake a dialogue with the words, in this case, the fragments, that come before and after them. To say that Kurtág's work is about failure because Kafka's diaries are full of self-reproach for his inability to sustain love misses the point that these fragments are now recontextualized by Kurtág, just as the *Diaries* are only part of Kafka's great oeuvre. Indeed, to call a piece *Fragmente* creates a paradox in itself, since they cease to be fragments as soon as they become part of a work that has closure, as this one clearly does.

As in many modernist works, however, there is no real plot here. This is not a "novelistic" song cycle, like Schubert's *Winterreise* or *Die Schöne Müllerin*. It is more reminiscent of Schumann's *Liederkreis,* op. 39 (another composer of fragments), in which there is a *thematic* unity within the cycle. Even so, it is not always clear why Kurtág has chosen the order he has,[13] or what specific relationship each fragment's setting has with the next. Like Nietzsche's fragmentary form, the order is a puzzle to be pondered with the texts. It is possible at the outset, however, to discern certain broader thematic patterns. (The texts of the forty pieces are found in the appendix to this essay.)

The work centers on three basic ideas—movement, illusion versus reality, and the fall from verbal communication to linguistic inexpressibility. These themes are related to one another by the central metaphor of the work—progression from one place to another, as progression is a metaphor for communication. In part 1, physical movement of one kind or another is the focus again and again. Part 2 considers the idea of the "true path" in the light of the difference between our perception of that path and the path itself, a Kantian distinction between perceived reality and reality. This distinction is at the heart of the fragments of the third section. The last part of the work focuses on the breakdown of communication, a fall from language, a confrontation with meaninglessness. It serves as an affirmation of the need for the fragment as a genre, a path, to remind us of the fragmentary nature of phenomenal reality—a path from Kant to Wittgenstein.

In the opening piece (part 1, fragment 1), "Die Guten gehn im gleichen Schritt," one of the recurring and, indeed, central images of the work is

---

13. The present order of the fragments is already a revision of the premiere and first performances of the work.

introduced—procession down a path. The text is simple: "Die guten gehn im gleichen Schritt. Ohne von ihnen zu wissen, tanzen, tanzen, tanzen die andern um sie die Tänze der Zeit—die Tänze der Zeit." The violin plays slow, repeated notes in stepwise chromatic motion, never varying to the end. This pattern represents "the good" as identity and repetition. The voice does the dancing of "the others." While the violin is instructed to keep the same *molto misurato* tempo with medium soft dynamics *indifferente al fine* (the same throughout the fragment), the vocal line is *staccato, capriccioso e leggiero* and finally *quasi niente, aereo*; the vocal line should vanish into breath and air as the violin stays firmly "on the ground." The movement from one point to another in space, music, or word is a trope of communication, just as metaphor is a communicative path from one point to another. The image of paths or ways [*Wege*], that ancient figure of human purpose and meaning, returns again and again in the work.

A great deal of Kafka's short fiction simply and literally describes how hard it is to get from one place to another (cf. "The Bridge," "A Common Confusion," "The Great Wall of China," "An Imperial Message," and so forth). Kurtág, too, is concerned with movement of one kind or another and has thus selected these particular fragments of Kafka's that center precisely on the *path,* the *way,* motion forward. In the first part, consideration of paths or ways [*Wege*] connects each individual fragment, forming a sort of path through the work as a whole. The path itself is the subject of the second fragment: "Wie ein Weg im Herbst: kaum ist er reingekehrt, bedeckt er sich wieder mit den trockenen Blättern." Here, voice and violin reverse their roles from the first fragment; the violin imitates the swirling leaves that "dance" without direction in the wind, to pick up an image of the first fragment, and the voice walks the path. A true fragment, this particular text never tells us what it is that is like a path in autumn. Following Richard Gray, we might call it "a 'ruptured' simile, one in which the tenor of the comparison is left unexpressed."[14] In keeping with the fragmentary nature of the text, the piece itself ends before one has a chance to reflect on its meaning; indeed, most of the fragments in this work are brief. As one critic writes about Kurtág's composition: "His pieces are brief not from 'moderation' but from a wholly immoderate facing-up to silence as the only alternative."[15] In the writing for the violin in this second fragment, harmonics abound from the middle to the end, giving

14. Gray, *Constructive Destruction,* 247.
15. C. Paul Griffiths, "Program Notes," Almeida Festival, England, June 18, 1988.

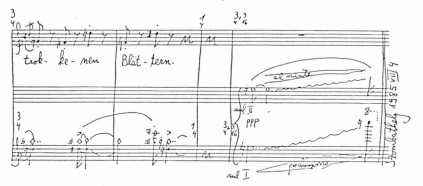

Ex. 1. Kurtág, *Kafka Fragmente,* end of part 1, fragment 2

the piece a ghostly sound; it ends with a glissando that vanishes into nothing, *al niente,* recalling the marking for the vocal line in the first fragment (see ex. 1).

"Verstecke 1," the third fragment in part 1, whose text is repeated verbatim in fragment 10 of part 3 as "Verstecke 2," concerns not so much a path one walks in life, but, allegorically, the possible paths to salvation. "Nimmermehr," the sixth song in part 1, describes a path that will never be traveled again—the path to the cities where chimes toll. The negativity of this verbal fragment couples with the image of the large tolling bell to announce the finality of death at the end of our forward movement. The music is to be played *doloroso* (mournfully); the subtitle is "Excommunicatio," suggesting a hopelessness and finality without salvation. Fragments 7, 8, 9 and 10 focus on diverse subjects, unrelated to the previous fragments. They move with great speed, like the first part in general, as if to emphasize the idea of motion that is central to this section. Motion is challenged in the tenth and eleventh fragments. The tenth fragment has to do with the path of a train observed as it passes. Here, the train moves, but the onlookers freeze, a suggestion that stagnation and fear of forward movement are death in life. The next fragment reiterates this idea in another way. "Sonntag, den 19. Juli 1910 (Berceuse 2) [Hommage à Jéney]" depicts a repetitive pattern of life that does not seem to move forward in its repetition and, therefore, is "elendes Leben" ['miserable life']. Ironically subtitled "Berceuse 2" (Lullaby 2), this piece is hardly that. In both the vocal and violin lines, dramatic changes highlight the different states of consciousness expressed by the words *geschlafen* and *aufgewacht*. The soprano dynamics range from *pianissimo* to *forte* with accents, and the violinist switches from *ppp* to *ff* and even *fff* several times throughout this short "lullaby." No one would be put to sleep by this dramatic and violent pronouncement of stagnation in life. The formal tension of the shrieking lullaby that announces peace as death reminds us that the path that the "good" walk in fragment 1 has exactly this anodyne repetitiveness.

The path comes into play indirectly once again in the first part in fragment 16, "Keine Rückkehr": "Von einem gewissen Punkt an gibt es keine Rückkehr mehr. Dieser Punkt ist zu erreichen." This fragment is an expression of triumph, not the failure that Walsh suggests. Although totality, the end of the path, is out of the question, a point beyond which despair is impossible is within our grasp; I believe that, for both Kafka and Kurtág, this point is the work of art.

Kurtág's music reflects the fragmentary nature of the texts. Each piece interrupts the expression of the last, and yet there are definite similarities in the compositions that bind the work together. Kurtág's vocabulary in *Kafka Fragmente* relies heavily on the open strings of the violin and on chords built from them. He continually urges the voice to imitate the violin and lose its human character; when this fails, the soprano lapses into "a rhythmically free semirecitative style" that Kurtág notates in a unique manner.[16]

Readers of Kafka know that the humor in his works is often overlooked, perhaps because of its darkness, but Kurtág understands this side of Kafka and sets it to music, reinforcing it with his own kindred sense of humor. In part 1 of *Kafka Fragmente,* there are several touches of black humor. Fragment 4 is less sung than acted. It consists of one word in the vocal line—*Ruhelos.* The directions in the score read: "Das Stück soll eine Art Pantomime sein. Die Sängerin folgt den Akrobatien und dem Wüten des Geigers mit wachsender Spannung, Erregung, sogar Angst, bis ihr am Ende wirklich auch die Stimme versagt." She utters the word *Ruhelos* without voice—*senza voce.* She cannot compete here with the violin that has been "strident" throughout, but she regains her voice for the next piece, "Berceuse 1" (much more a lullaby in both text and music than "Berceuse 2"), suggesting that the restlessness has been calmed. Kurtág's directions for fragment 13 are specifically "Mit Humor." The words are "Einmal brach ich mir das Bein, es war das schönste Erlebnis meines Lebens." Elsewhere, as we have heard in fragment 11 (and repeated in part 3, fragment 5), life is described as nothing but "sleeping and waking up— miserable life." No wonder breaking a leg can be something beautiful—it

---

16. Walsh, "'Kafka Fragments,'" 16.

breaks the monotony of life, of the path, as it is expressed in these fragments. The "broken leg" fragment is also characterized in the score by Kurtág's notation, in Hungarian, *chasszid tanc* (Chassidic dance), which makes the humor even more marked. The text of fragment 12, "Meine Ohrmuschel fühlte sich frisch, rauh, kühl, saftig an wie ein Blatt," is to be performed by the vocalist in what Kurtág describes as *Katzenartiges Sprechgesang* (catlike recitative). It moves so quickly that the only focal point of the piece is the last word, *Blatt,* which recalls the leaf-covered path of fragment 2.

Fragment 15, "Zwei Spazierstöcke," also picks up on the main theme and, at the same time, defines the nature of the fragmentary—the world that is all detail and no totality: "Auf Balzacs Spazierstockgriff: Ich breche alle Hindernisse. Auf meinem: Mich brechen alle Hindernisse. Gemeinsam ist das 'alle.'" Once again, the text indirectly deals with forward movement. Here, the walking stick becomes the metaphor for movement down a path filled with obstacles. Balzac has a handle on totality—everything is part of the human comedy. Kafka, on the other hand, is caught in the difficulties of basic existence—sleeping and waking, how his ear feels, breaking a leg, and so forth. He recognizes the enormous difference between himself and Balzac, but there is also a kind of pride and defiance in comparing himself in this way and coming up with a point in common. Kafka defines his success differently. Thus, it is not really failure that is the theme here, but, rather, a different kind of success. A "modernist" definition of success, so to speak.

Shortly before the end of part 1, Kurtág sets a fragment taken from the diary entry of November 15, 1910. He himself titles this piece "Stolz"; usually the titles are either the first lines of the fragment or Kafka's, so Kurtág has given us his interpretation of the fragment in the title. Here there is no real path; yet the way to proceed is clearly stated—a dive into the text itself. Once again, "Stolz," like many of the other fragments, expresses a different kind of success rather than failure. As in the preceding fragment, there is no turning back. A point of resolution is reached and pride is taken in precisely that resolution. The goal is a victory over the self, even at great personal cost—"und wenn es mir das Gesicht zerschneiden sollte." As if to emphasize the lacerations, the violin accompaniment becomes very harsh as the harmonies become more intense—*piu pressato*—and even the composer's direction for the violin is *gekratzt* when it accompanies "das Gesicht zerschneiden sollte."

The first part ends with "Nein! Nichtsdergleichen!" These words announce that what we are hearing is different, not like what has come

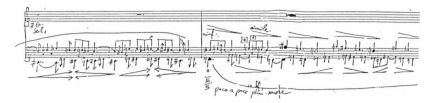

Ex. 2. Kurtág, *Kafka Fragmente,* part 2

before, as different as Kafka is from Balzac. As different as a Kafka fragment is from the more than forty volumes of *The Human Comedy,* which, uncompleted as it is, could technically also be called a fragment—in spite of Balzac's walking stick! The pieces in part 1 move by with enormous speed, and, as if to emphasize this swiftness, the last piece is marked *con moto, sempre piu e piu presto.* The music itself gets faster and faster, and the section ends on what would seem to be a particularly negative idea: "No, nothing of the kind!" (This was the first piece of the opus that Kurtág completed. Each song is dated in the unpublished score.) But the insistence that there is nothing of the kind can also be seen as a positive confirmation of the absolute originality of the subject.

Kafka entitled one of the collections from which several of the fragments used in Kurtág's piece have been taken "Betrachtungen über Sünde, Leid, Hoffnung und den wahren Weg." In various of the *Kafka Fragmente,* the "true" path is considered, as in part 2, where it goes over a rope that is strung barely above the ground and is almost sure to make you stumble, or, as in part 3, where "there is a destination, but no path; what we call a path is hesitation." These fragments stress a skepticism about human perceptions that hinder us and make an easy path difficult to walk. Part 2 is an adagio movement entitled "Der wahre Weg" and subtitled "Homage-message à Pierre Boulez." The voice sings long, sustained notes, while the violin writing, as in Boulez's school of complexity, is like a rather wobbly rope. This effect is achieved through quartertones, which give the piece a yearning quality (see ex. 2). Toward the end of this section, Kurtág has composed a short *Siciliano* in the vocal line that coincides with the word *stumble,* and musically recalls the "dances of time" of the first song in part 1. Perhaps dancing is the best way to travel the path, but dancing, of course, is precisely a kind of stumbling. As noted, this particular fragment marks a kind of transition touching on both the idea of path or movement, which was the basic focus of the first part, and introducing the problem of appearance and reality, the recurring theme of the third part.

Kurtág's part 3 is once again a sequence of short pieces ending with "Szene in der Elektrischen," the longest piece and most extended narrative of the entire work. The fragments in this part articulate the difference between reality and perceived reality in various ways. To quote Alice about Wonderland, "Nothing is as it seems." In fragment 1, "Haben? Sein?," existence means longing for suffocation. In the second fragment, "Coitus is a punishment for the happiness of being together." In fragment 3, the title song of the entire work, a prison cell is a fortress, and in the fourth fragment, "Schmutzig bin ich, Milena," the paradox of reality and perception is emphasized by Kafka when he writes about being dirty and, therefore, obsessed with cleanliness. To demonstrate this kind of obsession, he explains that the purest song is sung by those in deepest hell; we take that song from hell to be the singing of the angels. The fragments in this part all demonstrate the importance of perceived reality in our world. If there is a logic to our existence, it is an absurd one—the unsystematic system of modernism. As if to emphasize this, Kurtág uses scordatura in this section for the first time. The violinist plays a second instrument that is tuned differently from the first. For the voices of those in deepest hell, the tuning pegs on the violin are used in a glissando down to a low E and at the end of the piece, the tuning pegs are used again as if the instrument were being tuned. The violinist is to play the end *senza espressione,* intensifying the impression of tuning rather than playing something written. Thus, even in the performance of this work, perception differs from reality (see ex. 3). The fifth fragment in this section verbally reprises fragment 11 of part 1 about "miserable life." Kurtág calls it a "Double," but the music differs from the text's first setting. Here, the violin is lighter and less strident, as is the voice; perhaps because the tempo is not *andante* but *presto.* We have none of the roller coaster dynamics that marked the earlier fragment, but, rather, a steady crescendo from *pianissimo* to an accented *non forte* that complements a change in tempo in midpiece from *presto* to *piu presto.* Different, too, are the final two measures, in which the words *elendes Leben* appear. In the earlier fragment, the vocal line went up on the last note of "Leben," but here, both in the violin and vocal lines, the note progression is downward. So, although this fragment claims to be the double of the earlier piece, the reality is otherwise. There is little hope that this miserable life can go anywhere but downward.

The idea of the path returns in fragments 7 and 8 of part 3. In the seventh fragment, the words tell us that "There is a destination, but no path. What we call path is simply hesitation." This implies that existence

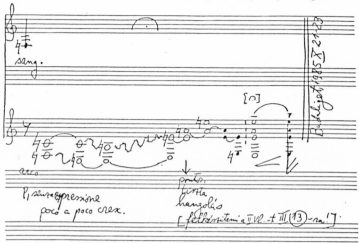

Ex. 3.   Kurtág, *Kafka Fragmente,* end of part 3, fragment 4

itself is without a path, without preordained purpose. Nonetheless, as long as we can name things, they seem to exist, and thus, even if our perceptions are wrong, they are the reality with which we must live. Once again, there is an affirmation within the negative implication of the words. This fragment expresses the belief that language itself causes our incorrect perceptions. We think there is a path, but we have misnamed it. The German word *zögern* (to hesitate) derives from the middle high and early new high German word *zogen,* which means to walk or move from one place to another,[17] and with this word, the theme of the first section returns. The dichotomy of appearance and reality typifies much of modernism and becomes clearly articulated in both words and music here. Fragment 8 confirms the idea that the path (as we call it) will lead to a destination, no matter how far away, in this case as far as the hand can throw a stone. Once again, this is one of Kafka's ruptured similes that has no expressed tenor of comparison. The first part of the fragment sets up a paradox in that we firmly hold on to something only to cast it away from us that much farther or with that much more intensity. In German, the word *verwerfen* can mean both cast away permanently and reject. The idea that the path will lead us back to the rejected object relates to the sixth fragment in this part, "Der begrenzte Kreis." The short fragment reads "Nur der begrenzte Kreis ist rein," which would indicate that circularity is purity.

---

17. *Der Große Duden: Herkunftswörterbuch der deutschen Sprache,* s.v. "zogen."

But if a path is nothing more than circular, progression is futile and merely illusionary. Kurtág, by choosing these fragments, has grasped the subversive nature of Kafka's writing. Meaning is constantly undercutting itself.

The ninth fragment, entitled "Penetrant Jüdisch," reveals Kafka's humor yet again and, with its title and ironic pose, reminds us of a Jewish joke. The reality of life is that we will lose whenever we do battle with the world. The advice of this fragment, to take the world's side against ourselves, is an impossible condition unless irony is the essence of our worldview, a worldview that is either "intensively" or "annoyingly" Jewish—the literal and figurative meanings of the word *penetrant*. Kafka and Kurtág obviously had both ideas in mind for this fragment. "Verstecke 2" reprises the text of fragment 3 in part 1. This text, like "Elendes Leben," is expecially important to Kurtág, otherwise he would not have used it twice within the same work. In its images, it reminds the listener of Kafka's man from the country in "Vor dem Gesetz," or the "ich" in "Gib's auf" or the animal narrator of "Der Bau"—three characters who might be said to lose in the struggle between perception and reality because they fail to progress along a clear path with true conviction.

The final two fragments in this part, one of which describes a large horse breaking through the roof, the other, a textual replication of the musical setting of Kurtág's voice-violin combination, are fragments that move us into the world of dreams. Like the penultimate fragment of part 1, the eleventh fragment in part 3 starts with a present participle, here "staunend," there "träumend," and deals with a dream. In part 1, the dreamer was a flower, here, although never said explicitly, the image seems dreamlike, almost hallucinatory.[18] Visions like that of the horse formed the basis for much of Kafka's literary activity. In his diaries, Kafka goes so far as to speak of his special talent of representing his "dreamlike inner life" that was the key to his writing.[19] Fear that this talent could leave

---

18. The close relationship between Kafka's writing and his dream life has often been noted. See particularly S. Fraiberg, "Kafka and the Dream," *Partisan Review* 23 (1956): 47–69.

19. Franz Kafka, *Tagebücher, 1920–1923,* ed. Max Brod (Frankfurt am Main: Fischer Taschenbuchverlag, 1980), 262. In the passage in which he writes of the talent, he also wonders whether it may not have already completely disappeared, leaving him unable to write. Kafka feels himself to be in a constant state of dying because of this insecurity: "So schwanke ich also, fliege unaufhörlich zur Spitze des Berges, kann mich aber kaum einen Augenblick oben erhalten. . . . Ich . . . schwanke dort oben, es ist leider kein Tod, aber die ewigen Qualen des Sterbens."

him at any time often made his life unbearable. Writing was Kafka's dream as well as his nightmare.

On Kurtág's facsimile, "Szene in der Elektrischen" has the subtitle "1910: 'Ich bat im Traum die Tänzerin Eduardowa, sie möchte doch den Csardas noch einmal tanzen,' . . ." a line that is actually part of a different fragment about Eduardowa, one of Kafka's earliest diary entries, and in the *Diaries* immediately precedes the one set to music by Kurtág as fragment 12. The two violinists sung about in the fragment represent the two instruments, the one tuned, the other mistuned, that the violinist of *Kafka Fragmente* plays. Not surprisingly, this piece took the longest for Kurtág to compose. The anecdote is once again typical of Kafka's less-acknowledged charming and humorous side and tells of the dancer Eduardowa, who travels everywhere, even in the streetcar, in the accompaniment of two violinists, whom she frequently has play. In part 1, Kurtág subtitled "Träumend hing die Blume," an homage to Schumann, but "Szene in der Elektrischen," with its changing rhythms and dance quality and subject matter, now even more audibly recalls that romantic composer. In the score, Kurtág has gone so far as to label certain parts "Eusebius" and "Florestan"—the two characters, one dreamy and one wild, of Schumann's musical imagination and *Davidsbündlertänze*. In terms of the Kurtág work, this fragment recalls the opening fragment, as we have a dancer. But this dancer is on a vehicle, thus moving on a path of sorts "at full speed" (perhaps passing by the frozen spectators of "Szene am Bahnhof"). There is a difference from the first fragment of the work, however; here, both vocalist and violinist(s) seem to dance. No straight line, march step accompanies the voice here. Perhaps, this means that "the good" of the first fragment was simply an illusion, like the voice of the angels in "Schmutzig bin ich Milena" and the uncovered path of "Wie ein Weg im Herbst." In reality, we are all "others," marking the dances of time, despite our perceptions to the contrary. Reality and perception are central to the way the music is written on the page in this piece. The violin line (see ex. 4) takes on great complication. For notating scordatura, the composer has the choice of writing the part as it should sound (*suono reale*) or writing the part as it must be played in the tuning he desires. Kurtág has chosen to notate both; thus, underneath the line *suono reale* are the notes that must be played to achieve the desired pitches on the violin. The score presents a double reality—reality of code and reality of act. (Of course, all musical notation is, in fact, a code for the real act. But usually the code corresponds to an expected reality, i.e., the note A in the score signifies production of

Ex. 4.   Kurtág, *Kafka Fragmente,* part 3, fragment 12

an A sound on the violin.) But the real sounds are not the real notes played (insofar as the real notes are equated with positions on the violin fingerboard); the real notes played are producing a sound not their own but a sound that is considered real. Scordatura necessitates an illusion of the "real" sound. Because the scordatura violin has a much tenser and thinner sound, the two violins become two different characters, possibly replicating Eusebius and Florestan, definitely representing Eduardowa's two accompanists. This fragment, perhaps better than any of the other thirty-nine, achieves a complete synthesis of words and music.

In Kurtág's part 4, the mood becomes much more melancholy than it has been. What can best be called the ironic stance of the previous section dissipates here and turns to brooding acceptance of the impossibility of communication through language. The first two fragments deal with a subject not yet broached in the work—love; but love here is past love, love that has been or perhaps really never was—another illusion, another perceived reality. Kurtág, in his setting of the fragment, has focused on the word *Liebe*. Both times it appears in the fragment the soprano sings the same notes, an interval of an augmented ninth. Real communication between two lovers in the first fragment is established nonverbally—with a smile—and that is the pinnacle of the relationship. As Kafka's words define it, love becomes a very solitary emotion that is worked through the self, not communicated to another, and Kurtág's music bears out this feeling.

The second fragment actually makes fun of love as an illusion and concludes that *looking* at a girl already creates a very long love story. In Kurtág's setting, which is to be performed *presto*, the singer must stutter on the words *Mädchen* and *Augen*, as if to indicate the embarrassment of the situation. The brief moment, a fragment out of time, the stuttering hesitation of expression, the full, extended meaning in an instant—this fragment recapitulates Kurtág's work: a long story, lived quickly, in stuttered moments, but unforgettable, "mit Donner und Küsse [*sic*] und Blitz." The somber mood returns in the third fragment, which is titled "In Memoriam Robert Klein." Dealing with hounds and their prey, the fragment suggests life (and, consequently, death) as a foregone conclusion. Although we see the dogs playing, we know that their prey, even with a head start, will not escape them. The fragment reminds the listener of Kafka's parable "Kleine Fabel," in which a mouse is cornered and devoured by a cat who gives it advice. There is no path of escape.

The melancholy mood and focus on nonverbal communication continue in fragment 4, where one hand expresses compassion for the other hand by enfolding it. The body parts take on identities of their own, almost as if they could think for themselves and more reasonably than the persona-narrator who writes and has "studied from six o'clock in the morning" till the evening. Of course, this, too, is illusionary. Nonetheless, as this section of the work develops, gestures increasingly signify more than words.

The ritualization of an amazing moment ultimately robs it of its meaning. An event as shocking as leopards breaking into a temple, as in the fifth fragment, can also become nothing more than ritual with its repetition. Common language, through its repetition, also becomes ritual—actually a breakdown of communication and expression. It loses its meaning and communicative power by being commonplace. We dwell under the illusion that we can really say what we mean, but having understood the nature of language, we should find it hard to say anything at all. In his fragments, Kafka often sought to express something that he felt was inexpressible. In a letter to Milena, he writes, "ich suche nur immerfort etwas Nicht-Mitteilbares mitzuteilen, etwas Unerklärbares zu erklären, von etwas zu erzählen, was ich in den Knochen habe und was nur in diesen Knochen erlebt werden kann."[20] One solution to this problem is to fall silent, as Hofmannsthal pointed out in the Lord Chandos letter or Wittgenstein at the end of his *Tractatus*. The other option is to use the metaphoric fragment that "represents a mode of expression which *shows* within its own structural patterns relationships about which it cannot directly *speak*."[21] In fragment 6, "In Memoriam Johannis Pilinszky," the music and the words describe this ultimate awareness of the breakdown of language. In words reminiscent of the letter to Milena, Kafka explains that he cannot really tell, "Ich kann nicht eigentlich erzählen"—the direct object that, if not grammatically necessary, would be syntactically helpful in both German and English is missing, so what it is is left open. Taken as a predicate alone without a direct object, *erzählen* (to tell) means to communicate (to tell) by speech or writing or to express with words; this is precisely what Kafka feels incapable of doing. So much so that he can hardly talk [*reden*] at all. Kurtág's music complements the ideas in the fragment. As in the opening piece of *Kafka Fragmente,* the violin plays a repetitive pattern, reminding the listener of walking, but, in this fragment, instead of quarter notes in very even

---

20. Franz Kafka, *Briefe an Milena,* ed. Willy Haas (New York: Schocken Books, 1952), 296.

21. Gray, *Constructive Destruction,* 169.

rhythm, Kurtág uses eighth notes with many rests, giving the sense of hesitant steps rather than confident marching (see ex. 5). The voice conveys the insecurity of speech by the many rests and pauses throughout the fragment. Comparing "telling" to the first attempts at walking that a child makes, Kafka and Kurtág unite the ideas of progression and communication that are central to the work.

"Wiederum, wiederum," the penultimate fragment, brings back the idea of movement. This time the walking or "wandering" is involuntary: a wandering of exile, an imposed wandering. If there is a path, its destination is uncertain. It leads away from "here." The exiled one has no choice but to wander; he has no "say."

Control over language reflects control over the pen, over the self, over the path, and this is precisely what has been lost by the end of Kurtág's part 4. The last fragment describes a pair of snakes crawling through the dust in blinding moonlight while birds shriek from the trees. Walking and dancing have given way to crawling, as Kurtág has staged original sin and the Fall as a large-scale aesthetic event leading from the path of the good in part 1, fragment 1, to the alienation of the serpents from the trees in the final fragment. As God pointed out to Adam: "You are dust, and to dust you shall return" (Genesis 3:19). There are sounds all around—birds shrieking, wind rushing—but there are no words exchanged by the pair blinded by the moonlight. Walking has served as the emblem of expression since the opening fragment. The good walk steadily there, we recall. The others do not. Communication, like walking, has become impossible. To underline this idea, the soprano abandons words at the end of the work and vocalizes for almost the entire piece in intricate melisma, until, at the end, she repeats the words *wir krochen durch den Staub, ein Schlangenpaar,* this time vocally white, and with the word *Staub* spoken, not sung to notes. In a sense, then, György Kurtág's *Kafka Fragmente* reenacts the Fall of Man from the goodness of regular meter. It also registers the triumph and success of art and artistic experimentation in describing the path—a way constructed of pieces or fragments—that cannot be followed, but that, paradoxically, leads us to modernism.

In my discussion of Kurtág's *Kafka Fragmente,* I have lightly sketched a path, a philosophical itinerary from Kant through Nietzsche to Wittgenstein. I mean no sense of influences here on either Kafka or Kurtág, but simply wish to point out that the *Kafka Fragmente* confronts the problems and ironies of a century and a half of Central European philosophy. Kant's attempt to save reality from our world of mere appearances so distressed

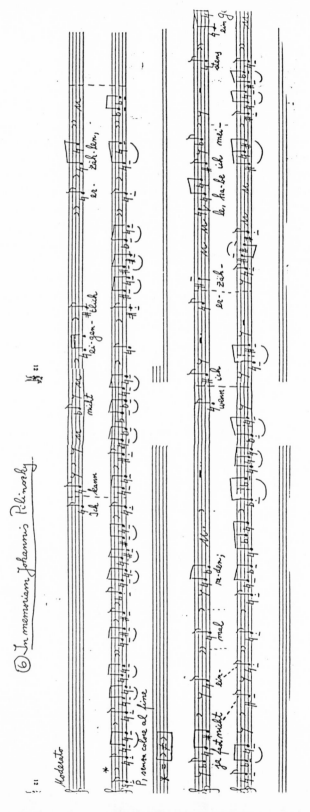

Ex. 5. Kurtág, *Kafka Fragmente*, beginning of part 4, fragment 6

Kleist, the German author with whom Kafka is often compared, that he had his own crisis of language. Nietzsche, who sets out from that crisis, concludes with his worship of a "dancing god," without ground or foundation, finding his own true path. And Wittgenstein, who starts his *Tractatus* with the confident assertion that "the world is all that is the case," concludes that carefully numbered path with his recommendation of silence on all we cannot know, which seems to be just what counts. (He later turns himself to a philosophy of fragments, bits of language.)

The concept of *Mitteleuropa* brings with it its own ironies. Kant, the German, lived his whole life in a city now in the Soviet Union. Nietzsche, who bore a Kaiser's first names and a Polish family name, spent his life escaping, to Switzerland, to Italy. And Wittgenstein, born a Jew in the Empire, like Kafka, had to escape, to find a path out of things. *Mitteleuropa,* a cultural world that Milan Kundera, among others, has poignantly lamented, was crushed, without identity or memory, for fifty years. It is hardly clear whether it can, or should, assume that middle ground of diversity, skepticism, and conflict again. But if it does, a work such as Kurtág's *Kafka Fragmente* might help point, ever so ambiguously, to the path.

Appendix:

Kafka Fragmente: Meine Gefängniszelle, meine Festung,
opus 24, by György Kurtág

Für Marianne Stein

PART 1

1. Die Guten gehn im gleichen Schritt
Die Guten gehn im gleichen Schritt. Ohne von ihnen zu wissen,
tanzen, tanzen, tanzen die andern um sie die Tänze der Zeit.

2. Wie ein Weg im Herbst
Wie ein Weg im Herbst: Kaum ist er reingekehrt, bedeckt er
sich wieder mit den trockenen Blättern.

3. Verstecke 1
Verstecke sind unzählige, Rettung nur eine, aber Möglichkeiten
der Rettung wieder so viele wie Verstecke.

4. Ruhelos
Ruhelos.

5. Berceuse 1
Schlage deinen Mantel, hoher Traum, um das Kind.

6. Nimmermehr
Nimmermehr, nimmermehr kehrst du wieder in die Städte,
nimmermehr, nimmermehr tönt die grosse Glocke über dir.

7. "Wenn er mich immer frägt."
"Wenn er mich immer, immer frägt." Das "ä" losgelöst vom
Satz, flog dahin wie ein Ball auf der Wiese.

8. Es zupfte mich jemand am Kleid

Es zupfte mich jemand am Kleid, aber ich schüttelte ihn ab.

9. Die Weissnäherinnen
Die Weissnäherinnen in den Regengüssen.

10. Szene am Bahnhof
Die Zuschauer erstarren wenn der Zug vorbeifährt.

11. Sonntag, den 19 Juli 1910 (Berceuse 2)
     Hommage à Jéney
Geschlafen, aufgewacht, geschlafen, aufgewacht, geschlafen,
geschlafen, aufgewacht, aufgewacht, aufgewacht, elendes Leben.

12. Meine Ohrmuschel . . .
Meine Ohrmuschel fühlte sich frisch, rauh, kühl, saftig an wie
ein Blatt.

13. Einmal brach ich mir das Bein
Einmal brach ich mir das Bein, es war das schönste Erlebnis
meines Lebens.

14. Umpanzert
Einen Augenblick lang fühlte ich mich umpanzert.

15. Zwei Spazierstöcke
Auf Balzacs Spazierstockgriff: Ich breche alle Hindernisse. Auf
meinem: Mich brechen alle Hindernisse. Gemeinsam ist das
"alle."

16. Keine Rückkehr
Von einem gewissen Punkt an gibt es keine Rückkehr mehr.
Dieser Punkt ist zu erreichen.

17. Stolz
Ich werde mich nicht müde werden lassen. Ich werde in meine
Novelle hineinspringen und wenn es mir das Gesicht zer-
schneiden sollte.

18. Träumend hing die Blume
     Hommage à Schumann
Träumend hing die Blume am hohen Stengel. Abenddäm-
merung umzog sie.

19. Nichtsdergleichen

Nein! Nein! Nein—nein! Nein—nein! Nichtsdergleichen.

PART 2

Der wahre Weg
Hommage-message à Pierre Boulez
Der wahre Weg geht über ein Seil, das nicht in der Höhe
gespannt ist, sondern knapp über den Boden. Es scheint mehr
bestimmt stolpern zu machen, als begangen zu werden.

PART 3

1. Haben? Sein?
Es gibt kein Haben, nur ein Sein, nur ein nach letztem Atem,
nach Ersticken verlangendes Sein.

2. Der Coitus als Bestrafung
Der Coitus als Bestrafung des Glückes des Beisammenseins.

3. Meine Festung
Meine Gefängniszelle—meine Festung.

4. Schmutzig bin ich, Milena
Schmutzig bin ich, Milena, endlos schmutzig, darum mache
ich ein solches Geschrei mit der Reinheit. Niemand singt so
rein als die, welche in der tiefsten Hölle sind; was wir für den
Gesang der Engel halten ist ihr Gesang.

5. Elendes Leben (Double)
Geschlafen, aufgewacht, geschlafen, aufgewacht, elendes
Leben!

6. Der begrenzte Kreis
Der begrenzte Kreis ist rein.

7. Ziel, Weg, Zögern
Es gibt ein Ziel, aber keinen Weg, was wir Weg nennen ist
Zögern.

8. So fest
Für Beatrice und Peter Stein
So fest wie die Hand den Stein hält. Sie hält ihn aber fest,

nur um ihn desto weiter zu verwerfen. Aber auch in jene Weite führt der Weg.

9. Penetrant jüdisch
Im Kampf zwischen dir und der Welt, sekundiere der Welt.

10. Verstecke 2
Verstecke sind unzählige, Rettung nur eine, aber Möglichkeiten der Rettung wieder so viele wie Verstecke.

11. Staunend sahen wir das grosse Pferd
Staunend sahen wir das grosse Pferd. Es durchbrach das Dach unserer Stube. Der bewölkte Himmel zog sich schwach entlang des gewaltigen Umrisses und rauschend flog die Mähne im Wind:

12. Szene in der Elektrischen (Ich bat im Traum die Tänzerin Eduardowa, sie möchte doch den Csardas noch einmal tanzen.) Die Tänzerin Eduardowa, eine Liebhaberin der Musik, fährt wie überall so auch in der Elektrischen in Begleitung zweier Violonisten, die sie häufig spielen lässt. Denn es besteht kein Verbot warum in der Elektrischen nicht gespielt werden durfte, wenn das Spiel gut, den Mitfahrenden angenehm ist und nichts kostet, das heisst, wenn nachher nicht eingesammelt wird. Es ist allerdings im Anfang ein wenig überraschend und ein Weilchen lang findet jeder es sei unpassend. Aber bei voller Fahrt, starkem Luftzug und stiller Gasse klingt es hübsch.

PART 4

1. Zu spät, 22 Oktober 1913
Zu spät. Die Süssigkeit der Trauer und der Liebe. Von ihr angelächelt werden im Boot. Das war das Allerschönste. Immer nur das Verlangen zu Sterben und das Sich-noch-Halten, das allein ist Liebe.

2. Eine lange Geschichte
Ich sehe einem Mä- Mä-dchen in die A- Augen, und es war eine sehr lange Liebesgeschichte mit Donner und Küsse [*sic*] und Blitz. Ich lebe rasch.

3. In memoriam Robert Klein

Noch spielen die Jagdhunde im Hof, aber das Wild entgeht ihnen nicht, so sehr es jetzt schon durch die Wälder jagt.

4. aus einem alten Notizbuch
Jetzt Abend nachdem ich von sechs Uhr früh an gelernt habe, bemerkte ich wie meine linke Hand die rechte schon ein Weilchen lang aus Mitleid bei den Fingern umfasst hielt.

5. Leoparden
Leoparden brechen in den Tempel ein und saufen die Opferkrüge leer; das wiederholt sich immer wieder, schliesslich kann man es voraus berechnen, und es wird ein Teil der Zeremonie.

6. In memoriam Johannis Pilinszky
Ich kann nicht eigentlich erzählen, ja fast nicht einmal reden; wenn ich erzähle, habe ich meistens ein Gefuhl wie es kleine Kinder haben konnten, die die ersten Gehversuche machen.

7. Wiederum, wiederum
Wiederum, wiederum weit verbannt, weit, weit verbannt. Berge, Wüste, weites Land gilt es zu durchwandern; Berge, Wüste, weites Land wiederum, wiederum, wiederum durchwandern.

8. Es blendete uns die Mondnacht . . .
Es blendete uns die Mondnacht. Vögel schrien, Vögel schrien von Baum zu Baum. In den Feldern sauste es, sauste es. . . . Wir krochen durch den Staub: ein Schlangenpaar.

Refiguring the Female Body: Two Romanian Avant-Gardists in Search of the Ideal Woman

Amy Colin

Unquestionably, the European avant-garde from Italian and Russian Futurism to German concrete poetry radically challenged literary traditions, subverted familiar modes of reading, and cut deeply into modern consciousness. Yet behind and beyond all attempts to break with the past run well-known poetic concepts, images, and ideas that counteract the avant-garde's linguistic upheaval, tightening its bond to tradition. In their search for new modes of writing, Zurich dadaists, for instance, reached back to the earliest poetic utterances of humanity, for they believed that only vowels and consonants had not lost their purity. Hence, Hugo Ball and his followers retreated into the "alchemy of sound," composing verse that recalled magic spells and the picture poems of the Greek Anthology (3 B.C.). A return to the past is also inscribed in Kurt Schwitters's "i-poems," in Guillaume Apollinaire's *Caligrammes,* as well as in post–World War II concrete poetry. Similar to German poetry of the baroque and to Christian Morgenstern's verses, these texts play with the pictorial dimension of words, turning them into "poem-objects" that could be hung on the wall.

As the history of such linguistic experiments as well as the title of the present volume suggest, antitraditionalism itself became a tradition. It is precisely the gradual metamorphosis of the avant-garde into a literary tradition that prompted archdadaists, including Tristan Tzara, to argue for the self-realization of dada through its self-destruction.[1]

Among the numerous examples that vivify the continuous existence of

---

1. Tristan Tzara, *Oeuvres complètes,* ed. Henri Béhar (Paris: Flammarion, 1980), 5:352.

literary traditions within modern linguistic experiments, there is the identification of language with the image of the mother and the woman in
general. In all cultures, the term *mother tongue* [*Muttersprache, langue maternelle,
lingua materna*] is used as a synonym for native language. In and of itself,
the simile implicit in mother tongue evokes a spectrum of potential relationships to the female Other from admiration and sexual desire to misogyny, prompting poets and writers of all time periods and cultures to play
with its connotations. Like the representatives of other literary movements,
the European avant-gardists also inscribed notions of sexual difference into
their innovative linguistic configurations, but they triggered an unusual
process of linguistic destruction, for in their verses, innovative avant-garde
metaphors and stereotypes of sexual difference mutually interact, constantly
reenforcing and subverting one another. In Kurt Schwitters's "Anna-
Blume" and André Breton's "Free Union,"[2] the linguistic upheaval is
intended to undo traditional images of the female, revealing the author's
critique of conventionality. In other texts, however, the stereotypes of the
woman undermine the writers' progressive attitudes, betraying disturbing
prejudices. Such intricate interplay of language experiments and stereotypical thinking in relation to the Other marks all European avant-garde
movements, but will be discussed here within the context of the less-known
Romanian avant-garde.[3]

The Romanian avant-garde looks back on a rich native tradition. Its
father was the legendary writer Urmuz (Demetru Demetrescu-Buzau,
1883–1923), whose enigmatic texts, characterized by absurd dialogues and
linguistic play, had a strong impact on modern Romanian writers from
Tudor Arghezi (1880–1967) to Tristan Tzara (1896–1963) and Eugene
Ionesco (b. 1912). In the 1920s, a considerable number of journals appeared
whose primary aim was to introduce the European avant-garde, in particular French surrealism and German dadaism, to a broad Romanian
public. They published articles and manifestos by Herwarth Walden, Max
Jacob, Pierre Reverdy, and Tristan Tzara in Romanian translation. In

---

2. See *The Poetry of Surrealism: An Anthology,* ed. Michael Benedikt (Boston: Little, Brown,
1974), 13–34.

3. For a detailed account of Romanian avant-garde literature, see Ovid S. Crohmălniceanu, *Literatura română şi expressionismul* (Bucharest: Editura Eminescu, 1971); Matei Călinescu, "Avangarda literară în România," in Saşa Pană, ed., *Antologia literaturii române de
avangardă* (Bucharest: Editura pentru literatură, 1969), 5–33. For another discussion of female
images and questions of gender within the European avant-garde, see Susan Suleiman,
Subversive Intent: Gender, Politics, and the Avant-Garde (Cambridge, Mass.: Harvard University
Press, 1990).

1923, the erudite Romanian writer Ion Vinea (1895–1964), a close friend of Tzara, started *Contimporanul* (1922–32), which became the model for such later avant-garde journals as *75 H.P.* (1924), *Punct* (1924–25), *Integral* (1925–28), *Urmuz* (1928), and *Alge* (1930–31).

The contributors to these journals—Ilarie Voronca (1903–46), Alexandru Philippide (1900–1979), and Stéphane Roll (1903–74)—gathered around surrealist Şaşa Pană (1902–81), a leading figure on the Romanian avant-garde scene. In their texts, Pană and his friends attempted to combine the style and language experiments initiated by Urmuz with Breton's reflections on dreams and automatic writing. Though playing with both the native Romanian as well as the French surrealist tradition, Pană succeeded in attaining his own innovative voice.[4]

World War II temporarily put an end to these literary activities, but, after 1945, another group of surrealist writers appeared on the Romanian literary scene. Poets Ghérasim Luca (b. 1916), Gellu Naum (b. 1913), Paul Păun (b. 1916), D. Trost (1916–66), Virgil Teodorescu (b. 1909), and others established a cenacle that engaged in surrealist poetic experiments. Eroticism, the creation of literary texts by dream strategies, and a provocative "black humor" characterize their writings. Like the French surrealists, they attempted to free language and thought from the restraints of rationality and convention. Their interest in problems of language was often linked to a strong political commitment, and they hoped to change the society of their time by challenging modes of thinking and reading. Ghérasim Luca, the leading figure of this movement, together with his friends—Gellu Naum, Paul Păun, D. Trost, and Virgil Teodorescu—published manifestos, theoretical texts, and literary experiments. Around the same time, Petre Solomon, Nina Cassian, and Ovid Crohmălniceanu also established an avant-garde circle of poets that engaged in *question réponse* and *cadavre exquis* plays.[5]

Time and again, modern Romanian literary critics, writers, and artists have insisted upon the rupture with tradition as a constituent of the Romanian avant-garde. In the preface to Şaşa Pană's anthology of Romanian

---

4. See Pană, *Antologia,* 302. Pană also published his own journal, *Unu* (1928–32), which included the linguistic experiments of his circle of friends.

5. Paul Celan occasionally participated in the meetings of this cenacle and translated some of Gellu Naum's and Virgil Teodorescu's poems into German. He also frequented Petre Solomon's, Nina Cassian's, and Ovid Crohmălniceanu's avant-garde circle of poets. At the insistence of his friends, Celan wrote a series of Romanian texts and poems in a surrealist style. See Petre Solomon, *Paul Celan: Dimensiunea românească* (Bucharest: Kriterion, 1987).

avant-garde literature, Matei Călinescu illuminates this crucial aspect of the European and, in particular, Romanian avant-garde, pointing to a strange paradox inherent in dadaist and surrealist language experiments. As Călinescu suggests, they attempt to destroy literary traditions by means of literary traditions, focusing more and more on the literariness of poetic language: " . . . the necessity . . . of human creation could not be abolished, and literature, like the bird Phoenix, was reborn from its own ashes, gaining perhaps a greater awareness . . . into its own literariness."[6] The surrealist manifesto "Strigăt" (Cry), published in *Alge* (1930), renders a powerful image that confirms Călinescu's ideas, suggesting that modernity and literary history exclude each other. "Abolish your roots in the past, which, rotting in you, will cause you to rot as well."[7] Through the fusion of heterogeneous images into unusual configurations, the Franco-Romanian surrealists seduced readers into creating links to known traditions and then destroyed these expectations. For instance, the title of Luca's early text, "Sfînta împărtăsanie" (The Holy Communion),[8] evokes the idea of a narration and confession; but the series of images or disrupted narratives metamorphoses into others, undoing all thematic linkages. In Luca's later *Paralipomènes*,[9] written in Paris in the 1970s, this surrealist language becomes increasingly dense; the poet reduces the sequence of metaphors to words or sound configurations, which generate other phonemes. His "La parole,"[10] for instance, reveals that words are verbal acts that exhibit the free play of *la langue* in Saussure's sense. The seemingly senseless interaction of everyday images culminates here in a powerful trope, which draws on the double meaning of *brûler* ['to burn/to skip'] and evokes the destruction of periods and, thus, perhaps traditions as well: "Brûler les états/brûler les étapes."[11]

Other Romanian avant-garde poets consciously used literary traditions as a means of annihilating them. Constantin Tonegaru's text, "Femeia Cafenie" (The Coffee-Skinned Woman, published in 1945),[12] is written in the style of a love song, but its metaphors gradually destruct themselves.

6. Călinescu, "Avangarda literară," 32.

7. Pană, *Antologia*, 567.

8. Pană, *Antologia*, 302.

9. Ghérasim Luca, *Paralipomènes* (Paris: Le Soleil Noir, 1976).

10. Luca, *Paralipomènes*, 36–37.

11. Luca, *Paralipomènes*, 37.

12. Constantin Tonegaru (1919–52), "Femeia Cafenie" (1945), in Pană, *Antologia*, 447–48.

Femeia pe care la Brăila am iubit-o într-o cameră de hotel
purta pantofi verzi de piele de şarpe
şi avea nasul turtit. Era o mulatră,
Cum venise aici, habar n-am.
Parinţii, bunici, purtaseră poate odată în nări un inel.
Gura îi era o ventuză.
   Sinii fierbinţi ca nişte pîini.
    Ochii tulburi.
Îmi era trupul claviatură pentru dînsa.
Numai mîinile îi erau reci,
    reci ca giaţă
şi degetele cu vîrfuri
alunecau pe mine ca boabe de struguri.
Îmi şoptea:
   —În Peru mi-a fost amant un spaniol.
    La Santa Clava avea plantaţii de zahăr.
Un altul cu favoriţi în U.S.A.
cincizeci de puţuri cu petrol la Smakover,
   dar amorul pentru pielea mea cafenie
s-a lichidat cu două destupări de pistol.

Am iubit la Brăila o mulatră.
   M-a iubit? . . . M-a minţit?
Vedea—cine ştie—în mine un altul?
Avea sîni fierbinţi şi mîini reci de ghiaţă.
Era prin noiembrie. Pe Dunăre dospea ceaţă.
În port la lumini de fanare
   robii descărcau un vapor cu lignit.

[The woman I made love to in a hotel room in Brăila / had green shoes
of serpent leather / and her nose was flat. She was a mulatto. / How
she got here, I really do not know. / Her parents, her grandparents
were wearing perhaps rings through their nostrils. / Her mouth was a
sucker. / Her breasts hot as bread. / Her eyes cloudy. / For her, my
body was a keyboard. / Only her hands were cold as ice, / and her
round finger tips were sliding on me like grapes. / She whispered: / —
In Peru, my lover was Spanish. / He had sugar plantation at Santa
Clava. / Another lover with connections in the U.S. / had fifty oil mines
in Smakover, / but his love for my coffee-colored skin / was wiped out
with two gunshots. / I loved a mulatto in Brăila. / Did she love
me? . . . Did she lie to me? / Perhaps she saw another man in me? /
Her breasts were hot and her hands cold as ice. / It was November.
Fog was bubbling over the Danube. / In the harbor, in the light of
torches, slaves were unloading a ship carrying coal.]

Karl Kraus's aphorism "Ich beherrsche nur die Sprache der Anderen, meine Sprache beherrscht mich" (I control only the language of others, my language controls [dominates] me) could well be the motto of this poem.[13] At first glance, the text vivifies a love scene between a white man and a mulatto in Brăila (a Romanian city on the Danube), placing the poem in the tradition of love songs. The powerful images of eroticism seem to assert rather than undo stereotypes of sexual difference, but the "black woman" portrayed as the epitome of lasciviousness and voluptuousness triggers such sexual desire in the speaker that he loses control, becoming the object of her sexual appetite, a mere instrument, "a keyboard." The latter image signals that the passionate black mistress is not just a woman, but an allegory for language itself, which turned the poet into its tool. Hence, Tonegaru's poem reverses not only the traditional male-female, but also the familiar author-text polarity, dramatizing the author's own poetic endeavor. The Romanian avant-gardist set out to radically transform literary language, assuming total power over words and metaphors. But language, once liberated from the restraints of tradition (here conventional sexual practice), becomes more powerful than its speaker. It metamorphoses into a "wild" and "passionate" black woman, turning the white master into a helpless "sex slave" who can no longer cope with the seductiveness of tropes and metaphors. The end of the poem seems to thematize such ideas, for it evokes the speaker's doubts in the authenticity of the woman's feelings for him, in her passion, and his own masculinity.

Tonegaru's text is an antilove song, which plays with traditions of love poetry as a means of destructing them. But the image of the "black woman" is so stereotypical that it undoes the subversive nature of the antilove song, revealing the author's own biases. All details of her portrayal—the huge, hot breasts, the flat nose, the ring her ancestors must have been wearing through their nostrils, her primitive sexual appetite and wildness—correspond entirely to the nineteenth-century clichés of black women, such as the Ashanti exhibited in London, Paris, and Vienna in 1816 and 1817. As Sander L. Gilmann, in *Difference and Pathology*,[14] pointed out, the black

---

13. Karl Kraus, *Werke*, ed. Heinrich Fischer (Munich: Kösel Verlag, 1952–62), 3:326.

14. See Sander L. Gilman, *Difference and Pathology: Stereotypes of Sexuality, Race, and Madness* (Ithaca: Cornell University Press, 1985), 76–127, esp. 81–87. Gilman analyzes not only the fin de siècle stereotypes of the black woman, in particular the Hottentot Venus and the Ashantis, but also the voyeuristic fascination with their body in Zola's and Altenberg's writings. It is Gilman who draws attention to the strange association of black sexuality with perversion and madness.

women, the "Hottentot Venus" and the Ashanti women in particular, were emblems of a sexuality inherently different than the "civilized" European sexual behavior. From the early nineteenth century to Freud's time, the sexualized black beauty was regarded as "wild," "primitive," and perverse. Her body not only fascinated the voyeuristic European public, but also inspired anxiety for, in the eyes of the righteous fin de siècle bourgeois as well as of intellectuals and artists, her anatomy—the "huge breasts and buttocks"[15]—denoted sexual anomaly, disease, and passion. As a source of dangerous attraction, the black woman, similar to the mistress in Tonegaru's poem, unsettles the hegemony of the white observer. Yet the Romanian avant-garde author not only criticizes the society of his time, but also betrays his own prejudices, for he borrows stereotypes of black sexuality without question. His attempt to create an innovative style by refiguring the body of poetry thus remains trapped within conventional images of the black female body that in turn subvert his progressive literary tenets.

Tristan Tzara's love poem "Am Sădit in Corpul Tău"[16] (In Your Body I planted) explores the psychoanalytic implications of the notion of mother tongue.

> Am sădit în corpul tău, iubito, floarea
> Ce o să-ți împrăștie pe gît pe-obraji pe mîini petale
> Și o să-ți înmugurească sînii mîine—primăvara
> Îmi plac sprîncenele și ochii tăi cu luciu de metale
> Și brațele ce ți se-ndoaie ca serpii, valurile, marea
> Din corpul tău aș vrea să fac palate, arhitectonice grădini
> Și raiuri pămîntești monumentale
> Și să mă îngrop în camera ta cînd voi muri
> Și în pămîntul lor să mă îngrop cînd voi muri
>
> În părul tău eu simt mirosul de struguri de portocale
> În ochii tăi cerniți văd soarele și-n buze pofta de mîncare
> Cu dinții tăi ai vrea să rupi din suflet carne
> Și unghiile să le prefaci în gheare
>
> Aș vrea să mușc din sînii tăi cum muscă pîinea
> Înfometații ce culeg pe-asfaltul străzilor parale
> Aș vrea să-ți înfloresc privirea cu-arhitectonice grădini
> Și să-ți aliniez gîndirea cu visuri pămîntești, mamie.

[In your body, my beloved, I planted a flower / which will scatter petals

---

15. Gilman, *Difference,* 87–89.
16. Tzara, *Oeuvres,* 1:71.

on your neck, face, and hands / and will make your breasts blossom tomorrow—spring / I like your eyebrows and eyelashes with metallic shine and your arms which bend like snakes, waves, the sea // Of your body I want to build palaces, architectonic gardens / monumental terrestrial empires / and to bury myself when I die // I sense the fragrance of grapes or oranges in your hair / I see sun in your black eyes and appetite on your lips / you would rip the flesh with your teeth, hardheartedly / you would turn your nails into crawls / I would like to bite your breasts the way starving people bite bread / the ones who gather pennies on the street / I would like to make your gaze blossom with architectonic gardens / and to align your thoughts with terrestrial dreams, mamie.]

Tzara's poem radically exploits the literal meaning of "dissemination." As the opening lines suggest, the woman's body is a "holy place" into which he implants the seed of poetic creation. Out of the fertile soil of femininity grows a gigantic flower whose petals cover up the female body— the face, neck, and breasts—recalling fin de siècle paintings of female nudes embedded in floral ornaments. Klimt's *Fish Blood* (1898) and *Watersnakes* (1904–7) portray the floating, sinuous bodies of women whose snakelike tresses (modeled after entangled water plants) draw the male swimmer into the depths of the lakes.[17] Similar to Klimt's women, Tzara's female Other, whose arms resemble waves and watersnakes, also inhabits a "liquefied world." Moreover, similar to art nouveau painters, the speaker hopes to use her to erect his temples of art, monumental edifices of eroticism: "Of your body I want to build palaces, architectonic gardens / monumental terrestrial empires."

An interplay of mutually exclusive fin de siècle clichés of femininity marks Tzara's poem. Seen through the prism of male prejudices, the woman is both the earth into which the speaker digs his grave, a symbol of death and destruction, but also the sun, and thus a source of light and

---

17. See the vivid descriptions of these paintings in Carl E. Schorske, *Fin-de-Siècle Vienna: Politics and Culture* (New York: Vintage Books, 1981), 222–31. "Klimt's women are at home in a liquefied world, where the male would quickly drown, like sailors seduced by mermaids" (224), writes Schorske, who underlines Klimt's attempt to subvert the conventional and realistic image of women by exploring their eroticism. Yet the sensual liberation evoked in Klimt's paintings as well as in the works of other art nouveau artists is subverted by the ornamental character of the female nude. As a "beautifying ornament," the woman's body suggests clichés of femininity prevalent in fin de siècle Viennese society rather than a radical break with the stereotypes of the female Other.

poetic inspiration. She is the passive instrument of the poet's creative energy, but at the same time an aggressive, "wild" animal that wants to rip the speaker's flesh.

In contrast to Tonegaru's text, Tzara does not allow the liberated "woman" to attack and destroy him. On the contrary, he is in full control of her, dominating even her thoughts and feelings. As the concluding metaphors of the text suggest, the speaker actually devours the female body, whose breasts he is eating up the way starving people eat bread. The romantic love scene that gradually turns into a perverse destruction of the beloved Other is not the final shock effect built into this text. It is the poem's concluding word that must have horrified his readers, for *Mamie* reveals that the mistress is not just a friend, *une amie,* but the mother herself.

Tzara's incest-poem, a provocation to the petite bourgeoisie, has its own contextuality. The adolescent Romanian dadaist wrote other variations on this theme—poems evoking the speaker's love affair with the mother, including "Mamie, You Will Not Understand" and "Friend Mamie."[18] One of these early poems contains the ironic consolation: "Mamie, you will not understand / But it is nice to be part of a poem."[19] Of course, the mother will never understand the son's oedipal fascination with her, but at least she should feel flattered, rather than shocked—the speaker argues—for, in his opinion, it should be a pleasure to inspire a poem— even as mere object of perverse sexual desire.

The identification of the mother with language is a key motif of Tzara's text. Similar to Tonegaru, Tzara plays with and subverts traditions of love poems that turn the image of the woman into an icon of the speaker's dreams and hidden wishes. Time and again, such love songs have presented the woman as constituting the speaker's world: she is the muse and object of sexual desire; the source of both creation and death, of happiness and suffering; the beauty and medusa; the mother and whore. Such binary oppositions, characteristic of traditional poetic representations of the female Other, are also inherent in Tzara's text, in his comparisons of the female body with both the grave and the sun, the peaceful flowers and wild animals. By playing with such mutually exclusive images, Tzara mimics traditional love songs, undoing their tropes of femininity. Moreover, Tzara's verses reveal that the traditional poet, who praises all qualities of

---

18. Tristan Tzara, *Primele poeme,* 70–73.
19. Tzara, *Primele poeme,* 73.

the beloved woman, in fact erases her individuality; she becomes an empty sign into which he projects his wishes, dreams, and hidden desires. He devours her, as he devours poetic language, since he believes himself to be in total control of words and metaphors. As a parody of traditional love poems, Tzara's early text does not attack art and literature itself, but its implicit assumptions, anticipating his later poetic tenets.[20]

Unlike Tonegaru's poem, however, Tzara's text does not even suggest the possibility of the female Other attaining her own voice. Her feeble attempt to show claws is immediately counteracted by the aggressive speaker, who rips her breasts. By suggesting the speaker's total control over the female body, the avant-garde author betrays, however, his own standpoint: he too remains trapped in the tradition he criticizes. The linguistic structures that posit the female as signifier of masculine sexual dreams and obsessions are so ingrained into consciousness that not even radical dadaist Tzara can evade them. As the reading of his poem shows, his innovative metaphors ultimately erase the female Other, disclosing that the focal point of his text is merely an empty sign that inhabits masculine imagination.

The destruction of the "promised land" into which the speaker implanted his poetic seed reveals yet another subtle aspect of the text. An author who no longer allows words and images to freely vibrate and engage in their play of differences is not in love with language but, rather, with his own linguistic power. Tzara's poem uncovers such narcissistic dimensions of the creative process, adding yet another shock effect to his provocative poem.

But there is still another subtext encoded in Tzara's verses with their repeated reference to the earth, the land, the soil. The pseudonym "Tristan Tzara" actually means "Tristan, the Land" as well as "Land of sadness." In light of these connotations, Tzara's poem appears to enact his name or, rather, his poetic development and quest for artistic identity within a new "land"—the unexplored terrain of avant-garde linguistic experiments. Tzara, who started out by writing verses rich in romantic images,[21] gradually turned away from the style of his early poetry, attaining an innovative poetic voice. But his poems bear his signature, his past. Thus, even such

---

20. See Tzara, *Oeuvres,* 5:353; "Dada a essayé non pas autant de détruire l'art et la littérature, que l'idée qu'on s'en était faite," writes Tzara in his later essay, "Dada Contre L'Art" (353).

21. See Tzara's "Verişoara, fată de pension" (Cousin, boarding school girl), in *Primele poeme,* 5–7.

provocative avant-garde texts as "In Your Body I planted," which are intended to subvert all bonds to literary traditions, are still entangled in those literary traditions. In this respect, both Tonegaru's and Tzara's poems illustrate the intricate ways in which innovative metaphors subvert and are, in turn, unsettled by the stereotypes of the woman prevalent in the literature and art of their time. They illustrate the impossibility of refiguring the body of poetic language without radically distorting the familiar iconography of femininity.

Schiller, Chicago, and China: The Function of Foreign Elements in Brecht's *In the Jungle of the Cities*

Walter Hinderer

Speaking in 1924 of his play *In the Jungle of the Cities*, Bertolt Brecht pointed out that there was no dramatic technique by which to express quotation marks. He added ironically, with regard to the quoted verses of Rimbaud and Verlaine, that if the stage had such a technique, "a great number of other beloved works would be perhaps more to the taste of the philologists, but rather unbearable for the public." He comforted the neglected fraternity, requesting sarcastically that "interested philologists . . . call again in eleven years' time. (I can, however, already tell you that the play, if it makes any strides at all, at any rate will stride over the corpses of the philologists)" (*W* 17:969). Forty-two years later, the members of our profession may put their minds at rest: the play certainly did not stride over the "corpses of the philologists." On the contrary, philologists have largely ignored the play, with the exception of a few pertinent studies.[1]

In his *Program Notes to the Heidelberg Production (Programmheft zur Heidelberger Aufführung)* of July 24, 1928, Brecht admitted in disappointment that "really, the play's total rejection by the public is understandable. This play

Brecht's works are quoted according to the *Gesammelte Werke in 20 Bänden: Werkausgabe edition Suhrkamp*, ed. Suhrkamp Verlag with Elisabeth Hauptmann (Frankfurt am Main: Suhrkamp Verlag, 1967); cited as *W*, with volume and page number, immediately after the quotation. Brecht's diaries are quoted according to the *Tagebücher 1920–1922: Autobiographische Aufzeichnungen 1920–1954*, ed. Herta Ramthun (Frankfurt am Main: Suhrkamp Verlag, 1975); cited as *T*.

1. In this context, see J. Knopf, "*Im Dickicht der Städte*," in *Brecht Handbuch: Theater*, ed. J. Knopf (Stuttgart: J. B. Metzlersche Verlagsbuchhandlung, 1980), 33–41, and Gisela E. Bahr, "'Und niemals wird eine Verständigung sein': *Im Dickicht der Städte*," in *Brechts Dramen: Neue Interpretationen*, ed. Walter Hinderer (Stuttgart: Reclam Verlag, 1984), 67–88.

depends on certain conditions, which is annoying and therefore avoided by the average production" (*W* 17:969). This supposedly most "incomprehensible"[2] of Brecht's plays does not reconcile the contradictions inherent in reality, nor does it smooth them over with a guiding moral or philosophical principle. It is interested in questions rather than solutions. At the end, only the faint-hearted principle of hope remains. In both the published version of 1927 and the first version of 1922, Garga's last reply is: "It is a good thing to be alone. The chaos is exhausted. It was the best time" (*W* 1:193). In the first version, however, the order of the first and third sentences is reversed. A vision of comfort—"Perhaps work will comfort me"—and a reference to the temporal situation of the main character are also interjected. Only then do the key words *east wind* appear with reference to the positive context of "south coast" and "Tahiti."

Both the "America" and the "South Sea" themes serve the obvious function of relieving the tension in Brecht's work from 1916 to 1924. During the same period they also provide a model for the new way of life of urban existence, for the isolation and alienation of the individual from the family and from the traditional behavior patterns, for the destruction of the old values, and for the scientific age. In part in reaction to his narrow Augsburg environment, Brecht wrote in 1920: "How this Germany bores me! It is a good average country, the pale colors and surfaces are pretty, but what inhabitants! A degenerate class of peasants whose crudeness creates no fantastical monsters, only a quiet brutalization; a fat middle class and an insipid intelligentsia! Remains: America!" (*W* 20:10). In the previously mentioned *Program Notes,* Brecht wrote that his choice of an American environment for *In the Jungle of the Cities* was not the result of any "romantic tendency," but served to clarify, through alienation, "the unusual patterns of behavior of great, modern types of people." The Chicago background of the play thus serves, on the one hand, as an aesthetic device and on the other as a model for the new, chaotic age that has destroyed the old way of life. As Brecht explained in the *Program Notes,* this was intended to disappoint the expectations of the "romantic public" and to alienate it from its customary environment. According to Brecht, the Asian quality of the Malaysian Shlink, and, in an early draft, of the Chinese Dschin-In, has an aesthetic function similar to "cold Chicago." It is intended to make the familiar recognizable and to correct habitual ways of perception, just as Shaw's plays did for Brecht at that time.

---

2. Knopf, "*Im Dickicht,*" 35.

In the preface to his *Phenomenology of the Spirit* (*Phänomenologie des Geistes*), Hegel had stressed epigrammatically the epistemological aspect of this method: "The known itself exists because it is *known,* not *recognized.*"[3] Brecht seeks new possibilities of perception and recognition through the "semantic" and topographical alienation in *Jungle.* After his conversion to Marxism, he considered this "produced alienation" to be an epistemological process that occurred in a sort of three-part dialectic: "Alienation as understanding (understanding—not understanding—understanding), negation of the negation" (*W* 15:360). In dramatic practice, this formula also can be expressed as the "amassing of the incomprehensible until comprehension occurs (reversal of quantity and quality)" (*W* 15:360). It is noteworthy that, in an unrevised version of the *Program Notes,* Brecht wrote that he had chosen the foreign milieu because he wanted, above all, "to make the action completely alien, that is, *conspicuous.*"[4] In *Jungle of the Cities,* Brecht consciously ignored psychological motivation because, in his view, the "behavior pattern of our contemporaries" could not be explained "by old motifs (often borrowed from literature)." His characters simply act differently than the audience expects. For this reason, as Brecht explained, "the philosopher is more at home than the psychologist in this world [and] in this drama" (*W* 17:970). However, in this regard, it should be added that he surely meant a philosopher who had not yet forgotten how to be open to new experiences and who thus had not yet fallen victim to his own philosophy.

The play *In the Jungle of the Cities* is, in form, content, and linguistic construction, one of Brecht's most interesting experiments in his dramatic work. Looking back, he remarked: "Before and afterwards I worked in a different way and according to different points of view and the plays were simpler and more materialistic" (*W* 17:950). This early experiment uses not only alien elements in order to make the known recognizable and the new visible, but it is also in direct opposition to one specific drama of the German tradition, Schiller's *Robbers* (*Die Räuber*). George Garga is intended not only to "look like A. Rimbaud, primarily a German translation from the French into the American," but also, as Brecht's working notes demonstrate, to be a "new Karl Moor."[5] Brecht stated this fact more clearly

---

3. Georg Wilhelm Friederich Hegel, *Werke in zwanzig Bänden,* vol. 3, *Phänomenologie des Geistes* (Frankfurt am Main: Suhrkamp Verlag, 1970), 35.

4. Patty Lee Parmalee, *Brecht's America* (Columbus: Ohio State University Press, 1981), 15.

5. Printed in Bertolt Brecht, *Im Dickicht der Städte: Erstfassung und Materialien,* ed. and commentary Gisela E. Bahr (Frankfurt am Main: Suhrkamp Verlag, 1968), 135.

when he said that "I wanted to improve on *Robbers* with *Jungle* (and to prove that battle is impossible because of the inadequacy of the language)" (*W* 15:69). The following remarks will consider the challenge presented by Schiller's first drama and its connection with the other elements of aesthetic alienation [*Verfremdung*] that I have mentioned above.

Bertolt Brecht told how, while writing *In the Jungle of the Cities,* he had been filled with certain desires and ideas brought on by seeing a poor production of Schiller's *Robbers.* In 1954, he wrote (in retrospect) that "in this play, an extreme, very wild, violent battle is waged for a bourgeois heritage, using unbourgeois methods at times" (*W* 17:948). However, his fascination at that time had another source as well: beginning in 1920, he was particularly intrigued by the sport of boxing, which he believed was one of the "great mythical pleasures of the big cities across the ocean." In his new play, he wanted to depict both a "battle per se," a "battle with no other cause than the pleasure of fighting," as well as "a story of ever more different, newer patterns of behavior" (*W* 17:948).

As in Schiller's *Robbers,* the battle in *Jungle of the Cities* represents the reaction and counterreaction of the warring factions. "At the end," Brecht wrote of his play, "the battle turns out to be . . . merely shadow boxing" (*W* 17:949). The fighters "couldn't connect with each other even as enemies." The same is true, albeit for different reasons, of Schiller's alienated brothers. In retrospect, Brecht criticized the "purely idealistic" dialectic of his early work and also the fact that he perhaps had "exaggerated slightly [its] formal aspects" (*W* 17:950). The characters of *Jungle of the Cities,* like Karl Moor, are unconscious of the difficulties of their very being.[6] As Garga apostrophizes the problem in the initial version, "language" is inadequate "for communication," and "animosity" cannot be executed because of the "eternal loneliness of man," as Shlink discovers in the same scene. The boxer becomes a "missionary, who is also an atheist" and the robber and noble criminal Karl Moor becomes the representative of a bourgeois law of morality to which no one else appears to adhere, while his atheist brother, the rogue Franz, falls victim to a divine judgment in which no one else appears to believe. It is no coincidence that, in Brecht's play, both fighters—in the initial version Garga, in the published version Shlink—call themselves "comrades in metaphysical action." In Schiller, the disappointed idealist Karl and the eventually

---

6. Knopf, *"Im Dickicht,"* 40.

despairing materialist Franz seem to trade their psychic and spiritual constitutions just as, in Brecht, the bookworm Garga and the successful self-made man Shlink switch their originally contradictory "patterns of behavior."

In his *Memories of Brecht* (*Brecht-Erinnerungen*), Hans Otto Münsterer included a photograph, taken in 1917, of the young playwright posed as the "new Schiller" in a niche in the Augsburg City Theater.[7] Evidently no conscious imitation, but a reforming challenge through Schiller himself was intended. Nevertheless, as a theater critic in Augsburg, Brecht protested the way that "Schiller is introduced to our youth" (*W* 15:22) in a bad production of *Robbers* on October 23, 1920. On November 16 of the same year, he reviewed a union production, summarizing the plot or "fable" of *Robbers* as if it were a *Moritat*,[8] a form that was, for Brecht at the time, another possibility of dramatic representation along with "sport theater" and the "revue." While the perspective on the content of *Robbers* in this review already indicated Brecht's asocial and antibourgeois attitude, his criticism of *Don Carlos* on April 15, 1920, demonstrated more clearly his antipathy to Schiller's idealistic concept. Here, he compared Schiller's text, which he "always loved, God knows," with Upton Sinclair's novel *The Jungle*, "the story of a worker who starves to death in the abattoirs of Chicago" (*W* 15:9–11). Because of this comparison, Brecht admitted that he could "no longer take Carlos's slavery seriously." He added parenthetically: "Freedom in Schiller is only postulated, in admittedly beautiful arias, but maybe it should also exist in at least one man" (*W* 15:10).

This criticism of *Don Carlos* is not only the verifiable juncture from which Schiller and Sinclair serve as points of departure for *In the Jungle of the Cities*.[9] It also indirectly indicates one of the tested devices to "alienate" or, most conspicuously, to alter and amend the aesthetic ideology of Schiller's text.[10] In addition to Sinclair's book, Brecht was influenced by the works of Rudyard Kipling and by *The Wheel*, a novel by the Danish author Johannes V. Jensen. In the latter, Chicago serves as the background

---

7. Gudrun Schulz, *Die Schillerbearbeitungen Bertolt Brechts* (Tübingen: Max Niemeyer Verlag, 1972), 6 n. 7.

8. Schulz, *Schillerbearbeitungen*, 22ff.

9. Schulz, *Schillerbearbeitungen*, 16–19; Knopf, *"Im Dickicht,"* 34f.

10. On this topic, see Walter Hinderer, "'Produzierte und erfahrene Fremde': Zu den Funktionen des Amerika-Themas bei Bertolt Brecht," in *Das Fremde und das Eigene: Prolegomena zu einer interkulturellen Germanistik,* ed. Alois Wierlacher (Munich: Iudicium Verlag, 1985), 47–64.

for a description of the American metropolis as a jungle.[11] According to a note of September 4, 1921, Brecht was inspired by reading Kipling to express poetically the "animosity of the metropolis, its vicious, stony consistency, its Babylonian confusion of language" (*T,* 145). This project went through a number of stages that Brecht called "In the Sticks" (*"Hinterwelt"*), "The Forest," "Jungle," "Animosity" (*"Die Feindseligkeit"*), and "George Garga." He was sure of only one thing: "It is a play about a battle, east against west, with a subterranean outcome" (*T,* 146). In the sketches for the *Play of Cold Chicago,* demonstrated by Seliger to have been the preliminary stage for the first version of *Jungle,* the main theme is presented logically as a "battle between an Asian and an Anglo-Saxon, a realist and an idealist."[12]

The battle theme found in Schiller and provided with a new function by the Chicago novels of Sinclair and Jensen underwent a further transformation under the influence of Alfred Döblin's Chinese novel, *The Three Leaps of Wang-lun* (*Die drei Sprünge des Wang-lun*), which Brecht read on December 14, 1920. (However, Münsterer indicated that the initial influence may have been that of the criminal play,[13] *Mr. Wu or the Revenge* [*Mr. Wu oder die Rache*], which was performed in Augsburg in 1919.) Perhaps Brecht's first concept of Taoist behavior was the result of Döblin's novel: "He, the Chinese, tried to conquer by remaining passive. To receive power by suffering."[14] Since the opponents, the idealist and the realist, the passive and the active character, switch positions in the course of the play, in *The Jungle of the Cities* it is George and not Shlink who speaks of the Asian strategy or type of battle: "I read that weak waters take on entire mountains. And I would like to see your face again, Shlink, your milky, glassy, damned, invisible face" (*W* 1:172). According to Seliger, the racial opposition becomes less pronounced from *The Play of Cold Chicago* (1921–22), to the first version, *In the Jungle* (1922), to the published version, *In the Jungle of the Cities* (1927).[15] Yet the cultural opposition between the Malaysian Shlink and the Anglo-Saxon Garga unquestionably continues to determine the battle throughout a large portion of the final version. The

---

11. Helfried W. Seliger, *Das Amerikabild Bertolt Brechts* (Bonn: Bouvier, 1974), 28f.

12. Seliger, *Amerikabild,* 37.

13. Seliger, *Amerikabild,* 28; Knopf, *"Im Dickicht,"* 33; Antony Tatlow, *The Mask of Evil: Brecht's Response to the Poetry, Theatre and Thought of China and Japan* (Bern, Frankfurt am Main, and Las Vegas: Peter Lang, 1977), 258ff.

14. Bahr, *"Im Dickicht,"* 130; see also Tatlow, *Mask of Evil,* 458ff.

15. Seliger, *Amerikabild,* 36.

antithesis of the strong and the weak is handled dialectically, of course, by Brecht. The idealist Garga, who will not allow the wood dealer Shlink to "buy" any "opinion" from him (*W* 1:127), goes on to explain to Shlink in the tenth scene that "the spiritual, you know, is nothing. It isn't important to be the stronger one, only to be the living one" (*W* 1:190).[16]

Contrary to *Don Carlos,* in *The Jungle of the Cities,* the older man simply makes way, "without putting up a fight," for the younger. Thus, the older, morally corrupt generation does not win over the younger, better, idealistic generation, as is the case in Schiller's tragedy, where, however, the outer victory of the Inquisition exposes ex negativo the inhumane system.[17] Instead of moral judgment, Brecht includes only the biological "natural elimination of the obsolete." The destruction of Garga's family occurs, however, in contrast to the similar scenes in *Don Carlos* and *Robbers,* as a result of hidden motives. As the foreword indicates, this is part of the constructive principle of the play. Brecht warned his spectators and his readers against "racking your brains about the motives behind the battle; instead, you should participate in the human efforts, judge nonpartisanly the fighting strategy of the opponents, and direct your interest to the finish" (*W* 1:126).

The finish in *Jungle* is as little tragic as it is dramatic. Shlink drinks poison, writes his own simple epitaph, and requests Marie to "throw a towel over [his] face, have pity!" Then he simply *collapses,* as the stage directions say (*W* 1:191f.). Brecht consciously transposes Schiller's pathetic depiction to the level of the *Moritat* or revue,[18] the sport theater,[19] polemically contrasting the "theater as moral institution" with the "theater as sport institution." As Brecht put it, the audience must "not watch for psychological shock and agree with the newspapers, but observe whether a man is doing well or badly, see how he is repressed or how he celebrates his triumphs, and they remember their own battles of the morning" (*W* 15:49). In this type of theater, the representation of patterns of behavior is more

---

16. See Jun-Yeop Song, *Bertolt Brecht und die chinesische Philosophie* (Bonn: Bouvier, 1978), 104.

17. Additional influences were Charlotte Westermann, *Knabenbriefe,* 2d ed. (Düsseldorf: Verlag der Rheinlande, 1908); George Horace Lorimer, *Briefe eines Dollar-Königs an seinen Sohn* [Letters from a Self-made Merchant to His Son] (1902); the German translation of *Old Gorgon Graham; More Letters from a Self-made Merchant to His Son* was published by E. Fleischel in 1905. Compare Schulz, *Schillerbearbeitungen,* 62; Knopf, *"Im Dickicht,"* 35.

18. See Brecht's criticism of the pathetic rhetoric of his time, "Über das Rhetorische," in *W* 15:45.

19. Schulz, *Schillerbearbeitungen,* 22ff.

important than psychological motivation and the reactions of the characters to the action is more decisive than the actual action. Brecht noted on August 21, 1920, that he did not want to create "great ideal dramas of principles, but simple plays that show men's destinies, men, who are intended to be the achievements of the plays" (*W* 15:50).

The play *In the Jungle of the Cities* tells of the decline of a family and the development of a new way of life. This new way of life is loaded with negative signals by Shlink in the tenth scene, such as the "splitting of language," "isolation," "loneliness," which is dismissed by Garga as "idle talk" (*W* 1:187f.). Garga wants what is physical, not spiritual, what is vital and alive, not elevated. In spite of all the negative omens, Garga considers "being alone a good thing." Just as the new way of life resulted from conflict with the old way, the new form of the play grew out of a critical discussion of the old form of drama. The construction of the battle in terms of content and aesthetics points clearly to the different ideological positions taken by the dramatists Brecht and Schiller. Nevertheless, the literary revolutionary from Augsburg knew that no innovations were possible in this area without knowledge of the established methods. Later, he expressed this opinion: "There are new things but they are created from conflict with old things, not without them, not out of thin air" (*W* 19:314).

The prosaic "cold Chicago" and the foreign Chinese or Malaysian element in Brecht's *Jungle* distances and corrects the old, pathetically elevated world of Schiller that Brecht used to contrast the new world. With his foundering heroes of *Robbers* and *Don Carlos,* Schiller demonstrated the autonomy and principal freedom of the human consciousness. Brecht's surviving hero in *Jungle of the Cities,* Garga, represents the direct opposite. In the third scene, Garga says: "We aren't free. It begins in the morning with coffee and with beatings, if you're an ape, and the mother's tears are the salt in her children's meal, and her sweat washes their shirt, and you're safe into the Ice Age, and the root is in the heart" (*W* 1:147). Although Garga claims that man "doesn't even have the freedom to perish," his opponent Shlink proves unpathetically, even banally, that freely chosen downfall is possible. His action, however, lacks Schiller's moral, idealistic foundation.

The slightly Oriental, epigrammatical style—"I, Wang Yen, called Shlink, 54 years old, died without an heir three miles south of Chicago" (*W* 1:191)—sounds like a critical parody of the Robber Moor's pathetic reply: "One thing is left me with which I can reconcile the injured laws and make the mistreated order whole again. It needs a sacrifice—a sacrifice that will unfold its inviolable majesty before all mankind—I myself am this sacrifice. I must die a death for it" (quotation from Schiller's *Robbers,* 5.2). The one appeals to a higher idea, the other dies purposely silent; he wants only to "save face." Through his death, Shlink escapes the lynch mob his opponent has unleashed on him, although he could have fled with Garga. However, Shlink considers Garga's flight an "error of calculation." Although he moves from Chicago to New York, Garga cannot escape the monstrous city (*W* 1:193). He referred to the problem in an earlier reply: "I will carry my raw flesh out into the icy rain," he says. "Chicago is cold. I'll go in. It's possible that I'm doing the wrong thing. But I still have lots of time" (*W* 1:190). It is Garga's reference to his youth, which allows him to make "errors of calculation," that results in Shlink's literally "*falling down.*" He understands Garga's statement as the "last stabs of the dagger," the "last words" in the battle, and he gives up, although not without warning Garga in a friendly fashion: "Don't stop because you're young. The woods are stripped of trees, the vultures are satiated, and the golden answer will be buried in the ground" (*W* 1:190). This last part of the reply is answered by Marie, who confirms: "I only see that you've lost ground. Have mercy on yourself" (*W* 1:191).

The two opponents end the battle, albeit with contrary motives. There is no "result of the battle" and no "understanding" (*W* 1:188); only the ambivalent "guarantee" (*W* 1:191) of "naked life" (Garga) or of death (Shlink) remains in the jungle of the cities, which, according to the surviving hero, Garga, is behind him and from which the dying hero, Shlink, escapes. Schiller's Moor also ends the battle, like Shlink, by deciding to die, although he tends toward pathetic self-elevation. There are many parallel details in the two plays.[20] Just as Karl Moor becomes a robber because of his brother's intrigues, Garga is nothing but a "rented fist-fighter," a "purchased idealist" of Shlink (*W* 1:189). Moor and Garga both want to "turn around," to return to their old "platform," but their crime binds each to his respective partner.[21] Both Brecht and Schiller shake the foundations of their main characters' beliefs. In Garga's case, the foundation is commercial; for Karl Moor, it is an ideal, a "belief in mankind."[22] Both shed their skins (*W* 1:135) and take on a different form of existence. The one becomes a criminal outcast, the other an egotistical

20. Schulz, *Schillerbearbeitungen,* 67–73.
21. Schulz, *Schillerbearbeitungen,* 69.
22. Schulz, *Schillerbearbeitungen,* 72.

opportunist who "introduces the lifestyle of the prairie" (*W* 1:133, 140). The vital difference, of course, cannot be ignored: Schiller's hero revokes his errors and atones for them, but Brecht lets them stand. Both dramatists test and critically judge the behavior of their characters. At the end, Karl Moor realizes that two such people as he "*would destroy the entire foundation of the moral world*" (*Robbers*, 5.2), but Shlink tells George Garga relatively early on: "You only realize the value of your inclinations when their objects are in the morgue and it's necessary for me to inform you of your inclinations" (*W* 1:160).

In fact, Shlink uses the members of Garga's family as "sources of help" (*W* 1:160), lives from his "supply," which he finally uses up, just as Garga exhausts Shlink's wood business and income. For this reason, Garga's reproach is applicable to both of the opponents: "That which is a human being to me you devour like a pile of meat." Later Shlink emphasizes the spiritual and Garga speaks of his "raw flesh." A similar change in position occurs between the idealist Karl and Franz, the materialist whose rationality at the end is negated by the irrational fear of punishment. Both Brecht and Schiller submit the two sides to a dialectical criticism, but Schiller's criticism aims at the character and Brecht's at the world to which the character is reacting with a specific type of behavior.

A path leads directly from *In the Jungle of the Cities* to *St. Joan of the Stockyards* by way of the thematic complex of Schiller and Chicago. In *St. Joan*, America is a model of capitalism that Brecht subjects to several levels of criticism. After the first version of *In the Jungle*, in which English and American environments intermingle,[23] Brecht continued to expand on the references to America. Chicago is the model of the gigantic asphalt jungle and of the struggle for life that takes place in it.[24] Garga's family, driven from the country in the south into the city, is threatened with disintegration in the dangerous city jungle, a disintegration that is accelerated by Shlink's passive action. The individual family members break away from the narrow community and become independent. Even the central figure of the traditional family, the mother, says: "I too must map out my years. Four years in this city of iron and filth!" (*W* 1:170). When she finally steals away, her husband states matter-of-factly: "That's the liquidation of the family" (*W* 1:175). On the subject of these occurrences, Wurm comments

23. Seliger, *Amerikabild*, 47.
24. Seliger, *Amerikabild*, 39ff.

sarcastically: "The moths have gotten into this family that would happily sacrifice its last cent to be told where the mother is, the pillar of the household" (*W* 1:180).

Garga blames Shlink for everything that happens (*W* 1:185) and takes revenge by ordering the lynching that his adversary escapes by committing suicide. The disintegration and perversion of Garga's family is Brecht's vehicle to show the alienation and isolation of urban man, just as Schiller had used the crimes against the idea of humanity in *Robbers* and *Don Carlos*. For Schiller, tears are a metaphor for the feelings of the heart, for empathic human expression. In *The Jungle of the Cities,* the cold of Chicago represents human coldness and the inhumanity of the large city.[25] For this reason, Gisela E. Bahr concludes her "evaluation" of the play with the view that it shows the negative aspects of the microcosm of the city.[26] The bestial, "wild" Chicago, where the law of the jungle prevails, does not allow a traditional solution of a conflict, not even a tragic solution, for "a return to old (bourgeois) values will not make the terrible condition of the world any more accessible."[27]

Brecht culled the basic material for his own work from Schiller's plays and was similarly generous in taking inspiration from the Chicago novels of Sinclair and Jensen. He was not interested in an accurate portrayal of American reality—this is obvious in his careless treatment of geography and terminology in the first version—but in the construction of an aesthetic model that rejected old models of experience and presented new perspectives on reality. The model not only provides the "patterns of behavior of our contemporaries which . . . old . . . motifs cannot explain," as Brecht wrote in the *Program Notes.* Instead, with the produced alien elements, the attention of the audience or reader is directed to a recognition of their own changed situation and problems. Brecht later defined the "alienating images" "as those that recognize the object but that [make] it seem strange" (*W* 16:680). In this connection, Brecht noted that antique and medieval theater alienated "its characters by using human and animal masks" and that Asian theater "still to this day [uses] musical alienation effects" (*W* 16:680).

There can be no doubt that the Asian elements in *The Jungle of the Cities* serve the same alienating function as the American elements. However, it was not until 1936 that Brecht began to see the progressive aesthetic position

25. Parmalee, *Brecht's America,* 22f.

26. Bahr, "Und niemals," 85.

27. Bahr, "Und niemals," 85.

of the "ancient Asian theater" (*W* 15:272) and to note the parallels to his own epic theater. At the beginning, he also confused Japanese and Chinese theater. Nevertheless, in *The Jungle of the Cities*, he correctly perceived the aesthetic possibilities of the Asian element. On the one hand, these possibilities enabled him to illustrate a certain type of behavior and, on the other, as Tatlow explains, he used the "'Chinese' nature as a means of making strange human behavior,"[28] or, as Berg-Pan puts it, in order to "'make strange' the familiar."[29] One can also argue the other way around, that both the Asian and American costumes represent an attempt to internationalize the problems of modern, European man. The Malaysian Shlink, whose exotic existence provides a mysterious quality,[30] an alien, not readily explainable type of behavior, says at one point that he spent his "youth in the row-boats on the Jantsekiang" (*W* 1:154). Another time, however, he introduces himself as "Wang Yen," "bred in Yokohama in the northern Peiho under the sign of the turtle" (*W* 1:191). At first, the exotic quality of alien names and places, and not an accurate portrayal of facts, seems to be the important aspect of this mixture of Japanese, Malaysian, and Chinese elements. With his team, including the Chinese Skinny, Shlink, the personification of the alien, breaks into Garga's apparently secure existence and changes his relationship to his family, his girlfriend, and himself. In his *Working Notes*, Brecht wrote that "with a spiritual system of apparent passivity, the man Shlink severs the young Garga's ties with his environment and forces him into a desperate fight for freedom against the ever denser jungle of Shlink's intrigues."[31]

Shlink represents the other, the sly, inscrutable one who consciously alienates Garga from his environment. The battle is for real things, "for the wood business, the family, a marriage, . . . for personal freedom,"[32] for commercial, social, and moral values that are destroyed or altered. A comment in the *Program Notes* stresses how close this battle is to "sport theater": "Here sport as passion is simply added to those passions that are already available to the theater" (*W* 1:971). "I have a taste for everything, my stomach digests gravel" (*W* 1:151) says the enigmatic Malaysian, who even employs such old values as goodness, altruism, and apparent

28. Tatlow, *Mask of Evil*, 260.
29. Renata Berg-Pan, *Bertolt Brecht und China* (Bonn: Bouvier, 1979), 60.
30. Berg-Pan, *Brecht und China*, 64f.
31. Bahr, "*Im Dickicht*," 136.
32. Bahr, "*Im Dickicht*," 137.

surrender in his battle against Garga. "I am an honest man, don't demand any words from my mouth, there are only teeth in it" (*W* 1:152) he says unequivocally to the father of his adversary, John Garga. His skin is not only yellow, a reference to racial prejudice, but also thick from experience (*W* 1:153f.). George Garga uses racial prejudice against Shlink with as little consideration as he uses his sister's love for the Malaysian (*W* 1:157). Shlink sees the battle as a possibility to break out of his loneliness and overcome the "splitting of language" (*W* 1:186f.), but Garga stresses the difference in their ages and the primacy of survival. In contrast to the Asian, who analyzes the situation intellectually and aims for the spiritual while his opponent answers with the physical and base (*W* 1:189f.), Garga either prefers a flat, low style, or expresses himself with quotations from Arthur Rimbaud's *Une Saison en enfer* and *Illumination* (*W* 1:134, 188f.). This not only points to the sheer impossibility of the "understanding" (*W* 1:187) that Shlink desires, but also to the general breakdown of communication and progressive isolation.

These traits reveal Garga as a "man without qualities," to use a key word of Robert Musil, who has only Shlink's actions to thank for his own existence as someone whom the Malaysian "bought for ten dollars," "an idealist who couldn't even tell his legs apart, a nothing!" (*W* 1:189). This inability to connect language, the world, and another human being is shown to be symptomatic of the jungle of the city, but also opportune. It is not fortuitous that the opponent who hopes for a "metaphysical" action or solution is the one who is destroyed, while the other, who is interested only in existence, bought, borrowed, or however come by, survives. Brecht's notation in his journal on September 6, 1920, reveals a critical stance with regard to this attitude: "One doesn't have one's own words and one never washes them. In the beginning was not the word. The word is at the end. It is the corpse of the thing. What a strange creature man is!" (*T*, 55). The crisis of language thus answers the crisis of the altered way of life that severs the individual from his bourgeois roots and places him in another environment. Looking closely, we see that the Asian opponent retains part of the old ideas and hopes after shattering the idealistic Garga's freedom of thought and world of books. Shlink relinquishes life when its substance is exhausted, while the supposed idealist Garga survives as a programmatic man of the jungle. Shlink's behavior can be interpreted critically and measured by Taoist criteria, as Alfred Döblin does in his novel, *The Three Leaps of Wang-Lun:* "To want to conquer the world by acting will fail. The world is spiritual, one should not touch it. He who acts, loses it; he who clings to it, loses it."[33]

It is noteworthy that not only the Asian, but also the Caucasian, George Garga, acts according to the precepts of the *Tao Te Ching*, thus proving that the alien elements in *The Jungle of the Cities* are exchangeable. This dialectical relationship of the two main characters elucidates Brecht's explanation in the *Program Notes* that he would be satisfied "to indicate Shlink's Asian-ness with plain yellow paint and furthermore [to allow] him to behave like an Asian, that is, like a European" (*W* 17:143). In this play, Brecht is concerned with creating a challenging comparison by means of alienation, but he avoids a possible identification with the alien element, or an illusion brought about by the fascination with the exotic. In a fragment from 1930, he warns against that "pompous and exotic facade . . . , that may spring up before the 'spiritual eye' of not only the *average* reader at the word *Asian*" (*W* 15:203). In order to "rob the term *Asian* of its last exotic pomp," he pointed instead to "the 'base' performances of the local Munich comedian Karl Valentin that . . . supposedly have something Asian about them, in order to understand [his] idea of theater" (*W* 15:204).

Brecht alienates the German and European situation with American and Asian dramatis personae, then alienates these, too, by tracing them back to German and European prototypes and problem complexes. In other words, the familiar is alienated in order to make it recognizable, and the alien is made recognizable by bringing it closer and making it understandable and familiar. This vision of Brecht's required a specific procedure that he called, simply but trenchantly in the *Little Organon for the Theater* (*Kleines Organon für das Theater*), an "alienation effect" ([*Verfremdungseffekt*]; *W* 16:680f.). Alien experience was ultimately the "best school for dialectic" for him because in it he saw the conditions that made changes possible (*W* 14:1462). "I have heard that Chinese poets and philosophers made a practice of going into exile just as ours go into the academy" (*W* 19:478). They chose the alien over home, over the familiar, over affirmation, in order to achieve a distance to themselves and the world they knew all too well and which they could recognize better and change critically from afar. Or, as Max Frisch puts it in one of his diaries, "The most alien moment you can experience is to see yourself and your own world from outside."[34]

33. Alfred Döblin, *Die drei Sprünge des Wang-Lun,* ed. Walter Muschg (Olten: Walter Verlag, 1960), 48.

34. Max Frisch, *Tagebuch 1946—1949* (Frankfurt am Main: Suhrkamp Verlag, 1972), 125.

Joyce Revoiced:
German Translations of *Ulysses*

Mark Harman

Translation is a useful prism for viewing Joyce's Irish-European web of words. Joyce himself was a translator in two senses of the term. As a young man, he translated two plays by Gerhart Hauptmann; as a seasoned artist, he translated Ireland into Europe and Europe into Ireland. In comparing three German versions of the "Nausicaa" chapter in *Ulysses,* I hope to keep in mind both the literal and figurative meanings of the term.

The Zurich Joycean, Fritz Senn, has argued that translations of *Ulysses* must inevitably lose the obsession of the original with the processes of language.[1] I am not quite as fatalistic as Senn and would argue that there is no reason why German translations of Joyce should not at least attempt to be as linguistically provocative for German readers as the original is for English speakers. Unless Joyce's translators set themselves that difficult task, the battle will be lost before it has even begun.

German has often been fortunate in its translators, and there have been figures such as Hölderlin whose radical translations suggest the outermost limits of what is linguistically possible. *Ulysses* calls for a translation that disassembles German just as Joyce deconstructs English. There is a German tradition of radical translation theory that could provide the framework for a bold attempt to create a thoroughly Joycean German. It is, characteristically, Goethe who sums up the issue most appositely. In his prose commentary on the *West-Östlicher Divan*, he argues that, if translators want to capture the provocative force of the original, they have to create a new linguistic entity, a seemingly non-German German: "und so entsteht ein

---

1. Fritz Senn, *Joyce's Dislocutions: Essays on Reading as Translation* (Baltimore: Johns Hopkins University Press, 1984), 28.

Drittes, wozu der Geschmack der Menge sich erst heranbilden muß."[2] Goethe is asking for the exact opposite of the "smooth," "fluent," and "readable" prose that many Anglo-American readers—and critics too, for that matter—look for, even in English versions of experimental texts.

Joyce's attitude toward English resembles that of certain German-Jewish writers toward German. When Kafka, for instance, asks himself whether he is a circus rider straddling two horses, one German, the other Jewish, he is using an image that also applies to Joyce.[3] There are, however, three horses at the very least in Joyce's ring; they represent the conversational culture of Ireland, the literary heritage of English, and the European mainstream. The "Nausicaa" chapter, for instance, translates the biographical experiments of James Joyce in Zurich into the fictional exploits of Leopold Bloom at Sandymount strand. Joyce's translators also have to weave a multilayered fabric out of these disparate cultural and linguistic strands.

The first German translation of *Ulysses* bore the proud imprimatur: "eine vom Verfasser autorisierte Ausgabe von Georg Goyert."[4] That claim was irresponsible because the publishers, the Rhein-Verlag, only left Goyert, the translator, and Joyce himself a few weeks to revise the draft. The revised version of 1930, produced at Joyce's insistence, was announced as the "definitive deutsche Ausgabe." In spite of the reservations expressed by such eminent Joyceans as Arno Schmidt, the Goyert version survived until 1976, when it was superceded by an entirely new translation by Hans Wollschläger.[5] Wollschläger's version has been generally well received. But, in 1983, Werner Gotzmann published an arresting counter-Wollschläger version of the "Nausicaa" chapter.[6] I would like to emphasize that my point in comparing these three versions is not to carp at three intrepid practitioners of a difficult art, but rather to uncover the radical quality of Joyce's challenge to German.

The translator of the "Nausicaa" chapter must recreate a purple prose

---

2. J. W. v. Goethe, *Werke,* ed. Erich Trunz (Hamburg: Wegner, 1965), 2:256.

3. Franz Kafka, *Briefe an Felice,* ed. Erich Heller and Jürgen Born (Tübingen: Fischer, 1970), 720.

4. James Joyce, *Ulysses,* vom Verfasser autorisierte Übersetzung von Georg Goyert (Zurich: Rhein Verlag, 1950). This edition is subsequently cited as Goyert.

5. James Joyce, *Ulysses,* Übersetzung von Hans Wollschläger (Frankfurt: Suhrkamp, 1976). This edition is subsequently cited as Wollschläger.

6. Werner Gotzmann, "Neuübersetzung: James Joyce *Ulysses,* 13. Kapitel," *Sprache im technischen Zeitalter* 86 (June, 1983): 138–67. This translation is subsequently cited as Gotzmann.

that is full of lyrical clichés. The narrator pokes fun at those hackneyed turns of phrase, while nevertheless milking them for what they are worth. Goyert is more successful at capturing that trite lyricism than he is at suggesting the narrator's tongue-in-cheek posture. I would like to compare Goyert's version of the opening paragraph, which describes Dublin bay, both with the original and with Wollschläger's later rendering.

> Far away in the west the sun was setting and the last glow of all too fleeting day lingered lovingly on sea and strand, on the proud promontory of dear old Howth guarding as ever the waters of the bay... (Joyce, 284)[7]

> Fern im Westen ging die Sonne unter, und lieblich lag noch kurze Zeit der letzte Schimmer des nur zu schnell schwindenden Lichtes auf Meer und Strand, auf dem alten, lieben, stolzen Vorgebirge Howth, das seit Ewigkeit die Wasser der Bucht schützt... (Goyert, 389)

> Fern, weit in Westen, ging die Sonne unter, und die letzte Glut des nur allzu schnell entschwindenden Tages weilte lieblich noch auf See und Strand, auf dem stolzen Vorgebirge des guten alten Howth, der wie eh und je über den Wassern der Bucht wachte... (Wollschläger, 481)

Goyert evokes well the ample rhetoric of the original and its self-indulgent fondness for alliteration. What he fails to suggest is the irony implied by the overinsistent use of clichés such as "all too fleeting day." Wollschläger captures the clichés by drawing on overused phrases and such slightly archaic words as *weilen*. He then mimes Joyce's euphonious yet hackneyed language far better than does Goyert.

Joyce experimented with some raw material for this chapter during encounters with Marthe Fleischmann in Zurich in 1918. The author of "Chamber Music," that ambiguously titled book of verse, first spied Marthe as she was pulling the toilet chain in her Zurich apartment, which was adjacent to his. The subsequent liaison was every bit as strange as that initial *coup de foudre*, according to Richard Ellmann's elegant account.[8] One

---

7. James Joyce, *Ulysses,* ed. Hans Walter Gabler (New York: Random House, 1986), 284. This edition is subsequently cited as *Ulysses.*

8. Richard Ellmann, *James Joyce* (New York: Oxford University Press, 1982), 448–52.

of Joyce's postcards to Marthe, now lost, was addressed by "Odysseus" to "Nausicaa."

Some of the kitschy imagery in the chapter is translated literally from Joyce's correspondence with Fleischmann, which is written in French, German, and even Latin. Although Joyce expresses a preference in one of the letters for French over German—"l'allemand ne me va pas"—his final letter to her is written in German, and ends with an invocation from the litany of Our Lady of Loreto: "O rosa mistica [*sic*], ora pro me." This mystical rose undergoes a sea change: the rose splits into the sentimental seductress, Gerty MacDowell, and the fulsomely praised Comfortress of the Afflicted, Mary, Star of the Sea. Joyce's description of Marthe in that last letter as "so blass, so müde, so traurig" reappears in the characterization of Gerty, in her "sad downcast eyes" and the "waxen pallor of her face." Besides, Joyce reaches heights of kitsch that would be the envy of Gerty, if she knew any German: "Und durch die Nacht der Bitterkeit meiner Seele fielen die Küsse Deiner Lippen über meinen Herz—weich wie Rosenblätter, sanft wie Tau."[9] The grammatical error in "meinen Herz" reminds us that Joyce picked up his German from books and on the street and never seems to have fully mastered the genders and the case system.

Ulysses is the symphony of a Catholic *Großstadt*, and so Joyce interweaves the prayers and singing at benediction with Gerty's novelette-ish gush. Instead of a literary expatriate experimenting coyly with the role of adulterer, we hear a congregation "kneeling before the feet of the immaculate, reciting the litany of Our Lady of Loreto, beseeching her to intercede for them, the old familiar words, holy Mary, holy virgin of virgins. How sad to poor Gerty's ears" (*Ulysses,* 290). There is no way of knowing how Joyce's invocation of the same litany struck Marthe, who seems to have been considerably more worldly-wise than her scatterbrained fictional counterpart. What the Fleishmann letters show is how crucial Joyce's multilingual environment in Zurich was to the composition of *Ulysses*. The language of the novel is always at several removes from standard English, and Joyce turns his Irishman's ambivalence about English and his versatility in other languages into a formidable artistic weapon.

Gerty thinks in phrases gleaned from the *Lady's Pictorial* and the novelettes of a Miss Cummins. While she is leaning back to watch the fireworks

---

9. James Joyce, *Selected Letters,* ed. Richard Ellmann (New York: Viking, 1975), 237.

and thus expose herself to Bloom's gaze, a relevant item of saucy gossip crosses Gerty's mind.

> ... because Bertha Supple told her once in dead secret and made her swear she'd never about the gentleman lodger that was staying with them out of the Congested Districts Board that had pictures cut out of papers of those skirtdancers ... (*Ulysses,* 299)

A glance at Goyert's version shows that he irons out the prose in order to make it reasonably correct syntactically.

> ... denn Bertha Supple hatte ihr einmal unter dem Siegel der Verschwiegenheit, und sie hatte ihr schwören müssen, nie ein Wort darüber zu sagen, von dem Logierherrn, der bei ihnen im Congested Districts Board wohnte, erzählt, und der hatte aus Zeitungen ausgeschnittene Bilder von Schleiertänzerinnen ... (Goyert, 412)

Goyert must not have known much about the Ireland of 1904, because he houses the Supple family and their pin-up loving tenant in the offices of the Congested Districts Board. The board was an agency set up to tackle the problems of the poor, densely populated Western counties. A trivial, if revealing, slip. Unfortunately, Goyert's rendering of the stream-of-consciousness flow of Gerty's thoughts is also clumsy. The postponement of the verb *erzählt* makes it difficult to say the phrases aloud, convincingly. And that is a key test for translations of such stream-of-consciousness passages in *Ulysses.* Goyert's concern with grammatical correctness is misplaced, especially in the last sentence of the chapter, which, in English, ends with "cuckoo, cuckoo, cuckoo." Goyert, feeling honor bound to respect the word order in relative clauses, ends the chapter instead with the verb *war,* thus weakening the effect of the playful allusion to Bloom, the titillated cuckold.

Goyert also tends to fill in the gaps that are so integral a part of the stream-of-consciousness technique. Whereas in the original we have to supply the missing phrase implied by "swear she'd never," in German, the translator has unnecessarily filled in the blank with "nie ein Wort darüber zu sagen." Here, as elsewhere, Wollschläger improves on the version of his predecessor. Incidentally, he also moves the Supple family out of the Congested Boards office and back into their own house.

Yet Wollschläger, too, often offers explanatory paraphrases rather than

German analogues to the verbal fireworks of the original. For instance, when Gerty is leaving, she takes out her handkerchief to wave to Bloom, "without" in the ambiguous phrasing of the original "letting him." Letting him what? It is up to readers to make up their minds, because Gerty does not complete the thought. Wollschläger eliminates all such uncertainty by stating his interpretation of what Joyce has intentionally left unsaid: "... ohne ihn aus den Augen zu lassen."

Joyce's father once said that the first thing James would do if he got dumped in the middle of the Sahara would be draw a map. One of the major challenges for the translator of *Ulysses* lies in Joyce's canny combination of underlying order and surface anarchy. Joyce buries his underlying diagram deep within the syntax, and reading aloud is one way of deciphering it. The preliminary translation from page to voice is itself an interpretative act. Decisions about pauses are also decisions about which phrases belong together semantically.

O sweety all your little girlwhite up I saw dirty bracegirdle made me do love sticky we two naughty Grace darling she him half past the bed met him pike hoses frillies ... (*Ulysses*, 312)

What, for instance, should the translator do with the strangely placed little word *up*? Bloom's voyeurism leads us to expect either "up all your little girlwhite I saw" *or* "your little girlwhite I saw up." Instead, Joyce unhooks it from the two phrases to which one would expect it to belong. The word *up* has, of course, recently been on Bloom's mind. A page earlier he had thought of a Dublin character who roams the streets trying to track down the source of postcards he has been getting bearing only the letters: *U.p.* Besides, up describes the trajectory of the fireworks Gerty has been pretending to watch as well as the erectile effect of her underwear on Bloom. The stylistic technique of the chapter, after all, is, as Joyce suggested to Stuart Gilbert, that of "tumescence: detumescence."[10]

Goyert avoids the complex resonance of "up" simply by omitting it from his version.

O Süsse all deine kleine Mädchenweisse sah ich schmutzig Bracegirdle liess mich lieben klebend wir beide böse Grace Darling sie ihn halb Bett Metimpikose Dessous ... (Goyert, 431)

---

10. Stuart Gilbert, *James Joyce's* Ulysses (New York: Vintage, 1958), 278.

Goyert inexplicably uses the English word *bracegirdle,* which automatically acquires a misplaced stylistic value as a *Fremdwort.* Wollschläger's version is far more meticulous and accurate than Goyert's. He comes up, for instance, with a satisfactory German equivalent for the pun on metempsychosis, the transmigration of souls, a term that, of course, recurs in various disfigurations throughout the novel. Nevertheless, this passage is flatter in Wollschläger than in Goyert. The fact that it is easier to understand than the original is a flaw rather than a virtue.

Ach du süßes Ding ich hab dein ganzes kleines Mädchenweiß rauf habe ich sehn können hab den schmutzigen Stützgürtel habe ich hat mich lieben lassen klebrig wir zwei beiden bösen Grace Darling hat sie ihn für halb nach vier wir für das Bett mit ihm zig Hosen Spitzenunterwäsche . . . (Wollschläger, 535)

Wollschläger imposes syntactical order on Bloom's jumbled thoughts, but the obtrusive scaffolding created by the repeated use of *haben* detracts from the desired detumescent effect.

According to Gotzmann, it is passages such as these in Wollschläger that prompted him to produce a countertranslation of the "Nausicaa" chapter.[11] His version of that passage runs as follows.

Oh Süßes all dein Mädchenweiß hoch sah ich beschmutzt Stürtzgürtel ließ mich lieben klebend wir zwei beide bösen Grace Liebling sie um halb nach ihm das Bett mit ihm zig Hosen Reizwäsche . . . (Gotzmann, 165)

This version challenges the German reader in a manner comparable to the effect of the original. It comes closer than Wollschläger's version to creating that "Drittes" of which Goethe speaks, a non-German German that only time will assimilate. This is surprising because Gotzmann is clearly not as experienced a translator as Wollschläger. There are other, less challenging passages in Joyce's text—such as the initial paragraph about Dublin bay—that are far less convincing in Gotzmann than in Wollschläger. Whenever he needs to get out of tight spots, Gotzmann resorts to ugly dashes, which interrupt the flow that was so important to

---

11. Werner Gotzmann, "Wer war M' Intosh?: James Joyce' Universalroman *Ulysses:* eine Partitur," *Sprache im technischen Zeitalter* 86 (June, 1983): 125–37.

Joyce. But his version takes greater risks with German than does Wollschläger's.

To revoice means to re-Joyce, and a translator who does not take creative risks will necessarily diminish *Ulysses*. At times, certain nuances of Dublin English and of the city's lore will be lost; translators ought to compensate for these losses by occasionally daring to push their versions further along Joycean lines than does the original itself. That is how Joyce himself translated a section of *Finnegans Wake* into Italian. The "carrying across" suggested etymologically by translation becomes, in Joyce's hands, a "carrying beyond." My Italian is not quite up to analyzing what he does to Italian, but, according to one critic, he offers "an exploration of the furthest limits of the Italian language conducted by a great writer."[12]

Joyce took delight in one compensatory strategy used by Goyert. In the 1927 version, Goyert had mistranslated the phrase "and that's the last of his nibs" as "und das ist das letzte, was er zu sich nimmt." In the 1930 edition, another version is substituted: ". . . und das ist das letzte Seiner Hochwohlgestorbenen." This pun on *Hochwohlgeboren* and *gestorben* goes beyond a literal translation; it turns Joyce's associative genius loose on German. Joyce uses the pun in a letter to Goyert of July, 1939: "Vielmals habe ich Sie wegen des hochwohlgestorbenen Johannes Jeep . . . ausgefragt."[13] There has not been enough of this compensatory play with language in the German versions of *Ulysses*.

There never will be a "definitive" German translation of *Ulysses,* not because individual translators are inadequate, but because Joyce is so inexhaustible that the translator's readings will inevitably fade with time and will be superceded by new interpretations and fresh recreations. If anybody ever musters the courage to undertake a complete translation of *Finnegans Wake* into German, I would suggest that he, she, no: they—the project would require a large team of polyglot translators—take a look at the musings of Walter Benjamin on translation.

There is a parallel between Benjamin's theory of translation and Joyce's implicit attitude toward language. For Benjamin, whose ideas about translation blend insights gleaned from the kabbalah, Goethe, and Hölderlin, the existing languages are merely fragments of an archetypal "reine Sprache." He sees translation as a potentially glorious enterprise that could heal the linguistic rift symbolized by the Tower of Babel.[14] Ideally, the task

---

12. Jacqueline Risset, "Joyce Translates Joyce," *Comparative Criticism* 6 (1984): 3.

13. James Joyce, *Letters,* ed. Richard Ellmann (New York: Viking, 1966), 448.

14. See the illuminating discussion of Benjamin's theory of translation in George Steiner,

of the translator is to integrate all existing languages and, thus, make tangible the presence of that "true" original tongue.[15]

Finnegans Wake represents the most radical attempt in modern literature to break out of the prison of a single language. Joyce's creative dissatisfaction with the limitations of English, which one can already sense in the "Nausicaa" chapter and elsewhere in *Ulysses,* is the driving force behind the *Wake.* In that formidable book, he sets out to accomplish an objective similar to the one that Benjamin envisaged for translation. By culling phrases from a multitude of local dialects, Joyce creates a metalanguage that mimics the sound of the primordial human tongue.

After Babel: Aspects of Language and Translation (Oxford: Oxford University Press, 1975), 63–64, 259–60.

15. Walter Benjamin, *Gesammelte Schriften,* ed. Rolf Tiedemann (Frankfurt: Suhrkamp, 1972), vol. 4, pt. 1:16.

Lüneburg Leatherstocking: Arno Schmidt and James Fenimore Cooper

Ellis Shookman

"Kennen Sie James Fenimore Cooper?"
Niemand kannte den großen Mann;
also ging ich zu Bett.

—Arno Schmidt, *Brand's Haide* (1951)

Tradition and experiment seldom mix as strangely as they do over and over in the work of Arno Schmidt. Throughout his life, Schmidt deeply admired writers who preceded him in numerous literary traditions. Such admiration, however, reflected and directed the unique course of his own narrative experiments. His work, grafting old on new, was therefore remarkably hybrid. As Peter Demetz has written of *Abend mit Goldrand* (1975), Schmidt's self-panegyrical, last complete text, "German provincialism, the pedantry of a vast antiquarian knowledge, and the literate genius for innovation have never been combined in a more provocative achievement."[1] Such unlikely yoking of provincial pedantry and literary genius is certainly not peculiar to Schmidt. Indeed, in the German tradition that he himself favored, combining those qualities put him in notable literary company. They do seem particularly incongruous in his œuvre, however, which Demetz censures for retaining "unquestioned assumptions" about the self, fiction, consciousness, and language, but which he admits anticipated the "systematic experimentation" begun by younger, more radical writers in the mid-1960s.[2] Schmidt's work, I think, can be explained as a more traditional, less systematic "experiment." He himself called his attempts to freeze the flow of consciousness in words "Versuchsreihen,"

---

1. Peter Demetz, *After the Fires: Recent Writing in the Germanies, Austria, and Switzerland* (New York: Harcourt Brace Jovanovich, 1986), 318.
2. Demetz, *After the Fires,* 320, 391.

and he even thought himself a kind of verbal test tube: "Vielleicht bin ich von Mutter Natur ausdrücklich als 1 Gefäß für Worte angelegt, in dem es schtändich probiert und rührt und komm-bieniert?"[3] Similarly, critics have found his phonetic spellings and Freudian neologisms signs of an extreme "Experimentierwut," though one strongly tied to mimetic concepts of language and thus "nothing if not tradition conscious."[4] The actual tradition of which Schmidt was so conscious stretches from around 1700 to about 1930, with high points in German romanticism and expressionism, one nadir in nineteenth-century realism, and many heroes whose senses of imagination and prose slowly cleared the way for its culmination in Joyce.[5] Scholars suggest that Schmidt used that tradition as both a literary ideal and historical justification for his own notions of fiction, and, though some fault him for distorting the authors whose work he examined, all agree that his citing them enriches the structure as well as the content of his texts.[6] Tradition and experiment thus seem heuristic concepts singularly suited to reading Schmidt's writing.

They especially help discover how Schmidt absorbed and transformed the work of James Fenimore Cooper. Research on Cooper's place in Schmidt's tradition is scant, but the fullest account of that tradition fittingly starts by mentioning him.[7] Few authors earned greater respect from

---

3. Arno Schmidt, quoted in Franz Lennartz, *Deutsche Schriftsteller der Gegenwart* (Stuttgart: Kröner, 1978), 645.

4. Werner Eggers, "Arno Schmidt," in *Deutsche Literatur der Gegenwart in Einzeldarstellungen,* ed. Dietrich Weber (Stuttgart: Kröner, 1976), 1:331; Siegbert S. Prawer, "Etyms and Endgames," review of *Abend mit Goldrand* by Arno Schmidt, *Times Literary Supplement,* September 5, 1980: reprinted in *Über Arno Schmidt: Rezensionen vom "Leviathian" bis zur "Julia",* ed. Hans-Michael Bock (Zurich: Haffmans, 1984), 303.

5. Wolfgang Proß, *Arno Schmidt* (Munich: Beck, 1980), 44–48.

6. Schmidt's tradition is cited as an ideal in Eggers ("Schmidt," 314), and as self-justification in Proß (*Schmidt,* 90). Criticism of his projecting his own subconscious onto the writers whom he analyzed is strong in Lenz Prütting, "Arno Schmidt," in *Kritisches Lexikon zur deutschsprachigen Gegenwartsliteratur,* ed. Heinz Ludwig Arnold (Munich: Edition Text und Kritik, 1981), 13. For appreciation of his allusions to other writers, see M. R. Minden, *Arno Schmidt: A Critical Study of His Prose* (Cambridge: Cambridge University Press, 1982), 38. Both those allusions and Schmidt's broader literary structures are respected in Thomas Wolf, *"Einmal lebt' ich wie Götter"!!!. . .—; Nachforschungen zu Arno Schmidts Gelehrtenrepublik* (Frankfurt am Main: Bangert und Metzler, 1987), 21.

7. Heiko Postma, *Aufarbeitung und Vermittlung literarischer Traditionen: Arno Schmidt und seine Arbeiten zur Literatur,* 2d ed. (Frankfurt am Main: Bangert und Metzler, 1982). One notable exception to the general lack of attention paid Cooper in Schmidt's work are remarks scattered throughout Horst Thomé, *Natur und Geschichte im Frühwerk Arno Schmidts* (Munich: Edition Text und Kritik, 1981). Specific glosses of references to Cooper in Schmidt's *Aus dem Leben eines Fauns* can be found in Dieter Kuhn, *Kommentierendes Handbuch zu Arno Schmidts Roman Aus dem Leben eines Fauns* (Munich: Edition Text und Kritik, 1986).

Schmidt, as the number, range, and import of his remarks on Cooper reveal. A biographical essay on Cooper, "Siebzehn sind zuviel!" (1955), began a series designed for radio broadcasts that Schmidt wrote about the lives and works of various authors dear to him. Articles that he published in German newspapers and magazines in the 1950s and 1960s similarly popularized Cooper while tracing his high standing in Schmidt's canon to their deep political, literary, and personal affinities. Several essays and books that Schmidt devoted to other writers—Stifter, Tieck, Karl May, and Fouqué—also shed direct and favorable light on Cooper. Finally, Schmidt translated four of Cooper's novels, *The Wept of Wish-Ton-Wish* (1829; *Conanchet oder die Beweinte von Wish-Ton-Wish,* 1962) and the "Littlepage Manuscripts"—a trilogy comprising *Satanstoe* (1845; *Satanstoe,* 1976), *The Chainbearer* (1846; *Tausendmorgen,* 1977), and *The Redskins* (1846; *Die Roten,* 1978).[8] In addition to all these efforts at winning Cooper more readers in Germany, allusions to him abound in Schmidt's own fiction, where they help make clearer sense of both men and their respective works on fundamental literary and psychological levels. Such reciprocal links need to be explained because scholars so far have failed to agree even on such basic questions as whether Cooper prefigured Schmidt's sense of modern prose.[9] My own approach here divides Schmidt's work into three parts: (1) his essays and articles mentioning Cooper; (2) his stories, novels,

---

8. Indeed, Schmidt claimed to have far surpassed Cooper as his ideal translator, one whose work—given Cooper's stylistic shortcomings—could not help being better than the original (Arno Schmidt, "Tausend Zungen," *Süddeutsche Zeitung,* April 30, 1955; Afterword, 384). In contrast, Schmidt wrote that the work of bad translators could seem like the work of madmen, a point that he illustrated by citing—though not naming—such a translation of Cooper's *The Monikins* in his ... *denn 'wallflower' heißt 'Goldlack': Drei Dialoge* (Zurich: Haffmans, 1984), 62. For a full account of Schmidt's translations, including Cooper, see Rainer Barczaitis, *"Kein simpel-biedrer Sprachferge": Arno Schmidt als Übersetzer* (Frankfurt am Main: Bangert und Metzler, 1985), 198. Barczaitis concludes that *Conanchet* is the least distinctive of Schmidt's translations, but that his renderings of *Satanstoe, The Chainbearer,* and *The Redskins* are his most successful and do, indeed, surpass Cooper's original.

9. Minden links Schmidt to Virginia Woolf by noting their common dislike of plot (Minden, *Schmidt,* 69), which Schmidt also attributes to Cooper in "Siebzehn sind zuviel!". The same passage in Schmidt's essay is taken to be evidence of his agreement with Cooper on "das Denkmodell von der als Raum gedachten Realität" in Reimer Bull, *Bauformen des Erzählens bei Arno Schmidt: Ein Beitrag zur Poetik der Erzählkunst* (Bonn: Bouvier, 1970), 57. In contrast, Boy Hinrichs cites Schmidt's afterword to his translation of Cooper's *The Wept of Wish-Ton-Wish* to show that Cooper lacked Schmidt's sense of the "Repräsentanzfunktion des Materialen" and the according "Primat der Prosa in der modernen Literatur" (Boy Hinrichs, *Utopische Prosa als längeres Gedankenspiel: Untersuchungen zu Arno Schmidts Theorie der modernen Literatur in ihrer Konkretisierung in "Schwarze Spiegel," "Die Gelehrtenrepublik," und "Kaff auch Mare Crisium"* [Tübingen: Niemeyer, 1986], 42 n. 129).

and other fiction—except (3) *Zettels Traum*. Since Cooper himself blended tradition and experiment by trying to write romances like Scott's suited to new American themes, these three instances in which Schmidt revived him show the tradition of experiment in its self-perpetuating complexity.

Schmidt's many essays and articles mentioning Cooper reveal what he thought of Cooper's reception and relevance, why he valued the style and tradition of Cooper's work, and how literary as well as philosophical leanings that he shared with Cooper mattered to him personally. To Schmidt, Cooper had been the first American author of international stature, one nearly forgotten by his compatriots, however, who had deliberately erased him from their national consciousness. Both they and most Europeans of his day, who had him to thank for what little they then knew about America, always seemed to regard him merely as the author of the juvenile Leatherstocking Tales. Such unfair reception was even worse in Germany, where Cooper receded into the shadow of Karl May, whose similar novels Schmidt thought hopelessly inferior as sources of cultural history.[10] Writing such history was Cooper's strength, Schmidt argued, and Germans should read him to orient themselves in the postwar world half-dominated by his United States. Indeed, Schmidt proclaimed: "Es gibt schlechterdings keinen besseren und müheloseren Zugang zum Verständnis der Mentalität der USA, auch ihren Ereig- und Erleidnissen, als das Gesamtwerk Coopers."[11] Schmidt thought such history lessons doubly relevant to his fellow Germans, whose knowledge of the United States he dismissed as superficial at a time when their own country suffered from political and social ills like those Cooper had diagnosed—"Erscheinungen, uns Deutschen des Neuen Bundes bis zum Kotzen geläufig."[12] This satiric criticism mirrors Cooper's own, which he leveled at a fatherland that he at once supported and decried, displaying a dual loyalty that Schmidt prescribed as an antidote to the patriotism more recently and disastrously shown in his own nation. Cooper's poor reception in America and the relevance that Schmidt hoped his work could have for Germany were therefore related when Schmidt quoted him in "Siebzehn sind zuviel!"

---

10. Arno Schmidt, "Abu Kital: Vom neuen Großmystiker," in *Das essayistische Werk zur deutschen Literatur in 4 Bänden* (Zurich: Haffmans, 1988), 4:133.

11. Arno Schmidt, "Das Amerika der Pioniere: Bahnt sich eine Cooper-Renaissance an?" *Die Zeit* (U.S. edition), June 22, 1962.

12. Arno Schmidt, "Amerika, du hast es besser . . . ," in *Der Triton mit dem Sonnenschirm* (Karlsruhe: Stahlberg, 1969), 397–98.

Das ist ... mein Ziel gewesen: eine richtige gegenseitige Schätzung der Völker anzubahnen. ... Ich schmeichelte weder nationalen Vorurteilen; noch schonte ich schreiende Fehler und Mißbräuche. Sollte man mich eines Mangels an Patriotismus bezichtigen, so stelle ich die Frage: Wer dient seinem Vaterlande besser: der, der den Mut hat, die Wahrheit zu sagen; oder der, der die augenfälligsten Gebrechen mit patriotischer Lüge übertüncht?[13]

Such honesty yielded self-righteous scorn for Cooper from many Americans, but Schmidt thought that Germans should emulate the civic skepticism motivating it. One of his reasons for recalling Cooper was thus political.

Schmidt also had other reasons, some more literary, for reviving contemporary interest in Cooper. The literary ones stress Cooper's style, which Schmidt criticized but nonetheless esteemed in his eclectic tradition. Noting cultural and historical details was not only Cooper's strength, he claimed. It also made up for Cooper's stylistic faults. Indeed, Schmidt repeatedly wrote that the value of Cooper's work lay entirely in its subject matter. Although he enjoyed its social criticism, minor characters, and fictional landscapes, he admitted that its major characters, metaphors, plots, and vocabulary were all hopelessly unpoetic. Such shortcomings sound dire as Schmidt summed them up in his long afterword to *Conanchet*. "Was die Konstruktion, das formale Gerüst, anbelangt, so ist Cooper ... nachweislich nie der Gedanke gekommen, daß es sich auch bei Prosagebilden um Kunstwerke handeln könne."[14] This severe judgment did not prevent Schmidt from admiring Cooper's fictional landscapes so much that he cited them as prime evidence of a prose style that he himself favored and named "Methode Brockes" after another of his literary heroes, the early eighteenth-century poet Barthold Hinrich Brockes.[15] That descriptive style suggests such land-

---

13. Arno Schmidt, "Siebzehn sind zuviel!", in *Dya Na Sore: Gespräche in einer Bibliothek* (Karlsruhe: Stahlberg, 1958), 299.

14. Arno Schmidt, Afterword to *Conanchet oder die Beweinte von Wish-Ton-Wish* by James F. Cooper, trans. Arno Schmidt (1962; Frankfurt am Main: Fischer Taschenbuch Verlag, 1985), 385.

15. This "Methode Brockes" is sometimes also linked to Schmidt's mania for accurate detail. Wolf-Dieter Krüger reluctantly admits that anachronisms in Schmidt's early works show that he did not practice such accuracy as strictly as he preached it to other writers (Wolf-Dietrich Krüger, "Bruch mit Brockes, Cooper und Co. ... Über Ungereimtheiten im Frühwerk Arno Schmidts," in *Zettelkasten 6: Aufsätze und Arbeiten zum Werk Arno Schmidts, Jahrbuch der Gesellschaft der Arno-Schmidt-Leser*, ed. Thomas Krömmelbein [Frankfurt am Main:

scapes, he claimed, by piling up pictorially minute details that slowly overwhelm their readers. It thereby differs from both the expressionists' equally graphic but more concentrated images and the breathless plots concocted by "Handlungsreisende" in the emphatic manner of Lessing and Hebbel. Schmidt disliked such improbable plots, preferring Cooper as part of "eine zweite Schule, bei der die Fabel nicht aus Taten und Handlungen, sondern aus Zuständen, Denkweisen, Funktionen und Befindlichkeiten besteht!"[16] This second, more deliberate kind of writing conveys a higher truth revealed in "Siebzehn sind zuviel!" when Cooper refutes criticism (by Scott) that his novels show too little action: "Die Wahrheit kennt doch gar keine Handlung, wie?!" (307). Schmidt thus squarely placed Cooper in a tradition of fictional experiment that downplayed plot. That tradition includes Stifter, whom Schmidt tirelessly accused of plagiarizing Cooper's *The Deerslayer* (1841) in *Der Hochwald* (1842), but whom he also commended for improving Cooper's style. It also includes Scott, Fouqué, and Freytag, who—like Cooper—recorded the history of their countries in literary forms. Such history—which Schmidt described as "eben nicht die 'Hohe Geschichte,' sondern die 'Privataltertümer'"[17]—is similarly part of Schmidt's own "historical" novels, so he, too, counts as Cooper's stylistic ally. Although left out of Schmidt's "Dichtergespräche im Elysium" (1940), Cooper therefore rightfully joins the literary underworld toured in its later revision, *Tina oder über die Unsterblichkeit* (1958). For Schmidt, being consigned to such purgatory was an honor.

Behind Schmidt's stylistic reasons for respecting Cooper lay even more revealing personal ones. Strong sympathy linked him to the Leatherstocking, Cooper's main character, as well as to Cooper himself. He extolled the Leatherstocking, also called Natty Bumppo, as a great and even archetypal figure in world literature, indeed as the equal of Faust, Parsifal, and the Wandering Jew. What is more, Schmidt felt akin to him because they both lived more-or-less splendidly isolated in nature. Therefore, he overlooked the odd disinclination to work that he regretted Bumppo (alias "Hawkeye")

Bangert und Metzler, 1988], 105, 112). Similar criticism is leveled at Schmidt in Fritz Senn, "'Entzifferungen & Proben': 'Finnegans Wake' in der Brechung von Arno Schmidt," *Bargfelder Bote* 27 (February, 1978): 12. Kuhn (*Kommentierendes Handbuch,* 213) notes that Schmidt even gives wrong directions from Cooperstown to Sarasota Springs. In contrast, Thomé explains that Schmidt—unlike Cooper—did not collect details for the purpose of reconstructing them correctly in historical novels (Thomé, *Natur,* 171).

16. Arno Schmidt, "Die Handlungsreisenden," in *Das essayistische Werk*, 3:158.

17. Arno Schmidt, *Fouqué und einige seiner Zeitgenossen: Biographischer Versuch* (Karlsruhe: Stahlberg, 1958), 346.

shared with his fictional peers. "Ansonsten fühle ich—dito entwichen in Absoliduden, wo sich andauernd = ähnlich Graue Neutra und die Gaspantomimen von Tiefdruckausläufern zusammenläppern—dem Falkenauge wirklich = täglich nach."[18] A sense of such shared isolation also bound Schmidt to Cooper himself in an account of how well he liked the "menschenleere Öde" that became his home on the North German plain. The motto opening that account of how his family had dispersed is a quotation from Cooper's *The Monikins* (1835): "Ich habe mich gemeiniglich als auf gleichem Fuß mit den ältesten Edelleuten Europas angesehen, da wenige Familien rascher und direkter in den Nebel der Zeiten hinaufgeführt werden können, als die, deren Mitglied ich bin."[19] Such family resemblances are not always so ominous. "Siebzehn sind zuviel!" reveals that Cooper, like Schmidt, enjoyed playing chess with his wife. Furthermore, to illustrate how rowdies abused Cooper's property by noisily playing baseball on his lawn, Schmidt called for sound effects like "Gebrüll, wie von Fußballspielern: <Toaaa!>" (302). This sound distinctly echoes the "Urlaute balltretender Menschheit" deplored as similarly vulgar in "Die Umsiedler" (1953; 1:284).[20] Schmidt's world corresponded to Cooper's seriously, however, when he commended Cooper's puritanism, by which he meant extreme diligence like his own devotion to work. Clearer still is the professional likeness implied when Schmidt explained that reading Cooper enables one not only to study but also to fortify in oneself the "Mentalität . . . des rüstigen Zukunftspioniers, der sich auf hübsche-kalte planetengroße Wildnisse angesetzt sehen und dort den <Isolierten Statt> zu bilden haben wird" ("Amerika," 115). Schmidt here posited his own mental utopia in future "Wildnisse" like Cooper's forests. Similarly, he revered "Pioniere, die vorn neue Formen und Sprachmittel ausprobieren," and he rebuked East Germany for rejecting every such "Pioniertat" as formalism (2:81, 105). By thus linking Cooper—renowned for *The Pioneers* (1823)— with his own notions of a writer's social calling and creative freedom, Schmidt declared himself, too, such an experimental, literary pioneer. Together with the Leatherstocking, Cooper thus shaped Schmidt's self-image.

The political, stylistic, and personal ties to Cooper so obvious in Schmidt's

---

18. Arno Schmidt, "100 sind zu viel!," *Der Spiegel,* February 5, 1964, 80.

19. Jan Philipp Reemtsma and Bernd Rauschenbach eds., *"Wu Hi?": Arno Schmidt in Görlitz Lauban Greiffenberg* (Zurich: Haffmans, 1986), 17.

20. Unless otherwise stated or obvious from my context, Schmidt's fiction is quoted from *Arno Schmidt: Bargfelder Ausgabe, Werkgruppe I, Romane Erzählungen Gedichte Juvenilia,* 4 vols. (Zurich: Haffmans, 1987).

essays and articles also occur in his fiction. From the early *Leviathan oder Die beste der Welten* (1949) to the posthumously published *Julia, oder die Gemälde: Scenen aus dem Novecento* (1983), allusions to Cooper recur on numerous levels of Schmidt's own narration. Indeed, those two works at the extremes of his career help locate such narrative levels in the many others that came between them. *Leviathan* not only includes his often noted charge of plagiarism against Stifter for copying Cooper's *Deerslayer*. It also describes the bloody loss of a child with biblical language that Cooper used to set a similar scene in *The Wept of Wish-Ton-Wish* (1:43).[21] *Julia* adds admiration for the hero of Cooper's *The Spy* (1821), notes sexual undertones audible in such characters' names, and itself mentions one named Nettchen Bumppo. It also shows prurient interest in Cooper's personal life and cites his *Wyandotté* (1843) to help explain the title of a book by one of its own characters.[22] Together, *Leviathan* and *Julia* thus suggest that Schmidt's diction, characters, settings, and emphasis on reading and writing can all be explained in terms of his sometimes sexually inspired allusions to Cooper. Setting aside *Zettels Traum* (1970)—which I shall later treat by itself—let us consider each of those several levels in turn.

At the level of diction, Schmidt borrowed phrases from Cooper that he initially used to make his stories sound racier and then altered to prove his pet theory of Freudian etymologies. In *Brand's Haide* (1951), postwar bathtub gin is "das schönste Feuerwasser" and a screech owl sounds like Cooper's *The Wept of Wish-Ton-Wish:* "Viermal schrie es ums Haus: Wish-ton-wish. Wish-ton-wish: Käuzchen. Großer Mann der Cooper" (1:175, 150). When the only female left in nuked and desolate Europe peels potatoes in *Schwarze Spiegel* (1951), moreover, its male narrator remarks (in English) "good for squaw to do that" (1:242). Scalps—something queasily noted in many of Cooper's novels—seem to have fascinated Schmidt, who often referred to them metaphorically. In *Kosmas oder Vom Berge des Nordens* (1955), he wrote "Der eisige Windstoß wollte uns beide skalpieren," and one of his characters in *Seelandschaft mit Pocahontas* (1959) "skalpierte Wurstecken mit scheußlich huronischer Technik" (1:495, 418). Scalping is more literal in *Das steinerne Herz: Historischer Roman aus dem Jahre 1954 nach Christi* (1956), where a character recoils in pain from pulling up his pants. Why? "Beim Hochziehen hatte er sich die Schamhaare eingeklemmt und unten halb

---

21. Such parallel use of the biblical passage (from Job) in both *The Wept of Wish-Ton-Wish* and *Leviathan* is cited in Dieter Kuhn, *Bargfelder Bote* 16 (April, 1976): 16.

22. Arno Schmidt, *Julia, oder die Gemälde: Scenen aus dem Novecento* (Zurich: Haffmans, 1983), 31–32, 86, 24, 7.

skalpiert" (2:21). Such genital associations of vocabulary like Cooper's soon came thick and fast thanks to the orthographical liberties that Schmidt took in *Kaff auch Mare Crisium* (1960). It, too, contains such simple cases as calling German Marks "wampum," but Schmidt's unorthodox spelling also produced the more complex "ß = Kallp" and "nattürlich (< Natty >)" (3:56, 262, 258). Spelling *natürlich* here with two *t*'s deftly conveys common sense, as Cooper's *Natty* Bumppo shows with his sincere respect for nature. Schmidt likewise coined an adjective from Natty Bumppo's nickname in *Die Gelehrtenrepublik: Kurzroman aus den Roßbreiten* (1957). "Es gibt ja Naturen, lederstrumpfig rundherum, die auch als Menschen sich freiwillig absondern" (2:339). Such new words show witty insights into Cooper's writing and can also offer sharp perspectives on Schmidt's own. In *Kaff*, for example, one character writes a novel in which his narrator rudely awakes "Aus nicht = unleckeren Träumen von einer huronischen Roothaariejen, ebenso kurzmähnich wie lang = lüstich." This choice of words offends the character's female companion, who mistakes "huronisch" for a form of *Hure* and prompts an explanation of what that term means: "ihr hatte der Ausdruck < huronisch > mißfallen; (obwohl ich nur, . . . zur Erhöhung des Oh = Guh ebbes Indianerinnenmäßiejes beabsichticht hatte: 'Ärroß der Ferne, Liebste—'" (3:137). Erotic connotations of foreign-sounding Indian names similarly enhance Schmidt's story when his second narrator reports on a "wyandottisches Kint—das sich eben an mir hochgeschob'm hatte. . . . Und mich lustvoll in die Nase bis; wie echte Wyandotten und Leghorns fleegen. . . . Wie = änd = Dottie, Hurohne, Iro + Keese & Feif Näischns!" (3:137, 143).[23] Schmidt thus used language like Cooper's to give his stories a dash of virility that became more sexual as his simple loanwords showed ever greater etymological license.

Schmidt's allusions to Cooper are equally creative at the level of his characters, who often seem much like the Leatherstocking, Cooper's proverbial loner. Such characters' fates in *Kosmas* turn on issues of ancient cartography, so one of them plausibly praises surveyors: "der Landmesser reinigt die Welt; von Wirrnissen, von Unübersichten, von Nurmythologischem" (1:486). This praise sounds genuine since Schmidt himself was fascinated by geodesy. It takes on new meaning, moreover, when one knows that he translated Cooper's *Chainbearer,* a novel named for a man who

---

23. Josef Huerkamp adds both that the red hair referred to by Schmidt's second narrator implies sexual liveliness and that Leghorns and Wyandottes are also breeds of chickens. See Huerkamp, *Bargfelder Bote* 23 (August, 1977): 10.

carries surveyors' chains to help plot terrain. With his aptly measured temper, Cooper's title character also restrains social unruliness. Related tensions in Schmidt's story, therefore, recall this social as well as symbolic characterization. Similarly, Cooper's Leatherstocking inspires the narrator of *Schwarze Spiegel,* who seems to enjoy being one of the few human beings left to roam a Europe blown to bits by nuclear war: "Natty hatte schon recht: Wälder sind das Schönste!" (1:211).[24] More obscure references link Cooper to the narrator of *Aus dem Leben eines Fauns* (1953). He is a loner, too, one named Heinrich Düring. Cooper resonates in this name because one Heinrich *Döring*—named as a translator of Horace in *Das steinerne Herz*—translated *The Last of the Mohicans* (1826) into German the very same year that it first appeared in English. This nominal link confirms the extreme interest taken in Cooper by Schmidt's figure of almost the same name. Düring confesses that Cooper can still move him to tears: "um Cooper kann ich heute noch weinen" (1:374). He even returns the grating greeting "Heilittler, Herr Düring" with a quip borrowed from Cooper's Indians: "Sagosago Paleface!" (1:368). Schmidt thus took some of his central characters' sympathies, habits, and names straight from Cooper.

The setting of Schmidt's stories can be even more reminiscent of Cooper. Düring quotes Cooper's Indians not only to distance himself from Nazis but also because he is lost in thought of a trip to Cooperstown in upstate New York. Cooper's hometown (named for his father) thus seems a utopia far removed from the everyday meanness of Hitler's Germany. Schmidt described it a second time in *Seelandschaft mit Pocahontas,* where it likewise inspires an imaginative foil to occupied Germany after the war.

> Der Prospekt von Cooperstown : Heimat des Baseballs *und* James Fenimore Coopers (Was ne Reihenfolge ! Und immer nur Deerslayer und Pioneers erwähnt. Ganz totgeschwiegen wurde das Dritte im Bunde, Home as found, wo er die Yankees so nackt geschildert hat, daß es heute noch stimmt, und das ja auch prächtigst am Otsego spielt : wenn der aus dem Grabe könnte, was würde der Euch Hanswürschten erzählen)! (1:394)

This setting of Cooperstown and Lake Otsego is not the only one so passionately invoked in *Seelandschaft mit Pocahontas.* Its narrator recalls

---

24. This self-styled description as the "Gestalt des einsam schweifenden, zivilisationsfeindlichen Trappers" is noted by Thomé (*Natur,* 82).

another, found in Cooper's *Oak Openings* (1848), as he dallies with a woman nicknamed "Pocahontas" along the shore of Schmidt's own, fictional lake: "Wie in den < Oak Openings >; vom ganzen Mittelmaaßbuch ist mir doch als Bild geblieben : Nachtfahrt durch die Schilfwildnisse des Kalamazoo" (1:429). By thus investing Cooper's surroundings and fictional landscapes with pleasant political and erotic connotations, Schmidt offset his own settings more clearly. With help from Cooper, he could even reflect on those settings ironically. His narrator in *Die Gelehrtenrepublik* can still dream of "blaue Boote und gelbes Wasser (dem sich wiederum Coopers < Glimmerglas > paarte : ich habe ihn immer für einen großen Mann gehalten)" (2:336). Other remarks on Cooper, though, reveal less veneration. A wealthy American widow once turned up inside a statue of Cooper sent to Schmidt's republic of letters, which outsiders secretly try to reach because it is safe from nuclear attack. The poets who live there, in contrast, can leave for Cooperstown on a literary whim: "Ab und zu bekamen die Dichter den bekannten Vogel vom < einfach leben > : prompt wurde ihnen eine Blockhütte am Otsego = Lake zur Verfügung gestellt" (2:309). Getting back to nature thus seems a poetic cliché, but Schmidt himself frequently did so, both in his fiction and in his solitude on the Lüneburg Heath. In literature as well as life, Cooper's settings inspired him.

Allusions to Cooper recur not only in Schmidt's diction, characters, and settings, but also in his stress on a literary tradition of authors whom he thought especially worth reading. Texts written by Cooper are read throughout Schmidt's own. In *Die Umsiedler,* Schmidt's narrator ranks Cooper first on a list of his small personal library: "Cooper, Wieland, Jean Paul: Moritzcervantestieckundsoweiter. Schopenhauerlogarithmentafeln" (1:291). That displaced narrator also offers to read the Littlepage Manuscripts with his mistress, just as the erotic quartet described in *Das steinerne Herz* settles down in the end with plans to read *Conanchet* together. Cooper is likewise among the authors whom Heinrich Düring reads in *Aus dem Leben eines Fauns.* Düring claims that he needs to read even more Cooper than he already has, but that does not stop him from judging Cooper, praising his male characters as superior to Balzac's while wondering whether he used Schnabel's *Insel Felsenburg* (1731–43) to write his similar *Mark's Reef* (also called *The Crater,* 1847). Such judgments are even more summary in *Schwarze Spiegel,* where Cooper is one of the few authors whom its narrator not only reads with enthusiasm but also imagines as critics of his own writing. He even respects Cooper and Poe as the height of American fiction and carries a copy of *Satanstoe* with him as bedtime reading. He is, therefore, glad to find books that complement his collection of Cooper, from which he gives two volumes as parting gifts to his female friend. No wonder that he conveys the courage taken to bear his solitude by exclaiming: *"Autores fideles und autores bravos* (wie die Spanier bei den Indios unterscheiden): mir fiels ein, als ich den Cooper aus dem Gesäck holte : wir sind beide bravos" (1:208). Reading Cooper thus amuses as well as sustains Schmidt's characters in extreme personal circumstances. Although hardly uncritical, they elevate Cooper to a prominent place in Schmidt's tradition.

As *Schwarze Spiegel* implies, Schmidt's stress on reading Cooper also extended to writing. Consider his late *Die Schule der Atheisten* (1972) and *Abend mit Goldrand* (1975), which both show Schmidt's own writing connected to Cooper's. A young man in *Die Schule der Atheisten* not only speaks in nautical terms said to come from Cooper's sea novel *Lucy Harding* (i.e., *Afloat and Ashore* and its sequel, *Miles Wallingford*, both 1844). He also tries to write such a novel himself—"halb SeeRoman, ('id Nachfolge COOPER's')."[25] Schmidt's main character, William T. Kolderup, praises Cooper as the first author of such sea novels, which seems appropriate since the main events shown in *Die Schule der Atheisten* occur during comparable voyages at sea. Many of Schmidt's characters in *Abend mit Goldrand* are remarkably like Kolderup, bookworms whose reading colors their writing. One quotes Cooper's *Oak Openings* as a source for a book by another, who, in turn, fondly recalls his youth as a time when just reading Cooper's nickname for the Leatherstocking could trigger his hormones: "selije Zeit. . . . Wo ich beim COOPER von der 'Langen Büchse' las & sofort eine Jägerin erblickte."[26] Knowledge of Cooper also reflects sharp political differences between young and old in Schmidt's story. As his alter ego A&O Glaser remarks, the young could take concrete plans for the utopia that they envision from *Mark's Reef.* Glaser also traces their radical term *EntrüstungsMeeting* to Cooper, whose fellow citizens accused him of cultural elitism, much like Glaser's young collocutors sneer at Glaser himself for respecting. A young woman who likes him doubts that another who objects to him has even read Cooper, moreover, and a third (with Schmidt's approval in parentheses) mocks such old men for resembling Cooper in their shift from political left to right with age: "(Jaja; mit dem COOPER

---

25. Arno Schmidt, *Die Schule der Atheisten: Novellen-Comödie in 6 Aufzügen* (Frankfurt am Main: S. Fischer, 1972), 170.

26. Arno Schmidt, *Abend mit Goldrand: Eine MärchenPosse, 55 Bilder aus der Lä/Endlichkeit für Gönner der Verschreibkunst* (Frankfurt am Main: S. Fischer, 1975), 108.

muß, jenseits der fuffzich, ooch nich mehr auszukomm' gewesen sein): "Iss das immer so : daß Mann in der Jugnd Links = , im Alter RechtsDrall hat?" (*Abend mit Goldrand*, 102). Finally, Glaser regards himself as part of a long literary tradition including Cooper: "Ich hab mich zeitlebms bemüht, meine 'TraditionsReihen', nach hinten zu, ausfindich zu mach'n; und mich (wenichstns zu Zeit'n) durchaus als 'KettenGlied' zu empfind'n : ich freue mich über Vorgänger" (153–54). Schmidt typed *aa* over the *au* in *ausfindich* here, so his spelling of *aus findig* can be read as *aasfindig* in the oversized typescript that is *Abend mit Goldrand*. This instance of the artful misspelling announced in its subtitle—*55 Bilder aus der Lä/Endlichkeit für Gönner der Verschreibkunst*—hints that Schmidt's own predecessors were "carcasses" on which he fed. The examples of his diction, characters, and settings given here together with his stress on the tradition of reading and writing confirm that he drew much sustenance from Cooper.

The texts cited thus far do not include *Zettels Traum* because it deserves special literary treatment. It, too, proves that Schmidt took much from Cooper. It does so, however, in ways all its own. Not only are its diction, characters, setting, and treatment of literary tradition all linked to Cooper. They thereby also offer insight into the highly literary and deeply sexual lives shown in its story. That story itself takes place on a day in 1968 that four characters spend together in a village near Celle. Its first-person narrator, Daniel Pagenstecher, is a writer and translator visited there by his married friends Paul and Wilma Jacobi and their sixteen-year-old daughter, Franziska. The Jacobis themselves translate Edgar Allan Poe, whose life and work quickly become the subject of their day-long conversation with the erudite Pagenstecher. At the same time, Franziska and Pagenstecher fall in love and lust together. Rather than have her stay with him in his oddly idyllic retreat, though, Pagenstecher resolves that her parents should take her away. In the end, he even gives them money to pay for her education on the condition that she never see him again. Schmidt describes these events at tremendous length and in a narrative voice, style, and textual layout that result from mixing Freud and *Finnegan's Wake* according to his own notions of fiction and his special interest in Poe. The end product is a behemoth that defies linear reading along with any attempt to make coherent sense of all its sprawling details. Many of those details become much more significant, though, when read as either references or allusions to Cooper. Schmidt himself furnished clues needed to recognize them as such, but fathoming their full import depends on knowing Cooper's work. Comments on Cooper and his dealings with Poe, etymologies showing Cooper's and his characters' sexual drives, and symbols and names suggesting the erotic collusion of Franziska and Daniel Pagenstecher reveal that import and, therefore, will be my main subjects.

In numerous statements on Cooper, Pagenstecher—referred to as Dän— shows the same political, literary, and personal interest taken in him by Schmidt. Dän takes such interest to new extremes, however, that reflect its major role in *Zettels Traum*. He, too, observes that the Littlepage Trilogy yields important details about the United States, some of which he weaves into his own conversation when he quotes *Satanstoe* to document the sorry state of higher education in nineteenth-century America and to suggest that Americans are overreligious. Similarly, he cites *The Chainbearer* to explain niceties of surveying. Such references are related to what Dän and the Jacobis see and do, as is his account of an early American flag, which he expressly takes from Cooper's *History of the Navy of the United States of America* (1839), a work coincidentally owned by a farmer whom they meet. The Littlepage Trilogy itself proves that the United States accomplished something worthwhile in the nineteenth century, Dän adds, and Cooper would be among the three authors whose books he would take with him to the moon (Nestroy and Freud are the other two). More seriously, he mentions Cooper in the same breath as Homer and Joyce, confirming the personal sympathy that he expresses when noting how Cooper rejoiced at being out of debt. Dän also praises Cooper's similes, subjects, and sea novels, though his statements about *The Water-Witch* (1830) show that he bestowed such praise for reasons that Cooper would have found dubious: "Ich verstehe wahrlich nichts von der Xlichen Seh = fart. . . . ach, WATER = WITCH! (:—alle Mädchen könn' schließlich mit ihrem Wasser hexn!)."[27] Dän does not display such irreverence without method, though. Explaining why he plays such etymological games, he argues that Cooper's heroes seem colorless because they are rarified products of their author's superego. As such, they result from masochistic creativity that drove Cooper as mercilessly as it did his colleagues Scott, Wilkie Collins, Stifter, May, Verne, and Poe. Indeed, Dän's interest in the national, literary, and personally appealing characteristics of Cooper's writing pales beside such psychological speculation.

It is, accordingly, no coincidence that Dän names Cooper along with Poe as an author whose psychobiography he expounds. Poe is the primary

---

27. Arno Schmidt, *Zettels Traum* (Karlsruhe: Stahlberg, 1970), 426, 560.

subject discussed in *Zettels Traum,* and Dän's further remarks linking him to Cooper reveal little-known facts about both their work and Schmidt's own. Dän notes that no one has studied connections between the two Americans and that reading Cooper might shed much light on Poe. He makes such connections himself by recalling their relationship and musing on Poe's use of characters who also occur in Cooper. Poe reviewed many of Cooper's works, Dän knows, specifically *Wyandotté* (1843) and *Sketches of Switzerland* (1836). Indeed, Poe's opinion of Cooper's work clearly fore-shadows Schmidt's own. In his review of *Wyandotté,* Poe praised Cooper's theme but faulted its form, much as Schmidt so often did. That theme of life in the wilderness is interesting, Poe wrote, though Cooper's syntax is sloppy and his diction inaccurate. Poe also found the plot of *Wyandotté* weak, but he did not think such weakness serious, and he even discounted it in terms strikingly like the ones used in Schmidt's essay "Die Hand-lungsreisenden": "Plot, however, is at best, an artificial effect. . . . Thus the absence of plot can never be critically regarded as a *defect.*"[28] Such general agreement on Cooper's pros and cons suggests that Schmidt saw him through Poe's critical eyes. At any rate, Dän knows that Cooper reviewed Poe, too, and calls their relationship mutually instructive. Cooper should be equally respected, he explains, not least for writing about the Revolutionary War and the Anti-Renter riots of the 1840s, events in Amer-ican history that Poe never treated. Dän also observes that the character Neptune in Poe's *Journal of Julius Rodman* (1840) recalls one with the same name in Cooper's *Headsman* (1833), and he finds several details of Poe's *Narrative of A. Gordon Pym* (1838) prefigured in Cooper's *Monikins.* Thanks to the extensive reading needed to pass such judgments, Dän can quote Poe to correct a poor translation in an old German edition of *The Deerslayer.* Similarly, Dän's views on Poe's feud with the critic Rufus Griswold prove that Schmidt knew the edition of Cooper's letters published by James F. Beard in 1960. As Schmidt described them, connections between Cooper and Poe thus show the erudition of all three men narrowly related in their respective fictions.

The enthusiasm—*mania* might be a better word—that Dän displays in reading Cooper and Poe together recurs in his pseudopsychoanalytic com-ments on Cooper and his characters. Their sexual drives seem plain to

---

28. Edgar Allan Poe, review of *Wyandotté* by James Fenimore Cooper, *Graham's Magazine* 24 (November, 1843); reprinted in George Dekker and John P. McWilliams, eds., *Fenimore Cooper: The Critical Heritage* (London: Routledge and Kegan Paul, 1973), 210.

him from etymologies even naughtier than the ones spelled out so oddly in *Kaff auch Mare Crisium*. When Paul and Wilma ask whether Cooper was chaste, remarking that the Leatherstocking practically dies a virgin and that Cooper was happily married and had many ideal children, such etymologies help Dän answer no. Cooper's wife and eldest daughter must both have attracted him, Dän thinks, for reasons like the one that explains why his characters in *The Prairie* (1827) always fear Indians called tetons: "Nu, er hatte doch 6 (oder 8?) Töchter : da wirds ganz schön von 'tetons' um ihn her gewüppert haben" (*Zettels Traum*, 553). No less scatological is the explanation that Dän gives for the nickname "Magnet" borne by the heroine of *The Pathfinder* (1840): "der weibliche Magnet, in deSSn Nähe alle männlichen 'Nadeln' zu delirieren beginnen. . . . der Ørt, wohin die nee/oodle sich richtet" (*Zettels Traum*, 1081, 873). Dän also observes that Cooper would have called buxom Wilma "Lange Büxe," misspelling one of the Leatherstocking's nicknames—"Lange Büchse" in German—almost as scurrilously as when he dubs a lustful country girl "Leda = strumpet." Dän takes even greater liberties with the Leatherstocking's real name by breaking "Natty Bumppo" into "nutty," "nuts," "bum," and "poo(p)"— syllables suggesting erotic, phallic, and anal levels beneath the virtuous surface of Cooper's main character. Rounding out this spree, Dän adds a final line about masturbatory impulses hidden in the name of an Indian tribe that Cooper respected: "Und was C.'s beliebte '*Onan*dagas' sind?:!" (*Zettels Traum*, 51). Such rabid debunking of Cooper and his characters shows how willfully Schmidt applied his theory of "etyms"—derivations that subliminally convey repressed sexual origins of literary language. Indeed, Dän derives such "etyms" so doggedly that he seems to lose sight of the historical Cooper.

Precisely because Schmidt strained evidence of the historical Cooper far more than in his other writings, however, his strictly literary uses of Cooper's work can assume meaning even more closely tied to his own narration. Dän knows that disproving Cooper's chastity turns Franziska's thoughts to sex, a narrative function assigned Cooper that proves crucial in Schmidt's story. Consider the doll that Franziska carries with her throughout *Zettels Traum*. It is an Indian maiden named Narra Mattah, a fact that Franziska and Dän note with embarrassment due to its sexual implications, which are vague at first but then become clearer as Schmidt gives more information and details about the doll. Franziska named it after reading *Conanchet,* where Narra Mattah is a young girl lost in an Indian raid on a Puritan settlement. This circumstance seemingly has less to do with Cooper than with Schmidt/Dän, who claims a major stake in that novel for having translated it and distorts its mention of a "Pallasch" (a broadsword), Dunbar, and Worcester (sites of Cromwell's victories) into a sentence about his own designs on Franziska: "In der Faust den, schweren, Pallasch/Phallus von Dänbare & Wust-hehr" (*Zettels Traum,* 716). Franziska herself attributes *Conanchet* to Dän no less than to Cooper, and she even praises Schmidt's afterword to it! The intimacy that she and Dän thus share thanks to Cooper goes so far that they speak in a voice and tongues like Narra Mattah's to hide their feelings for each other from Paul and Wilma. As Franziska adopts it, that voice is feminine, naughty, and passionate. Dän likewise speaks Sioux and Delaware to woo her as indirectly as she expresses her desire to sleep with him by saying: "NARRA hat Mir'n indianisches Sprüchwort gesagt;—übersetzt heißt's ungefähr : 'Wer allein schläft bleibt lange kalt : Zwei wärmen sich einander bald'" (*Zettels Traum,* 1225). Franziska's doll thus hastens her relationship with Dän and highlights their resulting intimacy. A prop borrowed, then, at least in name from Cooper helps navigate Schmidt's narrative labyrinth.

Franziska's doll serves other purposes that are not always so obvious but that betray Cooper's presence at deeper levels of her feelings for Dän. Schmidt tells how to find those levels when Dän explains symbols used by every "DP"—short for "Dichter-Prophet" or "Dichter-Priester," a writer who overlooks the repressed sexual longings implied by dead metaphors and dormant "etyms." Such symbols can be either general or specific, and Dän stresses the latter: "abgesehen von den allgemein = verbindlichen & verständlichen Symbolen, . . . hat jeder DP seine speciellen, nur ihm eigentümlichen; deren gesicherte Erkennung auch dem Unbegabten möglich ist, durch *a*) statische Erfassung der erstarrten Metaforik; und *b*) Etym = Häufung" (*Zettels Traum,* 743). Applied to Narra Mattah, this theory suggests the foolishness and eroticism of Franziska and Dän's affair. Foolishness is clear from many etymological changes that Dän rings on Narra Mattah's name. The *Narr* in "Narra" stands out when he calls the voice that he and Franziska so often borrow from the doll a "Narra/enstimchen." Franziska acts "Narr = sinnich," indulges in "Narrateyen," and entertains Dän "aufs NARR'ischsDe," moreover, and Dän knows that he is "1 = Narr(a)" to say "natürlich könnten Wir = Uns, eine zeitlang, ineinander verNarrân" (*Zettels Traum,* 744). Such verbal fooling around turns sexual when "Narrentaschen," a popular name for gallnuts, remind Dän of "NARRA's Täschel." Dän links Indians like Narra to other metaphors for female genitals as well, so it is hardly surprising to hear him say that she speaks "im faynstem Peep = Discunt." By means of a similar "etym," even Franziska admits to him that Narra's taciturn nature can hide devious sexual thoughts: "WeißD ja am besten, *wie* = lacunnysch diese Indiannerinn' sein könn'" (*Zettels Traum*, 745). Schmidt juggles metaphors and etymologies just as blithely to reinforce the eroticism motivating such symbols. Franziska and Dän find a niche for Narra in a fencepost that is sexually symbolic in Dän's own words: "Sieh ma : hier an der Seite hätt Sie [Narra] noch n Rundes Fenster drinne—", (und den Finger, dämonstratief, hineinstekkn :? / Sie [Franziska] nickte überaus bedeutsam") (*Zettels Traum*, 339). Phallic symbols surface as well when this "Zaunpfahl" later turns into an "EggPhall" and when Narra arrays herself among Dän's cigars. In stark contrast to repressed "DPs," Schmidt thus consciously exaggerates such symbols. Indeed, as soon as Dän defines them in terms of metaphors and "etyms," he shows what he means by describing Franziska's suggestive placement of Narra Mattah. "Sie setzte die lütte RothäuteRinne, behutsam, zwischen die Stricknadl = starkn Stämmchen" (*Zettels Traum*, 744). In its erotic context, then, symbolic connections to Cooper prove Schmidt's main theoretical point.

Narra Mattah's symbolic connotations seem more refined in other remarks on Franziska. Those remarks are oblique, however, and fully understanding them depends on knowing Cooper. Schmidt gives some hint of how they work when Dän discourses not only on symbols in general but also on dolls in particular. He explains that dolls have functions in a psychological "system" of Freudian "instances," most notably the superego (abbreviated "ÜI," for "Über-Ich") and unconscious sexual meaning ("ubw," for "unbewußt," plus "S = Bedeutung"). In the case of Franziska (Fr), this system makes Narra Mattah highly complex and overdetermined.

> Verwickelt : die Stellung der Pupp'n im System; (da von mehreren Instanzn her gespeist) : einmal Verputzijungn des ÜI; (die aber immer zú = sehen; und die man, ergo, bei böseren Tätlein, 'schlâfn = schäffn' muß); als Auto = Talismane strahlen sie Beruhijung aus. . . . —(hier, bei Fr, war NARRA ja wohl einwandfrei 'älter' (da schon 'ein Kind'); vom Typ 'Beraterin' demnach ?)—Andrerseits die, ubw = dirigierte mehrfache S = Bedeutung dieser Döckchin: . . . ja, die S = Püppchen. . . . Ich wollte 1000:1 wetten, daß manches Mädchin, mit der Puppe auf d Arm, an etwas ganz Anderes denkt, als ad Puppe! (*Zettels Traum*, 1223)

Schmidt thus assigns Narra Mattah two opposing roles: as advisor and talismanic charm, she embodies Franziska's superego; her protective vigilance must be made to lapse, however, during consummation of forbidden sexual longings, which she equally represents. Both these psychological levels and Dän's salacious summary of them seem plain in Schmidt's story itself. Franziska and Narra are related in Dän's mind when he urges Franziska to call herself "Narra," alludes to her as a "verpupptes Seelchen," and describes the ragged trim on Narra's moccasins as "Lederfränzchen." With Narra firmly in hand, moreover, Franziska approaches Dän "im süß = dämonischen Novizitat der Liebe" (*Zettels Traum*, 1228). She also holds and gapes at Narra when Wilma applauds her for seeing through men by inferring from Poe that sex with them is impersonal. In both her innocence and new experience, Franziska thus proves Dän's point that many a girl with a doll in her hand is really thinking of sex. Similarly, Narra also watches the two throughout their relationship, playing the role of Franziska's superego. Franziska affirms that role when she repeatedly asks Narra's advice, seeks her approval, and even puts her to bed when she and Dän need to be "evil" alone. Narra also shows Franziska's unconscious sexual urges. Franziska's rivalry with her mother for Dän's attention, her desire for him against her own better judgment, and her resolve to stay with him are all linked to her doll, which she addresses, sounds like, and quotes. Dän understands such gestures perfectly when he saves himself in the end by sending Franziska away with the words "Sieh zu, daß NARRA kein' Schaden macht" (*Zettels Traum*, 1319).[29] Narra thus shows Franziska's scruples as well as her desire according to Dän's psychological theory of dolls.

Just as dolls are only one example of Dän's symbols, however, "Narra Mattah" is one name among countless that Schmidt could have chosen for Franziska's. Why did he prefer it to all others? This question is crucial, not least since Dän himself finds naming dolls even more important than choosing them in the first place: "Ds Problem der 'Puppen Wahl' . . . (dh 'Wahl' insofern = incorrect, als man sie meist geschenkt bekommt; besser also; zu was das Gepupp' 'ernànnt' wird: there's the rub!)" (*Zettels Traum*, 1223). This statement applies to *Zettels Traum* itself, for the name "Narra

---

29. All along, tension in Narra's split personality is predictably high, as her reaction to fattening food indirectly demonstrates. When Dän first offers chocolate, to make conversation easier, Franziska answers that Narra adores it, thereby showing interest in his ulterior motives. As their relationship progresses, Franziska—in Narra's voice—warns herself against eating too much sugar. Finally, while they reflect on how Franziska has grown, Dän expresses similarly indirect doubts about taking their affair any further: "NAARA-MATTA soll sich ma auf de Briefwaage setzn : Gewicht controllieren; daß Se nich zu dick wird" (*Zettels Traum*, 638).

Mattah" connotes even more than the metaphors and "etyms" that it allows Schmidt to exploit. To appreciate it fully, one needs to observe the character who bears that same Indian name in Cooper's *The Wept of Wish-Ton-Wish*. She is not an Indian, and Narra Mattah is not her real name. Instead, she is actually Ruth Heathcote, youngest daughter in the family of Puritans whose life on the Connecticut frontier is Cooper's subject. Her wrenching story takes place at the time of King Phillip's War (1675–78), when native Indians and English settlers bitterly fought each other. Ruth, a small girl, lives with her family until she disappears during an Indian attack that destroys her entire settlement. Her relatives barely survive and gradually give her up for dead, but twelve years later she is returned to them by one of the Indians whom they are fighting yet again. That Indian is Conanchet, a young chief whom the Heathcotes gently held prisoner while Ruth was still a child. Although he escaped them then, he later took care of Ruth, who only had been captured by his tribe. Indeed, she has since become his wife and borne him a son. Even more incredibly, she has forgotten her family and their religious, civilized customs. Rather than return to them, moreover, she wants to stay with Conanchet. He feels strongly bound to her, too, but he is also mindful of the ethnic differences that divide their peoples, so he returns her to her parents together with their infant son. Not long after this separation, Conanchet falls prey to a rival tribe allied with the English and then sees Ruth one last time before being killed in her presence. Shocked, she briefly regains consciousness of her childhood but soon dies, unable to overcome her grief and her return to civilization. It is this sad character whose Indian name Schmidt gave Franziska's psyche. He thereby implied that the two share far more than that name itself.

Franziska and Ruth do, indeed, have feelings in common. Each wants to leave father and mother for a man from whom she is separated against her will. This similarity helps make sense of *Zettels Traum* when one knows why Ruth cannot go home again. She seems to have undergone some miraculous change, but her reluctance to rejoin her family actually results from more mundane causes. She betrays such causes when she claims to enjoy Conanchet's "warm wigwam," where she has more furs than any other warrior's wife. For the same reason, she even prefers it to houses built by the English "palefaces": "for the wigwam of her husband is warmer."[30] She rejects Conanchet's suggestion that she belongs to white

---

30. James Fenimore Cooper, *The Wept of Wish-Ton-Wish: A Tale* (New York: Stringer and Townsend, 1857), 383.

people more than to him, moreover, and when asked whether she is glad
to be back home, she answers that wives of men like Conanchet are happiest
with their husbands. She herself, finally, sums up her role in life with the
few words "Narra-mattah is a wife" (*Wish-Ton-Wish,* 461). In the dogmatic
climate of faith imposed by Cooper's Puritans, such hints of physical lust
for a savage amount to sexual thralldom. Beyond doubt, Ruth herself has
savage emotions that seem sexually laden and, thus, sharply at odds with
Puritan notions of morality. She bursts out in gleeful laughter when a
white man who had lived with her among the Indians simulates some
atrocity in a gruesome pantomime of an Indian triumph over the English.
Cooper did not describe that violence, saying only that it was even more
ruthless than the usual Indian habit of taking scalps. Ruth's sudden laughter, however, clearly bodes ill in the ears of her religious mother, after
whom she is named: "The soft, exquisitely feminine tones of this involuntary burst of pleasure, sounded in the ears of Ruth [her mother] like
a knell over the moral beauty of her child" (*Wish-Ton-Wish,* 413). Why is
young Ruth's laughter rejected as an immoral "burst of pleasure"? Why
does Cooper call it "soft" and "exquisitely feminine"? His text itself
furnishes no obvious answer, but the Schmidt of *Zettels Traum* would doubtless have found that Ruth here responds to some mimicked depiction of
rape. Lest this answer seem far-fetched, let us not forget that Schmidt
praised this scene as one of the most impressive in all literature (Afterword,
396). It would be especially suited to *Zettels Traum,* moreover, because Ruth
expressly represses English voices in her dreams since she has an Indian
chief for her husband. The name "Narra Mattah" thus suggests a dream-
work combined with sexual frustration. In Schmidt's own symbolic logic,
then, Franziska's similarity to Ruth implies that her desire for Dän is so
overwhelming that thwarting it will leave her psychologically ruined.

Franziska is not the only figure in *Zettels Traum* better understood against
a background derived from Cooper. Dän, too, often seems like characters
in novels that Schmidt himself counted among Cooper's best. Indeed, *The
Wept of Wish-Ton-Wish,* the Littlepage Manuscripts, and *The Monikins* show
why Dän is right to characterize himself as "'M/Dän, that gut = like Devil':
(COOPER)" (*Zettels Traum,* 54). To begin with, his side of Franziska's story
is like Conanchet's in *The Wept of Wish-Ton-Wish.* Like Conanchet, Dän
gives a young girl who adores him back to her parents. Both deny themselves
such willing companions because each cherishes his life of fierce independence led beyond the pale of mass civilization. The aging Dän differs from
young Conanchet insofar as he doubts his own virility, but he makes this

same sacrifice to his similar way of life. The Littlepage Manuscripts show another Indian forgoing a woman for reasons still more relevant to Dän's situation. That Indian, named Susquessus, survives almost the entire trilogy and dies a virtual legend thanks to his sexual self-control. As a young chief like Conanchet, he had desired an Indian woman captured from an enemy tribe by one of his warriors. According to tribal law, she belonged to her captor, but Susquessus could easily have forced him to surrender her. After great turmoil, however, and just as she offered to join him, Susquessus forswore her because he knew that even chiefs like him must obey the law. He then left his tribe forever in a fruitless search for peace of mind. This story of voluntary rectitude disbands a mob of tenant farmers whose claims to their landlords' property were Cooper's main concern. It thus is the climax of the entire trilogy. It thereby also offers insight into Dän, who likewise sacrifices Franziska to his special social—or rather *asocial*—status. By implication, that sacrifice is like Susquessus's—one from which Dän will never recover, however right it seems and despite whatever respect it earns. Dän's similarities to two of Cooper's Indians thus help explain why and how he forgoes Franziska.

Neither Conanchet nor Susquessus, however, is the character in Cooper related most tellingly to Dän. Schmidt invoked another, more revealing one with the very first word of *Zettels Traum*. That word—*king!*—is an oath that Dän uses when stuck climbing through a barbed wire fence suggested by two strands of *x*'s typed across Schmidt's page. A marginal note helps decipher this graphic construct: "(? : NOAH POKE? (oder fu = ?))." As a prefix to "-king," "fu-" implies an obvious compound. Who is Noah Poke, though, and what does he have to do with "king!" that it should thus introduce *Zettels Traum.*[31] Poke himself is a seafaring captain in Cooper's *Monikins,* a humorous, satirical, and ironic condemnation of faults that Cooper found with society in Europe and America. Amiable and direct to a fault, Poke conveys his wealthy young master to two Antarctic islands, where they see evils of aristocratic and democratic governments in two anti-utopias run by talking monkeys. He cries "king" at two turning points in this strange story. The first occurs when he meets his master in a noisy Parisian tavern. With the exclamation "King!," Poke cuts through a din of French that he does not understand but nonetheless derides: "I

---

31. For comments on the various scatological meanings of "poke," see Günther Fleming, "Noah Poke," *Bargfelder Bote* 1 (September, 1972). In another entry on "Noah Poke," Dieter Kuhn and Karl H. Brücher note that the name comes from *The Monikins (Bargfelder Bote* 2 [January, 1973]).

don't pretend to understand a word of what they are saying, myself; but it *sounds* like thorough nonsense."[32] He thus shouts "King!" out of frustration with words that he fails to comprehend but dismisses anyway. As a sign of such mixed feelings, "king!" is the perfect word to open *Zettels Traum*. Schmidt's text, too, often seems unintelligible, apt to frustrate readers and tempt them to dismiss it despite their ignorance of even its surface meaning. Indeed, "king!" itself frustrates one in Schmidt's initial line. Even if one knows that Noah Poke comes from Cooper, the meaning of "king" cannot be inferred from Schmidt's curious context. Since this single word thus sums up problems posed by the many that follow it, however, its speaker, Noah Poke, could be a key to the rest of *Zettels Traum*.

Schmidt's subsequent allusions to *The Monikins* confirm this possibility. Dän brings the novel to Wilma and Paul's attention, noting not only its similarity to Poe's *Gordon Pym* but also both the inadequacy of its single German translation and the phallic connotations of the tails attached to the monkeys inhabiting Cooper's fictional islands. Such tails helped Cooper raise his sexual attraction both to and with his wife and daughter, Dän insists, reason enough to retranslate *The Monikins:* "Mann kann schwerlich geschickter schwinigeln : und was *wérden* seine Damen sich nicht der schnurrhaarijen Erfindung gefreut haben : 'Och = páppa wie = *süüüß!*' . . . (& ihre für die Liebe bestimmten Teile ihnen nicht gekrimmert haben! Unbedingt neu zu übersetzen & kommentieren!)" (*Zettels Traum*, 53). The same tails that here reveal Cooper's sexual foibles are related to Dän's own desire for Franziska by the second episode in *The Monikins* that depends on Noah Poke and "King!" There the exclamation is also a form of address, since Poke uses it to greet the monkey who rules the island like corrupt Europe. Not knowing how to behave at court there, Poke commits a felony simply by implying that the monkey-king has a memory. He then breaks the Monikins' arbitrary law again by *not* attributing to their queen the very same memory that her royal husband lacks. The penalty for this second offense is decapitation, which Monikins think less severe than that for the first—"decaudisation," loss of one's tail. This odd priority makes sense to them because they bear their brains in their tails, an anatomical detail linking intellect to sex in both Dän's neologism "Männtailität" and Schmidt's view of the Monikins as "Affenmenschen . . . die das Gehirn nicht im Kopf, sondern (was dem ßesten passieren kann) im Schweif

---

32. James Fenimore Cooper, *The Monikins* (New York: Stringer and Townsend, 1857), 103.

tragen" (Afterword, 390). In this same metaphorical spirit, though, Poke's punishment distinguishes sex from intellect. He submits to "decaudisation," losing an ox tail that he had donned to appear presentable at the Monikin court. Precisely because he loses that tail, moreover, he is declared mentally incompetent and thus spared decapitation. Poke seems unmanned, then, but does not lose his head. Accordingly, the first word uttered in *Zettels Traum*—Poke's "King!"—connotes symbolic castration needed to rescue intellect. Dän makes such a trade-off by himself forgoing Franziska and thereby protecting the life of his mind. This symbolic connection to Cooper reveals psychological conflicts even more complex than Franziska's, then, which Dän himself frequently helps Schmidt's readers interpret. Dän and Schmidt cannot be equated, but the "etyms," symbols, and names cited in *Zettels Traum* plainly show Cooper's psychological-literary role at fundamental levels of Schmidt's own narration.

As singular and tortuous as it sometimes seems, Cooper's significance in *Zettels Traum* merely heightens his straightforward import in Schmidt's other writings. Essays and articles mentioning Cooper show that Schmidt respected him for reasons that were political, stylistic, and personal. Schmidt thought Cooper's aversion to facile patriotism politically wise, he praised Cooper's style for its truthful lack of plot, and he led the personal, literary life of a "pioneer" much like Cooper's Leatherstocking. His own fiction other than *Zettels Traum,* moreover, recalls Cooper in its diction, characters, settings, and emphasis on reading and writing.[33] Colorful words borrowed from Cooper assume brash new meanings in Schmidt's sexually charged phonetic spelling. Characters like Natty Bumppo often people Schmidt's texts, their stories set in fictional landscapes similar to Cooper's own. Not only do such characters also read Cooper's works; some even write in the literary tradition that Schmidt thought Cooper represented. These several levels of Schmidt's creative debt to Cooper overlap most tellingly in *Zettels Traum*, where they inform passages on Poe, Cooper himself, Franziska, and Dän. Cooper's historical import as well as his

---

33. References and allusions to Cooper at these several levels also occur in shorter works by Schmidt (not treated here). See "Der Sonn' Entgegen," "Schwänze," "Pipokramenes!'," "Die Abenteuer der Sylvesternacht," and "Caliban über Setebos," all of which appeared in *Kühe in Halbtrauer* (1964); "Schulausflug," containing similar references, appeared in *Trommler beim Zaren* (1966). All are contained in the *Bargfelder Ausgabe 3*. Josef Huerkamp notes both that the protagonist of "Schwänze" writes an essay on the regicides of Charles I—who figure in *The Wept of Wish-Ton-Wish* and are mentioned in *Das steinerne Herz*—and that Schmidt once started that same essay himself (*Bargfelder Bote* 43–44 [March 1980]: 7–8).

connections to Poe pale beside Dän's psychoanalytic craze for reading crimped sexuality into such authors' writings. Franziska's doll links her to Cooper's *The Wept of Wish-Ton-Wish,* showing her intimacy with Dän, the sexual meaning concealed in his metaphors and "etyms," and his theory of dolls as symbols of Freudian superegos and unconscious sexual urges. Maddening consequences of freeing but then frustrating such urges are clear in the figure of Cooper's Ruth Heathcote, who escapes her puritanical life by becoming the Indian "Narra Mattah." Since Schmidt gave Franziska's symbolic doll that same Indian name, an allusion to Cooper reveals the complexity of Franziska's sexual longing and thereby predicts psychological damage to her. Knowledge of Cooper reveals tension no less severe in Dän himself. Like Cooper's Indians Conanchet and Susquessus, Dän forgoes a woman to maintain a way of life run by rules other than those of mass civilization. Indeed, the very first word in *Zettels Traum*—"king!"—comes from Cooper's *Monikins,* where it both expresses impatience with unusual language like Schmidt's and connotes symbolic castration like Dän's for the sake of mental survival. Just as Schmidt's writing can tell us much about Cooper, then, knowing Cooper reveals much about Schmidt himself.

Such a reciprocal link between Cooper and Schmidt confirms how well tradition and experiment define their relationship. Schmidt's support of Cooper was highly traditional. Critics have long favored and faulted Cooper for reasons like Schmidt's: the energy of his low characters, the anemia of his high ones, his talent for describing nature, and his stylistic awkward-ness.[34] Those same critics have also often admired Cooper's stories for their suspense. Schmidt's praise for Cooper's artful lack of plot thus seems egregious, but *Zettels Traum* suggests that it derives from Poe. His pseudo-psychoanalysis of Cooper's sexual life and work has a similar forerunner in essays by D. H. Lawrence.[35] Likewise, Schmidt's enthusiasm for Cooper recalls a tradition in Germany, where Cooper's work was so well liked in his day that his "contemporary popularity nearly defies credibility."[36] Schmidt's efforts at popularizing Cooper extended that tradition. He even

---

34. Dekker and McWilliams, Introduction, 3–5. Schmidt was somewhat familiar with these traditional views of Cooper, as shown by his rejection of Mark Twain's famous essay "Fenimore Cooper's Literary Offenses" (1895). See "100 sind zu viel!", 80.

35. See Lawrence's "Fenimore Cooper's White Novels" and "Fenimore Cooper's Leather-stocking Novels" in his *Studies in Classic American Literature* (New York: Viking, 1923, reprint 1969).

36. Dekker and McWilliams, Introduction to *Fenimore Cooper,* 28.

praised Cooper's respect for such German faith in literature.[37] This traditional view of Cooper resulted in new experiments as Schmidt integrated it into his own narration. Those experiments succeeded in no small part, moreover, because Schmidt and Cooper resembled each other in numerous crucial ways. Both were at once social critics and literary pioneers, socially conservative and literarily radical. Both also felt torn between nature and civilization, nature representing order and civilization needing change. Thanks to such shared ambivalence, Schmidt's and Cooper's respective fictions are related in letter as well as in spirit. This similarity makes Cooper special in Schmidt's literary pantheon. More than just another writer among the many honored there, Cooper helped Schmidt discover realms summed up by a phrase that Schmidt himself first coined in *Schwarze Spiegel* and that transports his sincere respect for imagination to a better world as envisioned by Cooper's Indians: "die ewigen Jagdgründe der Phantasie."

---

37. In his radio essay on Tieck, Schmidt quotes Cooper's envious account of how Germans respected their writers and the fine arts. "Hierin ist Deutschland das Land der empfänglichen Gemüter; mögen nun Musik, Poesie oder mehr materielle Kunstgegenstände die Anregung zur Bewunderung hergeben. Dagegen können schwerlich Klötze unempfindlicher sein, oder weniger wahre Hochachtung für Wissenschaften, Künste, oder innere Ausbildung überhaupt haben, als der große Haufe in Amerika" (Arno Schmidt, "Funfzehn: Vom Wunderkind der Sinnlosigkeit," in *Das essayistische Werk,* 2:140). Günther Jürgensmeier traces this quotation to Cooper's *Sketches of Switzerland* (1836; "Meine Liebeserklärung," *Bargfelder Bote* 40 [October, 1979]: 4). Schmidt subtly integrated Cooper into that tradition with the subtitle of his translation of the Littlepage Manuscripts—"Bilder aus der amerikanischen Vergangenheit." Barczaitis notes the echo of Gustav Freytag's similar title, *Bilder aus der deutschen Vergangenheit* (1859–67; Barczaitis, *Schmidt als Übersetzer,* 177).

Berlin and *Böhmen:* Bachmann, Benjamin, and the Debris of History

Marilyn Sibley Fries

Zugrund gerichtet, wach ich ruhig auf.
—Ingeborg Bachmann, "Böhmen liegt am Meer"

Ingeborg Bachmann's "Büchner-Preis-Rede" of 1964, "Ein Ort für Zufälle,"[1] has only recently come to be regarded as an integral part of her oeuvre, despite its thematic linkage to prose works such as "Jugend in einer österreichischen Stadt" (1961), "Das dreißigste Jahr" (1961), or the "Todesarten" cycle (1961–78), and to several late poems, especially "Prag Jänner 1964" and "Böhmen liegt am Meer" (both published in 1968).[2]

Epigraph from Bachmann, *Werke,* ed. Christine Koschel, Inge von Weidenbaum, and Clemens Münster (Munich: Piper, 1978), 1:167. All subsequent references to Bachmann's works will be parenthetically cited in the text as *Werke,* with volume number and page.

1. Ingeborg Bachmann, "Ein Ort für Zufälle," in *Werke,* 4:278–93. The speech was also issued as a separate publication illustrated by Günter Grass (Berlin: Wagenbach, 1965). This edition omits the initial paragraphs that constitute Bachmann's direct address to the audience, thus, among other things, alleviating or deleting the tension between speaker and listener that I find crucial to the project.

2. Compared to her other works, there has been little critical analysis of this speech. The major analyses (Kurt Bartsch, "Ein Ort für Zufälle: Bachmanns Büchnerprcisrede, als poetischer Text gelesen," *Modern Austrian Literature* 18, no. 3–4 [1985]: 135–45; Bartsch, *Ingeborg Bachmann* [Stuttgart: Metzler, 1988], chap. 3.3.2.2; Hans Höller, *Ingeborg Bachmann: Das Werk, Von den frühesten Gedichten bis zum "Todesarten"-Zyklus* [Frankfurt am Main: Athenäum, 1987], chap. 6), locate the work within her oeuvre (that is, try to identify its *"werkgeschichtliche"* position) and lose themselves in the difficulties of genre classification and naming. Bartsch settles for "Groteske," while Höller, in his excellent and lengthy analysis, writes the following.
    Die Schwierigkeiten, den Text im Werk Ingeborg Bachmanns zu bestimmen, beginnen bereits mit der Gattungsfrage. . . . Der Begriff "Prosagroteske," den Kurt Bartsch vorgeschlagen hat, weist dem Text eine gattungsmäßige Sonderstellung im Werk Ingeborg Bachmanns zu. . . . Es spricht mehr dafür, die Bezeichnung Büchner-Preis-Rede beizubehalten, weil diese institutionalisierte Rede-Situation, denkt man etwa an die Reden von Paul Celan oder Günter Eich, eine Art des literarischen Diskurses hervorgebracht

This delay has much to do with its resistance to classification, and with the extreme structural complexities of the text, whose hermetic perspective and apparent lack of linear logic [*Konsequenz*] obstruct our approach. Indeed, after a few introductory paragraphs, Bachmann denies categorization and access by driving a wedge between herself and her audience. Signaling the first of many fissures in the text, this wedge is formed initially by the speaker's identification with Büchner's Lenz, by her apparent alienation from her German listeners, and by her retreat into the hermetic language of the dream. But the text's persistent ruptures have also to do with the confrontation it presents between deeply embedded structures of thought and language, in which a certain stratum adheres to a shared, and thus coherent, symbolic order, while another is rooted in the private articulation of the speaking subject. The intrusion of the latter into the former—its unwillingness or inability to be subdued by normative language and form—is the stuff, according to Julia Kristeva, of "poetic revolution," and of Bachmann's enterprise here.[3]

To be sure, Bachmann recognizes her audience in the opening remarks determined by the award reception situation. "Wie jeder, der hier gestanden ist und es nicht wert war, Büchner das Schuhband zu lösen, habe ich es schwer, den Mund aufzutun, den Dank trotzdem abzustatten mit einer Rede" (*Werke,* 4:278). But she also perceives her listeners in another, more personal way, one that retracts this ritualistic and formal acknowledgment and immediately creates a space between speaker and listener we had thought closed by the solemn award ceremony and a mutual respect for Büchner. "[I]ch vergesse nicht, daß ich in Ihrem Land bin mit seinen Zufällen, die sich der Diagnose nicht ganz, aber im Grunde entziehen,

---

hat, in der experimentierendes Denken, die Infragestellung des selbstbewußten Schriftsteller-Ichs und die Reflexion der Schwierigkeiten bei der Darstellung der geschichtlichen und gesellschaftlichen Wirklichkeit geradezu ein eigenes Genre entstehen ließen. Eine andere Möglichkeit . . . wäre die genrespezifische Einordnung als Essay." (Höller, *Bachmann,* 214)

Peter Beicken (*Ingeborg Bachmann* [Munich: Beck, 1988]) devotes less space than the others to this text, in which "die Dichterin [bietet] eine imitatio des Büchnerschen Lenz und seiner Passion. Sie spricht über den Wahnsinn, der von außen auf den einzelnen zukommt aus den Erbschaften dieser Zeit" (149–50). Although all of these, especially Höller, are useful analyses, their generally unquestioning acceptance of the notion of "Wahnsinn," among other things, limits their readings. I am not at all sure that Bachmann means this word as narrowly as they want to read it.

3. In the subsequent discussion, I refer to two of Kristeva's essays, "The System and the Speaking Subject" and "Revolution in Poetic Language," in *The Kristeva Reader,* ed. Toril Moi (New York: Columbia University Press, 1986), 24–33, 89–136.

wie alle Zufälle; Zufälle, die sich mitunter aber einer Optik und einem Gehör mitteilen, das sich diesem Zufall aussetzt, dem Nachtmahr und seiner Konsequenz" (278). Furthermore, this author identifies *not* with the great writer in whose name she receives the prize, but rather with his insane character, Lenz.

> "Konsequent, konsequent," sagte dann Lenz, und wenn jemand anderer was sprach: "Inkonsequent, inkonsequent." . . . Konsequenz, das Konsequente ist, wie Sie wissen, . . . in fast allen Fällen etwas Furchtbares, und das Erleichternde, das Lösende, Lebbare, das kommt inkonsequent einher. Konsequenz, das Folgerichtige, im Verfolgen des Risses—eines Risses, der für Lenz durch die Welt ging. (278)

And the *Ort* of which she speaks in the relatively complacent and provincial Darmstadt of the annual prize ceremony is *not* that place, but another, less secure and highly symbolic one: Berlin, the place in which Bachmann lived for two years (1962–64) as guest of the Ford Foundation, and from where she traveled to deliver her speech in Darmstadt.

In her apparently conventional opening paragraphs, then, Bachmann prefigures the narrative strategies of the text that will follow by denying her audience the pleasure of identifying with her "place." She is neither successor to Büchner nor is she a German writer; she is, rather, an *Ortsfremder* in every sense of the word—a Lenz who is befallen by the coincidences that reduce him to madness and to silence, an Austrian whose traumatic experiences in 1938–45 alienate her from Germany at the same time as they motivate her writing—a project that is itself "ein Ort für Zufälle." Addressing the audience of her Büchner Prize Speech, she establishes a barrier to accessibility that becomes a central structural device in this text, whose ruptures and discontinuities prohibit any generalizing analysis. Indeed, any generic classification misreads the poetic revolution of this work, whose texture is so clearly associative that the trope of the nightmare might explain it away, were it not for the sober and obvious alertness of the narrative voice to the social and political context of its delivery. For the piece, emerging from the reality of Berlin in the early 1960s (and its historical legacy), amplifies that reality with a narrative imagery and a poetic rhythm that are very much the personal reality of the speaking voice, juxtaposing and intertwining the notions of *Konsequenz* and *Inkonsequenz*. The *Konsequente* is the manifestly surreal dream, whose latent content tells of the overindulgent Germany of the *Wirtschaftswun-*

derjahre, in which repression and denial are symbolized by people who are enveloped in *Fettpapier,* who drown historical memory in beer and schnapps, whose raging consumerism would replace past horrors with present materiality. "In Berlin sind jetzt alle Leute in Fettpapier eingewickelt. . . . Myriaden von Bierflaschen stehen bis zum Wannsee hinunter, viele Flaschen schwimmen auch schon im Wasser . . ." (*Werke,* 4:280). Such descriptions of "people" are counterpoised throughout this text with moments of "excitement" among the "sick ones" in the asylum. The apparently seamless transitions between the *Leute* and the *Kranken* obscure the gaping fissures. Here is just one example: " . . . alle wollen auf einmal hinein in das *Kadewe* . . . die Leute sind nicht mehr zu halten, sie bedrängen die Verkäuferinnen . . . man reißt sich die Lottozettel aus den Händen und rennt an die Automaten, das Geld wird so laut hineingeworfen, daß die Kugeln durch die Kästen springen und in einigen Zimmern nach Schlafmitteln gejammert wird. Aber es gibt diese Nacht nichts mehr" (282).

The narrative is one of victimization, in which the speaking subject and the subjects of which she speaks are destroyed by the brutality of that which befalls them. The primary images of this destructive externality, of the *Zufälle* that dominate the *Ort* in and of the text, are derived directly from the historical and present reality of Berlin. There, an ominous hierarchy of chaotic hegemony obtains, a domination represented by airplanes—the machinery of civilization and of war—by various symbols of authority— the hospital chaplain in a green hunter's hat, the academy, American soldiers, Checkpoint Charlie, and a retinue of medical personnel—a chief physician and a series of nurses—who rely on injections and restraints to keep the unruly and excited inmates of the asylum Berlin under control.[4] It is clear that the speaking subject identifies with the patients, as it is that the world of this narrative is one of an unfinished—unanalyzed—history whose denial is a self-denial resulting in madness, and whose presence in Berlin (and in her own life) Bachmann denotes as "etwas in Berlin." This *es* or

---

4. In Bachmann's vocabulary, the physician figure is ominously linked to fascism and to the victimization of the concentration camps (see especially *Der Fall Franza,* in which Franza's husband is a psychiatrist for whom she is clinical experimental material). "Ein Ort für Zufälle" contains multiple allusions to the fascism that survives in the German society of the 1960s, among them the following: "Die Brandmauern am Lützowplatz werden beleuchtet von großen Scheinwerfern, es ist schon alles verraucht, der Brand muß vorbei sein. Und mit Taschenlampen wird noch genau zwischen die Grasbüschel geleuchtet, da ist nichts mehr, nur verkohlte Knöchelchen, angekohlter Boden, kein ganzes Skelett, nur Knöchelchen" (*Werke,* 4:281).

etwas, which cannot be more closely defined, is Bachmann's term for the disaster that befalls us but cannot be written.

This text has been read as dream and as grotesque. While elements of both are clearly present, neither term does justice to its sociohistorical stratum. For this is a work that "de-scribes the disaster."

> The disaster, unexperienced. It is what escapes the very possibility of experience—it is the limit of writing. This must be repeated: the disaster de-scribes. Which does not mean that the disaster, as the force of writing, is excluded from it, is beyond the pale of writing or extratextual.[5]

Bachmann's images move beyond metaphor into the realm of enigma and the surreal in a piece littered with the fragments of that un-writing, with a collection of impressions left by history in the individual life of the speaker and the collective life of the city. As such, it might be seen as a verbal pile of debris whose sorting out into a logical continuum (as in the practice of literary or historical analysis) would defeat the particular *Konsequenz* of this de-scription.

Rather than attempt the explication this text resists or even defies, I thus find it more useful to locate it within an accidental constellation of twentieth-century thinkers and writers, in particular Walter Benjamin, Maurice Blanchot, and Julia Kristeva, with some attention to Christa Wolf. In writing of the disaster that must remain "extratextual," Bachmann's uncanny text re-presents Benjamin's image of the angel of history,[6] while it enacts Kristeva's theories about the revolutionary aspect of poetic language. Taking its cue from Lenz's *Konsequenz* and the *Inkonsequenz* of those who surround him, it recognizes, with Lenz, the "[Riß], der . . . durch die Welt [geht]" at the same time that it telescopes and confuses the binary opposites of consistency and inconsistency, or continuity and discontinuity. It dismisses the causality of "progress" and replaces it with the chaos of simultaneity; it turns things on their head and at an angle, causing a slippage that deletes the boundaries of difference that divide the insane from the sane, the abnormal from the norm, the past from the present, the subconscious dream from the consciousness of wakefulness. "Wir schlafen ja,

---

5. Maurice Blanchot, *The Writing of the Disaster*, trans. Ann Smock (Lincoln and London: University of Nebraska Press, 1986), 7.

6. Walter Benjamin, "Über den Begriff der Geschichte," in *Gesammelte Schriften*, ed. Rolf Tiedemann and Hermann Schweppenhäuser (Frankfurt am Main: Suhrkamp, 1980), 2:691–704.

sind Schläfer, aus Furcht, uns und unsere Welt wahrnehmen zu müssen," Bachmann contends (*Werke,* 4:198). In this text, the crucial "Wahrnehmung" of "unsere Welt" can occur only in the "insanity" of the *Nachtmahr.*

The speaking, historical subject that identifies itself in the text's opening passages, only to disappear completely in what follows, is clearly the Austrian author Ingeborg Bachmann, who addresses her German audience. The "Sie" of the audience and the "ich" of the speaker appear once more before the "Gegend . . . auf die kein Finger mehr zu legen ist," the "Stadt, . . . die sich auf 'Teilung' hinausreden ließe" (*Werke,* 4:279), usurps the narrative. For "die Beschädigung von Berlin . . . erzwingt . . . eine Einstellung auf Krankheit. . . . Diese Einstellung kann jemand nötigen, auf dem Kopf zu gehen, damit von dem Ort . . . Kunde gegeben werden kann. Ein Kundschafter ist ein Ortsfremder" (279). The syntax of this paragraph, the third of the text and the last of the introductory remarks, demonstrates the breaks and ruptures, clustered around the word *Teilung,* that deny the omnipotence of what Kristeva identifies as the "transcendental ego,"[7] that mark both the fractured personal history of the speaking subject and the continuous/discontinuous sociopolitical history of the "Ort" of which Bachmann speaks. It also defines the narrative project at hand—a narrative dictated by the "Zufälle," by the "Wahnsinn," which "kann auch von außen kommen, auf die einzelnen zu, ist also schon viel früher von dem Innen der einzelnen nach außen gegangen, tritt den Rückweg an, in Situationen, die uns geläufig geworden sind, in den Erbschaften dieser Zeit" (278).

A statement of this kind emphasizes the text's (auto)biographical substratum. Bachmann implies, despite the shift from "ich" to the impersonal "Kundschafter," an extremely personal basis—an experiential foundation located not so much in history as in what "this age" [*diese Zeit*] has inherited. The *Teilung* that denotes the divided Berlin and is understandable in the spatial as well as the temporal sense of the word is transformed into *Riß* for the speaking subject; it abruptly divides the "ich" from itself, as the subject "ich" becomes the object "jemand," caused by a forced receptivity to disease to walk upside down. At the end of this passage, the almost absent speaking subject is an explorer, an alien or *Ortsfremder,* whose "Darstellung ist ihm ganz und der Sache nie ganz angemessen" (*Werke,* 4:279). The representation refers, in other words, immediately to the absent subject, but only by mediation through that subject to the object, the "Sache"

---

7. Kristeva, "The System," 27.

of the text. But the representation demands "Radikalisierung und kommt aus Nötigung" (279). Attempts to get at the ground of the text itself are fruitless, for it has none; like Berlin, the city of which it speaks, this text is the site of the rift in the world. Bachmann's "Nachtmahr und sein[e] Konsequenz" (278) are controlled by the *es*—by the *etwas* that overwhelms narration, which is to say, the orderly (hi)story that an inaudible voice wants to tell. In this instance, it is precisely *Geschichte* that undoes *Geschichten;* it is Bachmann's presentation of such unravelling that constitutes this remarkably cryptic and ominous text.

In "Fragen und Scheinfragen," the first of her *Frankfurter Poetik-Vorlesungen* of 1959–60, Bachmann echoes Kafka and Wittgenstein, among others, in claiming literature's affective and effective, that is, revolutionary, potential. "Was aber möglich ist, in der Tat, ist Veränderung. Und die verändernde Wirkung, die von neuen Werken ausgeht, erzieht uns zu neuer Wahrnehmung, neuem Gefühl, neuem Bewußtsein" (*Werke*, 4:194). Bachmann's revolutionary impulse is aesthetic and moral; hers is not a political agenda, at least not in the instrumental sense of that word. It involves politics, however, insofar as our social behavior is conditioned and controlled by the laws of our language, by our imprisonment in what she represents in *Der Fall Franza* as the colonizing and hegemonic sphere of "die Weißen," with whose victims she, as woman and as "stranger," identifies.[8]

In that same lecture, Bachmann speaks of the emergence of literature from historical conditions. "Daß Dichten außerhalb der geschichtlichen Situation stattfindet, wird heute wohl niemand mehr glauben—daß es auch nur einen Dichter gibt, dessen Ausgangsposition nicht von den Zeitgegebenheiten bestimmt wäre. Gelingen kann ihm, im glücklichsten Fall, zweierlei: zu repräsentieren, seine Zeit zu repräsentieren, und etwas zu präsentieren, für das die Zeit noch nicht gekommen ist" (*Werke*, 4:196).

From our perspective more than thirty years later, it seems odd that Bachmann's assertion should have had to be made at all, immersed as we are in the confluence of the personal and the social that has come to dominate so much of our contemporary discussion of "the text," whose definition by any given individual returns us immediately to that confluence.[9] Bachmann's insistence on acknowledging social and historical con-

---

8. Cf. Bachmann, *Der Fall Franza*, in *Werke*, 3:339–482.

9. On the theme of "the text," see Sandra Gilbert and Susan Gubar, "Masterpiece Theater: An Academic Melodrama," *Critical Inquiry* 17 (Summer, 1991): 693–717.

ditions in the production of literature must have had a different resonance in the literary-critical atmosphere of the late 1950s, however—in that time when "werkimmanente Kritik" held sway, when the analysis of the autonomy and form of the literary work enabled the avoidance of the treacherous realms of the social and historical conditions of the most recent past. In her own development, Bachmann's statement signals a shift to a prose that recognizes the conviction of that utterance and the gradual abandonment of the poetic works that first led to her acclaim as a "star" of postwar German lyric poetry. Recognized in 1953 with the prestigious prize of the *Gruppe 47,* by 1956–57 (her thirtieth year) Bachmann was composing stories, among them the title story of the 1961 collection *Das dreißigste Jahr* and, also in that volume, "Jugend in einer österreichischen Stadt." Subsequent works of prose, including the stories in *Simultan* (1972) and the unfinished *Todesarten-cycle* (*Malina,* 1971; the fragments *Der Fall Franza* and *Requiem für Fanny Goldmann,* both 1978), demonstrated, in ways that her poetry could not, her profound recognition of and dismay about the politics of social relationships, primarily as these are played out in language.

Most critics of Bachmann view one of her last poems, "Keine Delikatessen," as Bachmann's leave-taking from poetry, and are fond of quoting the familiar lines of the first stanza.

> Nichts mehr gefällt mir.
>
> Soll ich
> eine Metapher ausstaffieren
> mit einer Mandelblüte?
> die Syntax kreuzigen
> an einem Lichteffekt?
> Wer wird sich den Schädel zerbrechen
> über so überflüssige Dinge—
>
> (*Werke,* 2:172)

What, she asks here and in the following stanzas, is the validity of a poetic language that cannot speak of hunger, shame, tears, and despair? The poem was published in the 1968 issue of *Kursbuch* that proclaimed the "death of literature"; but Bachmann's apparent abandonment of the lyric form is in no way synonymous with this rumored demise—indeed, it signals a revolution in her poetic language, an upheaval that will affect much of her later writing. But perhaps the *Kursbuch* proclamation had to do not with the death of literature, but rather with the "death of the subject," in which case her inclusion in that issue is not so curious. For Bachmann's subsequent works will (continue to) focus on nothing other than death, or, as she puts it, "types of death," all of which involve the slow and tortuous murder of women by men.

Bachmann's gender politics, admittedly central to these works, are formed and informed by her entire life experience as an inhabitant of Central Europe in the mid-twentieth century, and her representations of the manner in which these hegemonous politics function have deep roots in her own intellectual preoccupation with language, epistemology, and psychology. This history allows the constellation I am constructing here: the experience of displacement joins together those otherwise foreign to each other—individuals from different places and different times. The contours are described by names whose sociohistorical resonances provide a kind of grid or network against which "Ein Ort für Zufälle" may be read. Surely these writers and thinkers—Blanchot, Benjamin, Kristeva, Wolf—are all stars that, although born at different times and different places, have wandered, most of them literally, some figuratively, sometimes to cross each other's paths, sometimes not, but ultimately to reside in that timeless and alien space of exile.

None of the connections I am suggesting is verifiable. There is, to my knowledge, no documentation of Bachmann's familiarity with Blanchot or with Benjamin. It is extremely unlikely that she could have known the latter's thesis "Über den Begriff der Geschichte" when she wrote "Ein Ort für Zufälle";[10] Blanchot's late works, which concern us here, postdate her death; and, of course, chronology denies the possibility of any knowledge of Kristeva, who arrived in Paris to begin her career in 1966 and published *La Révolution du langage poétique* in 1974, a year after Bachmann's death.[11] Bachmann will also have known little or nothing of Christa Wolf, one of her most sympathetic readers, who was beginning to gain international recognition only in the last four or five years of Bachmann's life. My approach may thus seem an argument for *simultaneity*, although I am reluctant to use that slippery term. I would rather argue that certain unique aspects of the shared experience of displacement engender a kind of community in which the unspoken is understood. It is not coincidental that

10. Although Benjamin's text first appeared in 1942 in "Walter Benjamin zum Gedächtnis," published by the Institut für Sozialforschung in Los Angeles, the now-familiar version was not available to the general public until the publication of *Illuminationen: Ausgewählte Schriften II* (Frankfurt am Main: Suhrkamp, 1969).

11. Toril Moi, "Introduction," in *The Kristeva Reader*, ed. Toril Moi (New York: Columbia University Press, 1986), 1.

Bachmann, for instance, identified with and *comprehended* the works of writers such as Wittgenstein, Kafka, Musil, Celan, Canetti, and Nelly Sachs. Nor does it seem out of order to suggest that her writing knows of the revelations that take a different form in the (revolutionary) philosophical works of Benjamin and Kristeva or reflects and is reflected in the writings of Blanchot.

All these writers, members of three successive generations, share certain fundamental experiences as inhabitants of that fragile geopolitical entity known as Central Europe.[12] Dwellers in this place have experienced the loss of center or of ground—displacement, exile, self-alienation—fundamentally, physically as well as metaphysically. Although the anguish of this experience and its representation in text is certainly not specific to Central Europe, it is, for historical reasons, here most extreme, and its precipitate in art and philosophy has produced a rhetoric of the subject that is quite unimaginable when we disregard that subject's geographic and historical positioning. The links to Benjamin and Kristeva, although initially more tenuous than those with Wolf, seem ultimately more fundamental in their shared insights. Just as Bachmann speaks of *Grenzen,* so Benjamin's angel stands at an (admittedly unstable) boundary between past and future. "Er hat das Antlitz der Vergangenheit zugewendet. . . . [Der] Sturm treibt ihn unaufhaltsam in die Zukunft, der er den Rücken kehrt."[13] And Kristeva writes of "frontiers": "All functions which suppose a *frontier* . . . and the transgression of that frontier (the sudden appearance of a new signifying chain) are relevant to any account of signifying *practice,* where practice is taken as meaning the acceptance of a symbolic law together with the transgression of that law for the purpose of reworking it."[14] I may, perhaps, be forgiven for dislodging these two thinkers from their places in contemporary theory and criticism—for lifting from Benjamin's well-documented and much-discussed writings on the philosophy of history that one famous passage from "Über den Begriff der Geschichte," inspired by Klee's painting, that transforms *Begriff* into *Griff,* that describes the angel of history—a passage and image whose essence is comprehended in Bachmann's text; or for seizing, in Kristeva, on the notion of poetic language "making free with the language code; music, dancing, painting, reordering the psychic drives which have not been harnessed by the dominant symbolization systems and

12. Blanchot may be the exception here, depending on one's definition of Central Europe.
13. Benjamin, "Über den Begriff," 697.
14. Kristeva, "The System," 29.

thus renewing their own tradition; and (in a different mode) experiences with drugs—all seek out and make use of this [postulated heterogeneity of semiotics] and the ensuing fracture of a symbolic code which can no longer 'hold' its (speaking) subjects."[15] My justification for such "lifting" has to do with the similarity of the questions asked by all these thinkers rather than with the specific disciplinary dress in which they clothe their answers— questions that have to do with theories of meaning, with language, history, the individual and society, with remembering and forgetting.

One can overmake the point of shared experience, of course, insistently locating (or attempting to locate) an author in her or his specific place and time for the purpose of allowing that location to explain the author's work. But such a project assumes the possible definition of a "subject" in a "place" and a "time"—a positive coherence undone by the slippage of the past into the present, by the mobility of borders and frontiers of all kinds, and by the discoveries of psychoanalysis. Lacking faith in such definitions, we find ourselves groping in a polysemous and heterogeneous morass of simultaneity, in which the never definable present moment (or, rather, definable only as "historical" *Augenblick,* in which case it is removed from the continuum of process) contains within it the waste and residue of all preceding moments.

Bachmann's project in "Ein Ort für Zufälle" recognizes and narrates this simultaneity in its attempt to speak a poetic connection between past and present, between here and there, to dismantle the boundaries erected by the force of language and by historical and political circumstances, in order, finally, to move *Böhmen* to the sea, to let land and sea merge. Thematically sketched and outlined in much of her early poetry, this project takes form and place in the prose works of her later years. It finds its sharpest and most revolutionary representation, however, in this text, in which (West) Berlin is the site of dis-ease, of a rupture signaled by the repression of history (i.e., of self) for the sake of material comfort, where Lenz's *Konsequenz* is truer than the *Inkonsequenz* that refuses to recognize connections between past and present. Berlin is the place occupied by Benjamin's angel of history, his back not only turned against the future, but literally up against the wall; it is the enclosure of "Wahnsinn," in which the presence of the "Krankenhaus" for the insane permits the illusion of difference between inside and outside or "them" and "us." Blanchot knows the truth of this illusion. "If it weren't for prisons, we would know

---

15. Kristeva, "The System," 30.

that we are all already in prison."[16] And Bachmann's text is the place that enacts the poetic revolution in an extreme fusion of the semiotic with the symbolic, paradoxically realizing Bachmann's poetic (utopian) project of merging land and sea in a work that "writes of the disaster," a text of utter alienation, despair, and anguish.

As is immediately evident from the foregoing, it will be difficult here to avoid metaphor in the discussion of a work that disclaims it.

> Die Beschädigung von Berlin, deren geschichtliche Voraussetzungen ja bekannt sind, erlaubt keine Mystifizierung und keine Überhöhung zum Symbol. Was sie erzwingt, ist jedoch eine Einstellung auf Krankheit, auf eine Konsequenz von variablen Krankheitsbildern, die Krankheit hervorruft. Diese Einstellung kann jemand nötigen, auf dem Kopf zu gehen. (*Werke,* 4:279)

This is the paradox of the work's poetic revolution: Bachmann denies herself and us the pleasure of the symbol while simultaneously calling into question the symbolic system that anesthetizes her German contemporaries, that encloses them in *Fettpapier,* but we must nonetheless mediate our reading with our own signs, having no other way to speak of the text. Our reading becomes an act of translation—a carrying over of a text that refuses the possibility of any such act, whose ground is a groundless and unbridgeable abyss, a text that enacts in its very writing the impossibility of transmission.

We can, of course, locate the work within the larger whole of Bachmann's project; we can attempt to categorize and classify it generically. The first procedure is helpful, the second quite useless, but neither assists in understanding the particular narrative gesture of this particular piece, unique among Bachmann's works and, because it refuses genre classification, also when (mis)aligned with any group from literary history. It seems to me more profitable to read this agonized text with respect to the constellation I have suggested, rather than in the traditional contexts provided by Bachmann's oeuvre or by German literary history. For lack of a better term, I should like to call this the constellation of displacement—and by this I mean not only that metaphysical or existential displacement/alienation that has become the cliché of the modern and postmodern (Western) world; I mean literal displacement, the personal historical experience of forced removal that is fundamental to the Central European in this century.

---

16. Blanchot, *Writing,* 66.

What makes Bachmann's prose revolutionary is her discovery of a system of signification that merges the rhythms of her personal language with the symbolic codes she has acquired and mastered via her immersion in the major strains of thought in her time. This constitutes the fusion and counterpoint of (at least) two voices. One is taught by what Kristeva describes as the "general social law" discovered by semiotics; of the fact of this law, Kristeva maintains "that [it] is the symbolic dimension which is given in language and that every social practice offers a specific expression of this law." It is precisely the expressions of such "social practice" that Bachmann questions and condemns in her prose; in the Berlin text, it is the (German) social practice of repression, of allowing the "industrious word," *Teilung,* to release us from necessary thought. Following Lacan, Kristeva calls the discovery of semiotics the "Law of the Father."[17] Opposed and juxtaposed to it is another voice, less univocal, that emerges from that region Kristeva designates as the *chora,* the realm of the semiotic, which is "more or less successfully repressed and can be perceived only as pulsional *pressure* on symbolic language: as contradictions, meaninglessness, disruption, silences and absences in the symbolic language. The *chora* is a rhythmic pulsion rather than a new language. It constitutes ... the heterogeneous, disruptive dimension of language, that which can never be caught up in the closure of traditional linguistic theory."[18]

I do not mean to suggest that Bachmann "finds her own voice" in the process of her later prose. I hold, rather, that a voice other than the acquired voice of "the law," of convention and tradition, finds *her,* and that it does so with a particular sort of vengeance in the Büchner Prize Speech. This highly intelligent product of the academy, a doctor of philosophy with a dissertation on Heidegger, for whom quotation from the philosophical and literary experiments of her time constitutes the intertext of many of her works, demonstrates, especially in her late prose, her bilingualism, her ability to be "hüben und drüben zu Hause" (*Werke,* 4:301), where "hüben" signifies the comprehensible, the "general social law" from which we swerve at our own risk, while "drüben" signifies the uncanny, the dangerous realms of the subconscious.[19]

---

17. Kristeva, "The System," 25.

18. Toril Moi, *Sexual/Textual Politics: Feminist Literary Theory* (London and New York: Routledge, 1985), 162.

19. The quotation comes from Bachmann's piece "Biographisches," whose opening is telling for our purposes here. "Ich habe meine Jugend in Kärnten verbracht ... an der Grenze, in einem Tal, das zwei Namen hat. ... Und das Haus ... trägt noch heute einen fremd-

It is, perhaps, not too extreme to claim that the writers and thinkers who concern us here are all "writing of the disaster." Bachmann certainly was: she records "the disaster"—her disaster—as the loss of any "zuhause" in "Jugend in einer österreichischen Stadt," on which she comments as follows.

Es hat einen bestimmten Moment gegeben, der hat meine Kindheit zertrümmert. Der Einmarsch von Hitlers Truppen in Klagenfurt. Es war etwas so Entsetzliches, daß mit diesem Tag meine Erinnerung anfängt: durch einen zu frühen Schmerz, wie ich ihn in dieser Stärke vielleicht später überhaupt nie mehr hatte. Natürlich habe ich das alles nicht verstanden in dem Sinn, in dem es ein Erwachsener verstehen würde. Aber diese ungeheure Brutalität, die spürbar war, dieses Brüllen, Singen und Marschieren—das Aufkommen meiner ersten Todesangst. Ein ganzes Heer kam da in unser stilles, friedliches Kärnten.[20]

The key concepts here—*Kindheit, zertrümmert, etwas, Erinnerung, Schmerz, Todesangst*—remain central to her discourse in "Ein Ort für Zufälle." Written some fifteen years after "Jugend" and located in another city, in the city that spewed forth the "entsetzliches Etwas" that destroyed her childhood and her city, the latter may be seen, in part, as a consequence of the loss of place portrayed in "Jugend," whose central figure is "die Kinder" in that Austrian city before and during the *Anschluß* and World War II, at the end of which these children "werden aufgefordert, ins Leben zu treten. . . . Sie gehen fort, die Hände in ausgefransten Taschen und mit einem Pfiff, der sie selber warnen soll" (*Werke,* 2:92).

Bachmann goes, taking *Erinnerung, Schmerz,* and *Todesangst* with her. The metaphors of her poetry of the ensuing years write repeatedly of this disaster, but in the Berlin piece, composed about twenty years after her departure from Kärnten, the collapse of the earlier experience with the later one—the *Konsequenz* that ties them together—leads to the abandonment

klingenden Namen. So ist nahe der Grenze noch einem die Grenze: die Grenze der Sprache— und ich war hüben und drüben zu Hause" (*Werke,* 4:301). Much has been made in the Bachmann literature of the notion of "Grenze," in both the senses she suggests here (the physical or geographic and the metaphysical), particularly because Bachmann is fond of quoting Ludwig Wittgenstein: "Die Grenzen meiner Sprache sind die Grenzen meiner Welt." The extreme form of "Ein Ort für Zufälle" dismantles language's boundaries even as it describes them.

20. Ingeborg Bachmann, *Wir müssen wahre Sätze finden: Gespräche und Interviews,* ed. Christine Kochel and Inge von Weidenbaum (Munich: Piper, 1963), 111.

of representation for the sake of presentation. In Berlin, history collapses upon itself in piles of debris, in which are buried the memories of the years 1918 to 1945. In Berlin, the telescoping of time repeats the childhood trauma of the war in "an Austrian city," and allows for the emergence of a language buried somewhere in that childhood. In Berlin, the denial of this *Konsequenz* engenders a treacherous disconnectedness. The geopolitical "hüben und drüben" in which Bachmann was at home in her youth is transformed to a temporal axis of then and now, marked by a divisionary tactic of repression that robs both spheres of any comfort: "zuhause" is displaced by "eine Einstellung auf Krankheit." At the risk of enormous misunderstanding, Bachmann's text retrieves the "drüben," the unspoken text on the other side of that dividing word, speaking it with the only language appropriate to its articulation: her own. One wonders, incidentally, how her speech was, as they say, "received" by the German audience in Darmstadt in 1964, or to what extent such a text is viewed as "loss of control" in the sense in which Christa Wolf means it in her own Büchner Prize Speech of 1980.

Die nach dieser Sprache fahnden wollen, müßten aber wohl ein beinah vollkommenes Schwinden ihres Selbst-Gefühls, ihres Selbst-Bewußtseins ertragen können, weil ja all die Muster, in denen zu reden, zu erzählen, zu denken und zu dichten wir gewöhnt sind, nicht mehr verfügbar wären. Sie würden wohl erfahren, was es wirklich heißt: die Fassung verlieren.[21]

We would, in other words, forfeit *Konsequenz* for the sake of *Inkonsequenz,* would suspend the linear "progress," the cause-and-effect continuum created by the historians, to replace—or displace—it with a chaos of indecipherable texts. We would be forced to "walk on our heads," be subjected to a simultaneity that gives equal presence to discrete historical events, experience a world in which we would be forced to relinquish the comfort of "eine Kette von Begebenheiten" to acknowledge the single catastrophe, to see the pile of debris at our feet, a world in which the waters overflow their banks and the streets raise themselves to forty-five-degree angles; we would become "ver-rückt." Evicted from the comfort of a realm made

---

21. Christa Wolf, "Von Büchner sprechen: Darmstädter Rede," *Die Dimension des Autors: Essays und Aufsätze, Reden und Gespräche 1959–1985* (Darmstadt and Neuwied: Luchterhand, 1987), 615.

"sensible" by narrative and label, our internal *Wahnsinn* would not remain contained, suppressed by the *Sinn* of the world outside, but would escape us to appropriate and define that world—"ein Ort für Zufälle."

Unlike Bachmann's previous public addresses, most notably "Die Wahrheit ist dem Menschen zumutbar" (her "Rede zur Verleihung des Hörspielpreises der Kriegsblinden" of 1959) and the *Frankfurter Poetik Vorlesungen* of 1959–60, this speech veers radically from conventional norms of the genre; it is neither didactic nor eloquent, neither learned nor theoretical, and any literary or philosophical tradition in which it embeds itself or to which it makes reference is immediately undercut and put into question by Bachmann's insistent identification with Lenz and his *Konsequenz*. At issue here is a tradition of another sort—the tradition of repressive forgetfulness that, transforming disaster into momentary "Aufregung," enables the "progress" of "economic miracles" and renders the speaking subject insane or mute. "[I]ch vergesse nicht, daß ich in Ihrem Land bin," Bachmann says to her audience, and the entire subsequent text is her exercise in not forgetting, undertaken in that land that ignores or avoids the signs of memory, thus lodging them more deeply in the dangerous realm of the "es." Bachmann's presentation of her memories as a nightmare—her recreation, on one level, of the scene of psychoanalysis that puts the audience in the position of analyst—is one way in which she hopes to effect change. By implying that the nightmare is not hers alone, however (it is a matter of "Wahnsinn" that "kann von außen kommen, auf die einzelnen zu, ist also schon viel früher von dem Innen der einzelnen nach außen gegangen, tritt den Rückweg an . . ." [*Werke*, 4:278]), she also suggests a reversal of position, where the German audience becomes the analysand and the speaker the analyst who articulates for the others what they cannot speak themselves.

One aspect of this tradition of repression lies in the elevation of "Berlin" to a symbol of division, of *Teilung*, endowing the place (or the concept of that place) with a symbolic function so overwhelming that the symbol tends to obliterate the signified. Maurice Blanchot reads "the word Berlin" in the following way.

Berlin . . . is . . . the symbol of the division of the world, and something even more: a "point in the universe," the place in which the question of unity which is both necessary and impossible confronts every individual who resides there, and who, in residing there, experiences not only a place of residence, but also the absence of a place of residence.[22]

But, Bachmann insists, "[die] Beschädigung von Berlin, deren geschichtliche Voraussetzungen ja bekannt sind, erlaubt keine Überhöhung zum Symbol" (*Werke*, 4:279). "*Teilung*," she maintains, "ist ein anderes, ein fleißiges Wort, es nimmt vieles ab, das Denken nicht zuletzt" (279). "Ein Ort für Zufälle" invalidates the "industrious word" *Teilung* in a text that presents fractured language to represent those "Erbschaften dieser Zeit" (278) that *Teilung* represses. Bachmann realizes in this text the goal articulated in her *Frankfurter Poetik Vorlesungen* of five years earlier. "Gelingen kann [dem Dichter], im glücklichsten Fall, zweierlei: zu repräsentieren, seine Zeit zu repräsentieren, und etwas zu präsentieren, für das die Zeit noch nicht gekommen ist" (196). She achieves this in "Ein Ort für Zufälle" by representing her "Zeit," that is, her personal history as a displaced [*verrückt*] Central European in this century who is confronted in Berlin by the massive collective repression of that history (and thus of that person). The representation thus grounded, however, is presented in a language for which "die Zeit noch nicht gekommen ist," in a text that demonstrates the loss or destruction of the speaking subject whose language will not correspond to the laws governed by that convenient word, *Teilung*. *Teilung* implies redeemable separation, reparable division. Bachmann refuses the solace of this word and opts for *Riß*, a sign of irreparable split that applies as much to the speaking subject as to the fragmented text itself.

The first rupture in the text occurs between what I have called the introductory remarks and this fourth paragraph, which loses the "ich" in a radical and unanticipated shift to an "es."

Es ist zehn Häuser nach Sarotti, es ist einige Blocks vor Schlutheiß, es ist fünf Ampeln weit von der Commerzbank, es ist nicht bei Berliner Kindl, es sind Kerzen im Fenster, es ist seitab von der Straßenbahn, ist auch in der Schweigestunde, ist ein Kreuz davor, ist eine Kreuzung davor, es ist so weit nicht, aber auch nicht so nah, ist—falsch geraten!—eine Sache auch, ist kein Gegenstand, ist tagsüber, ist auch nachts, wird benutzt, sind Menschen drin, sind Bäume drum, kann, muß nicht, wird getragen, abgegeben, kommt mit den Füßen voraus, hat blaues

---

22. Maurice Blanchot, "The Word Berlin," *Semiotext(e)*, The German Issue (1982): 60–61.

Licht, hat nichts zu tun, ja ist, ist vorgekommen, ist aufgegeben, ist jetzt und schon lange, ist eine ständige Adresse, ist zum Umkommen, kommt, kommt vor und hervor, ist etwas—in Berlin. (*Werke,* 4:279–80)

I do not propose here to guess *what* this ominous "etwas" is, for that would always be "falsch geraten"—mistakenly guessed as well as erroneously aimed: it would always go in the wrong direction. We are, after all, dealing here with *Zufälle,* with coincidences whose comprehension according to any normative standard is impossible, with the inexplicable accidents that befall us. The "es/etwas" moves in the internal realm of the unconscious (and it is surely not coincidental that Bachmann, who was a student of psychology, employs "das Es"—Freud's term for what English knows as the id), but it also dwells, as an element of the repressed collective unconscious, beyond and outside the individual. Bachmann's text presents the eruption of that which the individual unconscious has repressed (the earlier traumas of the "ich") in the face of the still-repressed collective memory: a jarring and incongruous confrontation of memory and forgetfulness or, in an extreme reading of Kristeva's theory, a veritable cracking-up of the semiotic on the rock-hard shores of the symbolic law of the existing social system—a system that refuses to acknowledge the traumatic past that the "ich" is forced to remember. The sign-system of the text demonstrates this collision in the imagery of the *Nachtmahr.*

The text presents a clash of image and function or of stasis and progress. The dominant image is that of the insane asylum that is Berlin, in which the loss of those coordinates that typically govern our social behavior reverses or confuses the notions of "consistency" and "inconsistency," or of logical cause and effect, in which the preexistent *Krankheit* of Berlin is brutally controlled by restraints of various kinds ("Die Nachtschwester . . . wendet den Griff an und gibt eine Spritze, die durch und durch geht und in der Matratze steckenbleibt, damit man nicht mehr aufstehen kann" [*Werke,* 4:280]). It is an enclosed world of absolute chaos and destruction, of historical debris thought buried but that, at least in the asylum, refuses to remain repressed. "Es muß eine 'Disharmonie' sein. In der ganzen Stadt sickert etwas durch, alle wollen 'Disharmonie' gelesen oder gehört haben, manche haben es sich schon gedacht. Aber es steht nirgends öffentlich" (284). The *inkonsequent* image, with its *Disharmonie,* calls to mind Walter Benjamin's angel of history, who sees "eine einzige Katastrophe"

(Bachmann: "Es ist eine Katastrophe" [283]) where "eine Kette von Begebenheiten vor *uns* erscheint."[23]

The static image is incompatible, however, with the narrative voice—
Bachmann's voice—the voice of a speaking subject that demonstrates its
own destruction in the signifying processes of the text. The intertextual
operations here have less to do with transfer and borrowing at the level
of the symbolic (allusion to or quotation from known and existing texts,
for example) than with the referential field of personal experience, especially
to the extent that that personal experience belongs to the "Erbschaften
dieser Zeit." The revolutionary aspect of this text lies less in the message
conveyed by the imagery discussed previously than in the radical ways in
which the unconscious realms of the individual are called into play against
and within the context of collective history. The "ich" that disappears
from the text after the third paragraph, only to let the narrative be "written" by an "es," remains nonetheless to generate the poetic language of
the text, to overthrow the "symbol" of the symbolic with the eruption of
certain elements of the semiotic, or what Kristeva calls the *chora*. Bachmann's narrative transforms the signs of progress—"das, was wir den
Fortschritt nennen"[24]—into process, or, more specifically, a "signifying
process."[25]

> Within this process one might see the release and subsequent articulation
> of the drives as constrained by the social code yet not reducible to the
> language system as a *genotext* and the signifying system as it presents
> itself to phenomenological intuition as a *phenotext;* describable in terms
> of structure, or of competence/performance, or according to other mod-
> els. The presence of the *genotext* within the *phenotext* is indicated by what
> I have called a *semiotic disposition.* In the case, for example, of a signifying
> practice such as 'poetic language,' the *semiotic disposition* will be the
> various deviations from the grammatical rules of the language: artic-
> ulatory effects which shift the phonemative system back towards its
> articulatory, phonetic base and consequently towards the drive-governed
> bases of sound-production; the over-determination of a lexeme by mul-
> tiple meanings which it does not carry in ordinary usage but which
> accrue to it as a result of its occurrence in other texts; syntactic irreg-
> ularities such as ellipses, non-recoverable deletions, indefinite embed-
> dings, etc.; the replacement of the relationship between the protagonists

23. Benjamin, "Über den Begriff," 697.
24. Benjamin, "Über den Begriff," 698.
25. Kristeva, "The System," 28.

of any enunciation as they function in a locutory act . . . by a system of relations based on fantasy, and so forth.[26]

Elsewhere in Bachmann's works, the pulsing realm of the *chora* is represented by the sea or water in general (see especially "Undine geht"), while *Böhmen*, that cipher for the Imaginary, expresses the desire for the wholeness of an earlier state of being. Bachmann's teleology, if such exists, is expressed in the poem "Böhmen liegt am Meer," where pulsing sea and solid land are merged, where word borders on word, and where the concept of "zugrunde gehen" revels in the positive and negative significations of "descent." This teleology of totality, of the merging of land and sea, is paradoxically realized in the renderings of the Berlin text—not as a utopian wholeness achieved by an "ich" (who is quite evident in the poem), but as a presentation of the sea's eternal pulsations against the less-than-solid social, linguistic, and narrative codes of the symbolic order. This work thus enacts—momentarily and despite the dominant discord of rupture— the meeting of land (the symbolic law's order of things, which is represented by the chief physician and the chaplain and is inevitably discontinuous) and sea (that covers everything, but buries nothing, whose signs are the unpredictable inmates of the asylum).

For Kristeva, this narrative gesture would constitute the intrusion of the semiotic *chora* into the Symbolic Order. Bachmann's understanding of this process, although not based in the linguistic theories that guide Kristeva's thought, nonetheless corresponds: "[die] Zeit zu repräsentieren, und etwas zu präsentieren, für das die Zeit noch nicht gekommen ist" (*Werke*, 4:196). Admittedly skewing somewhat Lacan's and Kristeva's Freud-based understanding of the developmental stages that move the individual from the semiotic (for Lacan, the Imaginary) and the symbolic (Lacan's "Symbolic Order"), I suggest that Bachmann's entry into the symbolic is described in "Jugend in einer österreichischen Stadt," and is fully established by her career as a student of psychology, philosophy, and literature and by her position within the intellectual currents of her lifetime—especially her preoccupation with the language philosophies of Wittgenstein and Heidegger. Her acceptance to this order is, paradoxically, confirmed by Heimito von Doderer's reference to her as "der Bachmann."[27] Her own denial of that childhood and youth is so complete that she must

---

26. Kristeva, "The System," 28–29.
27. Cf. Beicken, *Bachmann*, 68.

mask her autobiographical story of the thirtieth year with the use of the third-person-masculine singular—although, it must be added, that story acknowledges the destructiveness of repression and the concomitant loss of the Imaginary as its major theme.

By the time she embarks on *Todesarten,* and certainly by the time of the Büchner Prize Speech, Bachmann's perhaps intuitive recognition of the tension between the semiotic and the symbolic is the central theme of her exploration. This is quite explicit in *Malina,* whose chapter division and list of characters are signs for the impossibility of the coexistence of the two within one individual. The "Ich" in *Malina* lives one life (the life of the id) with Ivan, another (that of the ego) with Malina, who is, in his turn, the superego that finally destroys both aspects of the "Ich," who disappears at the end of the work into a crack in the wall—one could posit this as the always already existing gap in the life of this fragmented "Ich." "Ein Ort für Zufälle" rewrites the conflict of *Malina* with extraordinary economy; that novel's themes of fragmentation and destruction (murder) of the "ich" by "the law" that is embodied both in the "third man"— the father who incorporates the brutalities of fascism—and in the character Malina, who reduces the psychic anxieties of the *Nachtmahr* by naming them according to the ready terminology of psychoanalysis (just as I have done here for the sake of convenience and because, as I have said, we have only our own symbolic codes by which to describe the nature of this narrative). Blanchot writes of "psychoanalytic vocabulary (which, I believe, only those who practice psychoanalysis can use—only those, that is, for whom analysis is a risk, an extreme danger, a daily test—for otherwise it is only the convenient language of an established culture)."[28] In heeding his warning, we will only fall back on other convenient languages of established culture, or take recourse to the nonreferential metaphors that attempt to write of the disaster, such as Bachmann's image of the "crack" or "Riß."

Bachmann's perhaps best-known line—"Keine neue Welt ohne neue Sprache"—dates from the same period as her Frankfurt lectures. It marks the recognition of the "er" in "Das dreißigste Jahr" of the boundaries of thought and knowledge, a traumatic and sudden realization that is reached, notably, in the suggestive space of the Viennese National Library. There, where "er" has access to the accumulated works of "die Weißen" (read the heritage of Western Civilization), he reaches the limits of knowledge—

---

28. Blanchot, *Writing,* 67.

a knowledge that is paradoxically and tautologically limited by the accumulated knowledge in that space. Bachmann, for whom this "er" is a masculine mask, identifies (in the Frankfurt Lectures) with Hofmannsthal's Lord Chandos, accepting his language crisis as her own while, at the same time, implying that only a fundamental psychological crisis of this sort can give rise to a "neue Sprache." For, as she insists, ". . . die wirklich großen Leistungen . . . , die eine neue Literatur sichtbar gemacht haben, sind nicht entstanden, weil Stile durchexperimentiert werden wollten, weil man sich bald so, bald so auszudrücken versuchte, weil man modern sein wollte, sondern immer dort, wo vor jeder Erkenntnis ein neues Denken wie ein Sprengstoff den Anstoß gab—wo, vor jeder formulierbaren Moral, ein moralischer Trieb groß genug war, eine neue sittliche Möglichkeit zu begreifen und zu entwerfen" (*Werke*, 4:191).

"Sprengstoff," elsewhere referred to as "erkenntnishafter Ruck" (*Werke*, 4:192): this is the language of her revolution, and the demand and desire for a new language suggests, at first glance, a promise of revolution that would overthrow existing (linguistic) systems, would separate word from word, world from world. But just as "er" desires but does not believe in "[d]ie Kündigung der Geschichte, nicht zugunsten der Anarchie, sondern zugunsten einer Neugründung" (*Werke*, 2:132), he also comprehends the impossibility of overturning language, knowing of "das Fortbestehen der Worte" (132). Thus, the call for a new language to create a new world is at once utopian and paradoxical, just as the symbolic rupture of the thirtieth year denies the *Trauerarbeit* of Bachmann's enterprise, a work of mourning that is her work. She herself senses the paradox between this desire for rupture (interruption, discontinuity) and that rupture's ultimate threat— the uncrossable abyss formed by loss of memory, by denial of past. She articulates the paradox in what she identifies as her last poem, "Böhmen liegt am Meer," which writes a utopian image that displaces place to accommodate the person, moving the imaginary (the Imaginary) realm of *Böhmen* so that it merges with the imaginary realm of the sea.

> Sind hierorts Häuser grün, tret ich noch in ein Haus.
> Sind hier die Brücken heil, geh ich auf gutem Grund.
> Ist Liebesmüh in alle Zeit verloren, verlier ich sie hier gern.
>
> Bin ich's nicht, ist es einer, der ist so gut wie ich.
>
> Grenzt hier ein Wort an mich, so laß ich's grenzen.
> Liegt Böhmen noch am Meer, glaub ich den Meeren wieder.
> Und glaub ich noch ans Meer, so hoffe ich auf Land.

Bin ich's, so ist's ein jeder, der ist soviel wie ich.
Ich will nichts mehr für mich. Ich will zugrunde gehn.

Zugrund—das heißt zum Meer, dort find ich Böhmen wieder.
Zugrund gerichtet, wach ich ruhig auf.
Von Grund auf weiß ich jetzt, und ich bin unverloren.

. . . .

Ich grenz noch an ein Wort und an ein andres Land,
ich grenz, wie wenig auch, an alles immer mehr,
ein Böhme, ein Vagrant, der nichts hat, der nichts hält,
begabt nur noch, vom Meer, das strittig ist, Land meiner
    Wahl zu sehen.

(*Werke,* 1:167–68)

This poem, together with "Prag Jänner 1964," was written in the same
year as "Ein Ort für Zufälle"—"Keine Delikatessen" most probably a
year earlier—but all during the time Bachmann spent in Berlin. The
configuration that emerges when we view all these works together reminds
us, once again, of the temporal telescoping I have discussed. In the speech
about Berlin, there is no "ich" that speaks: the "es" overwhelms any
subject with its *Zufall.* In the two poems, however, the "ich" speaks
directly—in "Prag Jänner 1964," the "ich" speaks "böhmisch": "Seit
jener Nacht / gehe und spreche ich wieder, / böhmisch klingt es, / als wär
ich wieder zuhause, // wo zwischen der Moldau, der Donau / und meinem
Kindheitsfluß alles einen Begriff von mir hat" (*Werke,* 1:169). The retrieval
of childhood, of the mother, of the mother tongue, of *zuhause,* in short, of
Böhmen, stands here in direct contrast to the reminder of that childhood's
demise still present in Berlin. In that place, where no one has "einen
Begriff" of this "Ortsfremder," the connection between land and sea is
defeated by *Riß.* In her nightmare vision of the *Trümmerhaufen* that affords
a different view of *Geschichte* ("Die Geschäfte sind . . . geschichtet zu einem
Haufen"), Bachmann describes the loss of connection that forced forgetfulness of disaster imposes.

Die Geschäfte sind übereinandergelegt, geschichtet zu einem Haufen,
die Schuhe und Zollstöcke, etwas von dem Reis und dem Kartoffelvorrat
und Kohlen natürlich. . . . Die großen Schaufenster, obenauf die mit dem
Geheimnamen *Neckermann* and *Defaka,* sind als Glasdächer über allem,
man sieht durch, kann aber nur wenig erkennen. . . . Die Spree und der
Teltower Kanal sind schon vollgelaufen mit Korn, die Havel schäumt

bis obenhin vom Bier, niemand kann mehr deutlich reden unter dem
vielen aufgeschichteten Glas; alles, was gesagt wird, läuft zu den Mundwinkeln hinaus, fast unverständlich, es will auch niemand mehr reden,
nur noch so etwas sagen, an den Mundwinkeln läuft sowieso alles weg,
alles doppelt. Dann läuft es auch aus Augen heraus, es ist fast nichts
mehr zu sehen.

So still ist's geworden und Nacht. Seit damals war niemand mehr
auf der Straße. Versandet und verwachsen sind die alten Villen, sinken
immer tiefer ein in den Gärten. Am Knie der Königsallee fallen,
jetzt ganz gedämpft, die Schüsse auf Rathenau. In Plötzensee wird
gehenkt. In der Telephonzelle rollen die Pfennigstücke—alle umsonst
eingeworfen—unten wieder heraus. Es kommt keine Verbindung
zustande. (*Werke,* 4:287–88)

No connection can be made when Liebknecht's and Luxemburg's corpses
lie buried under glass in the Spree and the Teltow Canal, when the shots
that killed Walter Rathenau can still be heard, when the executions are
still going on at Plötzensee prison. Dialogue is impossible when that which
is said runs from the corners of the mouth, always double. We cannot
speak, we can only *say*, Bachmann tells us. We cannot tell a story when
history usurps all tenses and rhetorical figures.

In lieu of the dialogue, the *Verbindung,* that cannot be established, Bachmann attempts to say something. But saying does not tell—the disaster
cannot be written, it can only de-scribe—and the mouth remains closed
while the words run, double, from its corners, the focus blurs with double
vision, and "ich" is displaced by the "es" at the risk of becoming "ver-
rückt," of pitching the world at a forty-five-degree angle on which all points
of reference slip into each other in a giant heap of nonsignificance. "Wegen
der Politik," Bachmann writes, "heben sich die Straßen um fünfundvierzig
Grad, die Autos rollen zurück, die Radfahrer und Fußgänger wirbeln
zurück zu beiden Seiten der Straße, man kann nicht hindern, daß die
Autos Schaden anrichten. Die Fußgänger verfangen sich, halten ihr Gebiß
zusammen, sie sprechen nicht, aber sie schauen, mit den Händen fest
über dem Mund, schauen aus nach einem Halt" (*Werke,* 4:285).

Like Benjamin's angel, the speaking subject of Bachmann's narrative
sees only this *Trümmerhaufen.* That subject "möchte wohl verweilen, die
Toten wecken und das Zerschlagene zusammenfügen,"[29] but it succeeds

---

29. Benjamin, "Über den Begriff," 697.

in this only to the extent that it pauses to wake its own dead and repair what has been destroyed in a poetic signifying process to which inhabitants of the world of *Fortschritt* have no access. If there is no communication between this speaking subject and its audience, it is because the audience denies *Riß* and continues to believe in *Teilung*.

Breaking the Code of Fictional Biography: Wolfgang Hildesheimer's *Marbot*

Dorrit Cohn

In 1982, the *London Review of Books* featured a lengthy review by British Germanist J. P. Stern of a new work by Wolfgang Hildesheimer that tells the life of one Andrew Marbot, an unduly forgotten aesthetician and art critic of the younger generation of English Romantics who is presumed to have committed suicide in 1830, at the tender age of 29.[1] A later issue of the same journal published a letter to the editor that begins like this:

> Sir: to my dismay, I find that the reviewer of my latest book, *Marbot,* has missed the point of the book: namely the fact that the hero of this biography has never existed. He is purely fictitious. . . . The quotations from his writings, his letters, the letters from Lady Catherine, his diaries etc. are *my own.*

After further stressing his paternity of this impressive brainchild, Hildesheimer adds: "In my view, it speaks for the book that the reviewer has taken Marbot's existence for granted." To which the editor of the *London Review* appended the following reply: "It speaks for the reviewer that the author of the book should take for granted an assumption, on the reviewer's part, of Marbot's existence."[2]

Clearly an uncommon reception-historical instance: a reviewer pretends to be caught in an author's game only to find that he has caught the author in his own game. This singular imbroglio begins to suggest the uncommon nature of the work in question: the life story of an imaginary person presented

---

1. *London Review of Books,* August 5–18, 1982.
2. *London Review of Books,* September 16–October 6, 1982.

in the guise of a historical biography, a guise that the author evidently intended to be recognized and admired for what it is: a masterful *disguise*.

This disguise sports all the historiographic trappings of the biographer's craft: both the book cover and the title page are adorned with a portrait labeled "Sir Andrew Marbot (1827)," reproduced from a lithograph by Delacroix; the final pages consist of a carefully annotated *index nomini;* an inserted gallery contains paintings of family members (including one of Marbot's mother, the lovely Lady Catherine, by Sir Henry Raeburn), photographs of the family's manor houses, and portraits of friends, acquaintances, and mistresses (the former include de Quincy, Byron, and Leopardi, the latter Goethe's daughter-in-law Ottilie and Byron's one-time mistress Teresa Guiccioli). This pseudoauthentic iconographic documentation matches and sustains the textual documentation, a veritably luxuriant paper trail manufactured to interweave Marbot's life with the lives of his contemporaries: eyewitness accounts of meetings with the young Englishman are cited from such real historical texts as Henry Crabbe Robinson's and Schopenhauer's correspondence, Berlioz's and Delacroix's diaries, not to forget Goethe's *Gespräche mit Eckermann*. Conversely, autobiographical sources describe encounters with these and such other illustrious figures as Blake, August von Platen, Corot, and Turner. But these sources also contain documentation of a rather more intimate nature; notably tell-tale evidence, blacked out in a manuscript notebook but recently deciphered with the aid of quartz lamps, of Marbot's incestuous relationship with his mother. It is this discovery that has induced the biographer to write Marbot's life, since it alone can explain the originality of his works, notably his astonishingly proto-Freudian insights into the deep psychological roots of artistic creativity.

A few gullible early reviewers aside, critics quickly saw through Hildesheimer's mock-historiographic travesty. But the elaborateness of his performance had the effect of orienting its reception far more to the matter than to the manner of his generic trompe l'oeil. It was, in other words, reviewed in the manner *real* biographies are usually reviewed. For Stern, this approach was obviously dictated by his reviewing spoof. But other critics, too, have been most preoccupied by such issues as the accuracy of the historical data, the validity and originality of Marbot's aesthetic theory and art-critical practice, and, of course, the anomaly of his erotic life: the psychoscandal of an incest perpetuated (unlike its classical prototype) by a mother and son *en toute connaissance de cause*.[3]

---

3. Hildesheimer's historical data were checked by (among others) Peter Wapnewski in

Granting the interest of these historical and thematic questions, for me the true originality of *Marbot* lies less in its matter than in its manner, more precisely, in the way its matter relates to its manner. In my formalistic perspective, its distinction lies in the fact that it creates the life of a wholly imaginary character by way of the standardized discourse of historical biography.[4] In this respect *Marbot*—despite its conventional appearance—represents a generic anomaly, a one-of-a-kind experiment in fictional form that deviates from the entire novelistic tradition as we know it, including the tradition of the historical novel. That Hildesheimer himself thought of *Marbot* in these terms is confirmed by his cryptic announcement—in an interview two years prior to publication—that his work in progress would create a new literary species: "Es gehört einer Kategorie an, die es noch nicht gibt."[5]

Before I try to substantiate these large claims (Hildesheimer's and my own), I will enlarge them even further, in terms of the double meaning of my title. For even as I understand *Marbot* as a work that breaks the code of fictional biography, in the sense of departing from the norms that rule the genre, I also understand it as a work that can induce the reader to break this generic code, in the sense now of deciphering the way it functions.

To put it most directly, *Marbot* breaks the code—in both senses of the phrase—by excluding all the signal devices we have come to expect from fictional works. In this respect, Hildesheimer's work can be said to define the third-person novel by what it is not, by conspicuously excluding its distinctive features. This severe abstinence may be taken as both the

---

Der Spiegel, January 4, 1982, 109–12. For the most knowledgeable discussion of Marbot's aesthetics, see Ulrich Weisstein, "Wolfgang Hildesheimer's *Marbot:* Fictional Biography and Treatise on Comparative Literature," *Yearbook of Comparative and General Literature* 32 (1983): 23–38. Marbot's psychopathology is central to Hans-Joachim Beck, *Der Selbstmord als eine schöne Kunst begangen: Prolegomena zu Wolfgang Hildesheimers psychoanalytischem Roman* Marbot: Eine Biographie (Frankfurt am Main: Peter Lang, 1986); this monograph attempts a tracing of all the intertextual lines that connect Marbot's psyche to the various myths and archetypes of Western culture (more often than not by way of overinterpretations and tenuous analogies).

4. In this respect, my focus in this essay overlaps with Käte Hamburger, "Marbot—Eine Biographie," in *Romanistik Integrativ: Festschrift für Wolfgang Pollak,* ed. Wolfgang Bandhauer and Robert Tanzmeister (Vienna: Braumüller, 1985), 195–204. In this study—of which I was not aware until after I had completed my own—the author briefly applies to *Marbot* some of the basic generic criteria developed in *Die Logik der Dichtung,* Zweite, stark veränderte Auflage (Stuttgart: Ernst Klett Verlag, 1968), a work that has influenced my own thinking in such fundamental ways (acknowledged elsewhere) that the coincidence in this instance is far from coincidental.

5. "Gespräch mit Wolfgang Hildesheimer," *Deutsche Bücher* 9 (1979): 190.

necessary and the sufficient condition that enables Hildesheimer to create his "Kategorie, die es noch nicht gibt." Any slippage on his part into specifically fictional narrative discourse would have derailed his experiment, making *Marbot* into just another historical novel, remarkable only for its fancy presentation.

Hildesheimer's vigilance concerns, first and foremost, his epistemological credibility. He allows himself to include only biographical data for which he can plausibly claim documented knowledge. Marbot's physical appearance, his public bearing, even what he said to whom can be known quite readily from the fake entries quoted from real memoirs and letters. His intellectual portrait can be credibly drawn on the basis of quotations from his notebooks and correspondence. But Hildesheimer will allow his biographer no scenes of a kind that escape the gossip of witnesses or that would not or could not have been recorded by his subject himself. This applies, above all, to the two climactic moments of Marbot's life: his overstepping of the incest barrier and his—probable, never certified—suicide.

But the strictest prohibition enabling Hildesheimer's game is his pretended ignorance of Marbot's psyche. Lacking what he calls "Schlüssel zum inneren Erleben,"[6] his biographer refuses to force his way in by illegitimate—read fictional—means. This does not, however, prevent him from trying to penetrate Marbot's mind in the manner of modern psychobiographers: as a psychoanalytically trained observer who uses every shred of available evidence to build depth-psychological hypotheses. But these interpretations are insistently cautious, self-critically disabused, as befits a sophisticated psychobiographer in our age of suspicion. His psycholoquacious discourse is dotted with ignorance-asserting phrases: "wir wissen es nicht," "es bleibt ungewiss," "wir werden nie wissen, ob . . ." He modalizes almost every psychological interpretation: "so scheint es," "vieles spricht dafür," "ich bin nicht sicher, ob . . . " Many passages consist of a flurry of unanswered questions. Here is a typical instance concerning Marbot's possible relations with women (after circumstances force him to leave his mother-mistress and his homeland).

In seinen Aufzeichnungen findet sich . . . die verräterische Notiz, von der wir aber nicht wissen, was sie verrät: "He whose innocence is raped

---

6. Wolfgang Hildesheimer, *Marbot: Eine Biographie* (Frankfurt am Main: Suhrkamp, 1981), 156. Subsequent references to this work will appear parenthetically in the text.

by an angel loses by every novel experience." . . . Hat er daher auf die "neue Erfahrung" lieber verzichtet, um das wunderbare Bild des Engels nicht auszulöschen? Oder hat er den Verlust in Kauf genommen, im Versuch dieses Bild endgültig aus seiner Seele zu bannen? Wahrscheinlich doch das letztere, denn er hätte kaum von der Erfahrung gesprochen, hätte er sie nicht gemacht. Oder handelt es sich um eine Selbstwarnung? Wir wissen es nicht. (*Marbot*, 100)

The biographer's nescience is peculiarly in evidence as he approaches the *scène à faire*, the mutual seduction of mother and son. Distancing and modalizing phrases begin to multiply, leading eventually to a brief paragraph that opens with a promising "Ich stelle mir vor" (*Marbot*, 74)—a phrase that, ever since Max Frisch's *Gantenbein*, has come to function as a metanarrative topos for introducing an imaginary scene. But *what* he imagines remains singularly flat, almost clinically depersonalized. It concludes with the words: "wer wen ins Schlafzimmer zieht, ist ungewiss, das Unerhörte nimmt seinen Lauf—" (75). Inevitably the manner in which this scene is—or is not—told has drawn the attention of critics otherwise quite unconcerned with matters of narrative form; but only to voice their puzzled disappointment. Hanjo Kesting comments: "Völlig rätselhaft erscheint mir die Zurückhaltung, die er sich bei der Darstellung der erotischen Extremsituation auferlegt. . . . Kann man umständlicher, unerotischer erzählen?"[7] And Helmut Heissenbüttel: "selten habe ich ein so schwerwiegendes libidinöses, erotisches Ereignis so unerotisch beschrieben, umschrieben gefunden."[8] These comments betray the degree to which these critics have missed the crux of Hildesheimer's venture: the fact that it is wholly dependent on this self-imposed "Zurückhaltung," on inhibiting the narrative voice from telling Marbot's erotic experience—erotically.

We might remember in this connection what Henry James once, in an uncharacteristically libidinal image, described as the novelist's true achievement: "the intensity of the creative effort to get into the skin of the creature; the act of personal possession of one being by another at its completest."[9] Marbot's narrator could not allow himself to penetrate "into

---

7. Hanjo Kesting, *Dichter ohne Vaterland: Gespräche und Aufsätze zur Literatur* (Berlin: Dietz Nachfolger, 1982), 79.

8. Helmut Heissenbüttel, "Die Puppe in der Puppe oder Der Hildesheimer im Marbot," *Süddeutsche Zeitung*, November 21–22, 1981.

9. Henry James, *The Art of the Novel: Critical Prefaces* (New York: Charles Scribner's Sons, 1962), 37.

the skin of the creature," least of all at this supremely transgressive moment, without transgressing the biographer's norms. Such penetration would have been tantamount to admitting, precisely, that Marbot *is* his creature. In this sense, the fake biographer's failure to successfully "imagine" the bedroom scene spells the success of the real author's fictional experiment.

By now my insistence on the Marbot narrator's antiomniscient stance must have brought into view what I see as the deep chasm that separates the biographer's enterprise from the novelist's. To deepen this perspective still further, imagine for a moment the unimaginable: what the fictional lives of memorable characters would be like if their authors had treated them in the manner Hildesheimer treats Marbot: the lives, say, of Stephen Dedalus, Raskolnikov, Isabel Archer, Emma Bovary, or Aschenbach. Without episodes packed with their gestures and words, without moments of lonely self-communion minutely tracing spiritual and emotional conflicts, these characters would no doubt never have come to life or become engraved in our reading memories.

Among the memorable characters just mentioned, Aschenbach is an especially illuminating counterexample to Marbot, since his narrator does, at one point, take on the pose of a historical biographer (in the extended flashback that follows the opening scene, summarizing the life of the protagonist up to the moment when we first encountered him). The narrator's discourse in this section is quite comparable to that of Marbot's biographer: he analyzes, evaluates, and speculates on Aschenbach's works and ways, limiting himself strictly to what he may have learned from witnesses and inferred from documents, including Aschenbach's own writings; in short, he tells us only what a biographer can plausibly know about his subject. But this distanced account—confined to a single expository section— contrasts sharply with what precedes and follows. Had this biographical discourse continued throughout *Tod in Venedig,* we would carry a very different image of its protagonist in our reading memory: no prophetic jungle vision with crouching tiger, no magic transfiguration of time and space, no erotic ecstasy and shame, no Platonic meditation on the Lido beach, no Dionysian dream, no famous last thoughts. In sum, no *Tod in Venedig* if Mann had renounced the novelist's privilege of making his protagonist's mind transparent to his reader's eyes.

In all but its flashback section, then, Mann's novella follows the code of fiction cast in third-person form, more specifically, the focalization on and by a single character that gives its distinctive stamp to fictional biographies. The stability of this code is readily checked by running through

Matrix 1. Types of Life-Stories

Protagonist / Discourse	Historical	Fictional
Historical	Historical biography *Mozart*	Historicized fictional biography *Marbot*
Fictional	Fictional historical biography *Lenz*	Fictional biography *Tod in Venedig*

one's mind all the works of this type one knows—including those that center on the lives of actual, historical persons. In some instances, this biographical form of historical fiction features daring experiments in the presentation of the inner life. Büchner presents Lenz's bout with insanity by way of a pioneering venture in focalized narration; Mann condenses Schiller's life into a single *Schwere Stunde* of solitary meditation and treats us to an interior monologue of Goethe in person as he awakens from sleep in the seventh chapter of *Lotte in Weimar;* and Broch's *Tod des Vergil* may well be the most sustained exercise in free, indirect style in world literature. A few notches lower on the quality scale, we find the multitude of formally less ambitious best-sellers that grant us voyeuristic intimacy with the minds of heroes and geniuses—perhaps on the eve of a great battle or in the throes of creating a great work of art (as in Stefan Zweig's *Sternstunden der Menschheit*).

It now becomes clear that, in respect to the relationship between its matter and its manner, *Marbot* is the exact inversion of the type of fictional biography exemplified by *Lenz* and *Der Tod des Vergil*. In these works, distinctively fictional discourse narrates the life of a historical figure. In *Marbot,* in contrast, distinctively nonfictional (historiographic) discourse narrates the life of a fictional figure. To reflect this inversion, we might call the *Lenz* type fictionalized historical biography, the *Marbot* type historicized fictional biography (at least until someone proposes more elegant generic tags).

The relationship of *Marbot* to its three typological counterparts can be diagrammed as shown in matrix 1.

But valid as this schema may be on theoretical grounds, it is invalid on empirical grounds. Its symmetry obscures the fact that *Marbot* is—to date, to my knowledge—the lone inhabitant of its box, whereas the three other boxes are thickly populated. And it is this textual population that has inscribed in our reading minds the codes by which we read, activating different expectations according to whether we read (or think we read) fiction or history, fictional or historical lives.

Now I will not go so far as to claim that we had to wait for *Marbot* to decipher the generic code of fictional biography. The idea that free access to the minds of its characters is the distinctive feature of the novel has been around at least since the eighteenth century, when it was proposed by one of the earliest theorists of the genre, Friedrich von Blanckenburg. More recently (some thirty years ago) another German theorist, Käte Hamburger, placed this distinctiveness of fictional discourse at the vital center of a newly designed generic system in her *Logik der Dichtung.* If I nonetheless feel that *Marbot* has a heuristic role to play, it is because so many contemporary theorists of fiction have closed their eyes to the essential difference between factual and fictional narrative that *Marbot* brings into view. To cite a typical statement by one of these (in this respect) purblind theorists, the distinguished philosopher of language John Searle: "There is no textual property, syntactical or semantic, that will identify a text as a work of fiction."[10] To illustrate his dictum, Searle quotes the beginning sentence of a novel by Iris Murdoch.

> Ten more glorious days without horses! So thought Second Lieutenant Andrew Chase-White recently commissioned in the distinguished regiment of King Edwards Horse, as he pottered contentedly in a garden on the outskirts of Dublin on a sunny Sunday afternoon in April nineteen-sixteen.[11]

Searle tells us that he picked this example at random, and I am inclined to believe him. He could hardly have picked a novel opening that disproved his case more effectively, one that signaled its fictionality more emphatically: can one imagine a nonfictional work, say a biography, that sets out by quoting what a certain person thought (or, for that matter, by telling how he felt or what he did alone in his garden on a certain Sunday afternoon)?

---

10. John Searle, "The Logical Status of Fictional Discourse," *New Literary History* 6 (1975): 325. In fairness to Searle, I should make clear that this article is at pains "to explore the differences between fictional and serious utterances" (321) from a speech-actional perspective; it concludes, however, that these differences lie solely "in the illocutionary intentions of the author" (325) and leave no mark whatever on his discourse. An analogous view is taken by Barbara Herrnstein Smith in *On the Margins of Fictional Discourse* (Chicago: University of Chicago Press, 1978); see especially 29–31, where the author maintains specifically that third-person novels and biographies are look-alikes.

11. Cited in Searle, "Logical Status," 322.

Clearly, even if the cover page of this work—announcing a novel entitled *The Red and the Green*—were missing, we would still know that Second Lieutenant Andrew Chase-White must be a fictional character, for the simple reason that no real person can be known by a real speaker in the way this lieutenant is known by this speaker.

Searle's blind spot in respect to this passage—his missing the characteristically fictional omniscience of its narrator's discourse—is the obverse of the blind spot I noticed earlier in the critics of *Marbot,* who fail to recognize its narrator's pseudohistoriographic nescience as an essential strategem for breaking the generic code. Which perhaps goes to show, after all, that exceptions prove the rule only for readers already apprised of the rule.

I now pass on to another problem that opens to a somewhat less clearly encoded aspect of the generic code. It concerns the narrator—or, better, the reader's image of the narrator. Do we (and are we meant to) understand this biographer's voice as the author's own, or do we (and are we meant to) attribute it to a fictional person or persona of sorts?

We must note, first of all, that if *Marbot* were a real biography, this question would not arise. As in all nonfictional forms of discourse—not only historiographic narratives, but also philosophical treatises, cookbooks, travel guides, program notes, and so forth—the ideas and judgments expressed in a historical biography are unquestioningly attributed to the author whose name appears on the title page. The fact that he or she stands behind the work as its signatory instructs the reader to assume that he or she stands behind the views textually expressed.

There is at least one class of fiction where this is clearly not the case: novels and stories cast in first-person form. The way we recognize such a work—even when it does not announce its fictional status by way of a subtitle—is by the fact that its narrator bears a different name than its author. This is also the only way we can distinguish fictional from historical autobiographies on textual grounds, Thomas Mann's *Bekenntnisse des Hochstaplers Felix Krull,* say, from Rousseau's *Confessions.* And we are no more entitled to attribute Krull's opinions to Mann than those of any of his characters in third-person novels. Had Hildesheimer chosen to cast Marbot as the teller of his own life—perhaps under the title "Bekenntnisse eines romantischen Oedipus"—the problem of vocal attribution would not have arisen. Nor would the generic ambiguity: Marbot's life story would instantly have been recognized as a fiction; unless, of course, Hildesheimer had reverted to the early eighteenth-century practice of leaving his own name off the title page.

A distance—or at least a clearly marked distinction—between author and narrator would also have been created if Marbot's life had been told in the manner known from a number of historical biographies, for example, Boswell's *Life of Johnson*. These witness biographies, as they might be called, have their fictional counterparts in such novels as Conrad's *Heart of Darkness,* Grass's *Katz und Maus,* or Mann's *Doktor Faustus.* As the subtitle of the latter—*Das Leben des deutschen Tonsetzers Adrian Leverkühn, erzählt von einem Freunde*—clearly indicates, fictional biographies of this type are told by embodied narrators who have known their biographed subjects personally, in the only manner a human being can know another in real life: purely by his manifest behavior and without privileged inside views. Structurally, a fictional biography of this type therefore differs from its historical counterparts only in one essential respect: its narrator is (like Mann's Zeitblom) a named character, no less fictional than his biographed hero and, thus, ontologically set apart from the author who has created them both.

This clear fictionalization of his biographer, and the disengagement from the authorial self it entails, is a model Hildesheimer evidently chose *not* to follow in *Marbot.* That this was a deliberate choice is indicated in a prepublication interview. Referring to a conversation about his work in progress with his friend and fellow writer Walter Jens, he quotes the latter as saying: "da mußt du natürlich zwei Ebenen haben, die der beschriebenen Figur und die des Icherzählers, so daß eine Kontrastwirkung entsteht." Whereupon Hildesheimer comments: "Das wird mir schon wieder zu sehr Fiktion."[12] What he did intend—as he further explains in a postpublication essay significantly entitled "Arbeitsprotokolle des Verfahrens *Marbot*"—was to create the impression that he spoke throughout as himself, a process he calls at one point "meine Identifikationsakt mit dem Biographen," at another "meine individuelle Erzählerrolle des Ich."[13] What he does *not* say (but surely also intended) is that this voice would be recognized as his own by extratextual evidence that lay close at hand: his best-selling *Mozart* biography, published only four years before *Marbot* and similarly punctuated by a rash of "Wir wissen es nicht" applied to the psyche of the protagonist.[14] Hildesheimer could thus count on many of his readers

---

12. "Gespräch mit Hildesheimer," 189.

13. Wolfgang Hildesheimer, "Arbeitsprotokolle des Verfahrens *Marbot*," *Jahrbuch der deutschen Akademie für Sprache und Dichtung,* 1982, 27.

14. The biographer's inability to penetrate the consciousness of his subject is explicitly

perceiving the intertextual emulation of his own biographical stance in the earlier work, understanding that, as the biographer of Marbot, he was, so to speak, posing as himself. In this respect, the choice of his hero's name—nearly an anagram of Mozart's—was surely meant as an *avis au lecteur*. But more important, the self-pastiche is underlined by the Marbot biographer's almost verbatim repetition of the Mozart biographer's didactic comments on his craft in such adages as the following.

> Ich habe niemals die Ansicht vertreten, daß der Biograph vor dem Schlafzimmer haltzumachen habe, da das erotische Leben seines Helden zu ihm gehört und wesentlich—wenn nicht gar den wesentlichsten—Aufschluß vermittelt. (*Marbot*, 152)

> ...es ist der Welt immer schwer geworden, mit ihren Skandalen zu leben, daher ist es der Geschichte und Kulturgeschichte immer wieder gelungen, die Anomalien ihrer Helden und Opfer zu verdrängen. ... Auch die Biographie ist durchsetzt von diesen furchtbaren Vereinfachern, die schiefe und daher falsche Bilder entwerfen oder dafür sorgen, daß sie sich potenziert fortzeugen. (155–56)

What Hildesheimer, as he himself admitted, failed to foresee is that the readers' reception of such normative language is willy-nilly affected when it is transplanted to newly fictional surroundings. "Einige meiner Freunde," he tells us in "Arbeitsprotokolle," "haben . . . diese oder jene Passage, die ich als mein eigenes Ich durchaus ernst gemeint habe, für die Sprache eines ein wenig hochtrabenden, nicht uneitlen und ein wenig pedantischen Anderen gehalten. In diesen Passagen scheine ich also versagt zu haben. Ich war darauf bedacht, mein eigenes Ich als Objekt immer kontrollieren zu können, aber anscheinend wird es öfter ein anderer, als ich vorhatte." And he notes with particular distress that the comparison of *Marbot* with *Doktor Faustus*—which he himself encourages on other grounds—was applied to the neuralgic matter of his narrator. "Manch einer fühlte sich sogar hier und dort an Serenus Zeitblom gemahnt. Dieser Gedanke wäre mir niemals gekommen. Ich wollte ja keinen Roman schreiben, in dem auch die Rahmenfigur eine Fiktion ist."[15]

---

underlined throughout *Mozart* (Frankfurt am Main: Suhrkamp, 1977). See also Hildesheimer's remarks appended to *Mary Stuart: Eine historische Szene* (Frankfurt am Main: Suhrkamp, 1977): "Wie sah es in Mary Stuart aus? . . . Die Frage bleibt unbeantwortet, wie alle Fragen nach dem Innenleben einer historischen Figur" (76).

15. Hildesheimer, "Arbeitsprotokolle," 27–28.

Hildesheimer's surprise at what he himself calls his "failure" in this regard—"scheine ich versagt zu haben"—is not itself surprising if we believe his repeated assertion that he is not nearly as versed in literary theory as in the aesthetics of music and art.[16] Those of us acquainted with recent theoretical perspectives on fictional narrators and their potential unreliability will readily understand that the readers to whom Hildesheimer refers quite legitimately took advantage of an option he gave them by the mere act of becoming the narrator of a fiction: the option to disengage this narrator from the author, opening a gap that casts an ironic (and in this case also self-parodic) light on his normative discourse. There is no way Hildesheimer could have guarded against this critical move on his readers' part, save one: to limit himself to purely narrative language, strictly excluding his prominent "didaktisches Ich,"[17] with its normative language.

We owe the distinction between the two types of language to which I have just referred—narrative (or mimetic) language and normative (or nonmimetic) language—to Félix Martínez-Bonati, a theorist who has given particular attention to the author/narrator differential in fiction and to its weighty impact on the reading process. According to Martínez-Bonati, any competent reader of fiction distinguishes, on the one hand, mimetic sentences that create the fictive world itself: its characters, events, spatial setting, and so forth, and, on the other hand, nonmimetic sentences, which create in the reader nothing more nor less than the image of the narrator's mind. Unlike mimetic language, which is objective and "as though transparent," nonmimetic language is subjective and opaque, which means that, whereas the reader accepts mimetic sentences unreservedly as statements of fictional truth, he or she receives nonmimetic sentences with the qualified credence one grants to the opinions of an individual speaker.[18] A sense of narratorial unreliability will therefore arise whenever a work features "a perceptible difference between the impression of events derived by the reader solely from the mimetic moments of the basic narrator's discourse, and the view of the same events in the nonmimetic components of the

---

16. See, for example, "The End of Fiction" (*Merkur* 30 [1976]: 59), where Hildesheimer states: "Ich hätte lieber über bildende Kunst und Musik gesprochen. Beide Disziplinen sind Gegenstand meiner Reflexion und Spekulation gewesen, Literatur nicht. Ich bin ein Schreiber und ein mässiger Leser, aber kein Theoretiker."

17. " . . . als Verfasser eines Buches über ihn [Marbot], [bin ich] ein sozusagen didaktisches Ich, das seine Biographie schreibt" (Hildesheimer, "Arbeitsprotokolle," 30).

18. See Félix Martínez-Bonati, *Fictive Discourse and the Structure of Literature: A Phenomenological Approach* (Ithaca: Cornell University Press, 1981), 32–39.

same discourse (that is, in the narrator's general judgments, commentaries, expressions of feelings, etc)."[19] On this basis, the potential for unreliability is not limited to narrators embodied in the fictional world, but extends to the disembodied narrators of third-person novels as well, whenever they interlace their narratives with their own opinions.

Before returning to *Marbot* with this theory in mind, one more qualification must be added. As Tamar Yacobi has noted, a work that contains textual incongruities of the kind described by Martínez-Bonati does not *compel* the reader to construct the image of a narrator whom he or she differentiates from the author. This "unreliability principle"—or, as she also calls it, "perspectival principle"—is not the only "principle of resolution" for which a reader can opt. Another is the "genetic principle." A reader who resorts to the perspectival principle holds the *narrator* responsible for textual infelicities and, thereby, disculpates the author. A reader who resorts to the genetic principle, in contrast, holds the *author* responsible, on the assumption that various inner or outer liabilities attending the composition of his or her work are to blame for its flaws.[20]

It is surely significant that Hildesheimer attributes the (mis-)understanding of his narrator as a somewhat ridiculous Zeitblom-like figure to *friendly* readers—"einige meiner Freunde." For I would maintain that it opens to a far more positive evaluation of his work, by way of a reading that refers all the weaknesses in the Marbot biographer's performance to a fallible narrator of the author's own making.[21] Resolved perspectivally, the flaws in the narrator's discourse can now work in the author's favor.[22]

One of these flaws—which I will mention merely in passing—is this

---

19. Martínez-Bonati, *Fictive Discourse*, 35.

20. Tamar Yacobi, "Fictional Reliability as a Communicative Problem," *Poetics Today* 2 (1981): 113–26; see esp. 119–21.

21. The only critic who clearly adopts this reading is Kesting (see *Dichter*, 79–80). In my view, however, his characterization of the *Marbot* narrator as "ein Biograph, den selber nicht betrifft, was er redlich beschreibt" pushes the perspectival reading to inaccurate extremes. Nor am I convinced by the psychological motivation he ascribes to the author for resorting to this device: "Hildesheimer . . . schiebt seinen Biographen vor, um sich Marbot, den gefährlichen verführerischen Helden vom Leibe zu halten." This diagnosis leads Kesting to an unwarranted overall denigration of *Marbot*: "Durch den erfundenen Biographen ist die fiktive Biographie am Ende doch zum Roman geworden. . . . Und so ist ein gross gedachtes Buch in der Ausführung kleiner geworden." In my perspective, outlined subsequently, both a different cause and a different effect is attributed to the author/narrator differential in *Marbot*.

22. For a perspectival reading that "salvages" a much greater work than *Marbot* in this manner, see Dorrit Cohn, "The Second Author of *Der Tod in Venedig*," in *Probleme der Moderne: Studien zur deutschen Literatur von Nietzsche bis Brecht*, ed. Benjamin Bennett, Anton Kaes, and William J. Lillyman (Tübingen: Max Niemeyer Verlag, 1983), 223–45.

psychobiographer's rather shaky mastery of psychoanalytic language (notably his misuse of such Freudian concepts as "Verdrängung" and "Sublimierung").[23] Far more central to the thematic structure of *Marbot* is the incongruity that attends the narrator's stated reason for writing his psychobiography in the first place—*Schlafzimmergeheimnisse* and all. His motivation, as he tells us more than once, is that Marbot's aesthetic writings—about to be published for the first time in an undoctored edition—cannot be fully understood without knowledge of their depth-psychological genesis.

> Gewiß stellt sich hier auch wieder die Frage, ob Marbots Bedeutung, sein Stellenwert in der Kulturgeschichte, Angabe und Kenntis der letzten intimen Einzelheiten seines Lebens rechtfertige. Es dürfte sich aber schon bisher ergeben haben, daß diese Frage zu bejahen ist, denn ohne Kenntnis dieser Einzelheiten wären—und waren!—Marbots Schriften einer Tiefendimension beraubt. (*Marbot*, 153)

> Mancher Leser mag sich fragen, warum ein solcher biographischer Aufriß . . . vor der Neuausgabe der Werke und Briefe seines Helden erscheine. Die Antwort dürfte verständlich und eindeutig sein: diesmal mußte unter allen Umständen vermieden werden, daß Werk und Briefe unter einer falschen Prämisse gelesen werden. . . . [D]ie eingestandene, mitunter leidenschaftliche Subjektivität des Textes . . . [wäre] ungenügend erklärt, würde nicht der Hinweis geliefert, wie er zu lesen sei. (317)

The reader who repeatedly encounters statements of this sort naturally expects that they will be sustained by the wide sampling of Marbot's own writings directly quoted by his biographer. This is, however, far from being the case: Marbot's pronouncements on the process of artistic creativity, no less than his original interpretations of specific art works, are penetrating and illuminating in themselves, and in no sense dependent on—or even enlightened by—knowledge of his pathological love life. Accordingly, the biographer, who doth protest too much, stands exposed as something of a self-promoting fop, who—in a manner known from some of his colleagues—

---

23. Both these terms are applied to desires and fears, of which Marbot is fully conscious: for *Verdrängung*, see *Marbot*, 32 and 306; for *Sublimierung*, 120 and 179. The psychoanalytic shortfall of *Marbot* has previously been noted by Alexander von Bormann ("Der Skandal einer perfekten Biographie: Über *Marbot: Eine Biographie*," *Text und Kritik* 89/90 [1986]: 69–82 [see esp. 78–80]). In contrast, Beck paraphrases the psychoanalytic discourse of *Marbot* quite uncritically (see Beck, *Selbstmord*, esp. 25–27).

overinflates the explanatory value of biographical data for understanding the products of a creative mind.

Two further sources cast ironic light on the Marbot biographer's self-inflating discourse. The first stems from Hildesheimer himself, who defended a diametrically opposite thesis concerning the power of biographical explanations in his *Mozart*. Here he demonstrates precisely the un-bridgeable abyss that separates the life from the work, arguing that there is radical discontinuity between the Mozart we know from biographical and autobiographical sources and the Mozart we know from his music.[24] In this respect, the intertextual relationship between *Mozart* and *Marbot* is clearly antithetical, and readers who attribute the didactic discourse of these two works to the same mind—as they are encouraged to do on other grounds—cannot help but conclude that this mind has reversed itself in the four-year interval.

But this would be to forget that this same mind also created the mind of Marbot, a mind (clearly fictional this time) that, in turn, is made to create an aesthetic theory. And Marbot's theory matches the Mozart biographer's far more closely than the one held by his own biographer. For even though Marbot insists (like Freud a century later) that every work of art originates in its creator's unconscious conflicts—"das Kunstwerk als Diktat der unbewußten Regungen seines Schöpfers" (*Marbot,* 15)—he emphasizes the insoluble mystery of this psychic origin with at least equal force: "Bilder erscheinen mir immer wie gerahmte Rätsel. . . . [I]ch glaube der Art des Rätsels auf der Spur zu sein, nämlich der Seele des Künstlers" (119). Beyond this general intuition, the enigma will allow for no answer. It has a way of thickening whenever Marbot tries to decipher it in a specific work. A Giorgione self-portrait that he probes with particular intensity returns his gaze with the words: "In Wirklichkeit wirst du nichts über mich erfahren, du kannst es nicht" (185). Finally, on the last page of the biography, the following quotation from Marbot's notebook is prominently displayed.

. . . die Frage nach dem größten Geheimnis beantwortet es [das Kunst-werk] niemandem, nämlich die nach jener seelischen Notwendigkeit, dem es seine Entstehung verdankt. Daher werden wir mit Gewissheit nichts von dem erfahren, was im Künstler vorgegangen ist, außer sei-

---

24. See Hildesheimer, *Mozart,* 15f. and passim.

nem Gebot, was in uns vorzugehen habe. Der Künstler spielt auf unserer Seele, aber wer spielt auf der Seele des Künstlers? (320)

Geheimnis, Rätsel: these are of course the very terms Freud himself—unlike some of his followers—invariably employs when he speaks of the origin of a work of art. In this regard, the proto-Freudian Marbot is much more in tune with the master's voice than his post-Freudian biographer.

What I am suggesting is that Hildesheimer has endowed his imaginary protagonist with far greater wisdom and subtlety than his biographer. If we took the author at his word and understood his narrator as a self-impersonation, we would be forced to conclude that he has created, for Marbot, a mind superior to his own.[25] This unlikelihood points up, in a backhanded way, that the narrator of a fictional biography is, on principle, distinct from its author: a deep-seated tenacious feature of the generic code that even the code-breaking author of *Marbot* was not able to break.

Finally, surfacing from the deep, a few words about the most obvious, but perhaps also the most vexatious, of Hildesheimer's code-breaking practices: the duplicit nature of his text's paratextual presentation, which simultaneously asserts and denies its fictional status (and its historical status). This problem will lead me, in conclusion, to consider the class of modernist literary experiments with which *Marbot* could rightfully be classed.

Did Hildesheimer want his readers to be caught in his game? Not if we judge from his protest against Stern's (as he mistakenly believed gullible) review, quoted at the beginning of this discussion. Nor if we believe another, even clearer, postpublication pronouncement: "wenn mancher Leser und mancher Kritiker auf meine Täuschung hereingefallen sind, kann ich nur versichern, daß dies nicht meine Schuld ist. Zwar wollte ich Marbot zum Leben erweckt haben, aber ich wollte niemanden hintergehen." But, right after saying this, he concedes "daß meine Demonstration des Fiktionscharakters vielleicht allzu versteckt und schwach war."[26] This "demonstration," he now explains, consisted of two paratextual items: a single

---

25. Martin Swales reaches precisely this paradoxical conclusion when, after demonstrating the cogency of Marbot's aesthetic theories as compared to his biographer's simplistic psychologisms, he suggests (tongue in cheek?) that we need to defend Marbot against his creator— "ihn gegen seinen Schöpfer in Schutz nehmen" (review of *Marbot, Arbitrium* 3 [1983]: 322). Swales also remarks on the fact that Marbot's writings, as quoted by his biographer, can easily dispense with the depth-psychological explications proposed by his biographer (321).

26. Hildesheimer, "Arbeitsprotokolle," 28.

phrase in the first sentence of the jacket copy that reads: "Sir Andrew Marbot, der Held dieser Biographie, ist in die Kulturgeschichte des frühen neunzehnten Jahrhunderts gleichsam eingewoben"; and the omission from his *index nomini* of all the Marbot family members' names. What Hildesheimer does *not* mention here (or in any other place) is another paratextual item that easily outweighs the discreet and less than decisive signals he mentions: the subtitle "Eine Biographie" featured on the inside title page. (not on the book cover). This is surely the factor most immediately responsible for the fact that some readers and even some early reviewers were misled.

Generic subtitles, as Gérard Genette explains in a study that deals with the various verbal thresholds surrounding and supporting the body of a text, tend to play a decisive role in the reception of literary works. Their status is official, in the sense that the reader is meant to understand them as a kind of contractual agreement on the author's part. It signals the author's intention or decision concerning the generic nature of his or her work, with a view to determining a certain horizon of expectation.[27] In light of this convention, the tag "Eine Biographie" on the title page of *Marbot* would have to be understood as a deception on the author's part. But there is, of course, an alternative way of understanding it, the only way one *can* understand it once one has become apprised—by whatever means—of the real state of affairs: that *Marbot* is a fictional and not a historical work. The label "Eine Biographie" must then be understood not as a generic subtitle that follows the main title, but as part and parcel of the main title itself, which reads correctly: *Marbot: Eine Biographie.* Its appropriate generic subtitle—"Roman"—has simply been omitted: subtitles are not, after all, obligatory, for novels or any other types of publications. Another way of conceptualizing the ambiguity attending Hildesheimer's title page would be to say that it overtly frames *Marbot* as a biography—with the term *framing* here used in Erving Goffman's sense of contextualizing—but that this overt frame is surrounded by another, covert frame that, once it is discovered, transforms this biography (including its title page) into a novel.[28]

---

27. See Gérard Genette, *Seuils* (Paris: Éditions du Seuil, 1987), 89–97.

28. The relevance of Goffman's *Frame Analysis* (New York: Harper and Row, 1974) for ambiguous title pages is proposed by Lennard J. Davis in *Factual Fictions: The Origins of the English Novel* (New York: Columbia University Press, 1983), 20ff. Davis applies it to eighteenth-century fictional autobiographies whose title pages more-or-less "duped" the reader into understanding the work as the life history of a real person.

I doubt that Hildesheimer set up this titular prestructure inadvertently. Clearly, the effect of the work depended on a complex, if not a perverse, manipulation of his readers: explicitly inviting them to believe in the historicity of *Marbot* at the outset and sustaining that belief by all the means at his disposal; but inviting them as well, by fainter signals, to suspect its *counterfeit* historicity. He seems, in effect, to have aimed for an ideal reader who, Janus-eyed, could alternately conceive Marbot as a real *and* an imaginary figure, on the analogy with the viewer of the rabbit-and-duck in Gombrich's iconic illustration of absolute ambiguity. Such a reader, needless to say, could not survive the move of checking Marbot out in the *Dictionary of National Biography*. Still, a hypothetically innocent reading would create a condition of hesitation between two dissimilar visions of the world: one that does and one that does not include Andrew Marbot. Such an "ontological flicker" is the reader reaction Brian McHale attributes to the postmodernist genre of "apocryphal history," a form of historical fiction that "contradicts the official version [of history] . . . [by] claiming to restore what has been lost or suppressed."[29] *Marbot* could be regarded as a biographical variant of this genre by dint of the new look the existence of its protagonist gives to the history of aesthetics as well as to the history of the romantic movement.

But, at the same time, its mock-biographical presentation also affiliates *Marbot* with another postmodern experimental trend: the writing of lives that play on (and with) the border of history and fiction. The most prominent breakdown of generic distinction has lately been occurring between historical and fictional *autobiography*. Here, a number of crossbreeds have appeared—under such tags as "Autofiction" (Serge Doubrovsky, *Fils*, 1977), "A Fictional Memoir" (Frederick Exley, *A Fan's Notes*), or simply "A Novel" (Ronald Sukenik, *Up*, 1969)—that adopt the contradictory practice of naming their fictional self-narrators after their authors, thereby effectively equivocating the distinction between fiction and nonfiction for self-narrated lives.[30] But to subvert the codes that separate fiction from history in telling lives of *others*, more subtle rules must be broken. Here, experimental transgression has proceeded unilaterally, by appropriating fictional devices (including even stream-of-consciousness techniques) to tell about the inner life of real persons—movie actresses, convicted murderers,

---

29. Brian McHale, *Postmodern Fiction* (New York and London: Methuen, 1987), 90.
30. See Jonathan Wilson, "Counterlives: On Autobiographical Fiction in the 1980s," *Literary Review* 31 (1988): 389–402.

astronauts, sports heroes—in works that bear appropriately oxymoronic subtitles: "True Life Novel," "Novel Biography," "Non-Fiction Novel," and the like.[31] *Marbot* is the only work to date that clearly reverses this direction. Whether others will follow remains to be seen. But there is reason to doubt that it will be (or was meant to be) a pacesetter. Unlike the experimental biographies just mentioned, it depends, as we have seen, not on permissive freedom but on forbidding constraint: renunciation of the imaginative omniscience traditionally granted to the creator of imaginary beings. For this reason, *Marbot* may well remain the sole specimen of its species.

---

31. For a discussion of this contemporary practice, see Ina Schabert, "Fictional Biography, Factual Biography, and Their Contaminations," *Biography* 5 (1982): 1-16; Tom Wolfe, "The New Journalism," in *The New Journalism,* ed. Tom Wolfe and E. W. Johnson (New York: Harper and Row, 1973), 1-52.

Language, Text, and History in Russell Hoban's *Riddley Walker*

Judith Ryan

> Hear the voice of the Bard!
> Who present, past and future sees;
> Whose ears have heard
> The Holy Word
> That walk'd among the ancient trees,
>
> Calling the lapsèd soul,
> And weeping in the evening dew;
> That might control
> The starry pole,
> And fallen, fallen light renew!
>
> —William Blake

Can the modern world be restored to its prelapsarian condition? What Blake invokes with such desperate passion may appear even more remote to the twentieth-century reader; but those of us who work with literature still cling, by and large, to the notion that the voice of the bard has restorative powers, if only in some attenuated or metaphorical sense. But what if our own enterprise is somehow implicated in the very evils from which we hope it will release us?

This is the question that Russell Hoban, best known as a singer of innocence, asks in his extraordinary song of experience, *Riddley Walker*.[1]

Epigraph from Blake's *Songs of Experience;* quoted from John Sampson, ed., *The Poetical Works of William Blake* (1914; reprint, London: Oxford University Press, 1958), 81.

1. Hoban is mainly known as a children's writer. His series of books about Frances the badger, including, e.g., *Bedtime for Frances* (1960), *Bread and Jam for Frances* (1964), *A Birthday for Frances* (1968), and his book *Mouse and His Child* (1967), among many others, have been extremely popular with the very young. His adult fiction includes *The Lion of Boaz-Jachin and Jachin-Boaz* (1973), *Kleinzeit* (1974), *Turtle Diary* (1975), *Pilgermann* (1983), and *The Medusa Frequency* (1987). *Riddley Walker* (New York: Washington Square Press, 1980) won the John W. Campbell Memorial Award for the best science fiction novel in 1981. Page citations in the text refer to this edition.

Set almost twenty-five hundred years after the nuclear holocaust that has yet to destroy the world as we know it, Hoban's novel is written in a form of English none of us has seen or heard. His bard, Riddley Walker, the narrator of the tale, creates his own spellings of the language he uses in a world where literacy has virtually disappeared. Riddley's English contains vestiges of present-day, relatively uneducated Southern British English, a dialect appropriate to the geographic area where the story takes place, the region around what we know today as Canterbury. Alongside such easily recognizable forms as "gone ter morrer here today" (9), "you never know where it begun" (8), or "it aint ben beartht [= born]" (7), Riddley's language contains frequent phonetic renderings of colloquial speech, numerous degenerated forms of modern English words, several adaptations of present-day computer terminology, and a few words that have no modern English equivalent that I can identify. Thus, Riddley writes: "I cant say for cern [certain] no more if I had any of them things in my mynd" (7) or "it wernt you put that spear in your han it wer that other thing whats looking out thru your eye hoals" (6). "Lonesome" becomes "oansome" and "remembrance" becomes "memberment." The title Archbishop of Canterbury lives on as the "Ardship of Cambry," but no one quite knows what the Ardship's function is; England, or what is left of it after the holocaust, is ruled by a Pry Mincer and a Wes Mincer; Folkstone has become "Fork Stoan" and Dover "Do it Over." The descendents of those who caused the nuclear accident gather together each year to "do some poasyum" and, although they have lost all knowledge of science, they are convinced, like many today who attend symposiums, that they are "talking vantsit theary" (107). An obscure mythology surrounds their recollection of the time before the holocaust: it involves the "Puter Leat" and the "Power Leat" [computer elite and power elite] and, most particularly, the "Eusa folk," whose name suggests that they were working for the USA.[2] As for words we have not yet heard of, the wonderful coinage "zanting" (dancing or prancing) is one of the best examples.

All these forms suggest that Hoban has a good understanding of how language develops. He is familiar with the phenomenon of metathesis ("girzel" for "grizzle,"[3] "parbly" for "probably," "girt" for "great," "ter-pitation" for "interpretation"). He knows about linguistic leveling, in which

---

2. Hoban himself, though now living in Britain, is an American (born in Pennsylvania in 1925).

3. Riddley Walker's contemporaries use the word *girzel* to mean drizzle.

irregular forms are assimilated to regular ones and multiple forms reduced to a few. He knows, above all, that, however much we may be convinced that our language is becoming increasingly sophisticated, it is also perceptibly degenerating. In Hoban's novel, the decline of language comes to stand for the decline of civilization and humanity's increasing remoteness from paradise regained.

In *Riddley Walker*, the rulers of England ["Inland"] aim to recover the scientific knowledge lost at the time of the nuclear holocaust and restore the technological glories of that former age, which, in the baby language that infuses their speech, they call "time back way back." Tales of a past civilization that produced television and spaceships are linked in their minds with power and progress. Not realizing that it was nuclear fission that caused the destruction of technology and the loss of technological knowledge, they itch to possess the secret of the bomb, which they call the "1 Big 1." Riddley asks the pertinent question about the 1 Big 1:

Thats going to move Inland frontways is it? Thats going to get us out of the mud? Thats going to get us boats in the air and picters on the wind? (143)

The novel tells of this attempt to "move frontways" by finding the recipe for nuclear power: it is a search that ends with the rediscovery of gunpowder ("the 1 Little 1") and is attended by an accidental explosion that presages in miniature the larger disaster that we can anticipate at the end of the book. The illusion of progress is thus revealed as regress, and this, in turn, is seen as part of a vicious circle in which humanity is doomed to repeat its earlier mistakes.

Although the characters do not recognize that they are engaged in this fateful repetition, the knowledge of the vicious circle is, in fact, enshrined in what most of Riddley's contemporaries think of as a children's game. Called "Fools Circel 9wys," the game, accompanied by a rhyme that has been passed down by oral tradition, closely resembles "Oranges and Lemons."[4] One child is chosen as the "Ardship of Cambry" and goes "roun

---

4. For the text of "Oranges and Lemons," see Iona Opie and Peter Opie, eds., *The Oxford Dictionary of Nursery Rhymes* (London: Oxford University Press, 1952), 337. The commentary (337–39) reminds us that the game includes a tug of war between the "oranges" and the "lemons" to see which is stronger (338); in this sense, the rhyme manifests the war imagery that underlies *Riddley Walker*. The motif of iron and steel in *Riddley Walker* may allude to another, related nursery rhyme, "London Bridge is Falling Down," the fifth stanza of which notes that "iron and steel may bend and break."

the circel til it come chopping time," at which point he has to try to break out of the circle. Riddley tells us how much he enjoyed the game when he was a child:

> I use to be good at that I all ways rathert be the Ardship nor 1 of the circel I liket the busting out part. (5)

And indeed, Riddley Walker's role in the book is essentially the one he played in the children's game, an attempt to break out of the vicious circle of history and its disastrous illusion of progress. Along with the hideously deformed youngster who is the actual descendent of the Archbishop of Canterbury at the time of the nuclear holocaust, Riddley becomes the adversary of the two most powerful figures in England, Goodparley and Orfing. While Goodparley and Orfing try to find the combinations that will give them access to nuclear power, Riddley and the Ardship engage in a desperate race to avert disaster.

If *Riddley Walker* reduces to a simple moral tale in this way, why does it require us to take so much trouble deciphering its imaginary future language? Is Riddley's strange-looking English more than an amusing narrative trick? In fact, the invented language does much more than draw attention to the problem of history as progress or regress: it points up the fact that reading of any kind is always also interpretation. Questions of hermeneutics lie at the heart of *Riddley Walker*. The novel asks us not only to move between the language we know and the language it uses, but also between texts we are familiar with and other texts it reproduces, some oral, some written.

Besides Riddley's phonetic rendering of contemporary speech, there are two other forms of English it presents. One is standard, modern English, the other is the language of the time immediately following the holocaust. The former is the text of the legend of St. Eustace from a brochure describing the wall paintings in Canterbury Cathedral;[5] the latter is a

---

5. In his acknowledgments, Hoban tells us that he visited Canterbury Cathedral for the first time in 1974 and saw E. W. Tristram's reconstruction of the fifteenth-century wall painting *The Legend of Saint Eustace*. For an understanding of Hoban's novel, it is important to know that Canterbury has long been the primary ecclesiastical administrative center in Britain; that Thomas à Becket was murdered in Canterbury Cathedral in 1170; that the cathedral was half ruined in a terrible fire in 1174; and that, although the town of Canterbury was badly damaged during World War II, the cathedral (except the chapter library, which was blown up) received only superficial damage (*Encyclopedia Britannica*, 14th ed., s.v. "Canterbury Cathedral"). Its role as the destination of Chaucer's pilgrims in the *Canterbury Tales*

quasi-religious text narrating the events that led to the nuclear accident. Both texts are cited in full and subjected to detailed interpretation by Riddley and the other characters.

The legend of St. Eustace is placed at the approximate center of the novel. It is Goodparley who shows Riddley this text, obviously a relic from the preholocaust era. The leaflet, headed *The Legend of St. Eustace,* begins by explaining that "the Legend of St Eustace dates from the year A.D. 120 and this XVth-century wall painting depicts with fidelity the several episodes in his life" (123); it continues with a narration of the story of St. Eustace in six numbered paragraphs and concludes by noting that "the date of the painting is about 1480; the work is highly skilled in an English tradition and is a magnificent example of wall painting of this date" (124). Riddley is even more baffled by this example of our English than we are by his. Goodparley knows, however, that it refers to "some kynd of picter or dyergam" that they no longer have, but he understands the text, not as a transparent description of the lost picture, but as a kind of encoded writing, "some kynd of a seakert thing." With extraordinary ingenuity, he gives his own reading of the secret code:

A Legend thats a picter whats *depicted* which is to say pictert on a wall its done with some kynd of paint callit *fidelity. St* is short for sent. Meaning this bloak Eustace he dint just tern up he wer sent. A.D. *120* that the year they use to have it gone from Year 1 right the way to Bad Time. A.D. means All Done. 120 years all done theyre saying thats when they begun this picter in 120 nor they never got it finisht till 1480 is what it says here wel you know there aint no picter cud take 1360 years to do these here year numbers is about some thing else may be wewl never know what. (124–25)

Any scholar who has worked with older texts will recognize this parody of the academic method.[6] Goodparley continues with an interpretation of

---

is doubtless also alluded to in Hoban's novel when Riddley Walker and the Ardship of Cambry set out on their difficult journey toward Canterbury. For more information on Canterbury Cathedral, see Marian van Rensselaer, *Handbook of English Cathedrals* (New York: Century Co., 1893), 38–76.

6. Hoban may have been inspired here by the introduction to the Opies' *Dictionary of Nursery Rhymes,* which discusses the problem of interpreting these texts at some length. They are particularly critical of both the political readings proposed by John Bellenden Ker in *An Essay on the Archaeology of Popular English Phrases and Nursery Rhymes* (Southampton, 1834) and Katherine Elwes Thomas, *The Real Personages of Mother Goose* (Boston, 1930). Thomas regards

the entire text, assimilating the entire St. Eustace legend to the mythology of the postnuclear holocaust era with its dim reminiscences of a long-lost science and technology. "*Episodes,*" he explains, "thats when you do a thing 1 part at a time youve got to get the 1st episode done befor you go on to the nex. Thats how youwl do if youre working chemistery or fizzicks. Youwl do your boyl ups and your try outs in episodes" (126). St. Eustace himself is identified with the Eusa who had played such a fateful role in the nuclear accident. "*The figure of our crucified Saviour*" reminds him of the distorted scrap of information that still remains in oral tradition from the lost recipe for bomb making: "a littl salting and no saver" (128).[7] So convinced is he that the legend refers to "chemistery" that he reads the word "*crucified*" as "some thing you done in a cruciboal . . . thats a hard firet boal they use it doing a chemistery try out which you cud call that crucifrying or crucifying" (128). When the text describes how St. Eustace's wife is carried off by pirates, his first son by a wolf, and the second by a lion, Goodparley interprets this as an allegory of a chemical reaction in which the "*four souls*" who come together once again at the end are to be read as "4 salts" remaining at the end of the experiment. "Man and wife and littl childer coming back to gether for the las time thats your new clear family," he reasons (129).

This parody of textual interpretation is by no means isolated in the novel, however. Reading signs is an important aspect of the culture in which Riddley Walker lives. The novel opens with a cluster of three events that seem to him and his contemporaries to cry out for interpretation: his father dies while helping to dredge a rusted twentieth-century machine up out of the mud,[8] a baby is stillborn, and Riddley kills a wild dog with his spear. Using a word derived from computer technology, though no longer understood as such, the community describes random and inexplicable

---

Bo-peep, for example, as Mary Queen of Scots, Jack Sprat as Charles I, and so forth. The Opies comment: "The story of 'Sing a Song of Sixpence' . . . has been described as alluding to the choirs of Tudor Monasteries, the printing of the English Bible, the malpractices of the Romish clergy, and the infinite workings of the solar system" (27).

7. Gunpowder contains 75 percent saltpeter (the "little salting" of the formula given here), 10 percent sulphur, and 15 percent charcoal. The explosive is, of course, "no saver."

8. Just as Riddley Walker's culture is built on the ruins of twentieth-century technology, so Canterbury Cathedral is built on the ruins of its own former incarnation (the earlier cathedral that was severely damaged by fire in 1174). The motif of technology in *Riddley Walker* refers not only to the twentieth-century culture that Riddley's contemporaries are "unearthing," but also to the building of medieval cathedrals, which would not have been possible without advanced technology (see Jean Gimpel, *The Cathedral Builders,* trans. Teresa Waugh [New York: Grove Press, 1983], esp. 107–17).

phenomena as "blipful" (from "blips" on the screen). As he tries to work out the connection between these events, Riddley receives some helpful advice: "Every 1 knows if you get blipful things to gether you take the farthes out 1 for the nindicater" (13). Indeed, as any student of literature knows, an element that does not seem at first to fit with the rest is often the clue that yields a coherent reading of the whole.

The "farthes out" text in *Riddley Walker* is the *Eusa Story*. In Riddley's culture, the *Eusa Story* is a kind of Bible, and its form is that of thirty-three numbered verses "wrote down in the old spel" (29). Riddley and his fellows know this text by heart and can recite any verse on command. To give an impression of this quasi-biblical language, I quote the first verse, which tells of a time when technology was highly developed and spaceships and television sets were common; a time when the United States, allied with England, sets out to do war against England's enemies:

1. Wen Mr Clevver wuz Big Man uv Inland thay had evere thing clevver. Thay had boats in the ayr & picters on the win & evere thing lyk that. Eusa wuz a noing man vere qwik he cud tern his han tu enne thing. He wuz werkin for Mr Clevver wen thayr cum enemes aul roun & maykin Warr. Eusa sed tu Mr Clevver, Now wewl nead masheans uv Warr. Wewl nead boats that go on the water & boats that go in the ayr as wel & wewl nead Berstin Fyr. (30)

The story tells of the splitting of the atom, allegorized—with an unmistakeable allusion to our own Bible—as the "Littl Shynin Man the Addom" (30). We read how Eusa discovered the formula for the atomic bomb and Mr. Clevver dropped bomb after bomb on his enemies. We read about the "Bad Time," in which the whole earth is poisoned, people and animals are dying, and no food is safe to eat. In a parallel to the St. Eustace legend, Eusa goes off with his wife and two little sons to look for another place to live; but, just as Eusa has split the atom in two, so his sons are taken off in two separate directions by two mysterious dogs. In an extended visionary sequence, Eusa has an exchange with the Little Shining Man about the ontological status of his experience, which he would prefer to regard as simply a bad dream. The Little Man tells him, however, that it is part of a necessary and inevitable chain of events from which he cannot awake. Eusa, he says, must go through a series of changes whose number is determined by the nature of Eusa himself, or what he calls the "idear" of Eusa. "Eusa sed, Wut is the idear uv me? The Little Man sed, That we doan no til yuv gon thru aul yur Chaynjis" (36). The *Eusa Story* ends with this declaration that the meaning of humanity cannot be understood until we have come to the end of human history. Once again, the question of interpretation has been raised, but, despite the apparently transparent allegorizing of Adam and the atom, this text proclaims that we can never reach full understanding of experience until the totality of experience is complete. Thus, while Goodparley's reading of the *St. Eustace Legend* suggests that interpretations, imperfect though they may be, are readily available, the *Eusa Story* emphasizes the theoretical impossibility of interpretation within the finite frame of human experience.

The orally transmitted texts in *Riddley Walker* reveal a similar paradoxicality. At first, Riddley regards "Fools Circel 9wys" as simply a singing game for children, although the twentieth-century reader is more inclined to see in it allusions to sexuality:

> Horny Boy rung Widders Bel
> Stoal his Fathers Ham as wel
> Bernt his Arse and Forkt a Stoan
> Done it Over broak a bone . . .

(5)

When we look at the map of the area around Canterbury provided at the front of the book, however, we also note that the capitalized words are all place names from the region: Herne Bay, Whitstable, Faversham, Sittingbourne, Folkestone, and Dover are recognizable despite their post-holocaust distortions.[9] Both the sexual and the geographic implications are evident to members of Riddley's community, but they do not think of the rhyme as having any serious meaning. When Riddley finally meets the young Ardship of Cambry, however, he discovers that there is more to the rhyme than "jus a game" (80). The Ardship tells him that it is, in fact, the verse narrative of what happened to Eusa after the nuclear catastrophe, when he was beaten to death and his head, stuck on a pole, was taken

---

9. Such distortions are prefigured by "Oranges and Lemons" and a related rhyme, "The Bells of Shropshire" (Iona Opie and Peter Opie, *A Family Book of Nursery Rhymes* [New York: Oxford University Press, 1964], 46–47). Riddley's "Done it Over" is reminiscent of the lines: "Under and over, / Say the bells of Condover" in "The Bells of Shropshire" (47). Dover is important not only because it was the port by which stonecutters from France came to work on Canterbury Cathedral (cf. Gimpel, *Cathedral Builders,* 65), but also because, when St. Eustace landed at Dover, a brawl between his men and the citizens of that town broke out. This was ultimately to be the cause of his exile (*Encyclopedia Britannica,* 14th ed., s.v. "Eustace").

the round of the dead towns around the center of Canterbury. The rhyme remains as a reminder of that time, just as a small number of people deformed by radiation have been kept to continue breeding as a "memberment" of the misuse of knowledge that had led to the holocaust. The Ardship, with his spooky, eyeless face, is a descendent of that stock. Riddley's meeting with the Ardship marks an important phase in our narrator's attempt to follow the advice his elders have given him upon his father's death: "You bes start putting things to gether for your self you aint a kid no mor" (14).

As well as this and other rhymes passed down from mouth to mouth, there are a number of other stories that belong to the oral tradition of Riddley's culture. The first of these is *Hart of the Wood* (2–4).[10] This tale, which Riddley gives us at the very beginning of his narrative, hinges explicitly on the problem of ambiguity. The opening lines of the story discuss the multiple meanings of its title: a stag in the forest, a place in the center of the forest, charcoal (the heart of wood),[11] and—metaphorically—the "veryes deap of it" (2). The story itself is the tale of a man and a woman who, having killed and cut up their child to feed the devil in exchange for fire to keep themselves warm, end up burning to death in that very fire. What Riddley fails to recognize at first is that the story is a fairy-tale version of the nuclear catastrophe. Only much later does Riddley also realize that the word *wood* is homonymous with *would* and he comments: "You see what Im saying its the hart of the wud its the hart of the wanting to be" (165). As we know from countless fairy tales in our own culture—stories like *The Fisherman and His Wife,* for example—misplaced or overweening desire can have disastrous consequences, but this is a lesson that Riddley must painfully learn over again for his own time, in which the ability to interpret texts has shriveled to a very rudimentary capacity. Thus, although his culture accepts the notion that texts are powerful ("Words! Theywl move things you know theywl do things. Theywl fetch" [122]), it neglects or misunderstands the tales of warning that it possesses and that might save it from a repetition of disaster.[12]

---

10. The title of this tale recalls the nursery rhyme: "The hart he loves the high wood / The hare she loves the hill; / The knight he loves his bright sword, / The lady loves her will" (Opie and Opie, *Dictionary,* 200). The third line, which suggests a perennial love of warfare, is significant for *Riddley Walker.*

11. Charcoal is needed to make gunpowder; see n. 7.

12. The fire in Canterbury Cathedral in 1174; the fictional nuclear holocaust of around 1997; and the rediscovery of gunpowder twenty-five hundred years later are the major moments in the historical repetition upon which *Riddley Walker* is structured.

Another moral tale is told by the wise crone Lorna Elswint, whom Riddley describes as a "tel woman" (4). This story, called *Why the Dog Wont Show Its Eyes,* represents yet another version of how the nuclear catastrophe came to pass. It tells of a man and a woman inspired by the fire in the eyes of a dog at full moon to acquire the knowledge that seems to shine forth from them. Instead of being afraid of the darkness, they begin to regard night and day as essentially the same; they begin to keep livestock, grow grain, and think of land in terms of property. In a few sentences, the story covers the development of civilization from primitive to more advanced culture. Finally, the man and woman acquire what this story calls the "counting clevverness," the mathematical and astronomical knowledge that results in computer and space technology. The story tells how they used their counting cleverness to create the bomb and "woosht it roun there come a flash of lite then bigger nor the woal worl and it ternt the nite to day" and brought sickness and plagues to the earth (19). When Riddley hears this story, he is puzzled; he thought, from the *Eusa Story,* that it was Eusa who had made the bomb. But Lorna explains that the same thing can be told in many different ways:

> You hear diffrent things in all them way back storys but it dont make no diffrents. Mosly they aint strait storys any how. What they are is diffrent ways of telling what happent. (20)

She explains, furthermore, that there is no such thing as a straight story: many stories change over the course of their transmission, and even those that remain unchanged are more metaphorical than real.

Whereas the *Eusa Story* and *Why the Dog Wont Show Its Eyes* suggest that the nuclear holocaust could have been avoided if people had not been so intent on gaining knowledge and control, another story, *The Bloak as Got on Top of Aunty* (90–93), demonstrates that even a Schillerian acceptance of one's fate fails to free one from the clutches of inevitability. "Aunty" is a goddess of death in Riddley's culture: making love to Aunty is their metaphor for dying. The dread goddess is depicted as having "stoan boans and iron tits and teef be twean her legs plus she has a iron willy for the ladys it gets red hot. When your time comes you have to do the juicy with her like it or not" (90–91). This folk tale is the story of a man who thinks he can escape death by actively pursuing Aunty. Although he thinks he has "got on top" of her in both senses of the word, he actually succumbs to her twin sister, Arga Warga. Is our fate in our own hands or is it ineluctable? The tales Riddley hears present different possibilities without resolving this problem. Only by juxtaposing a number of stories that approach the question of responsibility, control, and power from various angles can Riddley begin to put things together for himself.

Through this multiplication of stories,[13] Riddley learns several important things about the interpretation of oral and written texts: he learns that narratives have meaning on many levels, that no narrative is anything more than one version of events among many possible others, and that narrative is not only our way of remembering but also our way of knowing.

But while Riddley spends a good deal of time listening to various stories, it is his friend, the Ardship of Cambry, who describes himself as the "Lissener" and who explains why listening is an important function. The Ardship tells Riddley a haunting tale from his childhood about an owl who swallows up the sounds of the world and replaces them with silence.[14] But all night long, while the owl is trying to obliterate audible reality, the "lissener" keeps it alive in what we might call his mind's ear: "he knowit wer on him to stop the owl so he begun to lissen every thing back" (86). In contrast to the story of the man and the woman who eliminate darkness by the questionable enlightenment of their "counting clevverness," the tale of *The Lissener and the Other Voyce Owl of the Worl* presents a countermyth that gives night a new and positive meaning. Russell Hoban exploits the full magic of his storytelling ability in this extraordinarily poetic and original tale.

Later, inspired by the ruins of Canterbury cathedral with its remarkable stone carvings, Riddley himself invents a similarly poetic text, which he claims is neither a story nor a dream. His text is called *Stoan* (163–64), and it invokes the silent speech of the inanimate:

Stoans want to be lissent to. Them big brown stoans in the formers feal they want to stan up and talk like men. Some times youwl see them lying on the groun with ther humps and hollers theywl say to you, Sit a wyl and res easy why dont you. Then when youre sitting on them theywl talk and theywl tel if you lissen. (163)

---

13. This multiplicity of stories with complex interrelations is characteristic of what Linda Hutcheon calls "historiographic metafiction" (*A Poetics of Postmodernism: History, Theory, Fiction* [New York: Routledge, 1988], 105–23).

14. This owl is a revocation of the nursery rhyme owl who lived in an oak: "There was an owl lived in an oak, / The more he heard, the less he spoke, / The less he spoke, the more he heard— / O if men were all like that wise bird" (Opie and Opie, *Family Book,* 35). The Lissener's story countermands this traditional "wisdom."

Here, Riddley combines two types of knowledge, the scientific and the aesthetic.[15] On the one hand he shows that, although stone seems to be immobile, it actually contains millions of tiny particles, the neutrons, protons, and electrons that make up the "girt dants of the every thing" (163). On the other hand he presents the stone carvings, in which bird heads grow on human bodies and vines and leaves grow out of human mouths, as part of another kind of great dance, this time an aesthetic one in which the stones seem to speak to us with their own silent symbolism. "They talk ther oan way which is stoan talk," he says (164). In his reflections on Canterbury cathedral, Riddley begins to put science and poetry together.

Thus, although Riddley spends a great deal of the novel looking and listening, he is himself a kind of incipient bard. Riddley Walker's father, Brooder Walker, had been a "connexion man"—a kind of priest or oracle—and Riddley takes over this function after his death. The big community gatherings take place at ritual puppet shows, put on by the government, that reenact the nuclear tragedy in symbolic form. Goodparley and his assistant Orfing go about from town to town presenting yet another version of the Eusa story known as the *Eusa Show*. With a great deal of slapstick and a certain amount of crude humor, this puppet show is the "parper stablish men story" presenting "trufax from the Mincery" (46) about how Eusa emptied all the knowledge in his brain into his "No. 2 head" (47), which is clearly a computer. Turning a crank on an iron hat, he is shown "inputting all kynds of knowing" from his head into a large, heavy box. Once the knowledge is no longer confined to his own head, however, it is accessible to exploitation by others, and the puppet show demonstrates that the "Bad Time" was the natural result of Eusa's computer foolishness. Although the *Eusa Story*, as a kind of biblical text, always remains the same, the puppet shows, we hear, are different all the time, constantly being adapted to the needs of "this here time weare living in" (52).[16] After

---

15. This integration of the scientific and the aesthetic forms a counterpoint to the critical view of technology in its relation to culture that predominates in *Riddley Walker*. It is significant that Riddley's new view takes place through what we might call the unconscious.

16. Puppet shows have traditionally been highly adaptable. They were especially useful as political commentary in periods when the theaters were closed, as in seventeenth-century England. Puppetry was an adult entertainment in England until about 1820 (see David Currell, *The Complete Book of Puppet Theatre* [Totowa: Barnes and Nobel, 1987], 37). In the eighteenth century, puppet shows were popular in Norwich, Kent, and Canterbury, and were used not only as entertainment but also to present social and political commentary (*Encyclopedia Britannica*, 14th ed., s.v. "Punch," "puppets").

each show, the local "connexion man" is supposed to go into a kind of trance and utter prophetic words that will reveal the meaning of the show. Riddley's first "connexion" is a failure, however, because, although he starts out with a perceptive interpretation of the smoke and flames on the backdrop used in the puppet theater,[17] his most profound revelation remains unspoken. He thinks he has said aloud what he has only thought to himself: "EUSAS HEAD IS DREAMING US" (61). This somewhat Berkeleyan idea is developed in a number of ways in the parts of the novel that follow and ultimately echoed in the Lissener's tale of the struggle between himself and the owl to think the world away or to think it present. Toward the end of the novel, Riddley has the terrible thought that everything may just be the result of his own consciousness: "What if its you whats making all this happen? What if every thing you think of happens?" (194). But he ultimately rejects this notion, reasoning that, in the last analysis, it makes no difference whether the events he experiences are his own or someone else's thoughts (19). This is not to say, however, that Riddley Walker is a pragmatist. He is, rather, a bardlike figure whose words are at once his own original creation and the medium through which another voice is transmitted.

Science fiction though it may on one level be, *Riddley Walker* is, on another level, the story of a poetic apprenticeship. It begins with Riddley's initiation as a "connexion man" upon the death of his father, describes his failed first revelation, traces his attempts to understand the relationship between language and history and to learn the art of textual interpretation, and concludes with his discovery of his own true vocation. It is no accident that the puppet show, which figures prominently in the opening pages of the novel Novalis called a "Candide against poetry," Goethe's *Wilhelm Meister,* plays such an important part in Hoban's plaidoyer for and critique of the poetic vocation. Whereas Riddley begins his career as a priestlike interpreter of the Eusa show, he concludes it by becoming a puppeteer himself. The shows he puts on at the end of the novel, however, are the result of a kind of textual archaeology. Fascinated by a hook-nosed puppet figure he has found miraculously preserved alongside some bog corpses from the preholocaust era,[18] Riddley begins to discover the subtext that

---

17. The smoke and flames of the theater's backdrop recall the traditional scene between Punch and the devil, which opens with Punch smelling smoke and fire (see Ed Kimberley, *Punch and Judy: A Play for Puppets* [Boston: Little, Brown, 1965], 25).

18. For pictures of the hook-nosed figure from various periods, see Currell, *Puppet Theatre,* 40.

underlies the puppet shows of his own time. The reader, who has already noticed (in the *Eusa Show*) a number of corruptions of the Punch and Judy show, is not surprised when Riddley reconstructs something very close to the familiar slapstick routine. It turns out that Goodparley's puppet kit has always contained two sets of figures: the Eusa figures, which he uses, and the Punch figures, which he keeps concealed. Common to both shows is the figure of the devil (Mr. Clevver in the Eusa show): "same red face and littl black beard and the same horns growing out of his head" (206). Finding the common element enables Riddley Walker to see that the later show is merely a variant of the earlier one. He ends up by presenting his own version of Punch and Judy, now called—to mark its differentiation from the original—Punch and Pooty. The final chapter of the novel includes a line-by-line account of this show, in which Punch, detailed to mind the baby while Pooty fries sausages, is constantly tempted to devour his own juicy little pigletlike infant. Reflecting on the puppet play with which he now travels from town to town, Riddley asks a crucial question about the nature of humanity: "Why is Punch crookit? Why wil he all ways kil the babby if he can?" (220). He suspects that he may never find out the answer, but knows that it is his task to ask the question.

The two parts of Riddley Walker's name suggest the questioning that characterizes his nature and the wandering route his search for knowledge takes. The novel parodies not only the novel of poetic apprenticeship, but the picaresque novel as well. At the end, we discover, along with Riddley himself, that, despite his honest intentions, Riddley Walker is also, if involuntarily, in league with the devil. In the popular mythology of Riddley's age, the devil is known as Drop John,[19] and, as Riddley leaves town after presenting his Punch and Pooty show, a mischievous youngster sings a taunting rhyme about him:

> Riddley Walkers ben to show
> Riddley Walkers on the go
> Dont go Riddley Walkers track
> Drop Johns ryding on his back.

> (219)

---

19. Drop John is clearly Jack Ketch, the hangman, who tries to hang Punch but is ultimately hanged by him. Punch comments: "You see, I'm smarter already" (this version of the wording is from Kimberley, *Punch and Judy,* 23), thus initiating the theme of "cleverness" that appears in *Riddley Walker.*

Horrified, Riddley nonetheless accepts this dreadful truth.[20] Like many a picaro, he has been, on one level, an artful trickster. Yet, at the same time and on another level, he is a grandiose and heroic figure. True to the character of a tragic hero, he claims in the last words of the novel: "Still I wunt have no other track" (220).

Seemingly just a quixotic linguistic experiment, Russell Hoban's *Riddley Walker* reveals itself as multiply intertextual.[21] It adapts the picaresque genre, revokes the novel of development, and puts the novel of poetic apprenticeship into question. It exploits or imitates such diverse forms as the tourist brochure, the biblical text, the nursery rhyme, the vulgar ditty, the cautionary tale, and the fairy tale. At the funeral of Riddley's father, the community sings something that sounds like a kind of hymn. The text, with its reference to sovereign galaxies and flaming nebulae, clearly owes its origin to the preholocaust era in which space technology had all but taken the place of conventional religion:

> Pas the sarvering gallack seas and flaming nebyul eye
> Power us beyont the farthes reaches of the sky
> Thine the han what shapit the black
> Guyd us there and guyd us back.
>
> (22)

The hymnlike sentiments and space-age vocabulary of *Savering Gallack Seas* conceal yet another textual model alluded to by the rhyme sound of the first couplet, the meter of the second, and the image of the shaping hand: Blake's poem "The Tyger."[22] The burning eyes, the forests of the night, the fire, the forging of the brain: all these have been motifs in *Riddley*

---

20. The image of Drop John riding on Riddley Walker's back is a revocation of the frontispiece of Blake's *Songs of Experience,* in which a shepherd, stepping forward out of the state of innocence into the state of experience, balances a winged cherub on his shoulders. The child's song about Riddley Walker suggests that the bard is accompanied not by an angel, but by a devil. The figure in Blake's plate is dressed in green, and a nearby tree is shown with ivy climbing up it: these motifs may be related to the stone figure with vines coming out of its mouth and to the motif of natural regeneration sounded in *Riddley Walker.* (For Blake's illustration, see Geoffrey Keynes, ed., *Blake: Songs of Innocence and Experience* [London: Oxford University Press, 1970], pl. 28).

21. Linda Hutcheon shows that postmodern texts are engaged in a "fundamentally contradictory enterprise" in which they "at once use and abuse, install and then destabilize convention" through "a critical or ironic re-reading of the art of the past" (*Poetics,* 23). The multiple intertextuality of *Riddley Walker* is a particularly apt example of this phenomenon.

22. Sampson, *Poetical Works,* 85–86.

Walker and its various inset stories. Hoban's novel can well be read as an extended meditation on Blake's question about the presence of cruelty and violence in a divinely created universe.

Blake's *Songs of Experience* and multiple other subtexts lie buried in *Riddley Walker* like the broken machines that strew its damaged and distorted countryside. In an impressive scene at the center of the novel, Riddley and the Ardship come across the ruins of giant machinery half hidden in great mounds of rubble. The enormous, shining objects are "broakin but not dead they cudn't dy there wer too much Power in them" (100).[23] From the darkness beyond the machines, the two young men can hear the sea: "breaving and sying and sying breaving and sying it wer like them machines were breaving and sying in ther sleap" (100). Riddley begins to apprehend something of the poetry of the atomic era, and he is profoundly moved. The long-time opponent of Goodparley and his attempt to recapture the lost science now sees the temptation of getting back "that shyning Power" (100). For the first time, Riddley hears the voice of the past and wants to bring it back into existence. In this visionary moment, he is overcome by the desire to "renew" "fallen light," as Blake puts it in the opening poem of the *Songs of Experience*. Yet the reader, who already knows where the knowledge of nuclear fission can lead, recognizes, at this point, the beginning of Riddley's secret collusion with Drop John the devil. For it is Riddley who finds the yellow sulphur stones that enable Goodparley's followers to make gunpowder and thus set in motion once again the vicious circle of history from which Riddley has been trying to break out.

Riddley Walker's narrative is the voice of a bard who sees present, past, and future, but who must inevitably fail to renew the fallen light. Its complex intertextuality is not one in which illustrious predecessors are outshone, but one in which their works remain as opaque and recalcitrant ruins.[24] Its technical innovations are designed not as harbingers of progress but as indicators of cultural degeneration. Its ravaged language and broken texts suggest that poetic monuments are not more lasting than bronze; insofar as they do survive, they remain grandly crippled, like the great machines of the space age embedded in the rubble. Like the great machines, too, these textual relics refuse to yield up their secrets: *Riddley Walker* puts

---

23. The power motif refers not only to the power of nuclear fission, but also to the fact that Canterbury was a center of spiritual power in the Middle Ages.

24. In this way, theories of intertextuality based on essentially progressive models, such as those of Harold Bloom (*The Anxiety of Influence*) or Wolfgang Iser (*The Implied Reader*) are effectively undermined in *Riddley Walker*.

the business of literary interpretation seriously into question by showing that the best intentioned of our attempts to understand texts from the past are contaminated by our own systems of thought, which, since they are anchored in the present, are always in some sense foreign to the object of interpretation. *Riddley Walker* reveals the tragedy inherent in culture and criticism. Borne along on his journey by a desire for regeneration summed up in the slogan "Hoap of a Tree" that Riddley once sees written on a wall (169–70), Riddley is repeatedly beset by despair: "O what we ben! And what we come to!" as he exclaims upon discovering the great broken machines (100). The powerful promise of imaginative language to redeem the world is constantly subverted in this novel; yet it is also through two texts, the puppet show and the taunting rhyme with which the novel ends, that Riddley Walker arrives at his most complex insight into his own unwitting culpability. The innovative language of *Riddley Walker,* with its strange combination of the primitive and the futuristic, imitates this ambiguity that lies at its center.[25]

25. I wish to thank Ruth Solie for drawing my attention to this novel. My essay was completed before the appearance of Peter Schwenger's article "Circling Ground Zero," *PMLA* 106 (1991): 251–61, which unfortunately could not be taken into account.

Experience and Reflection: Theodor W. Adorno's Literary Criticism

Peter Uwe Hohendahl

As a literary critic, Theodor W. Adorno is almost unknown in the English-speaking world. Although he wrote some fifty essays on literary topics—among them pieces on Goethe, Proust, Valéry, Kafka, Hofmannsthal, and Balzac—his reputation as a critic is largely based on his contributions to the field of music criticism. Among American musicologists, his work on Schönberg, Mahler, and Wagner, to mention just a few major composers, is well known. His music criticism has received an acclaim that has been denied to his literary essays, although these essays are by no means less important than his books and articles on music.[1] As far as the Frankfurt school is concerned, the literary criticism of Walter Benjamin has almost completely eclipsed the contributions of Adorno. This is ironic because it was Adorno who launched Benjamin's rediscovery after World War II. Without the two-volume edition of Benjamin's work that Adorno brought out in 1955, which incidentally emphasized, through its selection, Benjamin's early criticism and deemphasized the Marxist phase, Benjamin probably would be a forgotten author today.

How do we explain the absence of Adorno's literary criticism in the United States? The obvious but clearly insufficient answer is that most of his essays have not been translated. So far, various attempts to publish his *Noten zu Literatur*—four slim volumes of literary criticism in the broader sense of the term—in English have failed. While even his most complex work, *Aesthetic Theory,* was finally made available to English-speaking read-

---

1. For general information, see Martin Jay, *Adorno* (Cambridge, Mass.: Harvard University Press, 1984); Frederic Jameson, *Marxism and Form: Twentieth-Century Dialectical Theories of Literature* (Princeton: Princeton University Press, 1971).

ers in 1984, the resistance against his literary essays has not yet been overcome. In part, this has to do with their character. They are hardly conventional academic articles dealing with acknowledged research topics in an accepted academic manner. Instead, they are, almost without exception, highly personal, subjective, critical interventions written in a very uncommon style. In order to appreciate them, one has to pay attention to their form and manner of presentation as much as to their topics and arguments. Hence, it is very difficult to translate these essays without losing significant elements—precisely those elements that are embedded in their language. Any sensitive reader familiar with Adorno's original texts realizes that a translation that relies primarily on the transfer of ideas and arguments—as important as they are—misses the meaning of Adorno's literary criticism. As Samuel Weber, the translator of *Prisms,* pointed out, "Adorno's thought is inseparable from its articulation."[2] Indeed, the German language, as it is used by Adorno, and standard English prose are incompatible. Some of Adorno's German critics, to be sure, have always argued that his style lacks clarity and balance. It is apparent, however, that traditional notions of clarity and balance fail to grasp the force and structure of Adorno's prose, for Adorno's language means to capture the dialectical unfolding of the argument rather than the result, preserving in its articulation the tension that conventional discursive language wants to eliminate. Thus, Adorno's critical prose is, as Weber rightly observes, untranslatable. "The untranslatability of Adorno is his most profound and cruel truth."[3] Hence, any attempt to communicate the ideas of Adorno's essays must necessarily result in allegorical readings.

It is characteristic that the late Adorno, in an essay published in 1969 that clearly responds to the radical political demands of students, insisted on the democratic dimension of the concept of *Kritik*: "Kritik ist aller Demokratie wesentlich,"[4] thereby stressing the political aspect as well as the direction of his project. Where it is more than facile consumption, reading literature is neither mere appreciation nor mere explication, although both elements are, as Adorno emphasized in *Aesthetic Theory,*[5]

2. Theodor W. Adorno, *Prisms,* trans. Samuel Weber and Shierry Weber (Cambridge, Mass.: MIT Press, 1981), 11.

3. Adorno, *Prisms,* 15.

4. Theodor W. Adorno, *Gesammelte Schriften,* hrsg. Rolf Tiedemann (Frankfurt am Main: Suhrkamp, 1977), 10: bd. 2, 785; additional quotations will be identified in the text as *Schriften,* with volume and page numbers.

5. Theodor W. Adorno, *Aesthetic Theory,* trans. C. Lenhardt, ed. Gretel Adorno and Rolf Tiedemann (London and Boston: Routledge and Keegan Paul, 1984).

indispensable for criticism. Critical reading implies a critique of the artwork involved, of its technique, its formal structure, and, most of all, its *Wahrheitsgehalt* ['truth content']. This probing of the text, as we will see, is historical through and through—with respect to the situation of the critic as well as the genesis of the work of art. For Adorno there is no reading outside of history. Yet it would definitely be misleading to call Adorno a historicist. What distinguishes Adorno's method from the method of historicism is precisely the element of *Kritik,* the resistance to the act of historical empathy or the attempt at factual reconstruction. Adorno's literary essays consistently articulate their awareness of the historical force field, but they rarely provide background information on the particular historical circumstances. This lack of "research" is, of course, in part due to the essay form, that is to say, a generic characteristic that Adorno took very seriously, yet it also applies to much of his music criticism, where formal constraints would not be the reason.

The scope of Adorno's literary criticism is considerable, ranging from essays on Goethe and Hölderlin to such major writers of the twentieth century as Proust, Valéry, Kafka, Thomas Mann, and Walter Benjamin. His contributions to the nineteenth century focus on such authors as Eichendorff, Heine, Balzac, and (a rare excursion into English literature) Dickens. To these essays, we have to add his major theoretical and methodological essays, among them "Reconciliation under Duress" and "Commitment" as well as his famous "Lyrical Poetry and Society,"[6] which argues for an intrinsic sociology of literature. The center of Adorno's literary criticism is clearly the early twentieth century, his favorite authors are modernists, and his most pressing theoretical concern is a theory of modernism and the avant-garde. It is in this area that he particularly overlaps with and also—when one looks more closely—disagrees with Benjamin. A number of his essays, among them his essay on Brecht and his piece on Surrealism,[7] can be seen as responses to Benjamin's work—critical rereadings whose thrust remains concealed unless the reader remembers Benjamin's position. The essence of Adorno's rereading is typically a critique of his friend's arguments. The most obvious case is their different attitudes toward Brecht. Adorno's polemic against Brecht as theorist and playwright was, at least partially, motivated by the central role that Brecht's

---

6. Theodor W. Adorno, "Lyrical Poetry and Society," *Telos* 20 (Summer, 1974): 56–71; Adorno, "Rede über Lyrik und Gesellschaft," in *Schriften* 11:48–68.

7. Theodor W. Adorno, "Rückblickend auf den Surrealismus," in *Schriften* 11:101–5.

oeuvre occupied in Benjamin's definition of modernism. It is here that their most fundamental disagreement comes to the foreground. While Benjamin insisted on a break with high culture and, therefore, especially during the early 1930s, searched for a postauratic model of art,[8] Adorno consistently rejected this project as a dangerous regression to the level of pre-autonomous art. Adorno's concept of modernism is, as we will see, firmly based on the idea that art is an end in itself and must not be defined (as Benjamin did) in operationalist terms.

This interest in and concern with the autonomous status of art is also reflected in the horizon of Adorno's literary criticism. It places the emphasis on the nineteenth and twentieth centuries, avoiding for the most part any contact with premodern, that is, preautonomous literature. Unlike Benjamin, Adorno took no interest in the sixteenth or seventeenth century. It might be added that his attitude toward baroque music is equally ambivalent. Adorno never shared the postwar nostalgia for premodern music. His rigorous defense of Bach, directed primarily against the admirers of baroque music, stresses the modern character of Bach's compositions.[9] He argues that Bach's music is structurally related to the rise of industrial capitalism in the early eighteenth century. Similarly, his essay "Lyrical Poetry and Society" concentrates on the German tradition from Goethe to George, excluding the medieval period with the argument that our understanding of poetry is not really applicable to medieval literature.

To these historical boundaries we have to add the geographic borders of Adorno's criticism. For him, literature is tantamount to European literature, particularly the literature of Western Europe. Outside the German tradition, Adorno is primarily drawn to French authors. Excursions into English literature are rare (Dickens, Beckett). There is no indication that Adorno was ever interested in American literature, although he lived in the United States for more than a decade. The fact that he never wrote on major Russian or Spanish authors is possibly due to the fact that he did not feel comfortable with texts that he could not read in the original language. Clearly, Adorno's panorama of literature has blind spots, the most noticeable the absence of South American, Asian, and African literature, but, even within European literature, Adorno's preferences are unmistakable; it is obvious that English writers are marginal to his defi-

---

8. See Terry Eagleton, *Walter Benjamin, or Towards a Revolutionary Criticism* (London: Verso, 1981); Michael W. Jennings, *Dialectical Images: Walter Benjamin's Theory of Literary Criticism* (Ithaca, N.Y.: Cornell University Press, 1987).

9. Theodor W. Adorno, "Bach Defended against His Devotees," in *Prisms*, 133–46.

nition of literature. The same is, of course, true for Walter Benjamin, whose preference for the French tradition was even more outspoken. Yet Benjamin also showed a deep interest in Russian literature, a concern that Adorno did not share. No doubt, Adorno's point of view, which was largely determined by his fundamental theoretical assumptions about the autonomous status of art, resulted in a selection of texts and authors that is both very unique and—in terms of the European canon—fairly orthodox.

Adorno's literary essays clearly articulate his moral and aesthetic concerns. Seen together, they offer an answer to the question of modernism. On the one hand, Adorno stayed fairly close to the pantheon of great figures and masterpieces. There is no attempt to discover and come to terms with marginal traditions, for instance with proletarian literature or that of ethnic groups. These blind spots come out most clearly in his understanding of the German tradition, which is—at least by today's standards—closer to the mainstream than one would expect from a radical theorist like Adorno. With very few exceptions (Hölderlin, Heine, Wedekind), the radical tradition is missing in Adorno's criticism. There is no equivalent to Benjamin's essays on Jochmann. Authors such as Forster, Rebmann, Kleist, Börne, Büchner, and Heinrich Mann are not present. Even for Friedrich Schlegel and Novalis we would look in vain.

The attempt of the European avant-garde to break away from literature and art and its desire to reach a realm of utopian social practice mark the boundaries of Adorno's criticism. His skeptical position toward the margins of high culture is largely grounded in his understanding of modern mass culture, that is, the culture industry. In his early essay on the regression of listening (1938), he had already rejected Benjamin's idea of a postauratic popular culture.[10] The chapter on the culture industry in *Dialectic of Enlightenment* merely developed the idea that the ultimate threat was the leveling of cultural difference that would rob the work of art of its critical power. For Adorno (and Horkheimer of course), institutionalized modern mass culture not only reifies contemporary production and reception of art and literature but also undermines the cultural tradition by reorganizing it. It is this concern about the nonauthentic appropriation of the literary past that motivated and shaped Adorno's essays on the German literary tradition. His criticism had to be double-edged: it had to scrutinize and

---

10. Theodor W. Adorno, "On the Fetish Character in Music and the Regression of Listening," in *The Essential Frankfurt School Reader,* ed. Andrew Arato and Eike Gebhardt (New York: Continuum, 1982), 270–99; Adorno, "Über den Fetischcharakter in der Musik und die Regression des Hörers," in *Schriften* 14:14–50.

undercut the comfortable notion of a "kulturelles Erbe" that guides most of academic criticism; at the same time it had to rescue the literature of the past from the maelstrom of inauthentic appropriation through the culture industry. In other words, neither the academic nor the popular reception could be trusted. The concept of a literary canon could be acknowledged only in order to be questioned. The radical gesture of Adorno must, however, turn upon itself, because there is an equally strong desire to protect the tradition against misuse by the agents of the culture industry. Hence, for Adorno, reading the classics means to brush the text against the grain, stripping the text of layers of false appropriations and bringing out its authentic meaning.

The opening of Adorno's essay on Goethe's *Iphigenie* makes this quite clear: "Die stets noch herrschende Ansicht bringt Goethes Entwicklung unters Cliché eines Reifeprozesses" (*Schriften* 9:495). The close reading of a classic will necessarily encounter clichés, the sediments of previous interpretations. In the case of Goethe, as Adorno shrewdly observes, the author himself helped to establish his own canonization as a classic—a figure who not only transcends his own time but also becomes the cultural as well as literary model for future generations. Hence, it becomes the aim of Adorno's essay to undercut the notion of Goethe's classical maturity and serene harmony. This agenda could be carried out in different ways: the critic could emphasize Goethe's early work, for instance the poems of the Sesenheim period, *Werther,* or *Goetz von Berlichingen,* thereby shunning the mature work as a self-imposed regression to premodern classicism, or stress the importance of the late work, for instance *Faust II, Märchen,* and *Wilhelm Meisters Wanderjahre,* thereby arguing that the classical period of Goethe (1795–1805) was only a passing phase. Adorno chooses neither strategy. Instead, he deconstructs the notion of Goethe's classicism in focusing on the very drama that traditional criticism has viewed as its purest example.

Adorno's reading of Goethe's *Iphigenie* pushes aside its nineteenth-century reception with its insistence on *Bildung* through the Greek-German symbiosis. The concept of humanism [*das Humane*], unless it is critically reconsidered, becomes the stifling blanket that hides the real contours of the play.

Man pflegt diesen [*Klassizismus*], unter Berufung auf Goethes eigene Worte und gleichzeitige Schillers, Humanität oder das Humane zu nennen, gemäß der unverkennbaren Intention, die Achtung vor menschlicher Freiheit, vor der Selbstbestimmung eines jeglichen Einzelnen über

partikulare Sitte und nationelle Beschränktheit ins Allgemeine zu erhe-
ben. So eindeutig indessen die Iphigenie fürs Humane optiert, so wenig
erschöpft sich ihr Gehalt im Plädoyer, eher ist Humanität der Inhalt
des Stücks als der Gehalt. (*Schriften* 11:499)

Adorno's distinction between content [*Inhalt*] and *Gehalt* is strategically
significant indeed, for it allows the critic to reject the conventional reading
of the drama without losing an important category for his own interpretation. The concept of humanism becomes part of the material on which
the play is based—just as the Greek myth of Iphigenia's sacrifice is a
material element of the drama.

Adorno's reading owes its force to his concept of history, more specifically
to his understanding of the process of civilization. Its dialectic is reflected
in Goethe's play in such a way, Adorno argues, that the antinomies of
this process are split between two peoples—Greeks and barbarians. Yet
this opposition—and this is precisely the moment that the conventional
interpretation overlooks—cannot adequately be resolved by the victory of
civilization (and humanism) over barbarism, since Iphigenie and the
Greeks themselves are implicated in the process of guilt and retribution
from which they want to distance themselves. "Zivilisation, die Phase des
mündigen Subjekts, überflügelt die mythischer Unmündigkeit, um dadurch
schuldig an dieser zu werden und in den mythischen Schuldzusammenhang
hineinzugeraten" (*Schriften* 11:500). It is Hegel's philosophy of history that
Adorno confronts with Goethe's text without, however, basing his reading
dogmatically on Hegel's doctrine. Much more than Hegel ever did, Adorno
would place the emphasis on the price humanity has to pay for its own
"progress," a development where the European center displaces its own
problems on the "underdeveloped" countries. "Vag ist . . . der Imperialis-
mus des späteren neunzehnten Jahrhunderts antizipiert, der bis zum jüng-
sten Gegensatz hochindustrialisierter und nichtentwickelter Völker den
Klassenkampf in einen von Nationen oder Blöcken versetzte und unsichtbar
machte" (*Schriften* 11:507). In this context, Iphigenie's humanism, her
insistence on freedom and self-determination, appears, as Adorno suggests,
in a more problematic light. Ultimately, the text subverts itself. As much
as Goethe strengthens Iphigenie's position vis-à-vis King Thoas, it is Thoas
who is expected to show good will and generosity when Iphigenie and her
friends are leaving him.

Er [Thoas] darf, eine Sprachfigur Goethes anzuwenden, an der höchsten

Humanität nicht teilhaben, verurteilt, deren Objekt zu bleiben, während er als ihr Subjekt handelte. Das Unzulängliche der Beschwichtigung, die Versöhnung nur erschleicht, manifestiert sich ästhetisch. . . . Das Meisterwerk knirscht in den Scharnieren: damit verklagt es den Begriff des Meisterwerks. (*Schriften* 11:509)

The play's message, its official humanism, Adorno argues, fails; thus its most authentic figure is not Iphigenie but her brother Orest, whose utopian vision of *Versöhnung,* of peace and love, is at the same time the vision of a madman. He is still in the process of freeing himself from the realm of myth with its eternal chain of guilt and punishment. This very desire makes him, according to Adorno, a modern hero. Goethe's Orest "betritt sie [die Bühne] als Mündiger" (11:511). To put it differently, his thoughts and actions are the result of and reflect the ongoing process of Enlightenment.

Adorno's essay effectively turns the traditional interpretation of Goethe's drama inside out. Where convention saw the solution (in Iphigenie's position), Adorno discovers the problem; where the traditional reading recognized the problem (Orest's guilt and madness), Adorno finds at least the promise of a solution, since Orest overcomes the greatest danger, namely, the relapse into the configuration of mythic thought. Not surprisingly, then, Adorno's verdict is that Goethe is not the classicist whose oeuvre is far removed from today's concerns. Referring to the work of the "mature" Goethe, Adorno writes: "Dieser Goethe erst verkörpert den Einspruch gegen den Klassizismus, der, als sollte es nicht sein, schließlich doch die Partei des Mythos ergreift" (*Schriften* 11:514). This sentence is nothing less than a radical indictment of the entire construct of German literature as it was developed by the first generation of German literary historians during the early nineteenth century. This construct was based on the concept of classicism [*Klassik*] in which Goethe was ascribed a central position. To maintain, as Adorno does, that this classicism ultimately sustains myth rather than enlightenment casts doubt on the entire construct of a German tradition. If there is an authentic tradition at all, it must be one that can only be rediscovered through subversive readings.

One example may give us a more concrete understanding of the gains and limits of Adorno's counterreadings: it is Adorno's attempt to rescue Eichendorff's poetry from its conservative admirers. The basic structure of the Eichendorff essay is similar to that of the Goethe essay: the critic argues against a conventional appropriation of the romantic poet. Unlike Novalis or Hölderlin, Eichendorff has been a truly popular poet in Germany. His broad reception was due, at least to a large extent, to the fact that many of his poems were set to music by major German composers. Thus, Eichendorff's poetry became part of a major German as well as European music tradition. Its national popularity, as Adorno observes, confirmed a conservative agenda. Eichendorff scholarship has largely reflected the conservative Catholic bias of its author. On the other hand, Eichendorff has seldom found admirers on the Left. Lukács, for instance, gave Eichendorff no more than a cursory glance in his *Deutsche Realisten*,[11] dismissing him as a minor figure within the reactionary romantic tradition. This split leaves Adorno with a complex situation. "Eichendorff erkennend vor Freunden und Feinden zu retten, ist das Gegenteil sturer Apologie" (*Schriften* 11:71). Reading Eichendorff critically has to begin with a critique of conventional receptions. The ease and seeming triviality of Eichendorff's poems turns out to be the stumbling block. They can collapse, as Adorno admits, when they are reduced to an affirmative message; their authenticity would entirely depend on their language and what Adorno liked to call "metaphysical tact" [*metaphysischer Takt*] (11:73)—a special sensitivity to the historical feasibility of words.

Adorno's dialectical defense of Eichendorff is not without its problems when it is applied to Eichendorff's critical prose. The attempt, for example, to read Eichendorff's "Der Adel und die Revolution" as a progressive document has to discard most of the text and cling with vigor and determination to the passages where Eichendorff writes about the problems of the ancien régime.[12] It would be difficult, however, to read Eichendorff's concept of freedom as a supplement to the Hegel-Marx tradition, as Adorno wants us to believe. In his political writings, Eichendorff made it quite clear that he favored a hierarchical society under the leadership of a strong nobility. Although he did not participate in the wave of post-Napoleonic German chauvinism, he did not champion liberal democracy. It would be difficult, indeed, to rescue Eichendorff's political essays or his literary criticism from a conservative appropriation. In this respect, Adorno can only succeed by separating the author's life and opinions from his poems. Eichendorff's poetry owes its force and authenticity to its negative impulse, to its rejection of the security that conservative ideology wants to provide.

---

11. Georg Lukács, *Deutsche Realisten des 19. Jahrhunderts* (Berlin: Aufbau-Verlag, 1953), 49–65.

12. Freiherr Joseph von Eichendorff, "Erlebtes: I. Der Adel und die Revolution," in *Gesammelte Schriften,* bd. 10, *Historische, politische und biographische Schriften* (Regensburg: Verlag von J. Habbel, n.d.), 383–406.

Thus, Adorno calls Eichendorff an "unreliable conservative" whose poems tend to subvert his own system of beliefs in celebrating vagrants, soldiers, and outcasts who stand outside the social order that conservative doctrine typically supports. Through these marginal figures, Eichendorff approaches the utopian, a realm of *Erfüllung*. All of a sudden, the seemingly conservative romantic appears in a very different light: "Eichendorffs entfesselte Romantik führt bewußtlos zur Schwelle der Moderne" (*Schriften* 11:78). Eichendorff's poetry is closer to the *Fleurs du mal* than to Goethe's Sesenheim poems.

Again, Adorno's defense of the tradition ends up as an indictment of the tradition, an attempt to revise the conventional order of history where Eichendorff has had his place as a member of the second romantic generation. From a modernist perspective, Eichendorff's place, however, is closer to European symbolism (Baudelaire and Rimbaud). This postromantic character of Eichendorff's poems is not, Adorno argues, a matter of a new consciousness or attitude; rather, it is reflected in the poetic language itself. Language "als ein Autonomes, ist seine Wünschelrute. Ihr dient die Selbstauslöschung des Subjekts" (*Schriften* 11:83). Similar things could be said about Georg Büchner, who opposed the conservative position that Eichendorff adopted. Accordingly, Adorno tries to find a different, more suitable literary context for Eichendorff. In order to accomplish this he makes two suggestions that are not entirely compatible: on the one hand, he brings Eichendorff, as we have seen, closer to European Symbolism; on the other hand, he wants to place him within the anticlassicist German tradition that begins with the young Goethe and then includes authors such as Büchner, Hauptmann, Wedekind, and Brecht (11:79). But what about Novalis, Hölderlin, and Kleist? This typology undermines the essay's more important distinction between romantic and modern writers. Ultimately, Adorno does not argue rigorously in favor of either solution because he remains skeptical vis-à-vis any schematic principle. Thus, Adorno rejects conventional notions of tradition and literary history in general, yet his criticism cannot quite do without these concepts as long as Adorno is seriously involved in historical readings. Hence, he mocks the concept of periodization as inadequate for the language of Eichendorff and, at the same time, invokes the "break with tradition" in order to capture Eichendorff's historical situation (11:87).

Adorno's essay, searching for the authentic aesthetic moment, cannot do without the idea of a tradition as a negative element, the convention that blocks the access to the hidden meaning of the text. When Adorno reflects on the category of tradition in his essay "On Tradition," he is quite aware of the problematic nature of the concept for the analysis of modern history because tradition as a premodern category is hardly compatible with a social system based on a market economy.[13] Thus, modern art and literature respond to the loss of tradition (i.e., accepted cultural practices). This historical approach explains Adorno's ambivalence. Insofar as modern societies become rational and functional, they destroy cultural traditions. Under these circumstances, these traditions stand in opposition to the reification caused by modern rationalism. Thus, for Adorno, cultural traditions can also assume a critical role. However, the element of convention that is constitutive for traditions tends to confirm the status quo and therefore undercut the critical force that society needs. Tradition becomes false in two respects: first, as a remnant from the past, it is an inadequate guide for the future in a permanently changing social system, and, second, as a conceptual construct typical of a modern society, it is false and inauthentic. "Die falsche Tradition, die fast gleichzeitig mit der Konsolidierung der bürgerlichen Gesellschaft aufkam, wühlt im falschen Reichtum" (*Schriften* 10: bd. 1, 313). The concept of tradition developed in a capitalist society is subsumed under the concepts of property and exchange value. What they try to comprehend freezes—turning into inauthentic images. Consequently, Adorno calls for a Kantian approach to the problem of tradition. "Sie nicht vergessen und ihr doch nicht sich anpassen heißt, sie mit dem einmal erreichten Stand des Bewußtseins, dem fortgeschrittensten, konfrontieren und fragen, was trägt und was nicht" (10: bd. 1, 315). Yet this solution, I think, does not quite do justice to the contradiction involved in the category of tradition. Adorno's approach remains a balancing act that relies mostly on the tact of the individual critic. It avoids the radical question of whether the concept is fruitful for the interpretation of modern literature—particularly its inter- and contextual aspects. The reason Adorno did not eliminate the term in spite of its problematic character is probably his fear of a complete collapse of high culture. Brecht's vision of the literary past as a heap of building material could not entice Adorno, since it clearly degraded the works of the past to the status of mere material, thereby robbing them of their truth content. Therefore, he encourages a tradition of negation that defines intertextuality as a historical dynamic that forbids the repetition of the same techniques. The Adornian touchstone for this process is the concept of the authentic

---

13. Theodor W. Adorno, "Über Tradition," in *Schriften* 10: bd. 1, 310–20.

work of art: "Dichtung errettet ihren Wahrheitsgehalt nur, wo sie in eng-
stem Kontakt mit der Tradition diese von sich abstößt" (10: bd. 1, 320).

Adorno's essays point to a German literary tradition—in fact, to several
traditions—yet they never attempt to offer a complete account of the history
of German literature. In regard to their subject matter they remain fragmentary and suggestive rather than systematic. An academic reader might
be inclined to reproach them for their lack of interpretative rigor. It would
be too easy, however, to assume that such a highly self-conscious critic as
Adorno was not aware of this. More than once, the text of his essays
reflects on its own procedure by problematizing the task of reading literature. In his essay on Hans G. Helms, an avant-garde author almost
unknown outside of Germany, he confronts the question of understanding
head-on.[14] The hermetic text of the avant-garde, Adorno suggests, resists
easy understanding. "Ihm [dem Text] wesentlich ist der Schock, mit dem
er die Kommunikation heftig unterbricht. Das grelle Licht des Unver-
ständlichen, das solche Gebilde dem Leser zukehren, verdächtigt die
übliche Verständlichkeit als schal, eingeschliffen, dinghaft—als vorkünst-
lerisch" (*Schriften* 11:431). In this passage, Adorno suggests, first and foremost, that the modern, advanced work of art is so complex and strange
that it is not readily accessible. In this respect, Adorno comes across as a
typical modernist, a position that was still radical in 1960, but would
hardly offend mainstream criticism today. Furthermore, Adorno introduces
in an oblique way a distinction between the language of communication
and poetic language. While the former facilitates understanding (exchange
of meaning), the latter does not. It requires careful reading procedures.
In the Helms essay, which deals more with the idea of an avant-garde text
than with Helms's work, Adorno conflates these two aspects. Modern
literature calls conventional methods of understanding into question
because it has destroyed the illusion of "geschlossener Sinnzusammen-
hang" (11:431), which allowed the reader to situate the text. Yet this
conflation is problematic; it is by no means certain that older literature
is, by definition, more accessible than modern works. Ultimately, this
opinion does not reflect Adorno's own position; he consistently rejects, as
we have seen, conventional readings of classical texts. Thus, Adorno later
returns to his second distinction, that between communication and art,

---

14. Theodor W. Adorno, "Voraussetzung: Aus Anlaß einer Lesung von Hans G.
Helms," in *Schriften* 11:431–46.

between "normal understanding" and reading literature. As soon as we raise the question of what we mean by understanding a literary text, we realize, Adorno argues, that understanding cannot be equated with capturing the meaning [*das Gemeinte*]. "Kunstwerke versteht man nicht wie eine fremde Sprache oder wie Begriffe, Urteile, Schlüsse der eigenen" (11:432). Adorno refers to the understanding of concepts and arguments as rational *Verstehen*, because it deals with discourse matters. Literature, however, stands outside this realm; understanding a literary text can be accomplished only through a process of mediation. "[I]ndem nämlich der im Vollzug von Erfahrung ergriffene Gehalt, in seiner Beziehung zur Formensprache und den Stoffen des Gebildes, reflektiert und benannt wird" (11:433). Understanding, in other words, is based on experience [*Erfahrung*], yet it cannot stop there, it is incomplete without reflection on the material of the artwork and its relationship to form [*Formensprache*].

Adorno's definition of understanding literature, then, is wedged between two approaches that he rejects. Understanding can neither be a purely rational, conceptual translation nor a merely intuitive process of empathy (irrational). For Adorno, the irrational approach fails as much as the rational because the work is never fully accessible to immediate experience. Its element of self-reflection, an element that is independent of the intentions of the author, calls for a philosophy of art that will, by means of its conceptual work, overcome the blindness of the text. Hence, criticism is always more than reading a text, and the critic cannot pretend to be just a "reader." For Adorno, criticism participates in, but is not identical with, the philosophy of art.

What, then, is the difference? Why is literary criticism not simply applied philosophy of art? Traditional philosophy of art [*Ästhetik*], Adorno argues in his introduction to *Aesthetic Theory*, is at home in the realm of abstract categories and arguments, which can be derived from ultimate principles. Both Kant and Hegel keep their distance from the individual work of art. Criticism, on the other hand, begins its work within the text, using—and quite consciously so—the concrete experience of the reader or listener as a springboard for a close reading and subsequent reflection leading the critic back to the realm of philosophical discourse. What Adorno shares with formalism and post-structuralist approaches is his insistence on an intrinsic method. In his "Lyric Poetry and Society," for instance, in which Adorno outlines the principles for a sociology of literature, he argues that the deciphering of the social meaning has to begin with a close reading of the poem. Whatever the problems of this method may be, it emphasizes Adorno's concern with form and structure rather than content (themes and topics).

Considerations of theory and method obviously play a major role in Adorno's literary criticism, yet it would be misleading and ultimately false to appropriate Adorno's essays purely in terms of their philosophical rigor. Their formal structure is of equal importance. They are written as essays rather than *Abhandlungen* or articles, that is to say, they are not meant to be scholarly and scientific [*wissenschaftlich*]. It is not accidental, therefore, that the first essay of *Noten zur Literatur* (vol. 1, 1958), entitled "The Essay as Form," reflects on the formal problem of criticism. Adorno sees his own contribution in the tradition of a literary genre that was defined and also practiced by the young Lukács. Adorno's own concept of the essay form explicitly refers to Lukács's *Soul and Form* (1911) and systematically responds to Lukács's theory. As Adorno suggests, the essay "fängt nicht mit Adam und Eva an sondern mit dem, worüber er reden will; er sagt, was ihm daran aufgeht, bricht ab, wo er selber am Ende sich fühlt und nicht dort, wo kein Rest mehr bleibe; so rangiert er unter den Allotria" (*Schriften* 11:10). The essay wants to remain nonsystematic, playful, unbound by rules of rigor. For Adorno, the essay is the very form that allows the critic to explore the margins. Its strategies are suggestions and associations but not, as Adorno observes, fiction and "ästhetischer Schein" (11:11). The essay is informed by theory but it does not develop concepts and doctrines. In this configuration, therefore, reading and understanding take on a new meaning.

Occasionally, critics of Adorno have suggested that his method of reading lacks rigor, that he never works completely through a text. This observation is correct, especially for his essays on literature; they refrain from systematic readings and prefer a tangential method of allusions and cross-references that successfully avoids the heavy pedagogical turn of the explication de texte. Adorno's essays rarely present a straightforward argument using standard discursive prose. His style, highly mannered in its choice of words and syntax, compliments the structure of the essay. Its success depends on the tension between the individual, sometimes playful approach and the significance of the subject matter. Significance in this context, however, should not be confused with high seriousness. Adorno liked to write on marginal topics such as punctuation and *Fremdwörter*. Not only those pieces but also his essays on Balzac and Proust would hardly find the approval of the academy as serious contributions to Balzac and Proust scholarship. Quite consciously, Adorno entitled his collection of literary essays "Notes on Literature," hinting at their marginal character that would both accept and subvert the central position of academic criticism. His essays are supposed to remind their readers of the public function of criticism; they insist on the Kantian element of critique that is rooted in but not limited to the literary text. When Adorno's popularity was at its peak in the late 1960s, this method of reading was called *Ideologiekritik* ['ideology critique']. It became fashionable to take apart and dismiss authors and texts on the basis of their implicit ideology. Unlike some of his students, Adorno never applied his critical method of reading mechanically. In fact, it would be difficult to define his method in terms of academic schools and traditions. His concept of dialectical criticism, which, in principle, subverts overt meanings, owes its force to Hegel and Marx without accepting their doctrines as fixed norms.

In terms of his German contemporaries, the most interesting comparison would be that with Gadamer and the hermeneutic tradition. It goes without saying that Adorno had little sympathy for traditional hermeneutics. His scorn for *Einfühlung* ['empathy'] reminds us of Benjamin's frontal attack on German *Geistesgeschichte* that regularly invoked Wilhelm Dilthey for its own legitimacy. What distinguishes Adorno from this tradition is the polemical stance against the desire to objectify meaning and history. In this regard, he was rather close to Gadamer's critique of objectivity in *Truth and Method*. Still, the direction of their critique is hardly compatible. This is, of course, particularly true for their concepts of tradition. Whereas Gadamer wants to remind his readers that critique is not possible without prejudice and, therefore, stresses the priority of tradition over reason, Adorno consistently focuses his criticism on this conservative idea of tradition and continuity. His essays, as we have seen, quite deliberately subvert the notion of an unquestioned cultural tradition that gives us transhistorical values. If there is any truth in a work of art, it cannot be handed down through institutional channels. In fact, in dealing with classical texts, the unfolding of the truth content [*Wahrheitsgehalt*] has to begin with the removal of previous readings that have conventionalized the artwork. Truth in a literary work of art, apart from the fact that it simply cannot be spelled out in terms of concepts and ideas, escapes any attempt to pin it down and fix its meaning. Truth, Adorno maintains, becomes visible only in the moment of reflection on concrete experience, which, to be sure, is determined in history. Working out a method in terms of prescribed procedures—beyond the obvious requirement of reading— would disturb Adorno because it necessarily reifies the two essential elements of criticism: experience and reflection.

Acoustic Experiment as Ephemeral Spectacle?: Musical Futurism, Dada, Cage, and the Talking Heads

Steven Paul Scher

> Recklessness is what makes experimental art beautiful
> —John Ashbery

Looking back over the uncommonly varied and innovative aesthetic land-scape of twentieth-century Europe and North America, interdisciplinarity emerges most clearly as the overarching notion that seems to have governed both individual and collaborative artistic experimentation. While the bor-ders traditionally separating the individual art forms have not been elim-inated entirely, they have become less distinct than ever before. In rapid succession, avant-garde movements evolved in an intermedia context on an international scale and had a formative impact on the diverse cultural phenomena that constitute what Jean-François Lyotard calls the "post-modern condition." Indeed, the deep-seated interrelatedness of virtually all events and developments in our century—whether historical, political, social, economic, or artistic—remains unprecedented. Particularly when viewed in this wider context of cultural criticism, Lyotard's definition of the overworked concept "postmodern" acquires interpretive legitimacy. "The word [*postmodern*] is in current use on the American continent among sociologists and critics; it designates the state of our culture following the transformations which, since the end of the nineteenth century, have altered the game rules for science, literature and the arts."[1]

The aim of this essay is to contemplate, however provisionally, certain

---

Epigraph from John Ashbery, quoted in *The Craft of Poetry,* ed. William Packard (New York: Doubleday, 1974), 128.

1. Jean-François Lyotard, *The Postmodern Condition: A Report on Knowledge,* trans. Geoff Bennington and Brian Massumi (Minneapolis: University of Minnesota Press, 1984), xxiii.

evanescent and seemingly marginal transformations in early twentieth-century music and thinking about music and to draw attention to the perduring, as yet virtually unassessed, interdisciplinary consequences of these transformations.[2] More precisely, I shall argue that the portentous ideas about "noise as music" so assiduously promoted by the Italian Futurists were not conceived in splendid disciplinary isolation and that their impact was not confined merely to the realm of music. Not only have these ideas (along with some of their fascinating though short-lived technical realizations) profoundly influenced subsequent avant-garde *musical* experimentation down to our day, but, right from their conception, they were inextricably intertwined with—and became indispensable to—the theory and practice of mainstream Futurism, particularly *literary* Futurism. They have also left indelible traces in the ingenious sonic and linguistic strategies that have come to be associated primarily with dadaist and, later, concrete poetry.

Italian Futurism was the brainchild of Filippo Tommaso Marinetti (1876–1944), an angry young intellectual of moderate poetic talent but ample independent means who was set "on changing experience, and the world, society, as well as all the arts, totally."[3] As self-appointed chief ideologue, Maecenas, and impresario, Marinetti launched the movement with a real bang: on February 20, 1909, he published his infamous "Fondazione e Manifesto del Futurismo," conspicuously placed on the front page of the Paris paper *Le Figaro*. The shock effect elicited by this pompous and arrogant text couched in effusive poetic prose, the first of countless

---

2. Especially in recent decades, critical commentary on all possible aspects of Futurism—in many languages besides Italian—has been voluminous, and there seems to be no end in sight. Most of these studies are circumspect and informative but predominantly descriptive rather than analytically critical in nature and offer little more than occasional honorable mentions of musical developments. For a comprehensive bibliography, see Jean-Pierre Andreoli–de Villers, *Futurism and the Arts: A Bibliography, 1959–73* (Toronto and Buffalo: University of Toronto Press, 1975). Even Marjorie Perloff's admirably all-encompassing critical study *The Futurist Moment: Avant-Garde, Avant Guerre, and the Language of Rupture* (Chicago: University of Chicago Press, 1986) provides only passing references to musical matters. For specifically musicological studies, see Fred K. Prieberg, *Musica ex machina: Über das Verhältnis von Musik und Technik* (Berlin, Frankfurt, and Vienna: Ullstein, 1960); Otto Kolleritsch, ed., *Der musikalische Futurismus: Ästhetisches Konzept und Auswirkungen auf die Moderne* (Graz: Universal Edition, 1976); Rodney J. Payton, "The Music of Futurism: Concerts and Polemics," *Musical Quarterly* 62 (1976): 25–45; Karl Gustav Fellerer, "Der Futurismus in der italienischen Musik," *Mitteilungen (Mededelingen) der Königlichen Belgischen Akademie der Wissenschaften, Literaturen und Schönen Künste, Klasse der Schönen Künste* 39, no. 3 (1977): 1–68.

3. Peter Demetz, *Italian Futurism and the German Literary Avant-Garde*, 1986 Bithell Memorial Lecture (London: Institute of German Studies, 1987), 1.

more manifestos to follow, was just what its author hoped for. Significantly, it already contained the premises for enlisting music (along with poetry, painting, sculpture, architecture, and even film) in the all-out attack on traditionalism of every conceivable kind. As a result of this intellectual bombshell, though hardly of consequence when compared to its prominent predecessor, Marx and Engel's *Communist Manifesto* of 1848, "Futurism established itself as the most aggressive artistic phenomenon of its age in the least amount of time and on the widest possible international front."[4] Considering the febrile climate of proliferating artistic movements sketched by Diaghilev in 1913, such an astonishing success was no mean feat. "Twenty new schools of art are born within a month. Futurism, Cubism—they are already prehistory. One needs but three days to become *pompier.* Mototism overcomes Automatism, which yields to Trepidism and Vibrism and they in turn to Planism, Serenism, Omnism and Neism."[5]

Glorifying war and technological progress; rhapsodizing about speed and simultaneity; extolling the beauty of machines, cars, and airplanes; delighting in the cacophony of modern industrial cities replete with the rumble of traffic and factories; wanting to do away with libraries and museums—these key anti-*passatismo* sentiments and objectives of the Futurists are well known, as is their ardent nationalism and patriotism, which predisposed them early on to Mussolini's fascism and precipitated their demise.[6] Marinetti's founding document was followed almost immediately by the publication of two manifestos in a similar vein on Futurist painting (1910). They were signed by Umberto Boccioni, Carlo Carrà, Luigi Russolo, Giacomo Balla, and Gino Severini—extraordinarily gifted painters who were soon able to demonstrate their militant doctrines in artistic practice. This was certainly not the case with the proponents of musical Futurism, whose contribution to the movement turned out to be theoretical and visionary rather than work oriented, not least because they simply lacked sufficient talent to create a body of enduring works of art like those of their painter colleagues.[7] Boccioni's powerfully dynamic paintings, for example, are still regularly exhibited and valued the world over and con-

---

4. Max Kozloff, *Cubism/Futurism* (New York: Charterhouse, 1973), 118.

5. Kozloff, *Cubism/Futurism,* 120.

6. For a succinct discussion of these orientations and their consequences, see Demetz, *Italian Futurism,* 2–4.

7. "Die Russolos waren keine großen Komponisten, aber sie gehörten zu den sympathischen Fanatikern, die für eine Idee leben und kämpfen, gleichgültig, ob sie Bestätigung findet oder nicht" (Hans Heinz Stuckenschmidt, "Die Ordnung der Freiheit," *Melos* 29 [1962]: 265).

tinue to represent Futurist art at its best, while Futurist music has been virtually forgotten.

Francesco Balilla Pratella (1880–1955) was the only professionally trained musician among the Futurists. Directly inspired by Marinetti's first manifesto, the decidedly less belligerent and cosmopolitan Pratella came forward with no fewer than three manifestos of his own: "Manifesto dei musicisti futuristi" (1910), "Manifesto tecnico della musica futurista" (1911), and "La distruzione della quadratura" (1912). They were published together as prefaces to the piano score (cover design by Boccioni) of Pratella's *Musica futurista per orchestra* (1912), the first officially Futurist piece of music. In practice, however, this piece seems to have fallen far short of substantiating the novel compositional principles that Pratella proposed— atonality, rhythmic irregularity, microtonality, and enharmonicism. A contemporary reviewer found *Musica futurista* less than exhilarating. "Is it perhaps the march of the Futurists? Maybe. But rather than avant-garde music, I would say it was suitable to accompany dancing bears."[8] It is telling that perhaps the only programmatic prescription of truly Futurist flavor in all of Pratella's long-winded theorizing was added to his second, technical manifesto, in all probability by Master Marinetti himself: "Give musical animation to crowds, great industrial shipyards, trains, transatlantic steamers, battleships, automobiles, and airplanes. Add the domination of the machine and the victorious reign of Electricity to the great central motive of a musical poem."[9]

Even with all due respect for Pratella's role as the first theorist of musical Futurism, it is hard to comprehend today that it was as a composer that he ignited the keen speculative and experimental imagination of his painter colleague Luigi Russolo (1885–1947). During a performance of Pratella's *Musica futurista,* nonmusician Russolo hit upon the idea for his noise theory, which he first outlined in the 1913 manifesto "L'arte dei rumori." He addressed that manifesto personally to "Dear Balilla Pratella, Great Futurist Composer," and it became the first chapter of Russolo's 1916 book of the same title, translated only recently into English as *The Art of Noises* (1986).[10] In addition to a radically new musical aesthetics based on noises

---

8. A. E., review of *Musica futurista per orchestra* by Francesco Pratella, *Rivista Musicale Italiana* 20 (1913): 682.

9. Francesco Pratella, quoted in Michael Kirby, *Futurist Performance* (New York: PAJ Publications, 1986), 165.

10. Luigi Russolo, *The Art of Noises,* trans. Barclay Brown (New York: Pendragon Press, 1986). Brown's introduction provides the most illuminating critical-analytical overview of Russolo's thought to date.

of every perceivable and conceivable kind,[11] Russolo's pioneering treatise also offered a descriptive account of the series of new mechanical instruments called *intonarumori* ['noise intoners'] that he and his friend Ugo Piatti designed and actually constructed and that were capable of generating and regulating an astonishing spectrum of mechanically producible nonmusical sounds.[12]

By providing a theoretical and practical framework for the expanded musical realm of the future as he envisioned it, Russolo may also have paved the way for the unrelenting intermedia experimentation that has energized much of twentieth-century artistic avant-garde activity. His iconoclasm is as strong as it is suggestive.

> *We must break out of this narrow circle of pure musical sounds, and conquer the infinite variety of noise-sounds.* . . . We futurists have all deeply loved and enjoyed the harmonies of the great masters. Beethoven and Wagner have stirred our nerves and hearts for many years. Now we have had enough of them, and *we delight much more in combining in our thoughts the noises of trams, of automobile engines, of carriages and brawling crowds, than hearing again the "Eroica" or the "Pastorale."*[13]

Russolo privileged noise in order to legitimize it as usable artistic raw material; he even devised a classification of six major noise categories and proposed a new system for noise notation that, in modified form, is still used for the notation of electroacoustic music. His fundamental prescriptive insight implied nothing less revolutionary than the emancipation of noise from mundane acoustic confinement. Noise became musically composable and has remained very much so until today.

Wherever we are, what we hear is mostly noise. When we ignore it, it

---

11. "We will delight in distinguishing the eddying of water, of air or gas in metal pipes, the muttering of motors that breathe and pulse with an indisputable animality, the throbbing of valves, the bustle of pistons, the shrieks of mechanical saws, the starting of trams on the tracks, the cracking of whips, the flapping of awnings and flags. We will amuse ourselves by orchestrating together in our imagination the din of rolling shop shutters, the varied hubbub of train stations, iron works, thread mills, printing presses, electrical plants, and subways [and] the newest noises of modern war" (Russolo, *Art of Noises*, 26). Russolo's diction in this passage clearly shows signs of Marinetti's all-pervasive inspiration.

12. For reasons still unclear, none of the *intonarumori* seem to have survived World War II. Either they were accidentally destroyed during the war in France or they have not yet been rediscovered.

13. Russolo, *Art of Noises*, 25; italics in original.

disturbs us. When we listen to it, we find it fascinating. The sound of a truck at 50 mph. Static between the stations. Rain. We want to capture and control these sounds, to use them, not as sound effects, but as musical instruments.[14]

This Russoloesque passage, revealingly enough, comes from "The Future of Music: Credo," a lecture first delivered in 1937, but not published until 1958, by none other than John Cage, "one of the most important figures in twentieth-century music [and] perhaps the most influential and eloquent spokesperson for the musical avant-garde."[15] As relevant today as it was fifty years ago, his comment could just as well have been made in one of his Norton Lectures, given at Harvard in 1989.[16]

Apart from its potential for the twentieth-century musical avant-garde— which has been realized to an unprecedented degree by practitioners of musique concrète (Pierre Schaeffer and Pierre Henry), electronic music (Edgard Varèse, Karlheinz Stockhausen, Herbert Eimert, Luciano Berio, Luigi Nono, and Henry Pousseur), aleatoric music (John Cage, Pierre Boulez, Morton Feldman, and Christian Wolff) and, most recently, computer music[17]—the immediate practical benefits of Russolo's emancipation-

---

14. John Cage, "The Future of Music: Credo," in Richard Kostelanetz, *John Cage* (New York: Praeger, 1970), 54.

15. Daniel A. Herwitz, "The Security of the Obvious: On John Cage's Musical Radicalism," *Critical Inquiry* 14 (1988): 784. Cage's "contributions to music have included the vast extension of percussive means (most notably the invention of the prepared piano as we know it today), the development of new rhythmic configurations in composition, the early use of electronically processed sounds, and the early use of 'aleatoric' or 'chance' elements. He has reworked the Dadaist event into an occasion specifically for and about music, which produced the musical happening" (784–85).

16. According to Anthony Tommasini's report, in true "happenings" fashion, "The talks themselves struck listeners variously as a metaphysical meditation on the world, or Dadaist poetry, or gibberish" (*New York Times,* April 23, 1989).

17. For orientation about these movements, I have found the following titles most helpful: Frederick C. Judd, *Electronic Music and Musique Concrète* (London: Neville Spearman, 1961); Pierre Schaeffer, *La musique concrète,* 2d ed. (Paris: Presses Universitaires de France, 1973); Michael Nyman, *Experimental Music: Cage and Beyond* (London: Studio Vista, 1974); Jon Appleton and Ronald C. Perrera, eds., *The Development and Practice of Electronic Music* (Englewood Cliffs, N.J.: Prentice-Hall, 1975); David Keane, *Tape Music Composition* (Oxford: Oxford University Press, 1980); Michel Chion, *Guide des objets sonores* (Paris: Buchet Chastel/INA/ GRM, 1983); Barry Truax, *Acoustic Communication* (Norwood, N.J.: Ablex, 1984); Peter Manning, *Electronic and Computer Music* (Oxford: Oxford University Press, 1985); Simon Emmerson, ed., *The Language of Electroacoustic Music* (New York: Harwood Academic Publishers, 1986); and Ruth A. Solie, "When the Message Becomes the Medium: Text-Music Relationships in the Avant-Garde," *Ars Lyrica* 4 (1989): 7–18.

of-noise theory for the ongoing Futurist movement were enormous. Along with improvised incendiary speeches, poetry recitations, and exhibits of painting and sculpture, the scandalous Futurist soirees (precursors of later "happenings") regularly staged by Marinetti in cities all over Europe invariably included some sort of Futurist musical event. Marinetti's impassioned account of the first public demonstration of the clumsy battery of *intonarumori,* on April 21, 1914, in Milan, aptly captures the spectacle aspect of the concert-turned-riot and his obvious delight in the whole affair.

A huge crowd. Boxes and galleries full to bursting. Deafening uproar of conservatives who want at all costs to interrupt the concert. For an hour the futurists resisted imperturbably. At the beginning of the fourth piece an extraordinary thing happened: suddenly five futurists—Boccioni, Carrá, Armando Mazza, Piatti and myself—were seen to come down from the stage, cross the orchestral pit, and assault with punches, slaps and walking-sticks the hundreds of conservatives in the stalls, who were drunk with stupidity and traditionalist mania. The battle in the stalls lasted for half an hour, while Luigi Russolo continued to conduct his 19 *intonarumori* on the stage.[18]

Much of the noise (literal as well as musical) generated by Italian Futurism began to lose its shock value and quirky intellectual appeal after World War I, though it continued to be echoed for some time by subsequent avant-garde movements. With the advent of fascism, Marinetti sold his soul to Mussolini and his brainchild gradually slipped into oblivion.

"Futurism is dead. What killed it? *Dada.*" Thus spoke a pamphlet attacking Marinetti in 1921 from Paris.[19] The matter was surely not quite that simple, for many of the Futurist ideas and innovative artistic strategies, however altered in spirit and practical application, lived on in dada and beyond.[20] As Hans Richter reminisces in his *Dada: Art and Anti-Art,* "Like all newborn movements we were convinced that the world began anew in us; but in fact we had swallowed Futurism—bones, feathers and all. It is

---

18. Filippo Marinetti, quoted in John C. G. Waterhouse, "A Futurist Mystery," *Music and Musicians* 15, no. 8 (1967): 27–28.

19. Quoted in Pontus Hulten, *Futurismo & futurismi,* trans. Asterisco et al. (New York: Abbeville Press, 1986), 459.

20. For a succinct account of dadaism's Futurist legacy, see Hans Richter, *Dada: Art and Anti-Art,* trans. David Britt (London: Thames and Hudson, 1965), 217–18.

true that in the process of digestion all sorts of bones and feathers had been regurgitated."[21]

There was, of course, no such thing as dadaist music per se. Yet dadaist events, just as the Futurist *serate* before them, would have been inconceivable without some sort of specifically performance-oriented music or semblance of music as animating acoustic backdrop. Characteristically, though, no trace whatsoever remains of Berlin dadaist Efim Golishev's literally inimitable piano composition of 1919, which Raoul Hausmann introduced as follows.

Man spielt Ihnen *Die Antisymphonie* in drei Teilen (Die Kreisguillotine) *a*) Die provokante Spritze *b*) Die chaotische Mundhöhle *c*) Das biegsame super *fa*. Eh, Herr Johann Sebastian Bach, Ihre wohltemperierte Unordnung erlebt den Krach mit der dodekaistischen Antisymphonie! Aus und vorbei mit dem tönenden Zopf einer, ach so herrlich begründeten Tradition! Dada siegt auch in Tönen! Meine Herrschaften, Ihre eingerosteten Ohren klingen? Lassen Sie durch die musikalische Kreissäge zersägen! Spülen Sie die Reste Ihrer Stimme mit Golyscheff aus Ihrer chaotischen Mundhöhle![22]

Surely there must have been more to the musical Futurist legacy passed on to dadaism than promoting such sophomoric entertainments as Russian composer Golishev's rather forgettable recital (which we cannot even be certain actually took place).

What the dadaists did inherit from musical Futurism—or, rather, from Russolo's integration of Marinetti's boldly innovative poetic theory and practice into his own *L'arte dei rumori*—was an acute awareness of the unlimited possibilities of acoustic mimesis inherent in the sounds of language. Indeed, this heightened awareness has remained perhaps the single indispensable prerequisite for today's experimenters with phonetic poetry such as Austrian sound poet Ernst Jandl, poet-composer Gerhard Rühm, and other practitioners of concrete poetry the world over. It may not be an exaggeration to say that, without the impact, however indirect, of Marinetti's theory of "words-in-freedom" [*parole in libertà*] and of its first practical demonstration in his memorable "Zang Tumb Tumb" (1914), a

---

21. Richter, *Dada,* 43.
22. Raoul Hausmann, *Am Anfang war Dada,* ed. Karl Riha and Gerhard Käpf (Steinbach: Anabas Verlag, 1972), 105–6.

free-word poem-reportage attempting to recreate the experience of the World War I battle of Adrianopolis in the form of a "verbal score," twentieth-century avant-garde experimentation with the interface of text and music would have taken quite a different course. Practically all postulates of Marinetti's categorical *paroliberismo*—for example, abolition of traditional syntax, punctuation, and metrics; massive employment of onomatopoeia; introduction of mathematical and even musical notation; and the demand for a typographical revolution and "free expressive orthography"[23]—have been taken up in some form or other, if not outright adopted, by subsequent avant-garde artists.

Both despite and because of the undeniable link with Marinetti's pioneering efforts, dadaism's contribution to the world of sound proved to be far more inspired and lasting than that of Futurism. The dadaist counterpart to Russolo's rather vacuous and contrived "noise music" was the truly imaginative "word music" of Hugo Ball and Kurt Schwitters that consisted predominantly of ingenious onomatopoetic vocables and word clusters. Ball, Schwitters, and other dadaist poets invented such fascinating new forms of verbal composition expressly designed for performance as sound poems [*Lautgedichte*], simultaneous poems, noise poems [*poèmes bruitistes*], gymnastic poems [*poèmes mouvementistes*], and optophonetic poems.[24]

"Sound poetry as a conscious art form," as concrete poet, composer, and Cage disciple Dick Higgins defines it, "lies between music and poetry, and depends upon this acoustic element for its formal and aesthetic sense.... There may be considerable sense or logic in the acoustic structuring of a sound poem."[25] It took Kurt Schwitters more than ten years to complete his monumental sound poem "Ursonate" (1932), a unique example of the combined legacy of musical and literary Futurism and dadaism. Mindful of the potential of the human voice (preferably his own) to produce noise-sounds, Schwitters drew on traditional musical techniques and forms *and* utilized many of Marinetti's stylistic, typographic, and orthographic strategies, pushing the idea of "musicalizing" spoken text to its outer human limits. But in spite of all the serious effort, genuine engagement, and linguistic virtuosity that he invested in making "Urson-

---

23. See, especially, Filippo Marinetti, "Destruction of Syntax—Imagination without Strings—Words-in-Freedom" (1913), in *Futurist Manifestos,* ed. Umbro Apollonio (New York: Viking, 1973), 95–106.

24. For a useful characterization of these forms, see the preface in *113 Dada Gedichte,* ed. Karl Riha (Berlin: Verlag Klaus Wagenbach, 1982), 7–22.

25. Dick Higgins, "Early Sound Poetry," *Literature in Performance,* 1985, 42.

ate," it is difficult not to suspect that Schwitters, the supreme humorist and ironist, was fully aware of the ultimate absurdity of his grotesque creation. If the phonograph recordings on which he himself performs selections from the work are any indication,[26] he must have thought the whole affair hilariously funny: a serious jest bordering on parody and self-parody combined.

Since its founding in 1916 at the Cabaret Voltaire in Zurich, dadaism has never ceased to provide inspiration for generations of avant-gardists working in different artistic media. A recent, admittedly rare instance of this creative reception, cross-cultural as well as cross-disciplinary, deserves closer scrutiny: an obscure but timeless dadaist text was rediscovered and successfully integrated into postmodern popular culture (with mass appeal, no less). By way of an open-ended conclusion, then, I shall examine how Hugo Ball's sound poem "Gadji beri bimba" (1916) has been transformed into the influential classic hit song "I Zimbra" (1979) by Talking Heads, one of the finest rock groups performing today. Surfacing from the SoHo underground in the late 1970s and led by singer-songwriter-guitarist David Byrne, Talking Heads have been hailed for injecting fresh creativity into the popular music genre. Their song "I Zimbra" exemplifies a unique approach to the setting of text to music, reworking Ball's dadaist poem while preserving its original flavor and sonic and linguistic properties and using African polyrhythms and minimalist elements of musical texture.

Gadji beri bimba

gadji beri bimba glandridi laula lonni cadori
gadjama gramma berida bimbala glandri galassassa laulitalomini
gadji beri bin blassa glassala laula lonni cadorsu sassala bim
gadjama tuffm i zimzalla binban gligla wowolimai bin beri ban
o katalominai rhinozerossola hopsamen laulitalomini hoooo
gadjama rhinozerossola hopsamen
bluku terullala blaulala loooo

zimzim urullala zimzim urullala zimzim zanzibar zimzalla zam
elifantolim brussala bulomen brussala bulomen tromtata
velo da bang bang affalo purzamai affalo purzamai lengado tor
gadjama bimbalo glandridi glassala zingtata pimpalo ögrögöööö
viola laxato viola zimbrabim viola uli paluji malooo

tuffm im zimbrabim negramai bumbalo negramai bumbalo tuffm i zim

---

26. For a list of Schwitters's recordings, see Ernst Nündel, *Kurt Schwitters in Selbstzeugnissen und Bilddokumenten* (Reinbek bei Hamburg: Rowohlt, 1981), 150.

gadjama bimbala oo beri gadjama gaga di gadjama affalo pinx
gaga di bumbalo bumbalo gadjamen
gaga di bling blong
gaga blung[27]

I ZIMBRA

GADJI BERI BIMBA CLANDRIDI
LAULI LONNI CADORI GADJAM
A BIM BERI GLASSALA GLANDRIDE
E GLASSALA TUFFM I ZIMBRA

BIM BLASSA GALASSASA ZIMBRABIM
BLASSA GALLASSASA ZIMBRABIM

A BIM BERI GLASSALA GLANDRID
E GLASSALA TUFFM I ZIMBRA

GADJI BERI BIMBA CLANDRIDI
LAULI LONNI CADORI GADJAM
A BIM BERI GLASSALA GLANDRIDE
E GLASSALA TUFFM I ZIMBRA[28]

(Talking Heads)

Mindful of Peter Demetz's admonition—especially when dealing with such texts as Ball's poem and Byrne's song lyrics—that "we should be eager to feel the sensual pleasures yielded by art, rather than to exert our energies in the hermeneutic search for meaning,"[29] I shall, whenever possible, resist the temptation to find semantic content where there may be precious little or none. Yet I feel compelled to begin with the observation that the lyrics of "I Zimbra" possess a nonwestern flavor. In words such as *tuffm* and *gadjam,* the consonant groupings suggest African or Middle Eastern speech and the prominence of the high vowels *e* and *i* may infer Indian speech. There are neither diacritical marks characteristic of Western languages (such as circonflex or umlaut; Ball's "ögrögöööö"), nor words whose sounds or spellings specifically evoke Western words such as the programmatic title of Ball's better-known sound poem "Karawane," which instantly conjures up a particular context. Thus Byrne's lyrics intimate a non-Western setting but not an expressly African one.

---

27. Hugo Ball, "Gadji beri bimba," reprinted in Riha, *113 Dada Gedichte,* 34.

28. "I Zimbra" is the first song on the Talking Heads' album *Fear of Music* (Sire Record Company, 1979). Byrne's text is printed on the record jacket.

29. Peter Demetz, "Varieties of Phonetic Poetry: An Introduction," in *From Kafka and Dada to Brecht and Beyond,* ed. Reinhold Grimm, Peter Spycher, and Richard A. Zipser (Madison: University of Wisconsin Press, 1982), 33.

Perhaps not accidentally, then, Byrne shapes his lyrics out of material taken largely from the first five lines of "Gadji beri bimba," though more direct African clues such as "zanzibar" appear in the rest of Ball's poem. For example, "rhinozerossola,"[30] "elifantolim," and perhaps even "affalo" suggest African wildlife (Byrne's "Zimbra," derived from Ball's "zimbra-bim," may connote 'zebra'). Jungle calls such as "hoooo," "loooo," and "ögrögöööö" further evoke an African landscape. Also, the unusual consonant combinations occur less frequently as the poem develops and there is a greater proportion of the "African" low vowels *a, o,* and *u* toward the end.

With a stretch of the imagination, of course, "Gadji beri bimba" may be interpreted as a concise narrative. The poem possesses overall linguistic coherence and carefully avoids radical changes in sonority (except for the obvious onomatopoetic instances). Ball draws on a host of quasi-narrative devices to create the impression of a story: he emphasizes words and word clusters through repetition, and he consistently alters and modifies the shape and length of individual words to suggest elaboration and development of characters or events. There are perceivable hints of conflict ("rhinozerossola hopsamen . . . loooo") and climax ("ögrögöööö"); and, as the poem concludes, the lines grow shorter and shorter, intimating decay and death.

> gaga di bumbalo bumbalo gadjamen
> gaga di bling blong
> gaga blung

It is as if Ball had transcribed some anxious native's monologue about a jungle incident in a wholly contrived pseudo-African language.

For his musical setting, David Byrne has created a text of its own distinction: he has restructured Ball's poem and pared it down to singable dimensions. Paying little attention to the stresses and divisions within and between words, Byrne treats the text as a continuous series of syllables within individual lines, keeps the rhythm of each line consistent, and makes no effort to articulate the words as semantic entities. By combining and recombining words and syllables strategically extracted from the original, his streamlined version significantly enhances the effect of the song text,

---

30. Here, the veiled, punning allusion to Luigi Russolo, whom Ball must have known, is not inconceivable. The immediate contextual association is the German *Rüssel,* of course. The related form "russula" occurs in Ball's sound poem "Karawane."

while it still retains Ball's linguistic coherence, non-Western flavor, and, through the use of "I Zimbra" as title and refrain, the African allusion. The phrase "I Zimbra" is Byrne's own felicitous coinage, of course. He must have realized—correctly, I believe—that the vocables "zim," "zimbrabim," and "i zim" in various combinations served as the linguistic backbone to Ball's poem.

"Beschriebene Musik ist wie ein erzähltes Mittagessen," as Grillparzer adroitly remarked,[31] so I shall not dwell too long on what the Talking Heads' song sounds like; it must be heard to be appreciated, just as Ball's "Gadji beri bimba" was intended to be enjoyed in live recitation. The music of "I Zimbra," scored for multiple guitars, bass, percussion, and a small mixed chorus, consists of a series of repeated polyrhythmic textures comprising minimal motivic patterns. It begins with a section in which the textural elements are introduced one at a time and concludes with a recapitulation of the complete textural development. Each line of the song possesses a discrete rhythmic character and each stanza alternates with a movement to the subdominant and a repeated guitar figure. The second stanza conspicuously lacks a beat: with the omission of *bim* in the second line, there is no syllable on that downbeat. After setting up a specific pattern, Byrne intentionally violates it, but in so doing he effectively reinforces the rhythmic flow. The transition leading to the recapitulation in the final stanza consists of a repeated exchange between the bass and the guitar that is reminiscent of the call-response pattern found in West African drumming.

Talking Heads have recrafted Ball's sound poem into an effective song of their own: Ball tells a jungle story, Talking Heads transform it into a tribal chant.[32] As a chant, it need not tell the whole story but simply capture its essence. Ball's text is condensed in the Talking Heads' lyrics, which are then allowed to unfold in the more spacious musical setting. The listener need not be familiar with Ball's "Gadji beri bimba" to experience the dadaist flavor unmistakably present in the Talking Heads' "I Zimbra."

31. Franz Grillparzer, quoted in Karl Storck, *Musik und Musiker in Karikatur und Satire* (Oldenburg: Gerhard Stalling, 1913), 155.

32. David Byrne might have come across Ball's description of his own first recitation of "Gadji beri bimba" at the Cabaret Voltaire: "I do not know what gave me the idea of using this music, but I began to chant my vowel sequences like a recitative, in liturgical style, and tried not only to keep a straight face but to compel myself to be in earnest" (Hugo Ball, quoted in Richter, *Dada*, 43).

In a larger historical context, musical Futurism will be remembered as a revolutionary moment in early twentieth-century aesthetics: by championing the acceptance of noise as musical material, it initiated a radically new way of thinking about the essence of music and gave rise to parallel developments in, and reciprocal interactions with, the other arts, particularly literature. Ephemeral as the crude *intonarumori* and the scandalous spectacles that their repeated demonstrations precipitated may well be regarded today, the acoustic and later electroacoustic experimentation—not to mention phonetic poetry—unleashed by Luigi Russolo's intriguing *L'arte dei rumori* has certainly been more enduring. The key catalyst largely responsible for turning the revolutionary moment of musical Futurism into an ongoing evolutionary process of intermedia avant-garde activity has undoubtably been John Cage. In his "The Future of Music: Credo" of 1937, Cage prophetically outlined the course of experimentation for the second half of the twentieth century and beyond.

> I believe that the use of noise . . . to make music . . . will continue and increase until we reach a music produced through the aid of electrical instruments . . . which will make available for musical purposes any and all sounds that can be heard. Photoelectric, film, and mechanical mediums for the synthetic production of music will be explored.[33]

That a recently formed British rock group chose to perform under the name "The Art of Noise" is just one more indication that Russolo's curiously consequential legacy has not been entirely forgotten.[34]

---

33. Cage, "Future of Music," 54–55.

34. See also Jacques Attali's provocative *Bruits: Essai sur l'économie politique de la musique* (Paris: Presses Universitaires de France, 1977); translated by Brian Massumi as *Noise: The Political Economy of Music* (Minneapolis: University of Minnesota Press, 1985).

A Selective Bibliography of
Works of Peter Demetz

Books

1. *René Rilkes Prager Jahre.* Düsseldorf: Eugen Diederichs, 1953.
2. *Marx, Engels und die Dichter.* Stuttgart: Deutsche Verlags-Anstalt, 1959.
    2a. *Marx, Engels, and the Poets.* Chicago and London: University of Chicago Press, 1967.
    2b. *Marx, Engels y los Poetas.* Barcelona: Editorial Fontanella, 1968.
    2c. *Marx, Engels und die Dichter.* Berlin: Ullstein-Taschenbuch, 1968.
    2d. *Marukusu Enegrusu to Shijintachi.* Tokyo: Kinokuniya Shoten, 1973.
3. *Formen des Realismus: Theodor Fontane.* Munich: Carl Hanser Verlag, 1964.
4. *German Post-War Literature: A Critical Introduction.* New York: Pegasus, 1970.
    4a. *Die süße Anarchie: Deutsche Literatur seit 1945.* Berlin: Propyläen Verlag, 1970.
    4b. *Post War German Literature.* New York: Schocken, 1972.
    4c. *Die süße Anarchie: Skizzen zur deutschen Literatur seit 1945.* Enlarged ed. Berlin: Ullstein-Taschenbuch, 1973.
5. *After the Fires: Recent Writing in the Germanies, Austria, and Switzerland.* New York: Harcourt Brace Jovanovich, 1986.
    5a. *Fette Jahre, magere Jahre: Deutschsprachige Literatur von 1965 bis 1985.* Trans. Christiane Spelsberg. Munich: Piper, 1988.
6. *Worte in Freiheit: Der italienische Futurismus und die deutsche literarische Avantgarde, 1912-1934.* Munich: Piper, 1990.

Edited Books

1. *Franz Kafka a Praha.* Prague: Vladimír Žikeš, 1947.
2. *Neviditelný domov: Verše exulantů 1948-1958* (Poetry of exiled Czech writers). Paris: Editions Sokolová, 1953.
3. *Twentieth Century Views: Bertolt Brecht.* Englewood Cliffs, N.J.: Prentice-Hall, 1962.
4. *Lessing: Nathan der Weise, Dichtung und Wirklichkeit.* Berlin: Ullstein Verlag, 1966.
5. *An Anthology of German Literature 800-1750.* Edited with William T. H. Jackson. Englewood Cliffs, N.J.: Prentice-Hall, 1968.

6. *The Disciplines of Criticism: Festschrift for René Wellek.* Edited with Thomas Greene and Lowry Nelson, Jr. New Haven: Yale University Press, 1968.

7. *Karl Gutzkow: Liberale Energie, Eine Sammlung seiner kritischen Schriften.* Berlin: Ullstein Verlag, 1974.

8. *Proceedings of the AATG Annual Meeting (Bonn).* Edited with R. Grimm, E. Reichmann, and Walter Sokel. Philadelphia: n.p., 1975.

9. *Arsenal: Beiträge zu Franz Tumler.* Edited with H. D. Zimmermann. Munich: Piper, 1977.

10. *Theodor Fontane: Short Novels and Other Writings.* The German Library, vol. 48. New York: Continuum, 1982. Includes an introduction by the editor, xl–xvi.

11. *Alt-Prager Geschichten.* Frankfurt am Main: Insel Verlag, 1982. Includes postscript by the editor, 275–82, as well as three translations from Czech and bibliographical notes.

12. *Theodor Fontane: Delusions/Confusions, The Poggenpuhl Family.* Trans. W. Zwiebel and Gabriele Annan. The German Library, vol. 47. New York: Continuum, 1990.

13. *G. E. Lessing, Nathan the Wise, Minna von Barnhelm, and Other Plays and Writings.* The German Library, vol. 12. New York: Continuum, 1991. Includes an introduction by the editor, xxi–xxvii.

Translations from Czech Literature

1. Jiří Orten. "Gedichte." *Merkur* 4 (1950): 1267–71.

2. Božena Němcová. *Die Grossmutter.* Trans. Hana Demetz and Peter Demetz. Zurich: Manesse Verlag, 1959.

3. František Halas. *Poesie.* Frankfurt am Main: Suhrkamp, 1965. Includes postscript by the translator, 93–99.

4. "Neue Tschechische Dissidenten: Poesie von Karel Šiktanc und Jaroslav Seifert." *Kontinent,* 1976, 137–43, 144–52.

5. Svatopluk Čech. "Der Buchdämon." In *Alt-Prager Geschichten,* 81–116. Frankfurt am Main: Insel, 1982.

6. Jaroslav Durych. "Das Almosen." In *Alt-Prager Geschichten,* 132–51. Frankfurt am Main: Insel, 1982.

7. Jakub Arbes. "Die letzten Harfenspieler." In *Alt-Prager Geschichten,* 217–29. Frankfurt am Main: Insel, 1982.

8. Ludvík Kundera. "Zum Neuen Jahre." *Frankfurter Allgemeine Zeitung,* January 2, 1992; "Dreimal den Schlüssel Gedreht." January 21, 1991.

Selected Articles and Essays

1. "R. M. Rilke a Sidney Keyes." *Časopis pro Moderní Filologii* 31, no. 1 (1948): 28–31. "Oprava k článku >Rilke a Sidney Keyes<." *Časopis pro Moderní Filologii* 31, no. 2 (1948): 157–58.

2. "Franz Kafka a Hermann Melville." *Časopis pro Moderní Filologii* 31, no. 3 (1948): 183–85 and (Dokončení) 31, no. 4 (1948): 267–71.

3. "Franz Kafka a česky národ." In *Franz Kafka a Praha*, 43–61. Prague: Vladimír Žikeš, 1947.
4. "Kafka in England." *German Life and Letters* 4 (1950): 21–30.
5. "The Czech Themes of R. M. Rilke." *German Life and Letters* 6 (1952): 35–49.
6. "Goethes 'Die Aufgeregten': Zur Frage der politischen Dichtung in Deutschland." Hannover-Münden: F. Nowak, 1952.
7. "Early Beginnings of Marxist Literary Theory." *Germanic Review* 29 (1954): 201–13.
8. "Kafka, Freud, Husserl: Probleme einer Generation." *Zeitschrift für Religions- und Geistesgeschichte* 7 (1955): 56–69.
9. "Young Germany and Soviet Goethe Interpretation." *German Life and Letters* 9 (1956): 181–88.
10. "Englische Spiegelungen R. M. Rilkes." *Orbis Litterarum* 2 (1956): 17–30.
11. "Ezra Pound's German Studies." *Germanic Review* 31 (1956): 280–92.
12. "Počátky marxistické literární kritiky." In *Kulturní sborník Rok*, ed. Ladislav Matějka, 47–58. New York: Moravian Library, 1957.
13. "Zwischen Klassik und Bolschewismus: Georg Lukács als Theoretiker der Literatur." *Merkur* 14 (1958): 501–18.
14. "The Elm and the Vine: Notes toward the History of a Marriage Topos." *PMLA* 73 (1959): 521–32.
15. "Der Kritiker Holthusen." *Merkur* 14 (1960): 277–83.
16. "Über Fontanes Realismus." *Orbis Litterarum* 8 (1962): 34–47.
17. "Notes on Figurative Names in Fontane's Novels." *Germanic Review* 27 (1962): 96–105.
18. "Geschichtsvision und Wissenschaft: Über einige Arbeiten Hans Mayers." *Merkur* 15 (1961): 667–87.
19. "Introduction to Brecht." In *Twentieth-Century Views: Brecht*, 1–23. Englewood Cliffs, N.J.: Prentice-Hall, 1962.
20. "Literature in Ulbricht's Germany." *Problems of Communism* 11 (1962): 15–21.
21. "Flug und Flocke: Ein symbolisches Motiv bei Fontane." *Monatshefte* 54 (1962): 97–108.
22. "Defenses of Dutch Painting and the Theory of Realism." *Comparative Literature* 15 (1963): 97–115.
23. "Die Heilige Johanna." In *Johanna Dramen*, 9–28. Munich: Langen-Müller, 1964.
24. "Georg Lukács auf dem Wege zu Aristoteles." *Merkur* 19 (1965): 576–82.
25. "Lessings Nathan der Weise: Wirklichkeit und Wirklichkeiten." In *Lessing: Nathan der Weise*, 121–58. Berlin: Ullstein, 1966.
26. "Zur Definition des Realismus." *Literatur und Kritik* 2 (1967): 289–307.
27. "Eça de Queiròz as Literary Critic." *Comparative Literature* 19 (1967): 289–307.
28. "Balzac and the Zoologists." In *The Disciplines of Criticism*, 397–418. New Haven: Yale University Press, 1968.
29. "Karl Gutzkows 'Die Ritter vom Geiste': Notizen über Struktur und Ideologie." *Monatshefte* 61 (1969): 225–31.
30. "Wandlungen der marxistischen Literaturtheorie: Mayer, Fischer, Goldmann."

In *Der Dichter und seine Zeit: Politik im Spiegel der Literatur,* ed. Wolfgang Paulsen, 13–32. Heidelberg: Stiehm, 1970.

31. "Kitsch, Belletristik, Kunst: Theodor Fontane." *Anmerkungen zur Zeit.* Heft 44, 1–28. Published for the Berlin Academy by Gebr. Mann. Berlin, 1971.

32. "Die Folgenlosigkeit Lessings." *Merkur* 25 (1971): 727–42.

33. "Marxist Criticism Today." *Survey* 18 (1971): 63–72.

34. "Zur Situation der Germanistik: Tradition und aktuelle Probleme." In *Deutsche Literatur seit 1945,* ed. Manfred Durzak, 322–36. Stuttgart: Reclam, 1971.

35. "Till Eulenspiegel und seine Vetternschaft: Vom Überleben der Plebejer." *Literatur und Kritik* 8 (1973): 299–309.

36. "Der Literaturkritiker Karl Gutzkow: Eine Einführung." In *Karl Gutzkow: Liberale Energie,* 10–33. Berlin: Ullstein, 1974.

37. "Werkstattgespräch mit Franz Tumler." In *Arsenal: Beiträge zu Franz Tumler,* ed. P. Demetz and H. D. Zimmermann, 45–62. Munich: Piper, 1977.

38. "Die Fiktionen des Realismus." *Neue Rundschau* 88 (1977): 554–67.

39. "Introduction to Walter Benjamin." In Walter Benjamin, *Reflections, Essays, Aphorisms, Autobiographical Writings,* vii–xliii. New York: Harcourt, 1978.

40. "Die Literatur der Bundesrepublik in den Vereinigten Staaten." In *Perspectives and Personalities: Studies in Modern Literatures Honoring Claude Hill,* 110–17. Heidelberg: Carl Winter, 1978.

41. "Walter Benjamin als Leser Adalbert Stifters." In *Stifter Symposium: Vorträge und Lesungen,* 38–42. Linz, 1979.

42. "Postscript." In Max Brod, *Der Prager Kreis,* 241–46. Frankfurt am Main: Suhrkamp, 1979.

43. "Karl Gutzkow und Georg Büchner: Bilder aus dem Vormärz." In *Literatur und Kritik,* ed. Walter Jens, 205–18. Stuttgart: Deutsche Verlags-Anstalt, 1980.

44. "Eugen Gomringer und die Entwicklung der konkreten Poesie." In *Die deutsche Lyrik: 1945–1975,* ed. Klaus Weissenberger, 277–87. Düsseldorf: Bagel, 1981.

45. "An Inarticulate Society." *Yale Alumni Magazine and Journal* 45 (1981): 14–17.

46. "Laudatio Marcel Reich-Ranicki." In *Ricarda Huch Preis: Reden zur Preisverleihung,* 16–26. Darmstadt, 1981.

47. "Presidential Address 1981." *PMLA* 97 (1982): 312–17.

48. "Varieties of Phonetic Poetry." In *From Kafka to Dada to Brecht and Beyond,* ed. R. Grimm, 23–33. Monatshefte: Occasional Volumes, no. 2. Madison: University of Wisconsin Press, 1982.

49. "Lauter erfundene Geschichten: Über den Erzähler in der Fiktion." *Jahrbuch der Akademie für Sprache und Dichtung* 1982:9–23.

50. "Günter Grass in Search of Literary Theory." In *The Fisherman and His Wife: Günter Grass' 'The Flounder' in Critical Perspective,* ed. Siegfried Mews, 19–24. New York: AMS Press, 1983.

51. "Ein Nachwort." In Alfred Andersch, *Sansibar oder der letzte Grund,* 5–12. Bibliothek des XX. Jahrhunderts. Ed. W. Jens and M. Reich-Ranicki. Stuttgart: Büchergilde Gutenberg, 1983.

52. "On Stifter's and Fontane's Realism: *Turmalin* and *Mathilde Möhring.*" In *Literary Criticism and Theory: Festschrift for René Wellek,* 767–82. Bern: Lang, 1984.

53. "Deutsche Literatur in USA: Notizen zu einem Szenenwechsel." In *Gründlich Verstehen,* ed. F. Görtz and Gerd Ueding, 29–39. Frankfurt am Main, 1985.

54. "Postscript." In Theodor Fontane, *Stine,* 134–50. Frankfurt am Main: Insel, 1986.

55. "Der Kuckuck wie die Nachtigall." In *Goethe, Alle Freuden . . . ,* 154–56. Frankfurt am Main: Insel, 1986.

56. "Italian Futurism and the German Literary Avant-Garde." The Bithell Memorial Lecture. Institute of Germanic Studies, University of London, 1987.

57. "Der italienische Futurismus und Franz Pfemperts 'Aktion.'" *Jahrbuch des Wissenschaftskollegs zu Berlin* 1985–86:243–53.

58. "Laudatio auf Günther Kunert." *Heine-Jahrbuch* 1987:245–52.

59. "Postscript." In H. C. Adler, *Panorama,* 582–95. Munich: Piper, 1988.

60. "Postscript." In Theodor Fontane, *Mathilde Möhring,* 143–58. Frankfurt am Main: Insel, 1988.

61. "Foreword." In Max Frisch, *Novels, Plays, Essays,* ed. Rolf Kieser, ix–xii. The German Library, vol. 90. New York: Continuum, 1989.

62. "Die Literaturgeschichte Švejks." In *Literarische Symbolfiguren,* ed. Werner Wunderlich, 189–205. Bern and Stuttgart: Haupt, 1989.

63. "Postscript." In Theodor Fontane, *Grete Minde,* 141–54. Frankfurt am Main: Insel, 1990.

64. "A Conversation with René Wellek." *Cross Currents* 9 (1990): 135–45.

65. "Postscript." In Eça de Queiròz, *Das berühmte Haus Ramires,* 312–24. Munich: Piper, 1990.

66. "Introduction." In Golo Mann, *Reminiscences and Reflections,* ix–xiii. New York: Norton, 1990.

67. "Reflections of an Emeritus (To-Be)." *Profession* 90 (1990): 3–7.

68. "Second Conversation with René Wellek." *Cross Currents* 10 (1991): 235–51.

69. "Öffentliche und kapillare Geschichte: Über Literaten und sanfte Revolutionen in Berlin und Prag." *Transit* 2 (1991): 151–60.

70. "Prager Literaten in 'Sturm' und 'Aktion.'" In *Berlin und der Prager Kreis,* ed. H. D. Zimmermann and M. Pazi, 101–9. Würzburg: Königshausen und Neumann, 1991.

71. "German Literature under the Occupation in Germany: Memories of a Contemporary." In *Legacies and Ambiguities: Postwar Fiction and Culture in Germany and Japan,* ed. Ernestine Schlant and J. Thomas Rimer, 123–33. Baltimore, Md.: Johns Hopkins University Press, 1991.

Yale Dissertations in German and Comparative Literature Directed by Professor Peter Demetz

Günter O. Rebing, "Friedrich Spielhagens Apologie des Romans: Ein Beitrag zur europäischen Literaturtheorie des neunzehnten Jahrhunderts," 1965.

Steven P. Scher, "Verbal Music: Devices and Techniques, Evocations of Music in Modern German Literature," 1965.

Helene Scher, "The German Ballad: Tradition and Transformation, Münchhausen and Brecht," 1967.

Gisela Brude-Firnau, "Hermann Broch—Dr. Daniel Brody: Korrespondenz, 1930–33," 1968.

Robert R. Chase, "Adalbert Stifter as Historical Novelist," 1968.

Veronica C. Richel, "Luise Gottsched: A Reconsideration," 1968.

James Rolleston, "Rilke in Transition: A Study of His Poetry, 1896–1902," 1968.

Susan Abrams, "Communication and Narrative Structure in Two Contemporary German Novels," 1969.

David Connor, "Johann Christoph Gottsched and the Growth of German Literature," 1969.

John Flores, "Adjustments and Visions: Poetry in the German Democratic Republic (1945–1969)," 1969.

Gordon Nelson, "*Baal:* The Foundations of Brecht's Style," 1969.

Jean Friedberg Nordhaus, "The *Laienspiel* Movement and Brecht's *Lehrstücke,*" 1969.

Asta Lepinis, "Der Kritiker Robert Musil," 1970.

Volker Christian Wehdeking, "Über den Nullpunkt: Literatursoziologische Studien zur deutschen Literatur," 1970.

Rinehart Kyler, "Plievier's War Trilogy: A Critical Evaluation," 1971.

Elizabeth W. Harries, "Fiction and Artifice: Studies in Fielding, Wieland, Sterne, Diderot," 1973.

Linda M. Hill, "Language as Aggression: Studies in the Postwar Drama," 1973.

Luellen G. Lucid, "The Writer as Public Figure: Mailer, Sartre, Solzhenitzyn, An Essay in the Sociology of Literature," 1973.

Anne Close Ulmer, "A Doderer *Répertoire* with an Essay on Characterization in His Novels," 1973.

Krishna R. Winston, "Horváth Studies: Close Readings of Six Plays (1926–1931)," 1974.

Ruth Vera Gross, "*Plan:* An Austrian Journal of Literature, Art, and Culture," 1975.

Charlotte Carroll Prather, "Christoph Martin Wieland: His Philosophical Mansion," 1976.

David E. Wellbery, "Aesthetics and Semiotics in the German Enlightenment," 1977.

Neil Flax, "Written Pictures: The Visual Arts in Goethe's Literary Works," 1978.

Leigh Hafrey, "Intratextual Perspective: The Interpolated Tale as Parable," 1978.

Howard Stern, "Gegenbild, Reihenfolge, Sprung: An Essay on Related Figures in Walter Benjamin," 1978.

John Talmadge, "Narrative Artifice in the Literature of Exploration," 1978.

William B. Fischer, "Between Fantastic Fabulation and Didactic Disquisition: Kurd Lasswitz, Hans Dominik, and the Development of German Science Fiction," 1979.

W. Walter Jaffe, "Studies in Obsession: Otto Weininger, Arthur Schnitzler, Heimito von Doderer," 1979.

Page Laws, "Mythic Images of Four Recent European Novels," 1979.

George Newton, "Images of the American Indian in French and German Novels of the Nineteenth Century," 1979.

Willy Riemer, "Symbolism, Mathematics, and Monistic Thought: Contextual Studies in Hermann Broch," 1979.

Mark Harman, "Literary Echoes: Franz Kafka and Heinrich von Kleist," 1980.

Nancy Kaiser, "Social Integration and Narrative Structure: Patterns of German Realism," 1980.

Amy Colin, "Paul Celan: His Poetic Traditions," 1982.

Ellen Peel, "Both Ends of the Candle: Feminist Narrative Structures in Novels by Staël, Lessing, and Le Guin," codirector Peter Brooks, 1982.

Andrea Snell, "Die Franzosen and les Allemands: Cultural Clichés in the Making," 1982.

Kenneth Larson, "*King Lear* in German Translation," 1983.

Nancy Birch Wagner, "Stifter and Fontane: Encounters with Goethe," 1983.

Claudia Brodsky, "The Imposition of Form: Studies in Narrative Representation and Knowledge," codirector Peter Brooks, 1984.

Hugo Walter, "The Apostrophic Moment in Nineteenth-Century German Lyric Poetry," codirector Jeffrey L. Sammons, 1985.

Liselotte Davis, "History and Narrative Structure: *Ut mine Stromtid* by Franz Reuter and *Jahrestage* by Uwe Johnson," codirector Jeffrey L. Sammons, 1986.

Judith Cushingham, "On Lessing's Politics: His Dramatic Fragments and *Emilia Galotti,*" 1987.

Mortimer Guiney, "The Fictionalization of Experience in Rilke and Gide," codirector Peter Brooks, 1987.

Ellis Shookman, "Fictionality in the Novels of Christoph Martin Wieland," 1987.

Catherine LeGouis, "Three Versions of Positivism: Emile Hennequin, Wilhelm Scherer, Apollon Grigoriev," codirector Robert Jackson, in progress.

Tabula Gratulatoria

The following persons offer their congratulations to Peter Demetz on the occasion of his 70th birthday and the publication of this book:

Johannes Anderegg
Claire Baldwin
David P. Benseler
Clifford Albrecht Bernd
Nancy Birch-Wagner
Claudia Brodsky
Gisela Brude-Firnau
Robert Chase
Dorrit Cohn
Amy Colin
Judith Cushingham
Harry Deutsch
Thomas C. Fox
Marilyn Sibley Fries
Peter Gay
Mark Gelber
Ruth Gross
Mark Harman
Paul Hernadi
Linda M. Hill
Walter Hinderer
Peter Uwe Hohendahl
W. Walter Jaffe
Michael Jones
Mark H. Kadar
Nancy Kaiser
James E. Knirk
Diane Koester

Jocelyne Kolb
Kenneth E. Larson
Alan D. Latta
Frank and Waltraut Lehmann
Siegfried Mews
Gordon Eugene Nelson
Sela Condo Nelson
Heinz D. Osterle
Brigitte Peucker
Günter Rebing
Peter N. Richardson
James Rolleston
Judith Ryan
Thomas Saine
Jeffrey L. Sammons
Steven Scher
Leonard G. Schulze
Ernst Schürer
Barbara J. Seal
Ellis Shookman
Frank Trommler
Ann Close Ulmer
Mark Webber
Volker Wehdeking
Gerhard H. Weiss
David E. Wellbery
René Wellek
Susan Winnett

Index